The
Development
of
Education
in
Western Culture

The Development of Education *in Western Culture*

Ralph L. Pounds
University of Cincinnati

APPLETON – CENTURY – CROFTS

New York

DIVISION OF MEREDITH CORPORATION

6107–1

Library of Congress Card Number: 68–11098
PRINTED IN THE UNITED STATES OF AMERICA
E 71470

PREFACE

The purpose of this book is to present the development of education and schools from the time of nonliterate peoples on through, roughly, five thousand years of historic period. Our narrative is limited largely to the western world and to those events in the Middle East which gave rise to western civilization.

The author conceives it his job to trace the development of schools and those educational ideas underlying them as they were related to the social, cultural, and political events occurring at the same time. As it is his belief that the development of education can only be understood in the light of these other factors and that the breadth of scope of such investigations are tremendous, he has found it necessary to limit discussion of these factors.

Consequently, the outline for the book is as follows. The first four chapters accent education among nonliterate peoples and in those early civilizations of the ancient world. Chapter 1 covers literate peoples. Chapter 2 discusses those early historic cultures of the Nile River and Mesopotamia. Chapter 3 centers on Greek civilization as Chapter 4 upon the Roman. One chapter sums up medieval Europe and the rise of systems of education on a Christian basis, while a following chapter devotes itself to the period of the Renaissance. For the world since 1500, Chapter 7 examines religious reformation and scientific revolution. Chapter 8 looks into education and enlightenment, and Chapter 9 covers the development of national systems of education. So is our story down to 1930.

The most recent history of education in the Western World is presented by using a comparative approach. Our last two chapters examine the contemporary (1930 to present) systems of education in five of the major countries of the world: Germany, France, United Kingdom (emphasis upon England and Wales), the United States, and the Soviet Union.

The central theme of this book is the struggle which man has made to achieve freedom with security. The words "freedom" and "security" are, of course, difficult to define and no definition can be made which would be completely satisfactory to all. In this text *freedom* is equated with the concept of the ability and opportunity of man to make choices with increasing assurance due to knowledge of alternatives. As the number of areas in which choices can be made increases and man has the knowledge and background to make such choices intelligently, we then assume that he has, to that extent, achieved freedom.

Security or stability refers to the developing of institutions, or patterns of behavior, to protect man from too rapid changes or from institutional uncertainties which might force the individual to change too quickly or to feel too inadequate.

As greater freedom is accorded man, his security may be destroyed to the extent that he is not able to predict the future since his institutions ("agreed ways of doing things") are changing so rapidly. Therefore, he does not feel he is secure.

Throughout history there has been this struggle between freedom and security. The role that the school has played has been significant and it is hoped that this book indicates its potential.

To accomplish this, the debt any writer of such a textbook owes to the scholars who precede him is great. In American scholarship every educational historian owes a special debt to Ellwood F. Cubberley. His scholarship contribution was enormous in formulating the type of investigation needed to portray the history of education in the United States as well as the history of education in Western culture. This author wishes to acknowledge, also, his dependence upon the scholarship of R. Freeman Butts and James Mulhern, whose approaches are strongly parallelled by himself. He is indebted to Herbert J. Muller for assistance in the idea of man's struggle for freedom, and acknowledges a debt to Harry G. Good. To many others, a complete list of whose names it would be difficult to include here (but may be found in the bibliographies within the book) the author also would like to express his gratitude.

In particular the author wishes to express his thanks for the work of his editorial assistant, Mrs. Rebecca Pittenger. He also expresses his appreciation to Mrs. Mary Tull for reading and criticizing the manuscript and to Mrs. Mary Beckwith and Mrs. Jane Shreve for their help in getting the manuscript into the final shape for the publishers. The author is, of course, alone responsible for the final manuscript as you see it now before you.

R. L. P.

CONTENTS

The
Development
of
Education
in
Western Culture

Culture, Education, and Schools: Nonliterate Peoples

INTRODUCTION

This is a book on the development of education as found in Western culture from the nonliterate peoples to the present day. It is concerned with the history of schools as related to culture, and its point of view is that a story of education cannot be effectively written or studied except in relation to the social and cultural history of each of the peoples concerned. In this book, therefore, we constantly consider the interrelationship of three strands of history—culture, education, schools—and hope, by presenting a clearer picture of past events, ideas, and materials, to facilitate a better understanding of man's past, present, and future.

Culture, Education, and the Schools. Since the theme of this text is centered around the three topics of "culture," "education," and "school," it is necessary to define the ways in which these terms are conceived and used.

The word "culture" is used in many ways including both nontechnical and scholarly. Many of those meanings have quite a different connotation from that employed in this book and that used by most social anthropologists. In general, "culture" refers to the way of life which has been *learned* as opposed to behavior patterns and to other fixed aspects of the physiological structure or function which have been *inherited biologically*.

As Coon has said, culture may be viewed as the "sum-total of the

ways in which human beings live, transmitted from generation to generation by learning." [1]

This term, *culture*, then, includes a *wide range of social institutions
and behaviors*. While it is very difficult to develop an inclusive list, it
would contain *all of the customs and mores as well as the expectations of
a people, their tools and their ways of using them (technology), their
bodies of knowledge and their beliefs, their ideals and their values
(their aesthetic expression and recreational patterns), and their language,
literature and other modes of communication*. The use of the term here,
then, is all-inclusive, with all aspects, as such, being important to the
educator.

Three points illustrate the central nature of culture and demonstrate
how essential some form of education must be to any culture, simple or
complex. These points are: (1) Culture by its very nature must be acquired through some kind of a process of learning by the individuals in a
society. (2) Elements of a culture must be held in common by a sizeable
portion of the persons in that society (some elements of it will be universally held). (3) There must be some way of transmitting these from one
generation to the other.

Thus, while it is true of culture that its members must *learn* as they
participate in it as well as, in turn, *teach* by the kinds of expectations
which they hold for the other members of it, we, here, define *"education"*
by restricting its use to cases which involve the *consciously and deliberately planned processes whereby individuals or groups are helped to
"learn" the various aspects of their culture and to participate in it satisfactorily*. According to this definition, then, whenever an individual or
group makes a deliberate attempt to produce in some individual or group
a certain kind of desired type of behavior, this process is considered to be
"education." It may or may not involve an institution called a "school"
or specialized individuals called "teachers."

In considering the part which education and teachers play with regard to the development of the individual, we must not overlook the
importance of the family throughout history. Human beings, even before
the advent of Homo sapiens (modern man), apparently have always lived
in families. Because of the helpless nature of the human young, the child
is dependent upon the family. Consequently, the family has played a very
potent role in the early development of the child in determining his understanding of the whole culture and in his absorption of those values
paramount in his particular group.

Since the very nature of man and of the human situation is such that
education must play a very important part in any consideration of the
way in which culture is passed on from one generation to another and

1 Francis E. Merrill, *Society and Culture: An Introduction to Sociology* (Englewood
Cliffs, New Jersey, Prentice-Hall, 1957).

the way in which cultural change itself comes about from within the culture,[2] *school* is defined (at this point briefly and in a preliminary way) as a *social institution deliberately established by a group to carry out certain educational purposes.*

Although education is an integral part of all human culture everywhere—from the simplest to the more complex—and, while culture is inconceivable without the process of education to sustain and pass it on, schooling itself is a relatively recent occurrence in human history. Many other institutions were developed before the school. As such, apparently, the first schools date back only to the beginning of the historic period, i.e., as soon as there was a written language to be passed on. Now, whenever this separate institution, the school, has appeared, it has always been very much affected by the other deliberate and conscious educational activities within the culture. Both the school and those other means of education have been, themselves, influenced and molded by the characteristics of the total culture. It is held, then, that both the schools and education in general develop in relationship to the culture in which they are found and, consequently, it is necessary for educators to study the development of these educational processes in relation to the parallel development of the culture in general.

Nature of the School as a Social Institution.[3] All institutions as developed by different groups of human species are, of course, part of the culture and as such they must be called *social* institutions. As a matter of fact, the use of the word, "institution," when applied to the school, implies that the school is social in nature. To make more explicit these concepts, the word *school* is used to refer exclusively to *a social institution, whether under public or private auspices, which has been deliberately set up by a society. Its function is to carry on the processes of education with usually a selected group of the population. It is established to educate these persons in selected elements from the culture which the sponsoring group considers to be important and which can be best taught by the specialized school in that society.* Accordingly, the school is an institution developed by a people in order to carry out very consciously, and deliberately, certain action or purposes deemed appropriate by them. Quite often, however, as an institution, the school has lost contact with its culture as its society has changed. Therefore, the school has almost always tended to become a conservative force.

---

[2] The point of view which has been developed by the author may be compared to a quite similar point of view set forth by R. Freeman Butts in *A Cultural History of Education,* pp. 1–2.

[3] This section has been adapted from an earlier formulation by the author in Ralph L. Pounds and James R. Bryner, *The School in American Society,* 2d ed. (New York, Macmillan, 1967), pp. 51–52.

There is still another sense in which the school can be considered a social institution. Persons attending school learn certain patterns, methods, and attitudes of their society because the school *itself* is a miniature culture which reflects, at least partially, the society in which it is found. Lessons learned from the way in which the school itself is structured, or from the patterns of behavior within the school (reflecting those in the society), may quite often be very important in influencing the way in which the individual develops. His behavior and attitudes toward elements of his culture may be more strongly determined by the out-of-class experiences than by the official course content itself.

Quite often the course content is quite academic, very little related to life, and considered by many of the students to have little relationship to the real life outside of school. This is not just a recent phenomenon; this situation has been found in earlier schools as well as those of the immediate past. However, the importance of nonformal learning inside the schools has not been recognized clearly by persons studying or directing the schools until recently. It has, now, in many schools been given some sort of status in the form of organized extra-curricular (or co-curricular) activities and other student organizations.

Main Underlying Theme and Theses of the Book. Attempts at developing a theory or philosophy of history which can be substantiated in terms of causal relationships between prior events and later events have proven relatively unsuccessful. However, since the amount of possible material available for the historiographer in assembling the history of a certain period or theme is usually quite large, there should be some organizing principles or generalizations on the bases of which the historian selects his material. The basic theme or set of principles underly the selection of the material which indicate the threads of cultural development, as well as the material which relates to the development of education and schools.

From the standpoint of the present world situation and the current interest in man's successful development, the *main theme of human history* seems to be the *struggle man has to achieve freedom with security*. At the moment, throughout the world, human freedom, symbolized by faith and belief in, and struggle for democracy, seems to be in the ascendancy; however, in the long period of human history the pendulum has swung back and forth as groups have sought more security through giving up certain freedoms and then again sought freedom from the oppressions caused by the measures to insure that security.[4]

In furtherance of our discussion of the relationship between schools and their societies, there are two seemingly contradictory theses to be

[4] The theme of man's struggle for freedom has been fully developed in a series of books written by Herbert J. Muller. *Freedom in the Ancient World,* and *Freedom in the Western World.* Harper and Row.

considered. The first is *inter-action*. Schools tend to *reflect the society in which they are found and in turn do affect the changes in that society*. The second is *social lag*. *Schools tend to lag behind their societies, particularly in periods of rapid social changes*.[5] While the relationship between schools and their societies is examined in greater detail throughout the book, at this point it may be well to explain that the apparent conflict between the two can be resolved.

Although schools *do* reflect the cultures in which they are found, all cultures, all societies, tend to change, some more rapidly than others, some more rapidly at one time than at another. The institutions in a culture tend to change less rapidly than do other aspects of that culture. The school, being one of the many institutions, like them also tends to resist change. This resistance to change does not make much difference in times when the changes are occurring relatively slowly in the culture. In the recent history of most of the advanced countries of the world, however, change is coming about very rapidly. Consequently, the problem of the social lag of the schools becomes of great importance.

The Problem of Social Lag.[6] *Social (or cultural) lag may be defined as the uneven development of different parts of a changing culture.* This means that at any given time in the development of a culture some parts of the culture have not changed as rapidly as have others. This differential in the rate of development of the different parts of the culture is considered by many students of society to be one of the main sources of contemporary social problems. In this connection culture can be considered as being made up of three parts: the material aspects, the institutional part, and the ideological bases for the institutions. The third part gives the rationale underlying the material and institutional structure and changes in the culture.

Usually, changes in the material aspects of culture come about first and most readily. These are followed by a lag in those institutional changes which must eventually accompany them, and by a further lag in the development of ideas needed to provide a rationale for changes in institutions as related to the culture. Man seems to accept material changes more readily than he does institutional changes, and he seems to resist very strenuously any changes in his fundamental ideological conceptions. Some authorities do not accept the term, "social lag" or "cultural," but speak of societal breakdown as due to "disorganization"—a lack of the fitting together of parts.

Whatever it is called, the amount of social lag or "disjointedness" in a culture varies with the amount of speed of social change. If there is very

---

[5] These theses were formulated earlier by the present author in Pounds and Bryner, *op. cit.,* p. 55.

[6] This topic has been adapted from an earlier formulation in Pounds and Bryner, *op. cit.,* pp. 14–15.

little or no social change, obviously the lag, if it exists, is small. At times when social change was the result of a single force (which, when once applied, subsided as a force towards change) the lag was quickly reduced as the society adjusted to the relatively static new conditions following the initial impact. In Western civilization, there has been rather consistent change due to new events occurring largely from within the society. These have continually brought about changes in certain parts of society and thus lack of adjustment with the parts that did not change. As Western society has entered each new period of rapid social change, or when a particular change has set off a whole chain of new events, this lag has become acute.

THE NATURE OF MAN

Development of Man.[7]   The evolution of human society starts, at least as far back as modern man, the earliest known example of which is generally considered to be Cro-Magnon man. Cro-Magnon man is considered to have approximately the same biological structure (including the brain and nervous system) as does contemporary man. At least all men from Cro-Magnon on, including all contemporary groups, belong to the same species, Homo sapiens. The date of Cro-Magnon man usually has been placed back at least as far as 25,000 to 50,000 B.C.; however, earlier species of man may have existed on the earth as far back as nearly two million years.

On the basis of geological and other evidence, the earth is generally believed to have been in existence for at least two billion years, if not more (three or three and one-half billion years). Life has existed for over one billion years. The first mammals appeared on earth at least 150 million years ago. Man is thus a late comer on the earth's surface.[8]

The earliest known inscription or form of writing appears to be that from Sumeria. This has been dated around 3300 B.C. The nonliterate period (before written history) thus includes all man from at least approximately 25,000 B.C. down to 3300 B.C., since some groups became

---

[7] See also Pounds and Bryner, *op. cit.*, pp. 25–28.

[8] The cultural remains of early species different from modern man have been found, going back probably as far as one and three-fourths million years. Harry L. Shapiro, ed., *Man, Culture, and Society*, p. 21. The "potassium-argon" method, superior to the "Carbon 14" method for periods of one million years and over, was used to establish the age of Zinjanthropus, bones of an early species of man, whose discovery was announced in 1961.

historic at about that time. However, the nonliterate period also includes the story of many groups and tribes still living at the nonliterate stage in certain remote places on the earth's surface.

Early man solved his problem of living on a very precarious basis. He was able to get minimal food and shelter, but he did not understand the nature of his physical environment, nor the casual relationships that lay behind his successful attempts to provide for his minimal needs on a meager basis. Accordingly, he attributed much more to the "supernatural" than does contemporary man.

Knowing himself to be a creature that apparently could freely choose to do this and not do that, he tended to ascribe such freedom and personality to all other objects, animate or inanimate. This theory of the nature of the universe found almost universally among nonliterate peoples is called *animism*.

In the one form of *animism,* nonliterate man extended to inanimate objects the concepts formed as the result of his experience with animate objects: That is, a stone, like a person, possessed feelings of love or resentment and had the power to act on its feeling, just as his fellow men, himself, and other animals apparently did. Animism thus places a spirit in each inanimate object, and the object can then be controlled by cajoling, pleading, worship, or other means of manipulation.

The other aspect of supernaturalism, sometimes differentiated by terming it *animatism,*[9] seems to have been an extension of man's effort to control familiar objects by utilizing a supernatural science that can best be labelled magic. Man tried to control the forces in a supernatural cause-and-effect relationship by means of certain rituals or formulas that probably had at some time appeared, by coincidence, to work and thus became a part of his thinking and action. Incantations, sorcery, and divination were a part of the magic. Their use was quite prevalent in nonliterate man and persisted late into the modern period of civilized man. Failure of the method usually was ascribed to errors in the procedure rather than in the conception back of it. Skeptics existed, but they were usually merely skeptical of certain persons' power to use the ritual or of a particular formula used.

The use of taboo to control the behavior of individuals in the group has also become another aspect of dealing with the supernatural. Since the supernatural is power, it is dangerous. Whatever the actual origins of the taboos, such as a food taboo originating either in a coincidental or causally related sickness or death following eating certain substances, such origins in most cases have been forgotten. The reasons ascribed are almost entirely either the appeasement of a spirit or the avoidance of danger from the supernatural power involved.

9 Ruth Benedict, "Religion," in Franz Boas, ed., *General Anthropology* (Boston, Heath, 1938), Ch. 14.

Nonliterate man, living as he did in a world of precarious existence, got his security through his fixed mores, his myths to explain religious rites, the superiority of his group to others, and taboos of various kinds to enforce conformity. In many cases, primitive tribes lived with little change for thousands of years. It is this resistance, culturally inherited from the time that nonliterate man feared change as a threat to his security in a precarious world, that may be a basis for some of the unreasoned conservatism found in modern culture.

The Nature of Modern Man. The biological type, *Homo sapiens,* had been established through the evolutionary process of survival selection by 25,000 B.C. or before. The characteristics of the "human" developed since that time are held by most modern scholars to be almost entirely a result of cultural influence and change. The relatively great importance of culture on the development of man as opposed to the importance of biological evolution and inheritance on other animals is of great importance in education.

The human infant is born with a much more plastic nervous system as compared to other animals. All animals except the human are born with pre-formed behavior patterns that cause all animals of the same kind to develop very much the same behavior patterns regardless of environment. On the other hand, man tends to take on the patterns of the culture into which he is born and reared.

Man seems to differ from the other animals in at least these important characteristics:

1. He is born with a very few pre-formed behavior patterns.

2. The human infant is born helpless. He is absolutely dependent for survival on others. He is thus by nature socially dependent on others.

3. Humans are very sensitive to environmental stimuli. Some of their senses, such as smell, are not as well developed as other animals. However, they are sensitive to meanings as developed through experience with such stimuli.

4. Man has the ability to invent and to assimilate a language.

5. As a result of language capacity or the ability to use symbols in general, man is capable of problem-solving, both through thought and through experience.

The conclusions of modern students of man can be summarized as follows: All modern man belongs to the same biological species, Homo sapiens. Almost all development since about 25,000 years ago is cultural rather than evolutionary or biological. If, by some time machine, a baby from a nonliterate tribe of 25,000 years ago could be whisked to modern time and placed in any home, he would, aside from his individual physiological characteristics, grow up to become like the modern family rather than the nonliterate peoples from which he came. By the same token, a baby taken from the interior of—say South America—to France, would, if placed soon after birth with a French family, grow up to be in all respects a Frenchman (excepting certain physiological characteristics such as, possibly, skin color).

NONLITERATE SOCIETIES—CULTURE AND EDUCATION

Development of Tribes (Nonliterate Societies and Cultures). All societies, simple and complex, have folkways and mores which constitute important bases for their culture. Both folkways and mores involve established ways of behavior peculiar to a particular group. The *mores* are those aspects of culture to which all individuals are expected to conform. The mores are supported by the strongest of sanctions, in contrast to the folkways, which are desired but not compulsory. Violation of the mores are immoral acts in the broadest sense of the term. In Western society, monogamous marriage, right of private property, and prohibitions against murder, rape, or incest are part of the mores. *Folkways* are customs that persons are expected to follow, but violations do not involve serious consequences. Taking off your hat when addressing a lady is a folkway, but failure to follow it is not immoral.

Because of the precarious nature of their existence, strong feelings for conformity developed almost universally among the nonliterate groups. The very existence of the group seemed to depend on its preserving the successful way of doing which it had accidentally developed. Conformity thus became one of the goals of the culture and thus the central purpose of education. Each tribe sought security and perpetuation by teaching each individual the accepted folkways and mores. Excessive nonconformity was punished by death or exile.

Nature of Education in the Nonliterate Societies. Neither the school as an institution nor education as a function of society developed separately from other aspects and institutions of nonliterate man. Except that the family appears in all early human groups and that the separate offices of tribal government usually developed early, on the whole there was little separativeness about any of the institutions, customs, or ways of doing of nonliterate man. Life was fairly well integrated. Abstractions, specialization, and compartmentalization of life are results of a more highly developed society.

The education of the child came about naturally in his participation in family and group life. The purpose of education, had it been formulated, would have been to induct the young child into the ways of doing, thinking, and believing—the folkways and mores—of the group. In other words, conformity was taught. The method was imitation, learning by doing. However, in the "activity program" of nonliterate man, creativity was not encouraged. The child was expected to learn well to do things in the ways they had been done. In many groups, both competitive and cooperative, he was encouraged toward individual excellence; however, there was little permissiveness in experimentation with new techniques. Such new techniques as did evolve seem to have come about by unconscious drift, rather than by conscious effort toward improvement.

In almost all tribes there was no differentiation among persons responsible for teaching. Parents, other adults, and older children all participated in the effort to help the child grow into an adult. The ideology of the nonliterate group was instilled through conversation about such things as spirits and taboos, through a storytelling of tribal myths, and through religious ceremonies. Most nonliterate peoples were fairly indulgent with their children; however, the mores of the group seem always to have been thoroughly ingrained into those children by the time of adolescence.

The first vocation to become fairly sharply differentiated among nonliterate people was that of the medicine man or priest, who came to have exclusive knowledge concerning religious rites and exorcisings. These religious persons may be said to be the ones who first considered it a function of their office to play any special part in the education of the young. Many of the nonliterate groups had complicated rites at the onset of puberty in order to intellectualize the process of attaining the role of an adult and to dispose the youth emotionally toward complete acceptance of the folkways. The school as an institution seems to have appeared only after the development of writing and reading skills. Since the priests were generally the most literate group in this, the dawning period of the civilized era, these schools were usually closely tied to religious institutions and religious leaders. While the schools of Greece and Rome represented a more secular approach, education and religion usually have been very closely related in most cultures, even to the present time.

The education of nonliterate peoples was a tremendously successful process in accomplishing its goal of conformity to folkways. Since the society was practically united in respect to allegiance to its folkways and mores, and the child was immersed in them, he could do little else but be molded in conformity with the patterns of the tribe. A point worth mentioning here is that the method must always be considered together with the goal. In the nonliterate tribe, the complete activity approach—total participation in life situations—was used to develop a child who would be in complete conformity to the culture. There was little attention to creativity or to individual differences.

REASONS FOR SOCIAL CHANGE IN EARLY SOCIETIES

Some cultural cultural change existed at all times, even in those tribes that had the strongest antipathy toward change. This cultural drift in language, culture, social customs and institutions, and technology, while so slow as to be unnoticed in a generation, seems to have been universally present at all times in man's history and pre-history. "Nothing is constant but change."

Breakdown of Fixed Mores. It has been seen that, once a group has developed a certain type of culture, it tends to resist change in that culture. This resistance is probably due in part to fear of the unknown based on uncertainty of knowledge of the environment. Also the adults of the group who largely determine what mores are to be inculcated have fairly fixed habits. However, unless changes did occur, man would still be at a nonliterate level. Some groups improved technologically, achieved better standards of living, a written language, and creative arts before others. Some of these changes came about very slowly by a kind of cultural drift without any awareness of sudden change by the group.

Numerous reasons have been given to account for these changes and for the variation among groups with respect to the time of arriving at various levels of civilization. Among the reasons that have been advanced are: divine help, superior racial inheritance, and geographical conditions. The first two can be ruled out, inasmuch as modern biology and anthropology do not disclose racial differences sufficient to account for the progress, and most of the gods and myths have long since been discarded. Certainly favorable geographical conditions were helpful. The early Oriental-type civilizations developed in relatively fertile regions such as along the Nile and in the Tigris–Euphrates valleys. However, not all groups in the southern part of the North Temperate Zone developed at the same time, and most of them developed and then faded away.

The discussion thus far makes it apparent that the reasons for progress are multiple and involve much in the way of fortuitous circumstances or coincidences. The speed and type of the changes varied among the groups because of differences of internal social structure with respect to permissiveness toward slow cultural change of the drift type. This permitted changes to proceed along different lines in different groups. However, the large breaks with past mores or folkways were brought about by events most of which might be considered disasters: drought, famine, pestilence, fire, earthquake, war, and conquest. All served to force the group to move or change its ways.

In many cases, contacts with other groups led to adaptations using superior practices from either group. Sometimes the conquerors subdued the conquered but preserved selected parts of their culture. Sometimes as a result of these cataclysms, but sometimes independently of them, new inventions occurred. When these inventions met a need or answered a problem for the group, they would be accepted by it. It is true, of course, that certain actions carried out at too early a period might result in failure; but, when tried later after certain lines of development have ensued, would be successful. No one knows how many inventions "before their time" were rejected by the group.

Emergence of Civilizations.   When some of the nonliterate groups had developed sufficient technology to permit considerable travel for trade or for conquest, they subjugated other groups in wide areas, thus facilitating diffusion of cultural practices from many different groups. This stimulated further contact with still other groups and permitted cultural diffusions and accretions. It also probably further stimulated inventions and the acceptance of improved technologies and other folkways.

Out of this process of invention by diffusion, contacts with others and social changes within, the first cultures that might be termed civilizations finally emerged at around 3000 B.C. This stage in development can be measured by the development of a written language by means of which there appears a recorded culture usually spread over a fairly wide area.

With this emergence of civilizations, there also appears the possibility of changes brought by powerful leaders in accordance with their own desires. This type of dictatorial change can be seen in the contemporary world. Also, particularly in the modern world, changes may be brought about deliberately as a result of using increased scientific knowledge in attempts to improve a society.

FREEDOM VERSUS CONFORMITY IN THE NONLITERATE WORLD

The story of man's struggle for freedom and security in the world starts with the nonliterate peoples. As already indicated, as soon as a nonliterate people had developed any kind of a way of life which was at all successful in meeting at a minimum level the problems of their existence, there developed a strong drive toward conformity to that particular way of life. This meant that, contrary to prevailing ideas about the "free" way of life of the nonliterate peoples, they did live a very ordered and strictly governed life. The concept of the so-called free ways of the nonliterate peoples refers often to the imagined free sex life and marriage customs among some South Sea Islanders. This, of course, is misleading since the patterns of life, although different from those of the monogamous pattern of recent Western civilization, are as complexly ordered as is any culture with respect to all of the sex mores. They merely contrast with those of the people who are studying them.

The security of the nonliterate peoples lay in their their ability to live by established mores with practically no change over a great number of years. However, they also developed a mythology and a set of religious beliefs to bulwark these, and gave to them the security of the rightness of their points of view until they came in contact with others which conflicted with these. It was this contact with others which brought about catastrophic and sudden changes. The mingling of many mores and folkways finally led to the higher level of complexly organized oriental-type civilizations. In their outward characteristics, they had no more freedom—as a matter of fact they had much less—than those of the nonliterate peoples. Such examples of civilization are discussed more fully in the next chapter.

SUMMARY

The theme of this text centers around culture, education, and schools. *Culture* is defined as a "wide range of social institutions and behaviors; all of the customs and mores as well as the expectations of the people; their tools and their ways of using them (technologies); their bodies of knowledge and their beliefs; their ideals and their values; their esthetic expressions and recreational patterns; and their language, literature and other modes of communication.

Education is defined as the "consciously and deliberately planned processes whereby individuals or groups are helped to learn the various aspects of their culture and to participate in it satisfactorily." *School* is defined as a "social institution, whether under public or private auspices, which has been deliberately set up by a society. Its function is to carry on the processes of education, with—usually—a selected group of the population. It is established to educate these persons in selected elements from the culture which the sponsoring group considers to be important and which can best be taught by the specialized school in that society."

The main theme of this book concerns itself with the struggle man has had throughout the ages to achieve freedom with security, and to control the pendulum which has swung back and forth from time to time between extremes of anarchy or absolute freedom and security to the point of severe oppression.

It has been pointed out that, in general, the relationship between schools and society can be characterized by two rather paradoxical theses: (1) *interaction*—schools tend to reflect the society in which they are found; and (2) *social lag*—schools tend to lag behind their societies, particularly in periods of rapid social changes.

Man seems to differ from the other animals in that he has at least certain important characteristics. He is born helpless, with a very few preformed behavior patterns, and thus, by nature, is socially dependent on others. He is sensitive to environmental stimuli, i.e., sensitive to meanings as developed through experience with such stimuli, hence, he is able to invent and to assimilate a language. Last, he is capable of problem-solving, both through thinking and through tested experience.

Finally, it has been shown that neither the school as an institution nor education as a differentiated function of society developed in non-literate peoples. Education as an aspect of society and a part of the process of the whole life of the tribe, of course, did exist, but the purpose of this process was to produce conformity to ways of life.

SELECTED BIBLIOGRAPHY

Starred items represent books most closely paralleling chapter content.

General Books

Audrey, Robert, *African Genesis: A Personal Investigation into the Animal Origins and Nature of Man.* New York, Atheneum Publishers, 1961.

Bibby, Geoffrey, *The Testimony of the Spade.* New York, Knopf, 1956.

Brameld, Theodore, *Cultural Foundations of Education: An Interdisciplinary Exploration.* New York, Harper & Row, 1957.

*Butts, R. Freeman, *A Cultural History of Western Education: Its Social and Intellectual Foundations,* 2d ed. New York, McGraw-Hill, 1955.

Carrington, Richard, *A Million Years of Man.* Cleveland, World, 1963.

Coon, C. S., *The Story of Man: From the First Human to Primitive Culture and Beyond.* New York, Knopf, 1954.

*Durant, Will, *Our Oriental Heritage: The Story of Civilization.* New York, Simon and Schuster, 1954.

Eisenstadt, S. N., *From Generation to Generation*. Glencoe, Free Press, 1956.

Goldschmidt, Walter, *Man's Way: A Preface to the Understanding of Human Society*. New York, World, 1959.

*Good, H. G., *A History of Western Education*, 2d ed. New York, Macmillan, 1960.

Hart, Joseph Kinmont, *A Social Interpretation of Education*. New York, Holt, Rinehart, and Winston, 1929.

Hawkes, Jacquetta and Woolley, Sir Leonard, *Prehistory and the Beginnings of Civilization: History of Mankind*. Sponsored by UNESCO. New York, Harper & Row, 1963.

Heritage of American Education, Richard E. Gross, ed. Boston, Allyn and Bacon, 1962.

Kropotkin, P., *Mutual Aid: A Factor of Evolution*. New York, Knopf, 1916.

Lasker, Gabriel, *The Evolution of Man: A Brief Introduction to Physical Anthropology*. New York, Holt, Rinehart and Winston, 1961.

*Mulhern, James, *A History of Education: A Social Interpretation*, 2d ed. New York, Ronald, 1959.

*Muller, Herbert J., *Freedom in the Ancient World*. New York, Harper & Row, 1961.

New Perspectives in World History, Shirley Engle, ed. Thirty-fourth Yearbook of the National Council of the Social Studies. Washington, D.C., National Education Association, 1964.

Quennell, Marjorie, *Everyday Life in Prehistoric Times*. London, Batsford, 1963.

Shotwell, James T., *The Long Way to Freedom*. New York, Bobbs-Merrill, 1960.

*Smith, William A. *Ancient Education*. New York, Philosophical Library, 1955.

The Dawn of Civilization: The First World Survey of Human Cultures in Early Times, Stuart Piggott, ed. New York, McGraw, 1961.

The Evolution of Man: Man, Culture, and Society, S. Tax, ed. Chicago, University of Chicago, 1960.

Titiev, Mischa, *Introduction to Cultural Anthropology*. New York, Holt, Rinehart and Winston, 1959.

———, *The Science of Man: An Introduction to Anthropology*. New York, Holt, Rinehart and Winston, 1954.

Wallace, Anthony F. C., "School in Revolutionary and Conservative Societies," in Frederick C. Gruber, ed. *Anthropology and Education* (Philadelphia: University of Pennsylvania Press, 1961), pp. 25–54.

Wallbank, Thomas Walter, and others, *Civilization: Past and Present*. Chicago, Scott, Foresman, 1962.

Wendt, Herbert L., *In Search of Adam*. Boston, Houghton Mifflin, 1956.

White, Leslie A., *The Evolution of Culture: The Development of Civilization to the Fall of Rome*. New York, McGraw-Hill, 1959.

*Woody, Thomas, *Life and Education in Early Societies*. New York, Macmillan, 1959.

Pertinent Paperbound Books

Asimov, Isaac, *The Wellsprings of Life.* New York, New American Library, 1962.

Bobbs-Merrill Reprint Series in the Social Sciences.
> (Examples pertinent to history of education)
> Barnett, H. G. "Invention and Cultural Change."
> Herskovits, Melville J. "The Processes of Cultural Change."
> Holmberg, Allen R. "Adventures in Cultural Change."
> Meggers, Betty J. "Environmental Limitation on the Development of Culture."
> Sahlins, Marshall D. "The Origin of Society." Reprint.
> Steward, Julian H. "The Economic and Social Basis of Primitive Bands."
> White, Leslie. "The Symbol: The Origin and Basis of Human Behavior."

*Burrell, Sidney, *The Main Strands of Development from the Beginnings to the 18th Century. Elements of Western Civilization.* San Francisco, California, Chandler, 1959.

*Cheney, L. J., *A History of the Western World: From the Stone Age to the Twentieth Century.* New York, New American Library, 1959.

*Childe, V. Gordon, *The Prehistory of European Society.* Baltimore, Penguin Books, 1958.

——, *Man Makes Himself.* New York, New American Library, 1962.

——, *What Happened In History.* Baltimore, Penguin Books, 1961.

Darwin, Charles, *The Origin of Species: By Means of Natural Selection or the Preservation of Favored Races in the Struggle for Life and the Descent of Man: and Selection in Relation to Sex.* New York, Modern Library, 1871.

Dobzhansky, Theodosius, *The Biological Basis of Human Freedom.* New York, Columbia University Press, 1960.

*Frost, S. E., Jr., *Essentials of History of Education.* New York, Barron's 1947.

Frankfort, Henri, *The Birth of Civilization in Near East.* Garden City, New York, Doubleday Anchor Books, 1956.

Golding, William, *Lord of the Flies.* New York, Capricorn, 1955.

Howells, W. W., *Back of History: The Story of Our Origins.* New York, Doubleday, 1954.

Man, Culture and Society, Harry L. Shapiro, ed. New York, Oxford University Press, 1960.

Montagu, Ashley, *Man: His First Million Years.* New York, New American Library, 1959.

Montagu, Ashley, *Man in Process.* New York, New American Library, 1961.

*Ralph, P. L., *The Story of Our Civilization.* New York, Dutton, 1959.

*Sedillot, Rene, *History of the World in 240 Pages.* New York, New American Library, 1951.

Woolley, Sir Leonard, *Digging up the Past.* Baltimore, Penguin Books, 1960.

SELECTED FILMS

Journey into the Past (International Film Bureau) (30 min.)
> Story of ancient civilizations of the Mediterranean region told through a journey through their historic remains. Most notable architectural features of the past are pointed out and their historical significance is clearly established.

Man and His Culture (Encyclopaedia Britannica) (15 min.)
> Analyzes and describes culture. Defines culture as a system of behavior which includes all the things a group does to facilitate its continued existence.

Our Inheritance From the Past (Coronet) (11 min.)
> This presentation of the contributions of the past to our modern life creates a better understanding and appreciation of historic advances. The fact that our modern world is actually a product of the past is made clear by studying past civilizations and their accomplishments.

Paper (10 min.)
> From the series, *Milestones in Writing*. Shows the making of a piece of paper by the processes used when paper first arrived in the Western World.

Pictographs (10 min.)
> From the series, *Milestones in Writing*. The development of man's early efforts at written communication through picture writing and idea signs is discussed.

Story of Prehistoric Man, The (Coronet) (11 min.)
> This description of the life, appearance, habitat, and achievements of prehistoric man is reconstructed from authentic evidence: prehistoric tools and weapons, cave paintings and stone carvings, and skeletal remains. The periods of the Old and New Stone Ages are indicated and the geographical areas in which prehistoric man lived are mapped.

2

Early Historic Cultures
(3300 B.C. to 600 B.C.)

EMERGENCE OF EARLY HISTORIC CIVILIZATIONS

Where nomadic tribes finally settled down, civilizations developed. The earliest appeared in the "Fertile Crescent" (which includes what is now also called the "Mesopotamia" region along the Tigris–Euphrates valley) and along the Nile River. Through a simple agriculture, they started to meet their minimal needs. By settling, however, they became subject to conquest by nomadic tribes. The result was a mingling of the mores and folkways of the conquerors and the conquered over a considerable area and, usually, the consequent development of a higher level of culture. Indeed, culture became exceedingly complicated as the peoples of these regions developed the use of bronze (later iron metals) and worked out elaborate systems for writing down their languages.

There were also simultaneous developments of culture along the Indus and Ganges rivers of India and the Yellow River of China. Since, however, extensive information is not yet available concerning the early development of these civilizations, and since they do not affect Western civilization until nearer modern times, this study omits them.

Life along these two river systems was not simple and required a complicated social organization, from which strong leaders emerged. Powerful central authority seems to have been required to maintain the rigid social structure necessary to produce and maintain living conditions. The people were organized to repel invaders, to build a network of

canals and ditches to control the floods of the rivers, and to raise agricultural products. Because of the high fertility of the soil and of climatic
conditions generally favorable for this stage of human development, a
sufficient amount of food and other necessities were produced for a
relatively high level of well-being.

The leaders of the predominant tribes became the kings and the
religious leaders (or priests). These leaders organized the activities and
developed a complex government which commanded implicit obedience.
Their power was enhanced by the development of the beliefs that they
were divinely guided or even were actually gods (e.g., the pharaohs of
Egypt). There was a very close alliance between political and religious
leaders who supported the assignment of absolute power and divine
authority to the kings. At times, this divinity status extended to his
privileged class of office-holders and subordinate priests. Well-organized
political, economic, and religious institutions developed and centered
around the need of maintaining a way of life. These institutions welded
the people together in order to carry on the necessary corporate tasks.
Bodies of doctrine and dogma grew to provide the rationale underlying
the special techniques deemed necessary to maintain the established way
of living. Basic law codes were set up to maintain these rights. Commerce
and trade developed. There was also an increased development of the
arts, sculpture and painting, architecture, rudimentary science, literature, etc.

During the fourth and the third millenniums B.C., there was considerable improvement in the skills of manufacturing goods and an increase
in commerce and in communication between the distant peoples. The
continual wars brought the cities of the Mesopotamia area into even
larger empires so that eventually several millions of peoples came under
one rule. In the Nile River Valley, the kings (or pharaohs) were able to
bring the peoples living in widely scattered villages (rather than cities)
into a well-knit organized nation which quite often extended its jurisdiction over the neighboring states of the region to the east.

All of these developments eventually made life more complex and
made necessary a longer period of training to provide the requisite skills
to cope with the problems of living in this complex civilization. Schools
and, later on, the higher institutions of education were thus organized
to meet these needs.

Fertile Crescent.   In the Mesopotamia region of the Fertile Crescent,
the Sumerians (3000 B.C.), the Akkadians (2385 B.C.) and other peoples
successively dominated the area until finally a strong centralized government was achieved by the Babylonians (1800 B.C.).[1] Government and

1 Jacquetta Hawkes and Sir Leonard Wooley, *Prehistory and the Beginnings of Civilization,* pp. 384-6.

religion became so intertwined that the king's power was considered to be divine, and he exerted considerable control over every phase of life. In Babylonia, although the king was not divine, the actual ruler was the local city-god and the king himself was given divine power by this god. The inequalities were accepted as normal and right in the laws and customs which assigned very special privileges to the upper classes.

After the period of the Babylonian ascendency, whole series of kingdoms and peoples arose and fell during these early centuries of historic civilization. One city–state after another would become predominant. However, there was a continuity of civilization. The conquerors usually absorbed the older civilization and many times its language, particularly for official business and religious affairs, even though they used a different language among themselves. Two of the more important examples of such absorbing empires were the Assyrian and Persian.

The Assyrians dominated the area during the latter half of the second millennium B.C. and into the first. They created the first large-scale empire and used a conscript army from the masses, training them carefully. They developed improved iron weapons, a swift group of soldiers on horseback (or cavalry), and an artillery. The Assyrians can be compared to the totalitarian powers in the modern world. They perfected the practice of terrorizing the enemy through torture and annihilation. Sometimes they displaced whole nations by force.

The last great empire of the Mesopotamia area in this period was that of the Persians (now called Iranians), who conquered not only the Mesopotamia area and west to Egypt, but also most of the known world west of India (seventh and sixth centuries B.C.). The Persian Empire was the end of a long political development starting with tribal organizations of nonliterate man and progressing through the city and city–state stage to the kingdom state. Finally the many cities of the Persian area east of the Mesopotamia were united, culminating in a centralized empire covering an enormous amount of territory and ruling millions of people. Eventually this empire moved in and took over the peoples of the Mesopotamia area and, later, others to the west.

The Persians proved themselves to be more able empire builders than the Assyrians because they treated their subjects more tolerantly and humanely and also looked upon their empire as an integral whole. They introduced an empire-wide coinage system, built roads between parts of the empire, and granted a large measure of local autonomy for the different peoples in their local language, literature, and art. The uniform coinage, roads, and laws helped in the further development within the empire and the consequent exchange of culture. The political and economic forms which they developed for their empire were later adopted by Alexander the Great. Later adaptations were also used by the Roman Empire and eventually by many of the European emperors in the area of modern history well up into the latter part of the eighteenth century. The conception of government common to all these early kingdoms was that the power of the ruler was considered to be divinely ordained, absolute, and unlimited.

In spite of local autonomy, there was little tradition of democratic self-government of the people in any of these oriental despotisms. The Persians, and later on the Macedonian-Greeks and the Romans, gave a great deal of freedom to groups of people of different nationalities and cultures within the empire to develop their own institutions, provided they recognized the political sovereignty and superiority of the Empire rule. These local institutions were also authoritarian and absolute within their area of jurisdiction.

The Nile River. The development of the Egyptians along the Nile River was similar in many respects to those of the Middle East and Asia Minor. Because of Egypt's isolation, it was not as exposed to attacks; therefore, it developed a less highly militarized civilization. They had no walled cities, tended not to build large cities, and preferred to live in smaller villages, the king and his capitol being an exception.

Throughout its long continuous history (5000 B.C.–675 B.C.), Egypt was united politically under a long series of dynasties of pharaoh–kings. There was great cultural continuity from dynasty to dynasty. The pharaoh carried out his absolute rule, with the help of the religious leaders. These lived in specially assigned temples and took care of religious ceremonies, arranged from embalming the dead, and taught the people out of the Book of the Dead. This book included appropriate procedures for the day of judgment after death in order to be saved from eternal destruction. The king also had a large group of nonreligious officials to carry out his military commands, to construct public works, to collect taxes, and to maintain order. All these officials were accountable only to the king. He could dispose of their lives or property as he saw fit. The pharaoh, or sovereign king, was considered to be a god whose power was not to be disputed.

Other Ancient Civilizations. Besides the great empires already mentioned, there were many other civilizations which had their day along the Eastern shores of the Mediterranean and among the islands of the Aegean Sea. The Phoenicians along the Mediterranean shore were important for their wide-ranging commerce and trade. Of great significance was the fact that they were able to refine the alphabet which had developed among the Semitic peoples and use it in their written language.

The cities on the coast of Asia Minor, and particularly the inhabitants of Crete with their development of the Minoan civilization, likewise developed a remarkable ability in commerce, architecture, and engineering. The cities on the mainland and islands of Greece in the first millennium B.C. were developing a culture and forms of social organization more democratic than those of the oriental kings, and more in line with basic ideology of later Western civilization. These developments are described in greater length in the next chapter.

Important too, because of their impact upon the culture of the Western world directly and through the Christian religion (the Judeo–Christian element of Western civilization), was the development of certain wandering Semitic tribes, now called Jewish, which finally settled in Palestine approximately 1500 B.C. After settling here, there was a long period of rule under patriarchs, often called "judges." This was followed by a period of extensive kingdoms, under such kings as David and Solomon. Under Solomon, the Jewish nation became, for a time, an empire holding within its jurisdiction some of the neighboring groups in the fashion of other oriental states. However, it never became as extensive as the other empires of this area. Around 722 B.C., the ten northern tribes of Israel were conquered and transported to Assyria. The two remaining southern tribes were conquered in the early sixth century B.C. and taken in exile by the Babylonians. After about fifty years of Babylonian captivity, the Jews were released by Cyrus, the Persian king who had taken over Babylonia, and they were permitted to return to Palestine. Later, Palestine was conquered by Alexander the Great and finally by the Romans. The Jews were then dispersed as a nation by the Roman emperors starting about A.D. 100, and have not as yet been completely re-united. A part of the descendents make up the modern state of Israel.

The Jewish culture of this era of historic civilization, however, has influenced Western civilization at innumerable points, both in religious and other cultural and scientific matters. Since the Jewish people did not develop a highly complicated religion nor a complicated political state, they tended to emphasize, particularly in the period of their history called the "Era of the Prophets," individual morality. This affected the general level of morality of the Jewish people, and in turn had a strong influence on the early beginnings of Christianity.

EDUCATION IN EARLY HISTORIC CULTURES

Informal education, undifferentiated in function or in institutions from the rest of the culture, tended to be the predominant form here, just as it was in the nonliterate groups discussed in the first chapter. Very few individuals in these civilizations ever became literate. However, because there was a written language, the school as a differentiated institution for these few emerged as a necessity during this period.

Appearance of Formal Schools. Educational historians generally seem to agree that the formal schools as such appeared at that stage of culture when it became important to pass on a written literature, quite often related to the history and religion of the people, and to teach certain persons to write for religious or commercial reasons. These first schools grew largely under the control of the priestly class (in some few cases under "secular" scribes) to whom the art of writing was essential because of access to the sacred literature. The preparation of persons to become secular scribes was probably done through a type of apprentice education ("on-the-job" training) rather than a formal full-time school.

As the culture came more and more to deal with written material, it became more and more necessary to develop a formal education. In Egypt, for example, it seems that the schools developed in connection with the temples and, to a lesser extent, in the king's offices where writing was required. There is interesting archeological evidence both in Egypt and in Sumeria in the remains of the copybooks made by boys who were learning to write. This evidence makes it clear that such schools were not only set up in Egypt, but also in Sumeria and other parts of Babylonia to train priests for religious purposes and to train officials to take part in the affairs of the king. On-the-job training for writing in connection with commerce probably was practiced also at this time.

Up to the first millennium b.c., schooling was organized and controlled primarily for the upper class. Skill in the written language had a very great scarcity value for entrance into the religious, political, and economic life of the time. Certainly possession of these skills conferred status at the lower levels of officialdom or priesthood. But, for the great masses of people, there was no thought of any kind of formal schooling or learning to read and write language. Education for them still continued through nonschool agencies and would do so for two more millennia. The families reared their children to engage in whatever kind of occupation they knew, whether it was working the land, taking care of the animals, or some kind of skilled artisanship or trade. Education for the common people then, in Egypt and the Middle East during this period, was essentially like that of the nonliterate peoples.

Importance of Written Language. The school developed early as an institution concerned with the perpetuation of a language and literature. The development of a written language was probably one of the greatest steps that human social evolution ever took, because men could then preserve their acts and ideas for others to read.

While the invention of writing must be considered a very great step in terms of cultural development, an important educational problem was created which has plagued formal schooling ever since. A devotion to the mastery of reading tended to change education from the very informal and direct induction into the culture of the people of that time to something quite esoteric and academic. Schooling deals with written materials which have quite often come out of the past and may have little or no meaning for the present. Often the language of the books is a language no longer spoken by the people. In the history of the development of human culture, the problems, limitations, and restrictions in progress or change due to the development of a literature, and the rigid teaching of this literature, must be carefully assessed.

The development of writing came about as nonliterate man scrawled on walls crude pictures of the world which he saw around him. Although the pictures of these objects did not in themselves constitute writing, in both Babylon and Egypt this process finally took the form of picture-writing or pictograms.

These symbols represent a simplified or conventionalized drawing of actual objects to represent or substitute for them. Later, these came to refer not only to the object or action portrayed but to have a conceptual meaning beyond that object. Still later, the symbol came to designate the vocal sound of the name of its object and could then represent words not capable of being diagrammed (abstractions). Later these written signs, greatly stylized and simplified, referred to syllabic sounds combined to make up words standing for objects or ideas. Eventually, among the Semitic peoples and the Phoenicians, they were developed to represent the sounds of individual consonants and could thus be put into different combinations, thereby expanding still further the scope of the meaning. When these single letters were organized into an alphabet, the final stage in the evolution of writing had then taken place.

Although the Egyptians did use symbols to stand for a single sound, they never achieved a complete alphabet. This step was taken apparently by some unknown Semitic tribe and was transmitted to Western civilization through the alphabet used by the Phoenicians. The Greeks adapted and changed the Phoenicians' alphabet using letters not needed for their consonant sounds to indicate vowels.[2]

Writing, like most other inventions, was not a sudden inspiration springing from the intellect of man. It was a cultural development by which to make records necessary to maintain the rigid social structures. Written language, therefore, came about—at least on a permanent basis— only after culture became complex and there was a necessity for keeping records of governmental business, of religious affairs, and of communication between persons at a distance.

[2] Mario Pei, *The Story of Language,* pp. 72–80.

As far as is now known, the earliest written records apparently consisted of such things as accounts, property-holdings, legal documents, numerous medical formulas, and magic recipes. The oldest-known dated writing has been found in Sumeria and dates back to about 3300 B.C. Recent discoveries in Iraq have turned up cuneiform textbooks on mathematics used by schoolboys in Sumeria as early as 2000 B.C.[3] They have found also earlier tablets dealing with myths of the race, epic poems, and songs. The cuneiform writing was a stylized form of picture writing in which a wedge-shaped instrument was used to imprint into moist clay. These were then baked and consequently have been very well preserved.

The Egyptians had learned to make paper from the papyrus plant and this accelerated the process of writing as far as Egypt was concerned. Writing was thus developed to a very high state of efficiency in Egypt and was preserved by inscriptions cut into monuments so that they can be read by modern day archeologists. Many songs and stories which had been passed on by generations of oral discourse such as the *Egyptian Book of the Dead,* the Hebrew biblical literature, and the Homeric epic were preserved because of the development of the writing skills.

In general, the skill of writing was confined to the privileged few—largely the upper classes associated with the kings and priests. The ability to write, therefore, was a means of preferment and was very highly prized. The early writing was very complex, since without alphabets many symbols had to be learned, and its mastery took a long time. As the written language became simplified through the use of the alphabet and became available to greater numbers of people through mass printing, it made possible an extension of an influence toward greater democracy. This influence has not as yet been fully realized by the various world civilizations. It was only through a relatively simple system of writing using the alphabet developed in the Western world that education became intelligible enough that it could be extended to groups other than the elite or leisure class. It was through this that the foundations for a more widespread culture in the democratic spirit were laid.

The School and the Written Language. The development of written language and literature, and of formal schools in these civilizations to train certain individuals to write and to perpetuate the literature, had the effect of further stabilizing the culture and of slowing down change. The written book, particularly when tied in with religious sanctions, became the source of authority.

Ideas of the past, however, tend to be venerated. When there is no written literature, it is easier to bring about change. Since the past is not

[3] An interesting discussion of material found on these and other clay tablets from Sumeria at this date and somewhat later and on papyrus manuscripts from Egypt around 2000–1200 B.C. is found in V. Gordon Childe, *Man Makes Himself,* pp. 143–177. See also, Samuel N. Kramer, *History Begins at Sumer,* pp. 36–45.

recorded, the oral tradition can be easily modified. The nonliterate peoples are often not aware that changes have come about—they may be so gradual. The schools of the early historic cultures tended to be related not to the current culture, but to the past as recorded in the written literature. What changes did come about in the culture were the result of the forces outside the school and in many cases outside of the culture, such as conquests or cultural diffusion.

Because of the possible influence of Jewish schools upon early Christianity, it may be of interest to consider briefly education in this period of Jewish history. Early Jewish education was very similar to that of the nonliterate peoples surrounding them, that is, of a highly informal nature. Probably this persisted longer among the nomadic and relatively unsettled Jewish peoples than those of the Egyptian and of the Tigris–Euphrates civilizations nearby. However, development of a written set of laws with very minute prescriptions for the daily life of the Jewish people, and the later developments of the religious synagogue centered around the religious teacher, rabbi, caused the Jewish people at this later stage in their development to place a great emphasis upon education. Each head of the family had considerable responsibility in the appropriate inter-pretation of the complexities of Jewish laws. Formal schools of a higher educational nature were set up by the scribes (sofferim) in order to train students in the interpretation of the law.

Later the Jewish families were unable to continue the education of their children to any great extent, partially due to the fact that the spoken language became Aramaic rather than the Hebrew, the language of the law and the tradition. There began to be recommendations by Jewish leaders for special secondary schools around 75 B.C., and with the rise of the secondary schools, there was a need for elementary schools. By A.D. 64 these schools were established. They were closely tied in with the religious authorities and with religious education, at least regarding the interpreta-tion of the Jewish Law and traditions. These Jewish schools with their closer ties with religion came into contact with Greek learning as it had permeated throughout the area in the Hellenistic period. It was in this climate that early Christianity as a dissident sect of the Jews began to arise. While it was still an underground movement, it was necessary for the early Christians to set up certain kinds of educational facilities. At this time and also later, as a church responsibility in the early part of the Middle Ages, it is likely that some of the experiences of the Jewish people with their religious schools were utilized. There was no model for religious education among either the Romans or the Greek schools.

Curriculum and Methods. The curriculum involved in the formal schools of these civilizations was almost exclusively the sacred literature or at least the national epic (history). The emphasis in these schools was on the imparting of the sacred literature in its exact form. Many times this literature was written in a form of the language which was no longer spoken, or even in a markedly different language. Consequently, the emphasis upon form rather than meaning and the splitting of hairs concerning meaning was quite often the emphasis.

The methods of teaching stressed the use of the copy book in which the youngsters copied down the sacred literature as best they could. The use of continuous repetition or memory methods was continued until the student had completely mastered the original material. In this memorization, there was little or no emphasis upon meaning and no application to current life situations. It is true, of course, that where the laws did prescribe certain kinds of behavior, there was great discussion as to precisely what the laws meant. This was the case with Hebrew, which language prescribed the demands of the Jewish law.

FREEDOM VERSUS CONFORMITY IN ANCIENT CIVILIZATIONS

Actually, this period makes very little contribution to the development of man's freedom. It was a period when the very complex historic cultures with highly organized political governments and highly organized religions surrounded the individual with minutiae of specific requirements which prescribed very completely the nature of each individual's life. There was little gained by improvement in ancient literature, ancient laws, or ways of life. Everything was designed to hem the tradition in securely by political and religious requirements of the highest order.

Among the Jewish people an exception occurred when the prophets, with their emphasis upon principles of ethics rather than upon explicit prescriptions concerning human behavior, preached and denounced the religious and political authorities. It is, of course, important not to underemphasize the importance of this outlook on Western civilization, particularly since it was preserved in the ideals which influenced early Christianity and, through the preserved writings of the Jews and early Christians, reinfluenced later Christianity. However, it can be firmly said that the total emphasis of this period was upon preserving the security and the culture of the people through a tightly knit organization which effectively prevented individual choice. The individual was not encouraged nor permitted to make innovations which it was felt might jeopardize the civilization.

SUMMARY

Starting around 3300 B.C., civilizations which are termed "oriental-type civilizations" began to develop in the fertile river valleys. Because of settled agriculture and growth of the cities in the civilizations, there developed of necessity a complex government which commanded explicit obedience from the people in order to maintain the necessary agricultural, religious, political, and economic structures of life. In general, then, these civilizations contained essentially the following characteristics: There was a strong centralized rule with a very highly complex government which demanded complete obedience; there was a written dominant language and literature which enabled the civilization to develop a character and to maintain itself; there was a relatively high level of culture compared to the previous nonliterate peoples, manifesting itself in the development of art, architecture, a greater abundance of food and other more satisfactory living conditions; there was a high level of stability, at least for relatively long periods, and when the changes would occur in the dominant peoples, for example, those in the fertile crescent, there were few changes in the characteristics of the civilization involved; there was a prevailing attitude existing in these cultures as there had been among nonliterate peoples opposing any kind of cultural change; and finally as a result of these features, the individual came to be dominated by the social institutions because of their complexity and rigidity.

The development of common language and recorded literature was important in counteracting the cultural drift which might have occurred unconsciously without written language. In the story of freedom and conformity, there was little added during this period since conformity was the key word. Nevertheless, the stress laid by Jewish prophets upon principles of ethics and their denunciation of religious and political authorities did affect the preservation of the literature and acceptance of it by Christianity. Thus, through the dominant role of Christianity in later European civilization, Jewish ethical values effected the history of freedom in the Western world.

SELECTED BIBLIOGRAPHY

Starred items represent books most closely paralleling chapter content.

General Books

*Barclay, W., *Educational Ideals of the Ancient World.* London, Collins, 1959.

Bibby, Geoffrey, *Four Thousand Years Ago.* London, Collins, 1962.

Brewer, J. A., *Literature of the Old Testament,* 3d ed. New York, Columbia University Press, 1962.

Brinton, Crane, *A History of Western Morals, Vols. I, II.* New York, Harcourt, Brace and World, 1959.

Burrows, Millar, *The Dead Sea Scrolls.* New York, Viking, 1955.

Castle, E. B., *Ancient Education and Today.* Baltimore, Penguin, 1961.

Drazin, Nathan, *History of Jewish Education from 515 B.C.E. to 220 C.E.: (During the Periods of the Second Commonwealth and the Tannaim.)* The Johns Hopkins University Studies in Education, No. 29. Baltimore, Johns Hopkins, 1940.

*Durant, Will, *The Story of Civilization: Our Oriental Heritage.* New York, Simon and Schuster, 1935.

Frankfort, Henri, *Birth of Civilization in the Near East.* Bloomington, Indiana University Press, 1951.

Frost, S. E., Jr., *Historical and Philosophical Foundations of Western Education.* Columbus, Ohio, Charles E. Merrill, 1966.

Gaster, T. H., *The Scriptures of Dead Sea Sects.* London, Secker and Warlung, 1957.

*Gordon, Cyrus H., *The World of the Old Testament,* 2d ed. New York, Doubleday, 1958.

*Hart, Joseph K., *Creative Moments in Education.* New York, Holt, Rinehart and Winston, 1931.

*Hawkes, Jacquetta and Wooley, Sir Leonard, *Pre-history and the Beginnings of Civilization: History of Mankind,* Vol. I. Sponsored by UNESCO. New York, Harper & Row, 1963.

Heidel, Alexander, *The Babylonian Genesis,* 2d ed. Chicago, University of Chicago Press, 1951.

Heritage of American Education, Richard E. Gross, ed. Boston, Allyn and Bacon, 1962.

Hertzler, J. O., *Social Thought of the Ancient Civilizations.* New York, McGraw-Hill, 1936.

Keller, Werner, *The Bible as History.* New York, Morrow, 1956.

Kramer, Samuel Noah, *History Begins at Sumer,* 2d ed. London, Thames and Hudson, 1961.

Larson, Martin A., *The Religion of the Occident: The Origin and Development of the Essene-Christian Faith.* New York, Philosophical Library, 1959.

*McNeill, William, *History Handbook of Western Civilization.* Chicago, University of Chicago Press, 1953.

*Mulhern, James, *A History of Education: A Social Interpretation,* 2d ed. New York, Ronald, 1959.

Muller, Herbert J., *Freedom in the Ancient World.* New York, Harper & Row, 1961.

Mumford, Lewis, *The City in History: Its Origins, Its Transformations, and Its Prospects.* New York, Harcourt, Brace and World, 1961.

New Perspectives in World History, Shirley Engle, ed. Thirty-four Yearbook of the National Council of the Social Studies. Washington, D.C., National Education Association, 1964.

Ogg, Oscar, *The 26 Letters.* New York, Crowell, 1961.

Orlinsky, Harry M., *Ancient Israel.* Ithaca, Cornell, 1954.

*Power, Edward J., *Main Currents in the History of Education.* New York, McGraw-Hill, 1962.

Renan, Ernst, *Life of Jesus.* Cambridge, Massachusetts, Roberts Brothers, 1895.

Shotwell, James T., *The Long Way to Freedom.* New York, Bobbs-Merrill, 1960.

Smith, William A., *Ancient Education.* New York, Philosophical Library, 1955.

*Wallbank, Thomas Walter, and others. *Civilization: Past and Present.* Chicago, Scott, Foresman, 1962.

*Wilds, Elmer H. and Lottich, Kenneth V., *The Foundations of Modern Education,* 3d ed. New York, Holt, Rinehart, and Winston, 1961.

*Woody, Thomas, *Life and Education in Early Societies.* New York, Macmillan, 1959.

Pertinent Paperbound Books

Breasted, J. H., *Development of Religion and Thought in Ancient Egypt.* New York, Scribner's, 1912.

Building of the Human City: A Documentary Record of Western Civilization, Thomas P. Neill, ed. Garden City, New York, Doubleday, 1960.

*Burrell, Sidney, *The Main Strands of Development from the Beginning to the Eighteenth Century. Elements of Western Civilization,* Vol. I. San Francisco, Chandler, 1959. Pp. 57.

*Cheney, L. J., *A History of the Western World: From the Stone Age to the Twentieth Century.* New York, New American Library, 1959.

Childe, V. Gordon, *Man Makes Himself.* New York, New American Library, 1951.

————, *The Prehistory of European Society.* Baltimore, Penguin Books, 1958.

Cottrell, Leonard, *Anvil of Civilization.* New York, New American Library, 1957.

Frankfort, Henri, *Birth of Civilization in the Near East.* Bloomington, University of Indiana Press, 1951.

*Frost, S. E., Jr., *Essentials of History of Education.* New York, Barron's, 1947.

*Kirchner, Walter, *Western Civilization to 1500.* New York, Barnes and Noble, 1960.

Muller, Herbert J., *The Loom of History*. New York, Harper & Row, 1958.
Orlinsky, Harry M., *Ancient Israel*. Ithaca, Cornell University Press, 1954.
Pei, Mario, *The Story of Language*. New York, New American Library, 1949.
*Ralph, Phillip Lee, *The Story of Our Civilization: 10,000 Years of Western Man*. New York, Dutton, 1959.
Ryan, Patrick J., *Historical Foundations of Public Education in America*. Dubuque, Iowa, William C. Brown, 1965.
Sedillot, Rene, *History of the World in 240 Pages*. New York, New American Library, 1951.

SELECTED FILMS

Alphabet, The   (10 min.)
   From the series, *Milestones in Writing*. Traces the evolution of the letters from their Semitic origin through their Greek and Roman forms, to the forms we use today.

Ancient Egypt (Coronet)   (11 min.)
   Develops the way in which Egyptian civilization contributed to western culture—development of agriculture and community living, discoveries in the arts and sciences, and the development of religion.

Ancient Egyptian, The (International Film Foundation)   (27 min.)
   A picture of life in ancient Egypt based upon photographs of great painting, sculpture, and architecture.

Ancient Mesopotamia (Coronet)   (11 min.)
   The contributions of the Sumerians, Semites, Babylonians, and Assyrians are depicted against authentic locales that include Babylon, Ur, and Ninevah. These people were first to use the arch and the wheel and develop a code of laws, a system of writing, and military science.

Ancient Order, The: The Far East (Coronet)   (13½ min.)
   In India, China, and Japan, traces the growth of early oriental civilizations through re-enactments and authentic locales. The film is enriched with early manuscripts, paintings, sculpture, and architecture to show the heritage and ideas that have shaped oriental life and thought from ancient times to the present day.

Calendar, The: Story of Its Development (Coronet Films)   (11 min.)
   Traces the development of our calendar through Egyptian, Babylonian and Roman cultures outlining the steps that led to the Julian and eventually the Gregorian calendar which is used in most of the world today.

Early American Civilizations (Mayan, Aztec, Incan) (Coronet)   (13½ min.)
   Beautiful Mayan carvings, the Teotihuacanos' Pyramid of the Sun, the Aztec calendar stone, fine Incan weavings, and other art objects, ruins, and reconstructions attest today to the highly developed civilizations of the Mayas, Aztecs, and Incas. Influences of these cultures upon our own cultures are explained.

Holy Land, The (International Film Bureau)   (15 min.)
    This visit to the Jordan Valley, Sea of Galilee, Bethlehem, Nazareth, and Jerusalem is one of the best we have ever taken by film.

Holy Land, The: Background for History and Religion   (11 min.)
    Adding enrichment to the study of the geography, history, and literature of ancient Palestine, this film presents scenes where important historical events took place.

Papyrus   (10 min.)
    From the series, *Milestones in Writing.* Stresses the importance of the papyrus plant in the life of the ancient Egyptians, with emphasis on its use as a writing substance. A piece of papyrus is made in the ancient way, following directions left us by the Roman, Pliny.

The School (Gaumont-British)   (15 min.)
    Portrays educational methods of Jews in Palestine at the time of Christ.

3

The Development of
Greek Culture and
Education

GREEK CULTURE AND THOUGHT

The reasons for the development on the Attic peninsula of a different kind of civilization than those which had evolved in Far Asia, the Middle East, or the Nile area are difficult for the historian to formulate. Fairly advanced civilizations, the Minoan and the Mycenaean, had already developed in the vicinity of this peninsula prior to the invasion of the various Greek tribes. As was the case with other oriental-type civilizations of Asia Minor, levels of art and of culture were quite high. These areas were invaded by certain Aryan tribes from the north who called themselves Hellenes because, as they said, they were descended from a common ancestor, Hellen. In English and other related tongues of Europe they are called Greeks. The Greeks conquered the older civilizations, absorbed them and, in time, improved upon them. There was an early period (somewhat resembling the Medieval Period in Europe when civilization declined) but it did recover and, eventually, reach new heights.

Development of the First Western-Type Society. From around the eighth to the sixth century B.C., the Greeks developed from a loose city–state pattern of tribal political organization to a more advanced form in which full sovereignty was transferred to the state proper. The state, centering on its city, *city–state*, rather than the tribe, came to be more and more the political, economic, social, and religious center for the life of the people. This meant that the inhabitants of a certain territory no longer owed their allegiance and loyalties as members of a family or a related group of peoples, but as citizens of the state.

Also, during this time, the political power shifted from the old tribal king, first, to the aristocratic families; then, to the body of property-owners and, finally, to the citizens in general. This process, of course, was chaotic, irregular, and, actually it did not take place in all of the city–states. Sparta is an example of where the process of change stopped at aristocratic control. In Sparta, the number of people who had freedom to make a choice was probably always less than five per cent. The remainder were either free men who were not citizens or one of the vast number of slaves with no rights.

On the other hand, Athens is the best example of a Greek state in which the process continued on through to a democracy involving the entire citizens class, a large proportion of the inhabitants. The number of free men who had power to make decisions was always higher and became still higher in Athens' later history. Furthermore, the rights granted to the free men of Athens were much greater. A great deal more opportunity for each individual, whether citizen, "free" man, and slave, to make his own decisions was permitted.

One of the most important developments during this period was the maturation of the concept that law was a man-made affair. Growing out of the desire to regulate and to insure appropriate behavior, this development is a most important one in the history of culture and education. In all the oriental–type despotisms discussed earlier, the law was the word of a king or traditional law giver who either, claimed divine revelation or ruled in the name of a god. Thus, the law *absolutely* ruled *all men* and could not be changed readily by them. In Greece, the law, *binding* on men but being conceived as human in origin, could be changed by men if it became too irksome. Having this view of law, men began to exert control over man-made social institutions and practices in *their own* interests.

Another important factor which helps explain Greek history is that Greece developed from politically independent, small city–states. This meant that each state had developed and experimented with its own ideas. Although there were differences at many times among the Greek city–states, eventually a common spoken language, a common alphabet, and a traditional literature did take form.

There was, of course, a great contrast between the oligarchic, rigid type of city–state such as Sparta and the much more democratic one such as Athens. The two states were alike in that the power to rule was fairly widely dispersed within the oligarchy.

Although publicly the Greek state was religious, there was no dominant priestly class. There was no dogma which could place a restriction upon man's intellect. Students of Greek civilization, and of civilizations in general, are fairly well agreed that the Greek type and level of culture was achieved largely as an historical accident of social structure. Since the Greeks are very closely related to other European Aryans who did not accomplish nearly so much so early, it could not have been due to any superior or inherited characteristics of the Greeks themselves.

Two Contrasting Western-Type States. The political and social backgrounds of the two most important but contrasting Greek states, both of which can be called Western or occidental in outlook, were Sparta and Athens.

Sparta. Sparta was the most powerful state on the Peloponnesus, the lower area or peninsula of Greece. Sparta had been settled by Dorian tribes who had invaded around the eighth century B.C. At first there had been very little difference in their make-up from that of the other Greek tribes. After a rebellion by a neighboring city–state, Messenia, there was a change in the general attitude of the Spartans toward their government and military discipline. As a means to survival, due to the existence of a hostile population which outnumbered the Spartan citizens about twenty to one, they instituted certain constitutional reforms which made them, in modern terms, a totalitarian state based upon the conception of "master race" or an "elite" party.

These reforms or laws have been attributed to a man by the name of Lycurgus (*c.* 800 B.C.). This constitution provided for three well-defined classes: the Spartan citizens, the provincials (*Perioeci*), and the *Helots*. The Spartan citizens never numbered more than about nine to ten thousand families. They separated themselves and ruled the state vigorously by military power. The provincials, numbering of around 120,000, were the former masters of Laconia before its conquest by the Dorians but who retained their land, continued to till the soil and to engage in commerce. Probably, they were of Greek blood from earlier migrations. Given some freedom, the provincials furnished some troops for the Spartan armies, paid taxes, but had no rights of citizenship. The helots, about 250,000, were slaves and as such continually harrassed by the Spartans.

Within the citizen class of the Spartans, there was some semblance of democratic forms despite the totalitarian nature of the system as a whole. There were two kings who served as head of the government and ruled with the advice of a council of elders through the work of the "ephors" (magistrates). The council and the ephors were actually elected by the popular assembly, consisting of all adult male citizens. Since they were required to do so, these were the same adults who served in the army. Consequently, Sparta was a completely militarized state, run by the military—the citizen class—in its own interest.

The helots, or slaves, were assigned to work for these citizens, the Spartans themselves not being allowed to engage in commerce or work with their hands, or in any other activity but war and training for war. The helots were kept in a state of constant surveillance and could be killed on the slightest provocation. An active or intelligent helot, would very likely be "liquidated" as a potential threat. As a matter of fact, the young Spartan soldier was required to ambush and kill a helot as a part of his training.

Athens. One of the major historical differences between Sparta and Athens was that the territory around Athens was unified through agreement and cooperation rather than through military conquest. As a consequence, the citizens in the Athens city–state were a much larger percentage than that in Sparta, and included some persons who were not originally in the city itself.

By the beginning of the seventh century B.C., the rulers of the Athens city–state consisted of the king who was actually the leader of the army, and the magistrates who were the civil officials. After a time the king's power declined. The civil officials became more important and, gradually, they came to be chosen by the popular assembly which consisted of all citizens of the state. The magistrates themselves were assisted in their decisions by the Council of Elders made up of aristocrats. The kings finally disappeared.

Although there was a resemblance at this early period between the structure of government in Sparta and Athens, by the process of the widening base of Athenian citizenship, the whole general structure was gradually changed. At first, only the larger property owners made up the army and then, when they needed a stronger army, they added more citizens who possessed some wealth. Finally, groups of small land-owners and artisan-workers would sometimes be given more freedom and more rights after they rose up against the entrenched groups.

Solon, who has been traditionally given credit (and there is some historical basis) as the first great law-giver in Athens, can also be credited with the substantial improvement in the status of the lower social classes (the reforms of 594 B.C.). Under Solon's laws, the mortgages and debts were eased, the punishments of imprisonment of slavery for debt were abolished, the land speculations were regulated and export trade was favored, thereby encouraging its expansion. The lower classes were finally admitted to citizenship and thus were entitled to and given a place both in the army and in the popular assembly. This admission of the lower classes to citizenship helped to make the transition from aristocracy to democracy. Furthermore, some of the reforms of the later rulers weakened the hold of the aristocracy still more by distributing their land to the poor and limiting the power of the aristocratic institutions.

Almost complete democracy was brought about among the citizen class by the reforms of Cleisthenes whose constitution went into effect about 502 B.C. In order to break up the tribal groupings which had caused certain animosities, he divided the Athenian city–state into ten regions or districts which ignored the tribal groupings. From these geographical areas rather than the tribes, the citizens elected the various military, executive, and judicial branches of the government. The legislative branch was a popular assembly which all citizens could attend. The judiciary was a large elected law court; the executive consisted of an elected council of five hundred; and the magistrates executed the mandates of this council. These were the basic forms of the Athenian political democracy which were remarkably similar to modern forms of democratic government.

The aristocratic classes, however, still played a very important part because it was some time before the public officials were paid a salary, and therefore the wealthy people who could give full time to politics tended to take the more important roles. It must also be remembered that, while the population of Athens consisted of 90,000 to 125,000 free citizens, there were also 45,000 metics. These were foreigners who had settled in Athens, engaged in commerce and manufacturing, but who did not have the right to vote. In addition, 60,000 to 70,000 adult slaves, almost wholly prisoners of war, were entitled to no privileges of citizenship.[1]

In the period from the eighth to the sixth century B.C., there had taken place profound economic as well as political changes. The Greeks had made wine products that were superior to those of the rest of the world and so they could exchange these for the products of the Eastern cultures. There also developed the cultivation of olive trees which made large tracts of land more profitable than smaller ones. Thus developed the classes of large land owners and those who engaged in commercial trade, both of whom grew economically more powerful. Their supremacy led to conflict with, and the eventual restriction of, the power of the lower classes.

All over the area of Greece, under the influence of Athens, more so than Sparta, city life became more important than before. The people who were dispossessed from their land because of the increase in the large land-owning class went to the cities and tried to improve their economic status. The city–states came more and more into rivalry with other city–states and there was almost constant warfare between them. Within the city–states themselves there was conflict between the aristocratic land-owners and the new aristocracy of money, and also between these two and the common people. Later, as the common people gained more economic power (in the fourth century B.C., for example), they gained also more political power. It should be noted that when economic opportunity was

[1] James Mulhern, *A History of Education,* p. 137.

most widely available, the Athenian political democracy was, likewise, the healthiest.[2]

The "Golden Age" of Greece. Athens reached what was probably its political and military heights of power in the fifth century, B.C., and also this was the time of the greatest height of Athenian democracy. Athens had been involved in the war of the Greek colonies against Persia in the early years of the fifth century and had sent aid to them. This led to the Persian Wars in which the Greek city–states under Athenian leadership emerged victorious.

To ward off further invasions from Persia, they established the Delian Confederacy, and this was transformed by Athens from a league of independent states into an Athenian Empire in which eventually several states were under the hegemony of Athens. The creation of the Delian Confederacy then helped Athens to become the economic center of the Mediterranean world in the fifth century, B.C. The treasury was moved from Delos to Athens and the money pouring in quite often was used by the Athenians for their own purposes.

Athens was not only a political democracy but had a very strongly imperialistic foreign policy. This policy helped the commercial and artisan classes who joined forces to make up a democratic political party. The popular assembly then gained more power at the expense of the Council of Five Hundred and an even more extreme form of democracy took shape in which merchants, sailors, artisans, and small farmers opposed the ancient nobility and the large land-owners. Pericles was the leader of the "liberal democratic" party between about 460 and 430 B.C. This is the period often known as the Periclean or "Golden Age" of Athens.

Soon democratic and imperial Athens came into conflict with the other very strong state of Greece—the conservative and aristocratic Sparta. Athens was trying to get all of Greece united under her jurisdiction into a large political unit. Sparta opposed this by upholding the right of self-determination except for the states which were under her direct control.

The long rivalry for power led to the Peloponnesian War from 431 to 404 B.C. This was as much a struggle between Athenian sea-power and Spartan land-power as it was between a democracy and a military dictatorship. Athenian sea-power was destroyed by traitorous action, and finally Sparta was able to impose her peace upon Athens. Although democracy was now discredited, it was later restored for a brief time.

For several decades the political situation in Greece was very chaotic because one city–state fought another. The cities could not get together voluntarily, and no one city–state could impose military power long enough to bring about a consolidated empire. The essential weaknesses of

2 Butts, pp. 22–23.

Greek democracy seem to have been the excessive individualism and the inability of the Greeks to subordinate themselves toward a common good. There developed a wide gap in economic status between the lower and upper class citizens, and this led to constant conflict within as well as without the city–states.

Every so often representatives of the wealthy oligarchy would get in power and try to consolidate their own interests. When the popular movement gained power, attempts at retaliation upon the wealthy citizens were made. Citizens, in general, lost their interest in politics and tried to get out of their military obligations which meant that professional politicians and mercenary soldiers took over. There was an extension in the amount of slavery, the number of the citizens in the population then decreased, and the number of noncitizens increased. Patriotic zeal weakened and military preparedness rested upon a professional army of soldiers who were hired with the Athenian's increased wealth. This weakened the city–states, and confusion made way for the subjugation of Greece by Philip of Macedonia and his successors in the third and second centuries B.C.

Socrates, Plato, Aristotle. Any discussion of Greek education would not be complete without consideration of three outstanding teachers and intellectual leaders of this time who have had enormous influence on later Western thought.

Socrates, the first of these (469–399 B.C.), left no writings. Consequently, it is difficult to determine exactly what his ideas or methods of teaching were. About all of what is known is found in the writings of Plato and Xenophon. It is not known whether the Socrates in these writings is the real Socrates or a "Socrates" used by the authors to express their own ideas. Modern scholars hold that, in some cases, in Plato's dialogues, "Socrates" is a pseudo-Socrates created to voice Plato's own ideas.

The "real" Socrates taught primarily by a method that has become quite famous, known as the "Socratic method," a question–answer technique. A student would come to him with a question to be answered to which Socrates would respond with a question directed to the student. As soon as the student began to answer that question and those that followed, he eventually discovered that he knew nothing. The phase up to this point is known as the *ironic* or *destructive* stage. Then by a series of constructively worded questions, Socrates would build up the ideas he wished to place in the student's mind.[3] This is called the *maieutic* stage which is based upon the Greek word for midwife, thus, "giving birth to ideas." Socrates apparently thought he could get at truth by skillful handling of ideas. His questions were always related to life; consequently, he is considered among the Greeks to come the closest to the pragmatist (or the

---

[3] Some contemporary writers have referred to the teaching machine (i.e. programed learning) as Socratic. A careful study will show basic differences.

modern experimentalist) in method. However, he was not a thorough going pragmatist in the modern James–Dewey sense.[4]

Plato (427–346 B.C.), although a student of Socrates, represented a withdrawal from the emphasis upon the practical and the experiential. Plato soon moved his classes away from the market place to the Grove of Academius so that he would not be bothered by the practical things. Hence comes our word "academic"—relating to things that are not necessarily practical.

Plato went ahead to develop a philosophical point of view which held that truth was ultimately to be decided by reason alone. Ideas existed quite apart from man's experience with things. As a matter of fact, to Plato, the real world was a shadowy representation of the ideal world. The real end of education consequently must be to deal with these ideas apart from the material world. It must be abstract and intellectual.

Modern followers of Plato, however, should remember that Plato's concepts about education must be considered in the context of his time. Basic Greek education at that time allowed for the well-rounded development of the student, physically and mentally, through the songs of literature and athletic activities. As shown by his suggestions for education contained in *The Republic,* he assumed the existence of this broad emphasis in the early education of all students. Plato's emphasis upon the intellectual was of course the crowning part of the education he proposed for those few persons whom he believed capable of receiving it. Some of his modern followers have attempted to define education of the intellect as being the only kind that is worthy of the name education.

Plato's influence on the thinking of his time, and on the period which was to follow when Greek culture was disseminated throughout the Mediterranean region, was great. Through Neo-Platonism, a mystical form of Platonic philosophy that spread throughout the area soon after Plato's time, he exercised a profound influence upon Christianity and, of course, through Christianity on the whole Western World for centuries to come.

Aristotle (386–322 B.C.) was Plato's pupil. He agreed basically on most matters with Plato, but he had more interest in the things of the physical world than in immaterial things. In the first place, Aristotle was actively a great scientist. He wrote voluminously upon all matters which are now embodied in the various fields of knowledge. The modern organization of these fields of knowledge follows fairly closely that which was made by Aristotle in the fourth century B.C. Aristotle was primarily a collector of facts and a classifier of knowledge. Although he wrote many books in

---

[4] An excellent analysis of Socrates and an interpretation in light of the modern world can be found in Redmond, William K., *Socrates and the Western World* (London, A. Redman, 1954).

the different divisions of scientific knowledge, he did not understand nor accept the scientific method of experimentation as it was developed in the sixteenth century. Consequently, his work does contain many serious errors. Aristotle's philosophy as such did not influence early Western civilization and it might well be said that the civilization is still basically Platonic in form.

There were other forces in the Greek culture that contrasted with the ideals of the philosophers previously discussed. These showed themselves with the development of the Sophists and their ideal of expediency. This development also occurred at a time shortly after the Golden Age. As a matter of fact, some persons have held that Socrates, the first Athenian-born philosopher, was himself a Sophist.

Along with a social conception of citizenship previously indicated, there was a strong individualistic strain in the Greek character. This became even stronger when the economic conditions made material wealth a goal which could be realized by almost any citizen, and when democracy was discredited and put on the defensive by the Peloponnesian War. Some citizens desired to perform the duties as citizens more adequately through improving their ability to speak and think effectively in order to gain more personal power and advantage in their political and personal affairs. Sophism actually has two strains to it, both of them based on strong ethical sense, sophism tended to be beneficial; but when it did approach the extreme of opportunism, it tended to undermine the democratic way of life.

The sophists did not produce the changes in Athens, but they arose largely as a result of them. The arguments of the sophists went something like this: Laws and customs are really man-made "conventions." The individual man is "the measure of all things." The individual, therefore, need not be bound by conventional laws because they do not carry universal authority. Persons should individually set up their own standards of authority, do their own thinking, and make their own judgments. Grammar and logic then are the means by which an individual sets out to change or to avoid the conventional laws by making his arguments strong enough to prevail.

It has been noted that Socrates himself stressed the individual's thinking and judgment, but he felt that he could arrive at knowledge based on experience as opposed to knowledge based merely on someone's own desire or whim.

The Hellenistic Age and the Spread of Greek Culture. After the Peloponnesian War, Athens was in bad shape. With fleet and empire gone, it was forced to join the Peloponnesian League dominated by Sparta. Sparta was unable to exercise its leadership well and, for a while, Athens was able to stage a comeback in the latter part of the fourth

century, B.C. The time was then ripe for possible invasions from the outside since the Greeks were divided and somewhat weak. In this situation,
King Phillip of Macedonia defeated the Athenian and Theban forces and
became master of Greece in 338 B.C. Alexander the Great, after the death
of his father, followed in his footsteps and conquered not only the rest
of Greece, but all of Asia Minor, Syria, Egypt, and Persia, and over as far
as India. Upon the death of Alexander, three large units emerged: Macedonia, Syria, and Egypt. Each had its emperor and quite often they
carried on wars with each other throughout this period and until the
complete domination by Rome ended the conflict. The period starting
with the death of Alexander and ending after the Roman conquest is
known as the Hellenistic Age.

During this period Greek culture was diffused throughout the Orient
and south of the Mediterranean, and was itself modified through the
contact with the Oriental cultures. The Greeks themselves left their city-
states in large numbers and settled throughout the world. The Greek
spoken by the Athenian Greeks was somewhat modified and became the
prevailing language of the new Graeco–Oriental world. Important cities
were established, such as Alexandria in Egypt, Antioch, Seleucia and
Pergamum, as great intellectual and artistic centers. Athens was able to
maintain a form of democratic constitution during this period, but lost
the vitality of the earlier period and, of course, her political independence. The reestablishment of monarchy in Greece was the end of a long
process which had started with the kingly rule, then had gone to the
aristocracy and to different forms of democracy, and finally back to
monarchy.

During this period of time, there were also changes in education
which are described more fully hereafter, but it will be clear in such discussion that Greek education seemed always to be most rich and en-
lightening when Greek democracy was at its height. It tended to become
quite pedantic and academic when political democracy was discredited
or declining.

While the excessive Greek individualism helped to destroy democracy and alter education, it did not nullify Greek economic supremacy.
The establishment of Alexander's empire really laid the political groundwork for the expansion of Greek commercial interests. Consequently, this
expansion enabled not only the Greek culture to continue to prevail, but
also enabled the Greek language to dominate business and commerce during the Hellenistic period.

With the bringing of larger areas of land under cultivation, there
was an increase in numbers in the slave class. There were always very
great conflicts between the lower and upper classes, between the rural and
urban interests, and between the people interested in agriculture and
those interested in trade. The number of free citizens in the Greek state

became smaller so that the concept of leisure as such began to be praised by the philosophers who usually represented the thinking of the upper classes. Butts has pointed out that as the number of free workers increased, *manual* labor was looked down upon as *menial* labor by the leisure classes because their wealth and status freed them from work with their hands. This enabled them to develop their art and literature and have time to "philosophize." [5]

Many modern students of Greek thought feel that the groundwork was actually laid at this time for the distinction between the *liberal arts* suitable for the free man, and the *practical arts* suitable for the "unfree" man. This was actually a period of declining democracy as persons who no longer had to work with their hands were able to have leisure time for thinking. Modern students feel that this distinction of aristocratic class culture had an enormous influence upon educational theory and practices of the Western world, and of course, upon the whole Platonic-dualistic philosophy. Dewey, among others, has held that the rationale of the dualistic Platonic idealism was based upon the economic situation existing in the Greek world and the attitude when the intellectual Greeks took toward working with the hands.[6] The reluctance of Greeks to work with their hands also held back the development of science among the Greeks after the period of intellectual height. Science was not able to regain its standing until the scientific revolution of the sixteenth century because the advance of scientific knowledge does depend on working with material things.

GREEK EDUCATION AND SCHOOLS

Early Developments. Early Greek education, as is true of the early education in all nonliterate, indigenous cultures, followed much the same pattern described in the first chapter. After the Aegean and Homeric Ages, there developed in Greece formal educational agencies to teach the Greek alphabet. These were probably used first for commercial and other trade purposes, although they may have also been used early for recording the poetic and literary tradition. Around the seventh century, and continuing in the sixth and fifth, the school as a separate institution, specifically designed to teach in a formal way certain instructional skills to the young, began to appear. Actually, in the Athenian Greek situation, it

[5] Butts, p. 44.
[6] John Dewey, *The Quest for Certainty* (New York, Putnam, 1929). Chap. 2.

would be more proper to speak of the development of specialized teachers than of schools because the youngsters went to a teacher of a particular subject or curriculum. In the fourth, third, and second centuries B.C., elementary, secondary, and higher institutions took the form roughly similar to the levels of education found in most modern countries.

It has been stated earlier than one of the political developments which took place in all of the Greek states was the breakdown of the tribal organization and the centering of life in the city–state. When this happened, education dropped its informal nature and became more political in its basis. This was somewhat the same change as that which took place in the cultures as discussed in Chapter 2, the Egyptian, Babylonian, and Hebrew cultures.

However, the development in the Greek culture did differ somewhat. Rather than religion or service to the king being the primary motive of education in the Greek state, education became primarily an institution for the making of citizens. Although the concept of citizenship varied between the states, particularly between the extremes of Sparta and Athens, it was this dominant characteristic of each state and its ideals of citizenship, which determined the character of its education during the formative period of the ninth, eighth, and seventh centuries B.C.

This close identification of education with political developments carries with it, of course, certain advantages in keeping education very fluid and in line with certain needs. There was similar emphasis of this type in the Roman educational system, and it is found again in the development of the modern, national systems of education. What follows reveals some dangers which may develop when education is tied in too closely with the demands of a contemporary political situation.

Development of Spartan and Athenian Schools. Since Spartan and Athenian education and schooling represent extremes, we discuss each separately.

Spartan Education. It was noted earlier that when Sparta emerged from its nonliterate tribal organization and developed into an aristocratic, militaristic oligarchy as a dictatorship, the state began to control education very rigidly for its purposes, just as it controlled all the other phases of life in Sparta. The persons who ruled in Sparta, the ephors, also had general supervision of educational agencies along with their other authority. Later on they appointed a special educational officer who bore the name of "paidonomus," and who took over direct supervision of carrying out the educational regulations. It would perhaps be correct to say that Sparta was setting up virtually a state system of education under state control for state purposes.[7] This is quite in consistency with the institutions of the Spartan state because the Spartan child (by which, of

7 Butts, p. 34.

course, is meant only the child of a Spartan citizen) was considered as belonging to the state from the time of his birth to his death.

The supreme purpose of the development of the Spartan male was to become a brave and ruthless warrior; therefore, the content and method of education from beginning to end was determined by militaristic considerations. At birth the boy was brought before the ephors or the ruling class, and they made the decision as to whether or not he was healthy enough to become a strong male citizen. If he were not, he was exposed upon the mountains to die or perhaps given to a foreigner to be brought up as a tradesman, worker, or slave. If the child passed the rigid tests established by the ruling magistrates, he was returned to his father and mother who kept him until the age of seven. Although Sparta was more ruthless in this respect than the other Greek states, the leaving of the infants who were considered to be unfit to be exposed on the mountains or to be sold as slaves was a common practice of that day of the peoples of Asia Minor and the other Greeks as well as the Romans.

After the age of seven and until the age of 18, the boys were sent to a barracks away from home and were organized as a group on a militaristic basis. In this fashion they received basic training in physical fitness and morale. They were organized into bands or packs under the leadership authority of younger adults. These boys were very rarely permitted to go to their homes.

After age eighteen, there was a period of intensive military training, usually followed by ten years of active military service. It is not until age thirty than men became full-fledged citizens and were expected to marry. Sparta placed very little emphasis upon intellectual or aesthetic training. They were taught to read and write, and the rest of their education was picked up incidentally through observation of their culture.

The girls continued their education at home rather than living in barracks, but they were also organized into packs and were given physical training to build up their bodies so they could bear and rear strong sons for the army. They were also given special training for household duties and were taught how to control slaves. Surprisingly in this oligarchic, "totalitarian" state the women enjoyed a relatively high status compared to other women of this time. In managing the home, while the father was absent quite frequently on military or state duties, they had a great deal of authority and were therefore very important in the maintenance of the military machine which was the Spartan state.

Athenian Education. At no time in the history of the Athenian state did it exert as complete a control over education as was characteristic of Sparta. Because there was in Athens a very important tendency toward individual freedom and democracy, the provisions for education were left in the hands of the parents during most of the period up to the Macedonian conquest (338 B.C.). However, the state did concern itself with education. This was shown by the laws issued, in particular those of Solon in the early part of the sixth century B.C. containing numerous provisions for educational matters.

There were a great variety of schools found in Athens as compared to the monolithic educational structure of Sparta. Each of these schools was designed to take care of a certain aspect of the total development of the citizen. Very likely the first formal schools appeared in Athens some time in the seventh century B.C., although schools of a less organized nature must have existed earlier as in Sparta. It is definitely known that the schools were rather widespread by the end of the Persian War in 480 B.C.

There were three types of elementary teachers and they arose by degrees: the *kitharist,* or teacher of music, coming first; followed later probably by the *grammatist,* or teacher of letters (reading, writing, and some numbers); and, later still, the *paedotribe,* or teacher of gymnastics. However, these subjects or fields are not to be interpreted the same way as they would now be. The teacher of music, for example, would more likely be called a teacher of literature or the poetic tradition. Poems from Homer and others were recited accompanied by music. It is also known that the kitharist taught reading, writing, and rudimentary arithmetic along with the music before the development of the grammatist as a separate teacher. The grammatist appeared somewhat near the end of what is generally termed the "old Athenian educational period," replaced by the "new" about the middle of the fifth century B.C.

Music, or poetry, played a very important part in Greek life. It was tied in with both religious and civic matters. The kitharist did not attempt to teach technical excellence in music but used it for the molding of character. There is evidence to indicate that the Athenian students did learn to read and write well, and that they were thoroughly imbued with the tradition and ideals of Athens and of Greece generally. Illiteracy was extremely rare among the citizen class in this early period. There was probably very little training in arithmetic or numbers because of the complicated number system; so, very likely they learned to count with the aid of the fingers or probably on an abacus.

The Greeks took great pride in their physical excellence, and gymnastics were a very important part of the education of children. In the elementary age, from about seven to fifteen, the boys frequented a private institution called the palaestra. This was probably developed from an informal playground to a more organized institution. At age fifteen, and sometimes much earlier if the parents were quite poor, the elementary education came to a close. The boys were then free from the surveillance of the pedagogue who had supervised their education up to that time. The school day was quite long and the discipline strict, and they emerged usually as well-rounded individuals. If they belonged to the poorer of the citizen classes, at the age of fifteen they would start to work. If they were well-to-do, they would go to one of the public gymnasiums to work on physical exercise beyond that of the palaestra. The gymnasiums were supported and controlled by the state with a state official in charge and, along with the gymnastic program, there were also free discussions and public lectures.

As is well known the gymnasiums later developed into an almost completely intellectualistic type of institution. Consequently, the word *gymnasium* has come to mean, in modern Greek and in certain Teutonic languages (German and Scandinavian), an academic secondary school as opposed to the common use of the term in English-speaking countries as a place for physical exercise.

At age eighteen, the young Athenian, whether having been in the home or gymnasium, became an "ephebus." At this time he took the famous Ephebic Oath, was paraded on the streets of Athens, began to bear arms, and there followed a period of two years of military training. Later, after 335 B.C., there was an Ephebic College which carried on a much more formal training than the period of military training prior to this time.[8]

The so-called new Athenian education which developed after the fifth century B.C. was called new by scholars because there was a different attitude toward the ancient tradition, a drifting away from the ancient moorings, and a greater emphasis upon the teaching of the sophists. Along with this, there arose a more clear-cut distinction between the teacher of music and the teacher of letters. The sophists or wandering scholars who came in from the colonies gave instruction for fees to the young men from fifteen on, particularly very extensive training in speech, emphasizing grammar, rhetoric, and oratory. However, the sophists did more than merely make students into orators. They were keen students and critics of the social order, and they tried to develop persons who could think and become leaders in the new society. The sophists made a very deep appeal to the young Athenians. The students left the gymnasium in great numbers and sought out the sophists. This resulted in the development of two new higher institutions of education, the rhetorical schools and the philosophical schools.

The rhetorical school continued on a higher plane the sophist idea of preparing young men for public careers. The philosophical schools were developed to elaborate the philosophical tradition initiated by Socrates, who himself was a sophist, although not entirely typical of the other sophists. The first of the rhetorical schools was founded by Isocrates, a sophist, about 390 B.C. By and large, he drew those students from all over the Greek area who planned to become the politicians and statesmen of their day. These schools continued to exist on through the next period

[8] *Ibid.*, p. 22.

and had a very strong emphasis on subsequent Roman education which also placed a strong emphasis upon political and rhetorical education.

The first of the philosophical schools growing directly out of the Socratic tradition was the Academy founded by Plato about 386 B.C. How the educational approach in this Academy, however, differed from that of Socrates has already been discussed. Three additional philosophical schools were established about the close of the fourth century B.C. They continued on into Roman times and were the Lyceum, founded by Aristotle in 335 B.C.; the Stoa, founded by Zeno in 308 B.C.; and the School of Epicurus, founded in 306 B.C.

The Lyceum, although it also included philosophy, placed more emphasis upon the natural sciences. Alexander the Great showed a strong interest in this school and, for this and other reasons, the Lyceum achieved early success and wide-spread recognition. The Stoic and Epicurean schools placed more emphasis upon human conduct and less upon logic and metaphysics. Out of these latter, two schools developed the great philosophical traditions of the Stoics and the Epicureans. These two philosophical traditions were to persist until the development of Christianity, but the Platonic and Aristotelian traditions were to continue and influence the Western world down to the present time.

One consequence that arose out of the philosophical schools and the "philosophic era" was the development of educational theory. Plato himself was very much interested in education and wrote his *Republic,* in part, to set forth his educational ideas. Aristotle did not write a book specifically on education, but references can be found throughout his many works which do imply educational principles. Plato gave his ideas on education in describing utopia, a "republic" which was not a republic in the modern sense, but actually an oligarchic state ruled by an elite-selected educational system.

Plato felt that there were three different kinds of (free) men in the world. He did not discuss the education of those who were not free citizens. The three kinds, he called "men of gold," "men of silver," and "men of iron." The "men of gold" were the outstanding intellects who should be trained to become rulers. The "men of silver" were the courageous types destined to be the soldiers and guardians of the security of the country. The "men of iron" were to be the artisans or the workers. The early education was to be much the same for all, and the ones who were to go on were to be selected on a basis of their success in the rather rigid intellectual education given to all.

It is well to remember that in Greek education there were never any prescribed curriculum, diplomas, or degrees. Also, it is probably incorrect to think of levels of education in Greece as elementary (seven to fifteen) and then the more advanced education (up to age eighteen) as secondary in the modern sense. Organization was very informal in Greek "higher" education and it cannot be compared to current higher education.

As time went on, the higher philosophic institutions became quite esoteric and even monastic in their emphasis upon a selective membership, or a group of initiates with an inner circle, similar to modern fraternal orders. These were located at or near the gymnasiums from which they took their names. The School of Cynics founded by Antisthenes, for example, is named from the gymnasium, Cynosarges, which has its origin in the Greek word for dog. The foundations for the higher education of tradition which was laid in these philosophical schools incorporates the Pythagorean and non-Platonic monastic ideals of the late Grecian period and forecasts the monastic ideals of the monkish orders of the Christian era.

Education in Hellenistic Times.   As has been said earlier, the period after the conquest by Alexander the Great is known as the Hellenistic Age. At this time, Greek culture became diffused throughout the Mediterranean area, and Greek education became quite widespread. There were, however, some changes occurring in Greek education during the Hellenistic Period. During the third and second centuries B.C., education became more systemized and there was some increase in state or civil control. There was probably more nearly a definite pattern of elementary, secondary, and higher education similar to the later modern period. Much less emphasis was placed upon gymnastics and music for the younger boys. The school of the grammatist became common and almost exclusively the elementary school. As the fields of knowledge became more extensive during this period, the school of the *grammaticus* was recognized as the accepted secondary school for boys from about thirteen or fourteen to sixteen or eighteen years of age.

The disappearance of the gymnastic and physical training came about largely because of the lack of necessity for military training. The conquest of the Greek states, and the development of the armies directly under the Macedonian rulers and their successors, were the important factors in this change of emphasis. Beyond the school of the grammaticus, there were higher education centers, the schools of philosophy and rhetoric, mentioned in the discussion of the earlier periods. These schools were also carried over into the Roman period, and were eventually either closed or reconstituted by the Christian church in the early medieval European education. The Ephebic College, set up primarily for physical and military training, but which had some intellectual content, took on more and more intellectual content after 300 B.C. The requirement for physical training was first reduced to one year and then made voluntary, and thus philosophical and rhetorical studies became the major part of the curriculum. The Ephebic college thus became more like a fashionable semimilitary academy rather than a democratic civic institution which it had been in the earlier period.

During the Hellenistic Era, there was an increase in the public support and control of education. Some cities chose an administrator of schools who resembled the modern superintendent of schools. Some teachers were appointed by the state and their salaries were paid out of public funds or from endowments. There was more supervision of the curriculum. The philosophical and rhetorical schools expanded and attracted students from all over the Hellenistic area. At the time of the height of Rome, they were spread over the entire Roman area.

Some historians have used the name, "University of Athens" for the group of philosophical schools in Athens. These schools were early examples of higher education but were much different from the university as developed in the late Middle Ages. The word "university" or its equivalent in Greek or Latin was not applied to these institutions at this time. As the Greek or Macedonian leaders carrying the Hellenistic cultures established cities such as Alexandria in Egypt and certain cities in Asia Minor, they quite often *also* established centers (often libraries and museums) for advanced study and research. These have also been termed universities by some modern historians, but they were really centers of libraries, museums, and groups of scholars engaged in a particular kind of research more than educational institutions as such. By the end of the Hellenistic period, there was a considerable number of well-educated individuals due to the general wealth and prosperity brought about by development of commerce and trade. Very likely within the area of Hellenistic influence is found the most highly educated population that had existed in any time up to the period of the advanced countries in the twentieth century. Furthermore, this Hellenistic education laid the groundwork in content and organization for the Roman system, and this in turn influenced the educational institutions of the medieval world and, through them, the modern world.

The Teaching Profession. The status of the teaching profession in Greek society was a tenuous one. In Sparta the teachers were appointed by the government and certainly would have had some type of official status on a subordinate level. Spartans, however, placed the educational responsibility on all male citizens. This had been true also in the non-literate tribal period. The idea of having all parents responsible for the education of the young, of course, would be quite democratic if it were directed toward democratic goals.

In Athens there were some teachers who had an extremely low and some who had an extremely high status. For example, elementary teachers were usually in low regard because being poor, they had to accept fees for instruction. Also, it was quite often felt that a person "who cannot do, teaches." This is found in statements quite frequently concerning the Greek grammatist [9] indicating that many persons teach because they can-

9 E. B. Castle, *Ancient Education and Today,* p. 65 *and passim* cites an example of such a reference.

not make a success of any other occupation. The assignment of slaves as teachers to young boys also indicates the low estate of teaching. These "slaves," however, sometimes had been citizens of a foreign state who had been quite well educated and sometimes they may have been outstanding persons. The sophists actually were foreigners who were held in very high regard by the Athenians even though they had no citizenship status. At the height of democracy in Athens outstanding persons flocked in, both to teach or to pay fees to study with the great sophists and other teachers.

Certainly great men like Socrates, Plato, and Aristotle as well as Epicurus and Zeno, had high social status in Athens. Of course, Socrates was condemned to death because of the threat of his popularity to the authorities, and Plato and Aristotle were each ostracized from Athens for a while. Such social pressure and demand for conformity, of course, are not rare by any means. In a similar situation the teacher in the Oriental-style cultures across the Mediterranean area would have been completely dominated. Quite often in the cities of the Hellenistic era, teachers were appointed to government posts or elected to office by the citizenry, and sometimes wealthy persons endowed funds for the support of teachers. The great Athenian schools of philosophy and rhetoric lasted for some eight hundred years, indicating a high respect for teaching certainly at the upper levels.

Out-of-School Education. In all societies, both simple and advanced, the culture itself constitutes a very important means of providing directly for many educational needs. Since the Greek city–state was very compact, and since the citizens themselves engaged very actively in the political machinery, the citizens learned much directly from their participation in civic activities. Particularly in Athens, where there were great master-pieces of art in buildings and temples, the citizens lived in the presence of many educative influences. The development of dramatic performances, and various athletic, musical, and poetry contents, were also the sources of many direct educational benefits. The people living outside the cities quite often could also participate in these public festivals, go to the theatre, and engage directly in many other activities so that the educational influence was widespread. The richness of cultural life of Athens itself *then* contributed to the general education of the Athenian citizen quite apart from the schools.

There was preparation for occupations through an informal system of apprenticeship. This method dates back to the days of the nonliterate era. The Athenian education continued along the lines set in the non-literate tribes in that the vocational aspect was carried on by family groups with father usually teaching his son the task. Later, apprentice-ship became somewhat more specialized when the children were sometimes taken into shops and households other than those of their own family to learn a new trade. After the sixth and fifth centuries, B.C., there was a heavy demand for skilled laborers, therefore a need among the members of the lower groups to be prepared for highly specialized tasks. Sometimes in this early period specialized agreements were set up by which the worker would be examined by his teacher and later he would use the approval by such a teacher as proof of his skill. Some of the areas in which apprenticeship training was available were sculpture, stone masonry, carpentry, shoe-making, medicine, law, household affairs, and cooking.[10]

Arts and crafts were necessary for providing consumer goods and these were handed down from generation to generation outside the schools. In the olden days even the kings and noblemen had to work with their hands, and in Solon's laws the parents were required to teach their children a trade. However, later in Athens, education was held to be more aristocratic in nature and educated gentlemen of leisure were not expected to work with their hands. This emphasis became even stronger from the fourth century, B.C., on.

EDUCATION, FREEDOM, AND CULTURE AMONG THE GREEKS

The age of ancient Greek culture is also an important one in the history of the advancement of human freedom. A great number of the concepts which are the progenitors in the freedom fabric of Western culture have their origin in the ancient Greek culture. Yet, there is much conformity as well as freedom in Greek ideas and practices.

The development of the concept of human freedom and the concept that laws are made for man was a product of the peculiar social circumstance under which the Greek civilization developed. There were, however, times in Greek history when it was dangerous for an individual to speak out in favor of change or innovations on penalty of death or exile. At other times, the forces of reaction were very much in retreat.

Although the Greeks had great traditions which strongly influenced their culture, such as Homer and other oral traditions of the pre-literary period, religious literature did not have the status of divine sanction binding contemporary Greek ideas or political patterns. Even the gods were not perfect models to emulate. They were much like men with their

10 Butts, p. 44.

noisy quarrels and other weaknesses. Consequently, it was left to each generation to make its own decisions and to change its decisions if it seemed to be worthwhile.

There was also the possibility of improvement of man's state through exploring the advantages in possible changes in man's institutions. This is the "idea of progress."

Interestingly enough, the great Greek philosophers, Socrates, Plato, and Aristotle, who were to so strongly influence Western culture later, were not complete believers in political democracy. Aristotle and Plato, in particular, were very much opposed to democracy. Plato's *"Republic"* pictures the ideal state composed of the rule of the few, the philosopher-rulers. However, both Aristotle and Plato believed in the freedom of the spirit—that is, in the right of each individual to attempt to arrive at truth by the power of his own mind and logic. This freedom of seeking the truth did not carry over to freedom of action in the political world.

Nevertheless, it can be said that the Greeks had achieved, at the height of their culture, a greater amount of individual freedom and a greater insight into the values inherent in man's choosing for himself than had any of the civilizations before or afterward, down to the advent of democracy in modern times in the Western world.

SUMMARY

The development of Greek culture, from around the sixth century B.C., provides an example of the first Western-style society. The Greeks, through an accident of history which permitted them to form fairly small, autonomous city–states, and through the social situations which caused them to come to believe that "laws" were man-made and could be changed to their benefit, developed a fairly flexible situation which provided the variety of cultural patterns among the different city–states. Sparta represented the extreme of the relatively rigid city–state ruled by an oligarchy with heavily prescribed behavior patterns. Athens represented the more liberal city–state still ruled by an oligarchy not only representing a higher percentage of its population but permitting still more individual freedom within its group.

In the period of the Golden Age of Greece in the fifth century B.C., Greek civilization rose to a very high peak which has probably never been equalled in artistic and intellectual productivity at any other time since. Greek civilization is responsible for the great philosophers and teachers, Socrates, Plato, and Aristotle, whose teachings in turn have so strongly influenced the whole Western civilization. With the decline of the Greek civilization due, among other things, to the Greek's inability to solve the problem of wars among themselves, they were conquered by an outside semi-Greek civilization, the Macedonians. Through additional conquests by the Macedonians, Greek culture was carried throughout the remaining world, and was the dominant culture when Christianity made its way through the Roman Empire. This, together with the remnants of the Roman culture, mingled in the medieval culture which in turn provided the European background for later Western civilization in general.

In Greece, during the periods of relative prosperity, the development of a relatively informal and nongovernmental basis of a rather widely dispersed education system provided an opportunity for a majority of the Greek voting citizens to become fairly well educated. This school system was secular, but private. There developed a series of beginning (or local) schools devoted separately to the teaching of reading, music (or literature), and physical education. There later developed a school at the level which the later Western world would be called "secondary," concerned with the study of the Greek classical literary works.

Still later there developed the philosophical schools found around some of the great teachers such as Plato, Aristotle, Zeno, and Socrates. Greek education was never at any of its stages formal or prescribed. There were no diplomas, degrees, or prescribed curriculum. Teaching was at times an occupation of very high status but at the elementary level it was relatively low. Much of Greek education occurred with the participation of the child in the rich culture of the community itself. Greek education strongly influenced Roman education and both directly influenced the education developed under Christian auspices during the early part of the medieval period. Later in the revival during the Renaissance and the centuries immediately following the reading of the old Greek and Roman classics further influenced the education and educational views of that time toward those favored by the writers of those classics.

SELECTED BIBLIOGRAPHY

Starred items indicate references which closely parallel this chapter.

*Barclay, W., *Educational Ideals of the Ancient World.* London, Collins, 1959.
Beck, Frederick, A. G., *Greek Education, 450–350 B.C.* New York, Barnes and Noble, 1964.

Bonnard, Andre, *Greek Civilization: From the Iliad to the Parthenon.* London, George Allen and Univin, 1957.

———, *Greek Civilization: From the Antigone to Socrates.* New York, Macmillan, 1961.

———, *Greek Civilization: From Euripides to Alexandria.* New York, Macmillan, 1961.

Boyd, William, *The History of Western Education,* 7th ed., revised and enlarged by Edmund J. King. New York, Barnes and Noble, 1965.

———, *Plato's Republic for Today.* London, Heinemann, 1962.

*Butts, R. Freeman, *A Cultural History of Western Education: Its Social and Intellectual Foundations,* 2d ed. New York, McGraw-Hill, 1955.

*Cubberly, Ellwood R., *The History of Education.* New York, Houghton Mifflin, 1920.

Dampier, William C. and Dampier, Margaret, *Readings in the Literature of Science: Being Extracts from the Writings of Men of Science to Illustrate the Development of Scientific Thought.* New York, Harper and Brothers, 1959.

Duggan, Stephen, *A Student's Textbook in the History of Education.* New York, D. Appleton and Company, 1927.

Durant, Will, "The Life of Greece." *The Story of Civilization.* Part Two. New York, Simon and Schuster, 1939.

Freeman, Kathleen, *God, Man and State: Greek Concepts.* London, McDonald, 1952.

Frost, S. E., Jr., *Historical and Philosophical Foundations of Western Education.* Columbus, Ohio, Charles E. Merrill, 1966.

Good, H. G., *A History of Western Education,* 2d ed. New York, Macmillan, 1962.

Hart, Joseph K. *Creative Moments in Education,* pp. 27–85. New York, Holt, Rinehart and Winston, 1931.

———, *A Social Interpretation of Education.* New York, Holt, Rinehart, and Winston, 1929.

Hatch, Edwin, *The Influence of Greek Ideas and Usages Upon the Christian Church.* London, Williams and Norgale, 1904.

Heritage of American Education, Richard E. Gross, ed. Englewood Cliffs, New Jersey, Allyn and Bacon, 1962.

History Handbook of Western Civilization, William McNeill. Chicago, University of Chicago Press, 1953.

Hutchinson, R. W., *Prehistoric Crete.* Baltimore, Penguin, 1962.

Kirchner, Walter, *Western Civilization to 1500.* New York, Barnes and Noble, 1960.

Lodge, R. C., *Plato's Theory of Education.* London, Kegan Paul, Trench, Trubner, 1947.

Meyer, Adolphe E., *An Educational History of the Western World.* New York, McGraw-Hill, 1965.

Myer, Frederick, *A History of Educational Thought,* 2d ed. Columbus, Ohio, Merrill, 1966.

*Mulhern, James, *A History of Education: A Social Interpretation.* New York, Ronald, 1959.

Muller, Herbert J., *Freedom in the Ancient World*. New York, Harper and Row, 1961.

Mumford, Lewis, *The City in History: Its Origins, Its Transformations, and Its Prospects*. New York, Harcourt, Brace and World, 1961.

Neill, Thomas P., ed. *The Building of the Human City: A Documentary Record of Western Civilization*. Garden City, New York, Doubleday Dolphin Masters, 1960.

New Perspectives in World History, Shirley Engle, ed. Yearbook of the National Council of the Social Studies. Washington, D.C., National Education Association, 1964.

*Power, Edward J., *Main Currents in the History of Education*. New York, McGraw-Hill, 1962.

Readings in the History of Education, Ellwood R. Cubberly, ed. Cambridge, Houghton Mifflin, 1920.

Richmond, William K., *Socrates and the Western World: An Essay in the Philosophy of Education*. London, A. Redman, 1954. Pp. 214.

Robinson, C. E., *Hellas: A Short History of Greece*. New York, Pantheon Books, 1948.

Rusk, Robert R., *The Doctrines of the Great Educators*. New York, St. Martins', 1965.

Shotwell, James T., *The Long Way to Freedom*. New York, Bobbs-Merrill, 1960.

Smith, Morton, *Ancient Greeks*. Ithaca, New York, Cornell, 1960.

Stobart, J. C., *The Glory That Was Greece: A Survey of Hellenic Culture and Civilization*, 3d ed. New York, Grove Press, 1962.

The Birth of Western Civilization: Greece and Rome, Michael Grant, ed. New York, McGraw-Hill, 1964.

The Educated Man: Studies in the History of Educational Thought, Paul J. Nash, and others, eds. New York, Wiley, 1965.

The Greeks, Hugh Lloyd-Jones, ed. Cleveland, World, 1962.

Wallbank, Thomas Walter, and others. *Civilization, Past and Present*, Chicago, Scott, Foresman, 1962.

*Weimer, Herman, *Concise History of Education*. New York, Philosophical Library, 1962.

*Wilds, Elmer H. and Lottich, Kenneth V., *The Foundations of Modern Education*, 3d ed. New York, Holt, Rinehart, and Winston, 1961.

*Woody, Thomas, *Life and Education in Early Societies*. New York, Macmillan, 1959.

Pertinent Paperbound Books

Building of the Human City: A Documentary Record of Western Civilization. Thomas P. Neill, ed. New York, Doubleday Dolphin Books, 1960.

Beck, Robert H., *A Social History of Education*. Englewood Cliffs, New Jersey, Prentice-Hall, 1965. Pp. 149.

Bowra, Cecil Maurice, *The Greek Experience*. New York, New American Library, 1958. Pp. xii + 215.

Broudy, Harry S. and Palmer, John R., *Exemplars of the Teaching Method*. Chicago, Rand McNally, 1965.

Burrell, Sidney, *The Main Strands of Development From the Beginnings to the Eighteenth Century. Elements of Western Civilization*. San Francisco, Chandler, 1959.

*Castle, E. B., *Ancient Education and Today*, pp. 106–153. Baltimore, Penguin, 1961.

*Cheney, L. J., *A History of the Western World: From the Stone Age to the Twentieth Century*. New York, New American Library, 1959.

*Cordasco, Francesco, *A Brief History of Education*. Paterson, New Jersey, Littlefield, Adams, 1963.

*Frost, S. E., *Essentials of History of Education*. New York, Barron's, 1947.

*Kirchner, Walter, *Western Civilization to 1500*. New York, Barnes, Noble, 1960.

*Ralph, Philip Lee, *The Story of Our Civilization: 10,000 Years of Western Man*. New York, Dutton, 1959.

*Sedillot, Rene, *History of the World in 240 Pages*. New York, New American Library, 1951.

SELECTED FILMS

Acropolis, The (International Film Bureau)   (11 min.)
      This study in depth of the Acropolis as it remains today opens a new appreciation of the arts of Greece. Models of the buildings are used to contrast the remains with their probable original appearance.

Age of Sophocles, The (Encyclopedia Britannica)

Alphabet, The   (10 min.)
      From the series, *Milestones in Writing*. Traces the evolution of the letters a–d from their Semitic origin through their Greek and Roman forms, to the forms we use today.

Aristotle's Ethics, Book I—The Theory of Happiness (Encyclopaedia Britannica)

Athens—The Golden Age (Encyclopaedia Britannica)

Plato's Apology—The Life and Teachings of Socrates (Encyclopaedia Britannica)

4

The Roman World
and Education

THE DEVELOPMENT OF ROMAN GOVERNMENT
AND CULTURE

Early Development of Rome and the Italian Peoples. What happened
on the Italian Peninsula is similar to that which took place in Greece,
the Fertile Crescent, and many other places throughout the world at the
same stages of development. There were migrations of people, there were
conquests, and there was the mingling of various cultures until there
developed a higher level of culture which can be called a "civilization."

The peoples of Rome were actually constituted from a mingling of
many stocks. They were primarily of the Indo-European stock which for
some time had lived in the area around the Tiber River. The Etruscans,
who probably came from the Danubian area into the central area above
the Tiber River around 800 B.C., developed a fairly high level of civilization before the Latin tribes did. Although the origin of Etruscans is not
certain, recent discovery has indicated that they had developed a much
higher level of civilization than had been earlier thought. There were
also Greeks, who settled in the area in the seventh and sixth centuries
B.C., and Gauls, who entered the northern part of the peninsula in approximately the fifth century B.C. The Latin tribes, who were eventually
to give the language and much of the basic civilization to the area where
Roman culture was to develop, lived in the central portions of the west
coast below the Tiber River. In this area, the city of Rome, according
to tradition, was founded in 753 B.C.

Some time between the eighth and sixth centuries B.C., both the Etruscans and the Latins passed out of the nonliterate stage and settled down to a political organization something similar to the early Greek city–state. The rulers of Rome, for example, were the kings and noble families of the Latin tribes which became amalgamated. Like the Greeks, the Romans had developed an advisory council to the king made up of the noble families. They called this the *Senate*. These families and their descendants became known as the "patricians" and were of the hereditary aristocracy. In the sixth century, B.C., the Etruscans came down and conquered the city of Rome and held it for approximately one century. Then the Latin tribes overthrew them and Rome, the capital of the Latin peoples, emerged as the leading military and political center of this area. Eventually Rome became the military and political center of Italy and, finally, of the then-known world.

The Roman Republic (Fifth to First Centuries B.C.). Again, according to tradition, the ruling patrician groups among the Latins not only threw off the rule of the Etruscans and the Etruscan Kings, but they also did away with their own kings. They established a "republic"—actually an aristocratic oligarchy. The patricians continued to be the main political force throughout the fifth and fourth centuries, and ruled through the former advisory body, the senate, which now became the legislative body of the republic.

The senate established a constitution, the so-called Laws of the Twelve Tables, approximately 450 B.C., and in place of a king chose two consuls to be joint executives for a period of one year. During their term of office, these consuls were given complete power. But since they were elected by the senate and served for short terms, Rome has been considered to be a republic. However, the form of government established by the Romans was actually much less democratic than Athens of the same period, since the control of the republic was at first entirely in the hands of the patricians who were really a very small minority of the total Roman population.

As Rome developed and became more prosperous, the plebian (or commoners) class of citizens began to increase in numbers and began to exert its political influence. These plebians were free citizens of the Roman republic and many of them were holders of land, but they were not of the older patrician or noble class. Rome was very successful and became very wealthy as the result of its wars rising out of conflict with the other tribes of the Italian Peninsula and with the Gauls to the north. The "plebs" also became important in the military forces and since these were so successful, they thought they deserved the rights to demand more privileges for themselves. In the fifth century B.C., the plebs organized themselves and chose representatives called *tribunes* who finally won the right to speak for them in the senate. These rights were included in the code of civil law known as the Twelve Tables. These Tables dominated the political form of government of the Roman republic.

In the fourth and the third centuries B.C., a popular Assembly was organized which consisted of all the citizens who had served in the army or held land. Eventually this assembly won from the senate the right to propose legislation and even to elect the consuls and to decide on matters of war and peace. Again, however, Rome never became as democratic as Athens, even among the minority of persons who were citizens. Through a system of voting whereby the patricians' vote counted more than the plebians, the patricians always could out-vote the commoners. Of course, Rome, like Greece, always had a sizeable group of slaves who had no rights whatsoever.

As the control of Rome over the Italian peninsula was extended during the fourth and third centuries, B.C., there was also an improvement of economic democracy and the total well-being of the peoples. An increasing number of plebs continued to become land owners. As the influence of Rome became more widespread and the products were widely dispersed, other plebs took advantage of commercial trade and crafts opportunity and became the shopkeepers and the skilled craft workers of the area.

The second century B.C., saw a slowing down of the trend toward economic well-being and economic democracy. Rome had engaged in the costly Punic Wars which, although they were eventually successful, bled the resources of the Roman Empire considerably. Also they had participated in the so-called Eastern Wars around the Mediterranean. So the number of plebs decreased and some of them, having fallen into debt, lost their land to the wealthy people. This meant that the plebs had to become tenants living on the land. The wars also led to an increase in the number of slaves available so that the wealthy businessmen were able to buy slaves and consequently did not have to hire pleb labor.

While these events were occurring at home, Roman military and political power was being established throughout the Italian and Mediterranean area. It is generally considered that by 275 B.C. Rome had under its control all the Italian Peninsula. By the end of that century, it had gained control of the islands of Corsica, Sardina, Sicily, and the peninsula of Spain. Finally, Rome was successful in the East and conquered Macedonia, Greece, Asia Minor, and the entire Mediterranean world. The Greek states had been conquered by Macedonia and at first had welcomed the Romans as liberators. But Rome did more than liberate. It stayed on as the ruling power.

However, at home on the Italian Peninsula, Rome's power was challenged by numerous struggles for power and civil wars lasted for over a century. Finally, the Senate representing the patricians became victorious over the Assembly, representing the commoners. In the first century B.C., there were struggles between important army generals including the famous one between Pompey and Julius Caesar. Caesar won and became a complete dictator under the legal sanction of the Senate, although he was never emperor in name. He was assassinated in a conspiracy of a group of leading persons in the Senate who wished to reassert their original rights. After Caesar's death, there were additional struggles in which Octavius was victorious. He changed his name to Augustus and took the title of *Imperator* or *Emperor*. This is the date of birth of the Roman Empire, 27 B.C.

The Height and Decline of the Roman Empire (27 B.C. to A.D. 500). At least on the surface it appeared that the new Emperor Augustus intended to restore the constitution which had lapsed under Julius Caesar. Since, however, he had complete control of the army and was the real ultimate source of authority, the Senate was very much a figurehead organization. Even so, Augustus continued to have respect for it and it remained nominally in authority. The emperors who were to follow maintained their power and authority largely as long as they controlled the army or at least the imperial guards located in Rome. For a number of years they permitted the Senate to stay in session and all acts of the emperor had to be ratified by the Senate. After a while, this pretense of maintaining the authority of the Senate began to lapse until the emperors ruled more arbitrarily without any pretense of submitting their edicts to the Senate. The fall of Rome became imminent when the emperors could no longer control their armies and lost their power which had been based upon military strength.

During the first and second centuries A.D., the Roman Empire was at the height of its cultural and political strength in the Mediterranean area. Because of the enforced *Pax Romana* during most of this period, there was a flourishing of commerce and trade throughout the area. Many of the towns in the provinces outside of Rome maintained the high level of cultural living comparable to that which had been maintained in the cities within Rome itself. Still, even during the earlier prosperous period of the Roman Empire when culture was at its highest, there were things happening which might have given a clue to the eventual deterioration of Rome. These have been fully set forth by Gibbon.[1]

To name a few, there was a decline in the number of middle-class Romans and an increase in the size of the larger estates. Instead of the farms being operated by the owners who lived on them, by and large the landlords were absentee and the farms were actually run by managers

---

[1] A good edition of Gibbon's book is the abridgement by Edward Gibbon, *The Decline and Fall of the Roman Empire*, abridged by D. M. Low. New York, Harcourt, Brace and World, 1960.

with the work being done by slaves or hired hands. These became more and more inefficient and the production and quality of the farm products deteriorated during the period of the first few centuries A.D. This was also true of the products in the shops in Rome and elsewhere. There was no organized dissemination of technical information and there were no vocational schools. Also, because sons no longer wished to pursue the vocation of their fathers unless they had to learn from him directly due to their low estate, wasteful methods in the production of goods gradually developed.

After the second century A.D., the Empire became politically weaker and, in time, broke into the East and West divisions (fourth century A.D.). Because it was militarily weaker, the Germanic tribes to the north began making increasing incursions into the Empire. Historians generally give the date of A.D. 476 as the date of the Fall of Rome because at this time a leader of a Germanic tribe actually became emperor. It is, however, a purely arbitrary date. Long before that the Empire had ceased to exist as a strong political force; law and order having broken down considerably throughout the various parts of the Empire.

Books have been written and lengthy discussions held concerning the reasons for the decay and fall. Certainly, the prosperity and general cultural level of the Roman nation was highest when the economic ownership of farms and shops was broad and not concentrated in the hands of a few. Economic deterioration was the result of limited and concentrated ownership, and this was the same development that had occurred in the latter and declining days of Greece.

It is to be noted that, during the periods of economic democracy (by which is meant the widespread ownership and decision-making by a great number of people), there was also a larger measure of political democracy. As the upper classes gained economic superiority, and social prestige was almost entirely theirs, the power of freedom diminished for the great mass of people. Through the disorders occurring in Rome, the emperor became stronger and, finally, he destroyed the aristocracy becoming the supreme dictator of the country, in theory as well as in fact.

When the people had participated directly in the government, they had had a sense of self-realization and attained, therefore, freedom of thought and action. With the lessening of these freedoms, self-realization was no longer possible, and the incentive to think independently in matters of politics, economics, and commerce diminished. During this period, the rural lower classes (later on to be called serfs) became almost completely subservient to the emperor. Laws were passed restricting them to their job so that they would not migrate to the city and become problems. Out of this practice of the later Roman Empire some of the basis for medieval feudalism was laid.

Due to the deterioration in the general attitude and morale of the

Roman people, there was a decline in the birth rate, particularly among the aristocracy. Upper class families were no longer able to maintain extensive courts which had resembled elaborate oriental establishments. A major factor contributing to the straightened circumstances of the wealthy was their inability to meet the severe taxes imposed on them. For the lower classes, of course, there was no self-maintenance at all, except by being bound to the land or by some form of relief passed out in the cities.

During this time, the old social structure of the Roman Empire was like that of an enormous pyramid with the emperor and his family, high-ranking persons, including the priestly class, at the top, widening out through the wealthier class, finally coming to rest upon the broad backs of the serfs and slaves. Because the poorer classes of people had no real stake in the prosperity and well-being of the country, when the Germanic tribes came in, the emperors were not able to get them aroused enough to fight against the invaders. They had to hire mercenary soldiers from the Germanic tribes already there in order to fight off other Germanic tribes. It was in this period of discouragement and degradation that the people turned to various mystical religious ideas which were competing with the developing Christianity that was to win out in the end.

A general summation of these years of the Roman Empire indicates that, as in Greece, the basic reason for decline was that Rome failed to establish a truly genuine democracy with a sound socio-economic and political base. This failure, of course, has significance. More and more the wealthy classes had gained the exclusive privilege of education. Had the Roman Empire placed emphasis on continued education and training (vocational and otherwise) of the masses, high standards of workmanship might have been maintained thus preventing the cultural deterioration characteristic of this period.

ROMAN EDUCATION AND SCHOOLS

Family Education in the Early Roman Society. During the period of the Republic, education was controlled and dominated by the family. This process was similar to that of the nonliterate peoples studied earlier. The purpose was to induct the children into the customs and life of the group in order to preserve their ideals and way of life. Among the Romans, children were held in very high regard. The mother was charged with the responsibility for the care of the children and usually for their early training and education. After this period, the girl was taught how to run a home, to be a mother, and to take care of a household, while the father took over the boy. He taught through permitting the boy to observe and participate in the activities of the family, and various local groups. Of course, he was given some direct instruction. After the codification of Roman law in the Laws of the Twelve Tables, the boy was required to memorize them. He was inculcated with the predominant ideals of the Roman State, such as piety, courage, and prudence. The general aims of the family were to teach the boy to be healthy and strong; to revere the gods; to know how to fight; to engage in various sports, such as boxing and swimming; and to develop other necessary skills.

Sometimes the son of a wealthy family would serve an apprenticeship in a public office so that he would be able to hold office and serve the state later. The boy of the privileged class at about age sixteen or eighteen would put on the dress of the citizen and then accompany his father to the Forum and to various public religious ceremonies and festivals. This type of education was reserved for the people of the senatorial class. The children of the lower classes and the slaves received only minimal instruction and, where skill training was required, this was given by on-the-job training for whatever their particular station or status in life might be.

Private Schools Under the Republic.   There were practically no formal schools existing in Rome before 300 B.C. Some time shortly after 300 B.C., due to the spread of Greek influence within Rome, they began to appear and by the end of that century, they had become fairly common. Many of the early teachers were the Greek captives, some slave and some free, who came to instruct in the homes of the wealthy Romans. Later on, some men began to establish schools and to teach for fees. There was a period of time in which Rome opposed the spread of Greek culture; but, in spite of much discussion and the passage of laws opposing it, Roman civilization took on much of the culture of the Greeks.

The elementary school, designed to teach reading skills in the Latin language, came to be known as the *Ludus* (originally from the Latin word for games). This was presided over, as the school took form, by a teacher eventually known as *Ludi Magister* or sometimes called the *Litterator*. The latter is the Latin equivalent of the Greek *Grammatist* in the Hellenistic schools which had developed in the East. During the ages of seven through twelve, children (girls were often included) were taught to read and write Latin and to do some simple counting. Unlike Greek education of the similar period, instruction in music (in reality literature) and gymnastics was not found in these early Roman schools. These schools were all private schools; there was no compulsory attendance and practically no supervision by the state. The Greek slave, the *pedagogue,* quite often took the children to their private schools and acted as their supervisor. Even this elementary education was still designed only for the upper classes and provided an exclusive education available only for those who could afford to pay for it.

The secondary school came into Rome also during the third century B.C. and its form was completely Greek in character. It was essentially a transfer of the Greek *Grammar School* taught by the *grammaticus*. Later on, the Roman equivalent, *Litteratus*, was used for the name of the teacher. In these schools the Roman boy was taught Greek grammar and literature, without the attention which the Greeks had given to broad backgrounds. There were at this time no Latin language schools since Greek was used as the basis of instruction and there was as yet no good Latin literature. The grammaticus was a private teacher supported by fees until the time of the empire. He was not controlled or supervised by public authorities.

Finally by the first century A.D., the Latin language improved and a Latin literature began to emerge. Consequently, a few Latin grammar schools were established. By the beginning of the period of the Empire, there were Latin grammar schools existing alongside the Greek grammar schools. So for a long period of time there existed within the Roman Empire the two kinds of grammar schools, and many boys who had sufficient money and time could attend both schools and get a very well-rounded education. It was necessary to attend one of these grammar schools in order to get the best types of jobs in the public offices in the republic.

A supplementary education, roughly equivalent to secondary education, was also established as in the Republican period, and was usually pursued by those persons who had completed grammar school education, but was roughly equivalent to a kind of secondary education. These Roman advanced schools were called the rhetorical schools, whereas those in the Hellenistic centers of the East under Roman control were usually called the philosophical schools. The rhetorical schools did not become prominent in the western half of the Roman nation until during the time of the Empire. The emphasis of the schools of rhetoric was quite different among the Romans of the West than in the philosophical schools of Athens, since the Romans did not place emphasis upon philosophy. This development is discussed more fully hereafter.

It should be remembered by students of history that the schools described thus far were only for the very few, that most of the children in the Roman period had no formal school education as a part of their life, and the only education they received was an informal education from their family or environment. In some cases, an informal apprenticeship education was available for the craft vocations.

Schools under Civil Control in the Empire.   The political and social events which occurred during the latter part of the Republic, and which lead to the breakdown of the Roman government and to the eventual establishment of the Empire, also brought about the rise of the Latin grammar school. The popular party, which represented several of the lower classes along with the upper classes, was very favorable toward the development of the so-called Latin grammar school to promulgate the teaching of the Latin language and literature throughout the Roman Empire. So by the end of the Republic, the Latin grammar school had risen to a position somewhat comparable to that of the Greek grammar school.

With the change of government from Republic to Empire, there were very few changes in the basic patterns of the schools. There were some changes in the matters of emphasis and support. The *School of the Litterator,* as the elementary school was more frequently called now, was used throughout the Empire primarily to teach reading. The *School of the Grammaticus* was the common secondary school throughout the Empire and, increasingly in the Empire period, it was devoted to the study of Latin grammar and literature in the West, and Greek in the East. Eventually, the Greek grammar schools disappeared entirely in the West. The Rhetorical School now became the most popular advanced school. So there was a decline of the philosophical schools even in Greece, with rhetoric being emphasized both in the East and West schools, but with each using the Greek and Latin languages, respectively.

From time to time sporadically throughout the period of the Empire, the emperors gave support to the teachers and, in several cases, the municipal authorities helped to support town schools, or gave aid to some children of the upper classes. Actually, the giving of money to the schools by the emperor was on a very haphazard basis. It was usually done through the special grants by the emperor to particular teachers in certain centers. As the support of the emperors and the town governments became greater, they began also to exercise more control in the appointment of the teachers and in what was taught. However, it must not be thought that there was any such thing as a universally established public school system. These schools were still for a very few of the upper classes.

There was some increase in the number of schools throughout the Empire after A.D. 100. Eventually teachers had to have the approval of governmental authority. Finally, under the Emperor Theodosius (during the latter part of the fourth century), a state monopoly of education was developed. This state monopoly of education was probably not completely enforced; however, it did become the dominant principle which was to be utilized by the established Christian religion later in the Christian era. With Constantine (fourth century A.D.) came the recognition of Christianity, later to be established as the only religion. The ensuing struggle between Christianity and lingering paganism (as the Christians called the old Roman religion and culture) helped to bring about a further decline of education, already languishing over a long period of years.

Finally, the Emperor Justinian, early in the sixth century, ordered all of the pagan schools closed. At this time no Christian schools had been established with equivalent standards of the old classical schools. So the effect of the decree was to destroy almost completely what formal education there was. The emperor then ceased all contributions to the schools, and their maintenance was assumed directly by the church. It is interesting to note, however, that a few Italian towns managed to continue to maintain publicly supported schools throughout all these changes and exigencies well into the Middle Ages, and they were not affected greatly by the controversy between the new religious authority and the old pagan, classical writers. However, the number of these schools was small, and their effect upon education was somewhat negligible.

Education, by and large, during the fourth and fifth centuries A.D., was quite literary in nature and very much divorced from current trends. There were apparently a few schools teaching "practical" subjects. These were usually of a much lower standard than the classical schools.

Characteristic Patterns of Roman Schools. As we have seen, since Roman civilization throughout the period, Republic or Empire, was largely aristocratic in character, the attendance at schools, or education of any sort, was always confined in a large measure to the upper classes. It is true that in the period of the Republic, when the economic and political life was on a much broader base, the number of people who probably actually went to school was relatively larger. In the latter days of the Empire, education became almost exclusively limited to the senatorial or to the knightly classes (the *equites*). While there was some development during this period in making public money available for teachers and, in a few cases, there were scholarships granted by emperors to poor but promising students, there was not much opportunity for the children of the lower classes. Even this little opportunity became very much less after the third century A.D.

The Roman pattern of schools was carried over largely from the influence of the Greek. This pattern was to influence strongly the late medieval schools once they recovered from the period of the educational decline following the fall of Rome. The development of the medieval university is a story in itself. Any really fundamental changes in the conception of the elementary school and the secondary or grammar school was not to come about until the modern period.

Status of Teachers. At previous points in the discussion of Roman education, the role and status of teachers have been implied. It is certainly true that the teachers of the elementary school were, during this period and previously (and almost ever since), held in fairly low repute and received very small fees. Quite often in Rome, the teacher was a slave or at least a captured freeman of some country which had been conquered by Rome. In some cases, these persons may have had a high level of culture but the level of their status was rarely very high.

The teachers in the higher schools were sometimes held in high repute. Many times foreign teachers in the higher schools with backgrounds of Greek scholarship were made Roman citizens before many others of their same group. This illustrates the regard with which the Romans held the Greek culture. In this respect the Romans were somewhat ambivalent since they feared Greek culture, yet they respected it. Sometimes the Greek scholars were actually made the center of attention in intellectual circles, receiving special privileges and patronage from the Senate and, later on, the Emperor. Some of the teachers were given special civic offices in order to support them in their teaching work. Quintilian, one of the great Roman teachers, held a fairly high public office under the Emperor Vespasian (d. A.D. 79) in the fairly early days of the Empire and there are other examples of teachers who held high office.

Nonschool Agencies and Influences.   As already indicated, the most important educational influence on most of the Romans was nonschool in character. By and large, this was the Roman family. The higher the socio-economic status of the family, the more it was able to provide the adequate introduction of the child to the culture and to give him some understanding of it. The attention of the Roman family was directed toward broad development in respect to all aspects of his life—religious, political, economic, and social.

There were other agencies during this period which helped in educational development. In Rome, itself, there was the Forum, the Senate, and the popular Assembly during the better days of the Roman nation. Even in the smaller towns, there had developed small replicas of the Forum and of the educational, recreational, and other cultural centers. Under the Empire, though the Senate began to decline, there were still great architectural, sculptural and artistic monuments which were a part of the daily life. The sponsorship of theaters, festivals, and holidays which were public in character, was very influential. Libraries and museums were also developed during the Empire days, for the continued education of the intellectual classes even after their formal schooling.

One of the agencies for the education of people was the army. A great number of persons of the lower classes eventually served in the army. The persons of the upper classes who joined the army had been educated for leadership and were given leadership training on the job. In the lower classes at least the development of skills and physical training was carried on by the army.

The second type of education carried on outside the school was skill training of the lower classes to be tradesmen and craftsmen. This was done through an apprenticeship. Although this was not as well organized as it was during the guild period of the later Middle Ages, this form of apprentice education saw to it that the new entrant in the skill was thoroughly trained before he could take his place as a regular worker. During the latter part of the Roman Empire, there was some decline in the quality of this apprenticeship.

Now, in considering an over-all evaluation of Roman education, it is necessary to look at the educational ideas found in the writings of two of the most influential teachers and thinkers in Roman education, Cicero and Quintilian. The education of the Roman nation as that of most countries failed to live up to the ideals of its great thinkers. However, these writings were also important in their later influence on the education of Europe, particularly during the period of the Renaissance.

Cicero (106–43 b.c.). Cicero, one of the leading Roman orators and statesmen, was well-trained in Greek rhetoric and philosophy. In addition, he was one of the greatest influences on educational theory in the Roman state during that period of the Republic influenced by the Hellenistic civilization. His books also provided the ideal for the education of the Middle Ages, particularly of the classical or grammarian type of education. His main educational ideas were set forth in the book, the *Orator*. In this book, he outlined his conception of the skills of rhetoric and oratory necessary for the development of the public leader or orator. It was felt at this time that the ability to speak and to persuade persons was of the greatest importance in professional and public life. Cicero felt that the orator should have a well-rounded education in what would now be called the "liberal arts" as well as training in the platform skills. The orator should also be a man of wide practical experience in order to provide a sound basis for his philosophy. The emphasis was a practical one rather than theoretical. Cicero developed a conception of the studies proper to humanity as a basis for the orator. This combination is the outstanding contribution in Cicero's theory of education. Of course, the word, "humanities" comes into the literature much later.

Cicero's listing of these subjects (the "humanities") is sometimes vague, but he did include the following: grammar (this was primarily classical literature), rhetoric, logic, geometry, astronomy, music, physics, history, civil law, and philosophy. These studies were somewhat more inclusive in scope than the traditional seven liberal arts which were recognized during the later Medieval period as constituting the whole of liberal education. Astronomy, music, and civil law were not included in the seven liberal arts. Cicero, unlike his imitators of the later Middle Ages, constantly stressed the point that the purpose of pursuing these was not simply for intellectual or spiritual exercise, but that they would be useful in giving the person breadth and skill in public affairs. The whole focus was on the art of leadership in public life.[2]

Quintilian (c. A.D. 35–97). The outstanding Roman thinker in education in the early period of the Empire was the teacher and orator, Quintilian. His views on education in this period are important because, like those of Cicero, they revealed the highest ideal of Roman education (seldom achieved), and also because there are certain aspects of it which are very "modern" in form. They were rediscovered during the Renaissance when they became an important source for the ideas of certain individualistic humanist educators.

In his most important book, *Institutes of Oratory,* Quintilian pictured the orator in somewhat the same way as Cicero did—as a well-rounded man of affairs or public leader. The orator's role of leadership in public policy should rest not only upon his ability to speak, but upon his intellectual background and knowledge and upon the integrity of his personality or character.

Quintilian sounds strangely like modern educators when he talks about the necessity for teachers to take into account the different individual capacities of boys. He not only felt that the majority of boys were capable of being educated, but that there ought to be a possible choice of studies in order to develop the special talent of each individual. He recommended, in ways strangely predictive of some ideas of Froebel and others in the early modern period, that plays and games should be used for relaxation and to stimulate interest. He suggested competition and awards as a basis for motivation rather than corporal punishment.[3] However, in spite of a modern quality to his emphasis upon recreational pursuits and material awards, Quintilian did stress memory and used moralizing as a main basis for motivation.

One interesting thing in line with the later development of public education was that he felt that group (or class) instruction was preferable to individual tutoring even though the parent could well afford a private tutor. He was able to see that there were certain things which the boy learned in the class, but which he could not learn alone. Friendships and the cross fertilization of ideas through class discussion would make learning in classes superior in its advantages to private tutoring. Some of the arguments against class teaching was that the association with others might hurt the morals of the boys. Also the teacher might not be able to be fair to all individuals. Quintilian argued, however, that if the classes of the schools were not unduly large, the teacher would be able to give his attention to individual pupils.

2 Thomas Woody, *Life and Education in Early Society,* pp. 598–601.

3 James M. Starr, "Marcus Fabius Quintilian (35–95 A.D.) Laid the Foundations for Modern Educational Methodology." *The Journal of Teacher Education,* Vol. 14 (December, 1963), 429–434.

Quintilian went into much greater detail on the educational curriculum and methods than did Cicero; although, with the exception of the points above mentioned, his recommendations for the curriculum were not too greatly different from those of Cicero. Very young children in the elementary school, after instruction in reading and writing, would go on into grammar school education (secondary) with the emphasis upon grammar, composition and the reading of the outstanding Latin poets. Quintilian, like Cicero, wanted music both to train the voice as a basis for speaking and also as a part of singing the lyrics. He did stress mathematics and a minimal amount of physical education in order to provide for the development of those body skills necessary in speaking. Like Cicero and the other Romans, Quintilian did not strongly emphasize the study of philosophy. Romans tended to be concerned about practical affairs and to develop his individual ideas out of experience.

Quintilian, and to some extent Cicero, with all of his concepts of the classical and literary nature of education, tried to tie education fairly close to life's affairs. After their time education moved farther away from life, and when their ideas were revived in the later Middle Ages, the close relationship of education to culture as they had recommended was quite forgotten by their imitators.

EDUCATION, FREEDOM AND CULTURE

The Romans, by picking up and maintaining the Greek culture with its ideas of challenging the established order, made a contribution indirectly to the preservation of certain ideals of freedom. During the period of the domination of the Senate in the Roman Republic, the Senate, representing only part of the population, made decisions for the country with complete freedom of debate, rather than this being done on an authoritarian basis. However, under the Empire, Rome soon lapsed into an authoritarian state with the authority and divinity of the emperor thoroughly established. The emphasis on Roman laws for governing persons rather than the arbitrary wish of the emperor was at first respected. However, in the later part of the Roman Empire period, this was quite frequently overlooked particularly at the top level since the emperors often flaunted the Roman law. In local administration the citizen, during most of the period of Rome, was well protected in his rights by the thoroughness and efficient operation of the system of Roman law. Freedom under law, of course, is later to be one of the basic aspects of the protection of human freedom.

In the area of education, education reflecting as it did the predominant utilitarian philosophy, there was very little freedom of the student. However, in some of the pronouncements of the outstanding thinkers of this period, such as Quintilian, there was some emphasis toward adapting the education to the particular individual characteristics and needs of each student. Although this was not put into practice widely at this time, when these classical writings were read later in the Renaissance period, it did influence the individual humanists.

Although the issue of freedom versus conformity was not sharply or clearly defined during the Roman period, the widespread protection of the Roman citizen, broadly conceived for most individuals within the sway of Roman influence, tended to establish the idea of citizen rights. This constituted a basis for the later precedent in jurisprudence for the protection of human freedom.

SUMMARY

The history of the development of the Roman nation and culture ran the whole gamut of human experience from the early prerepublic, nonliterate Roman or Latin tribes, through the Republic with some semblance of "democratic" procedures on through, of course, to the most absolutist of political empires with a god–emperor. The Roman Republic was established to carry out the domination of the upper class, but through a period of reforms gradually admitted some members of the lower class into a partial involvement in the processes and actions of government.

The Roman world at this time became tremendously successful from the standpoint of its military and political conquests, and came to dominate the entire then-known world, spreading its ideas of culture as these matured, and influencing that of the leading nations of the time. Part of this was due to the absorption of aspects of the Hellenistic culture which had permeated the region under the Macedonians in an earlier period. Rome rose to its height early in the empire period. It then began its slow decline toward its fall due to its own internal deterioration and through the pressures from the Teutonic invasions from the north. This provided an opportunity for the Christian church, as it developed and became organized within the Roman Empire, to take the place of the previously unifying force of the Roman State.

Many different kinds of education was found in the Roman Empire.

This ranged from education carried on by the family through the private schools of the Republic which gradually became modeled after the Greek schools. However, the Romans did not emphasize philosophy but rather placed greater emphasis upon utilitarianism. The Romans never developed a system of state schools or any kind of a universal system as extensive as that of the Greek education at its height. It might well be contended that one of the causes of the eventual deterioration of the Roman Empire was its failure to establish an educational system which might have preserved Roman values and those technological achievements which had been developed in the formation period of the Roman State. There was some interest in education on the part of some of the emperors and, to some extent, the town authorities; however, this did not play any consistent or sizeable part in Roman education.

The Roman period did give currency to the educational ideas of two scholars, Cicero and Quintilian, whose influence affected later educational history. As Roman deterioration set in and the educational system declined, the way was left for the almost complete redevelopment of education by the Christians. However, many of the practices of the Christians were a continuation of the ideas of the pre-Christian Romans. Furthermore, the adoption of Roman practice was accentuated later in the early Middle Ages when many classical documents were rediscovered, further influencing textbooks and other educational ideas.

The Romans were the first people to make any attempt to provide a kind of secular, publicly supported education without its main emphasis being upon religion. But, of course, this did not reach many people. The Romans played down philosophy and placed more emphasis upon grammar and upon the ability to speak. In the highest conception of Roman education—the very broad liberal-arts conception—Roman education was at its best. At the other end (frequently as is the case with the ordinary teachers and schools), it deteriorated into an emphasis upon form, memorization, and the formalities of Latin grammar as opposed to meaning.

SELECTED BIBLIOGRAPHY

Starred items represent books most closely paralleling chapter content.

General Books and Periodicals

Barclay, W., *Educational Ideas of the Ancient World*. London, Collins, 1959.
Barrow, R. H., *The Romans*. Baltimore, Penguin, 1949.

Boyd, William, *The History of Western Education*, 7th ed., revised and enlarged by Edmund J. King. New York, Barnes and Noble, 1965.

Brinton, Crane, *A History of Western Morals*. New York, Harcourt, Brace, and World, 1959.

*Butts, Freeman, *A Cultural History of Western Education: Its Social and Intellectual Foundations*, 2d ed. New York, McGraw-Hill, 1955.

Cordesco, Francesco, *A Brief History of Education*. Paterson, Littlefield, Adams, 1963.

*Cubberly, Ellwood R., *The History of Education*. New York, Houghton-Mifflin, 1920.

Durant, Will, *Caesar and Christ* in *The Story of Civilization, Part Three*. New York, Simon and Schuster, 1939.

Frost, S. E., Jr. *Historical and Philosophical Foundations of Western Education*. Columbus, Ohio, Merrill, 1960.

*Good, H. G., *A History of Western Education*, 2d ed. New York, Macmillan, 1962.

Heritage of American Education, Richard E. Gross, ed. Boston, Allyn and Bacon, 1962.

Kirchner, Walter, *Western Civilization to 1500*. New York, Barnes and Noble, 1960.

Laffont, Robert, and others, *A History of Rome and the Romans from Romulus to John XXIII*. New York, Crown, 1962.

Low, D. M., *Gibbon's The Decline and Fall of the Roman Empire*. One volume Abridgement. New York, Holt, Rinehart and Brace, 1960.

McNeill, William, *History Handbook of Western Civilization*. Chicago, University of Chicago Press, 1953.

Meyer, Adolphe E., *An Educational History of the Western World*. New York, McGraw-Hill, 1965.

*Mulhern, James, *A History of Education: A Social Interpretation*. New York, Ronald, 1959.

Muller, Herbert J., *Freedom in the Ancient World*. New York, Harper & Row, 1961.

New Perspectives in World History, Shirley Engle, ed. Yearbook of the National Council of the Social Studies. Washington, D.C., National Education Association, 1964.

Power, Edward J., *Main Currents in the History of Education*. New York. McGraw-Hill, 1962.

Readings in the History of Education, Ellwood R. Cubberly, ed. Cambridge, Riverside, 1920.

Rusk, Robert R., *The Doctrine of the Great Educators*. New York, St. Martin's, 1965.

Starr, Chester G., Jr., *The Emergence of Rome: As the Ruler of the Western World*. Ithaca: Cornell, 1950.

Starr, James M., "Marcus Fabius Quintilian (35–95 A.D.) Laid the Foundation for Modern Educational Methodology" in *The Journal of Teacher Education*, Vol. 14 (December, 1963), pp. 429–434.

The Building of the Human City: A Documentary Record of Western Civiliza-

tion, Thomas P. Neill, ed. Garden City, New York. Doubleday, Dolphin Masters, 1960.

The Birth of Western Civilization: Greece and Rome, Michael Grant, ed. New York, McGraw-Hill, 1964.

Wallbank, Thomas Walter, and others, *Civilization: Past and Present.* Chicago, Scott, Foresman, 1962.

*Weimer, Hermann, *Concise History of Education.* New York, Philosophical Library, 1962.

*Wilds, Elmer H. and Lottich, Kenneth V., *The Foundations of Modern Education,* 3d ed. New York, Rinehart and Winston, 1961.

*Woody, Thomas, *Life and Education in Early Societies.* New York, Macmillan, 1959.

Pertinent Paperbound Books

A History of Rome: From its Origins to 529 A.D. as told by the Roman Historians, Moses Hadas, ed. Garden City, New York, Doubleday Anchor Books, 1956.

Burrell, Sidney, *The Main Strands of Development from the Beginnings to the 18th Century. Elements of Western Civilization,* Vol. I. San Francisco, Chandler, 1959.

Carcopino, Jerome, *Daily Life in Ancient Rome: The People and the City at the Height of the Empire.* New Haven, Yale, 1940.

*Castle, E. B., *Ancient Education and Today.* Baltimore, Penguin, 1961.

*Cheney, L. J., *A History of the Western World: From the Stone Age to the Twentieth Century.* New York, New American Library, 1959.

*Cordesco, Francesco, *A Brief History of Education.* Paterson, Littlefield, Adams, 1963.

Dill, Samuel, *Roman Society from Nero to Marcus Aurelius,* 2d ed. London, Macmillan, 1925.

————, *Roman Society in the Last Century of the Western Empire,* 2d ed. New York, Macmillan, 1921.

Dudley, Donald R., *The Civilization of Rome.* New York, The New American Library, 1962.

*Frost, S. E., *Essentials of History of Education.* New York, Barron's, 1947. Pp. x + 206.

Grant, Michael, *World of Rome.* New York, World, 1960.

Hamilton, Edith, *The Roman Way.* New York, Mentor Books, 1960.

*Kirchner, Walter, *Western Civilization to 1500.* New York, Barnes & Noble, 1960.

*Ralph, Philip Lee, *The Story of Our Civilization: 10,000 Years of Western Man.* New York, Dutton, 1959.

*Sedillot, Rene, *History of the World in 240 Pages.* New York, New American Library, 1951.

SELECTED FILMS

Ancient Rome (Coronet)   (11 min.)
　　Remains of the Forum, the Baths of Caracalla, the Colosseum, the palaces of Palatine Hill, and the Sacra Via and Appian Way recall a culture that contributed many ideas to our modern civilization. Advancements in law, language, literature, architecture, and engineering are studied as are many features of government and daily life.

Decline of the Roman Empire (Coronet)   (13½ min.)
　　Actual settings in France, England, the Near East and Rome to present the political, social, and economic forces which weakened the Empire from within and the forces from without which brought about its decline.

Rise of the Roman Empire (Coronet)   (13½ min.)
　　Development of Rome from a group of early tribal communities to a mighty empire which embraced a large part of the Western World.

Education in Medieval Europe
(A.D. 500 to c. A.D. 1300)

MEDIEVAL EUROPEAN CULTURE

To understand the structure of education in medieval Europe, it is first necessary to study the essence of the cultural and social developments during this period, A.D. 500 to around A.D. 1300. This study is divided into two parts: Early Middle Ages, A.D. 500 to c. A.D. 1100, and Later Middle Ages, c. A.D. 1100 to c. A.D. 1300.

Early Middle Ages (A.D. 500 to c. A.D. 1100). Quite often historians and others have labeled this period, the early medieval era in European history, as the "Dark Ages" because of the confused cultural and political situation at this time, and also because there was a decline in learning and general culture following the invasions of the Teutonic tribes. In the period of struggle between the old Roman, or what the Christians of this era termed the "pagan," culture and the new culture of Christianity, much of the Greek and Roman culture was discarded for a number of centuries.

This was a period in which there was very low interest in any kind of new learning; however, it is not correct to label this period completely "dark." Traditional learning was preserved in the monasteries and, in some cases, was taught practically unchanged in the schools of this era. Also during the latter part of the Middle Ages, the twelfth and thirteenth centuries, learning became quickened in preparation for the renaissance of Greek and Roman culture (A.D. 1300–1500).

As the various Christian sects or congregations in the first two centuries of the Christian era gained followers, they began to come in conflict with other religions, and eventually they came to the notice of the emperors of the Roman Empire. It is not altogether clear why the Christians were persecuted so severely by the emperors, since the Empire was quite tolerant toward most of the many religions within it.

However, the Christians did insist upon the worship of one God, refusing to honor or worship the emperor, and this refusal was regarded by the Romans as an illegal or traitorous act. They also refused to engage in civil ceremonies and games which often, although quite casually, exalted the emperor and the old pagan gods. In addition many of these early Christians refused to serve in the army because it involved killing which they at that time believed to be contrary to their religious ideals. The early Christians lived rather strict moral lives. Their meetings and ritual were held in secrecy. They therefore were regarded with suspicion and were considered dangerous as far as the state was concerned.

Whatever may have been the more important reasons for their persecution, the growing Christian sects became of increasing concern to the public officials of the state. The Emperor Nero (A.D. 54–68), in particular, found them a useful scapegoat on which he blamed the burning of Rome.

By the third century, because of the difficulties which the Empire was having with various groups, and because the strength of the Christians seemed to be increasing, the emperors felt that the time had come to call a halt to further Christian growth. So they tried from time to time to reassert the absolute power of emperors in an effort to wipe out the Christian congregations. However, the Christians were not stopped and, as the Empire came out of the third century into the fourth, the church was much stronger than ever. This was only the first instance in which the church won its battle with the state.

It was in the fourth century that the attitudes of the emperors changed. The imperial throne was becoming a precarious one. The emperors may have seen a way of gaining additional support in return for giving protection to this now large sect of Christians. In A.D. 313, through the Edict of Milan, the Emperor Constantine (A.D. 306–337) gave the Christians full legal rights and, in A.D. 325, he recognized Christianity as the official state religion.

This recognition made a very great difference in the character and attitude of the Christian church. Many of the church leaders, instead of arguing for complete separation of church and state, as they had previously argued, now began to assert that the church and state should cooperate. The church leaders claimed that the state should protect and support the church and that, in points of conflict, the church should be supreme. Hence, a contention was raised for the first time concerning the state establishment of religion which was to be such a controversial matter in Christendom from this time on.

There was a temporary setback in the fourth century (A.D. 361–363) under an apostate Pope, the Emperor Julian, who brought the pagan gods back again into prominence. However, Christianity soon triumphed when Theodosius (A.D. 379–395) determined that to worship the old Roman gods was a crime and gave legal religious protection only to the Christians. Eventually, then, this left the Roman Catholic (or Christian) church the greatest power in the western empire of the fifth century.

The eastern Emperor Justinian (A.D. 483–565) made a strong attempt in the sixth century to unify the empire once more into a great single world state. Justinian was, like Theodosius, a very strong believer in using Christianity as a means of strengthening the empire. In A.D. 529, he showed his desire to stamp out completely any remnants of paganism by ordering the Philosophic Schools of Athens closed. These schools had existed since the time of Plato and Aristotle. This was just another sign that the classic culture was finally giving away in part to medieval culture.

The Christian church rose to power because of the force of its high moral and ethical doctrines and the intensity of the faith of its adherents. However, it managed over the centuries from A.D. 313 on to gradually structure its organization on a pattern similar to that of the empire, becoming very hierarchal in nature. Back in the days of early primitive Christianity, there were a number of fairly independent communities of believers, but gradually over the years they began to build up a central organization. Two of the steps in this change were to differentiate the priesthood from the layman, and to develop a hierarchy among the clergy.

Local small districts or communities of believers within the city were established and the joint churches of that city would appoint the priests or clergy for the local churches. The church established the office of bishop to take charge of all the churches in that particular city and its surrounding area, the diocese. Then in the various provinces of the empire the archbishops (sometimes called metropolitans or primates) were established, and these governed over the bishops and their territories. Over a group of provinces the church then appointed patriarchs. Even preceding the direct influence by Roman officialdom, by the fourth century A.D. this process had become very well established.

Finally, sometime in the fourth and fifth century A.D., the bishops of Rome were able to press their claim to jurisdiction over the entire western church and to exert their power as popes over all. The fact that the bishop of Rome was located in the old center of Roman power, and that Rome was still looked to as a very important center of the decaying empire, helped in establishing this supremacy. There was a theological and historical argument based upon the claim that the church at Rome had been founded by St. Peter, designated in scripture as Christ's chief apostle. For this reason it was held that the bishops of Rome should be considered as the successors of Christ. The conception of a united Christendom prevailed in the Christian world, and gradually spread into northern and northeastern Europe as the Roman (and Christian) civilization spread into that area. It was to play a very important part in governmental and in theological affairs. It would also influence very heavily the intellectual education and educational decisions of the empire, as well as the total culture of the Middle Ages.

The breakdown of the Roman Empire into the eastern and western parts was followed by a breakdown of the western part into smaller political divisions. After A.D. 476, the gradual process of breaking up began, even though this is not easily recognized except in historical perspective. The political authority first began to move northward into the kingdom settled by the Frankish tribes located in what is now France and the western part of Germany. Finally, many of the small Frankish kingdoms were brought together under a line of kings known as the Merovingian.

Charles Martel, who is given the credit for the defeat of the Moslem invasions of Europe through Spain at the Battle of Tours in France in A.D. 732, also brought most of western Europe under one rule, and strengthened the position of the Christian church. It was his grandson, Charles the Great, or Charlemagne (A.D. 742–814), who extended this empire still further and finally asked the pope to crown him emperor of the Holy Roman Empire in A.D. 800.

Charlemagne, probably an unlettered man but greatly interested in the education of the clergy, became the towering figure of the early Middle Ages. He made great strides in establishing a strong central government over most of western Europe. There was considerable intellectual achievement during this time with an interest in and an emphasis on learning stimulated by Charlemagne (discussed later in the section on education). The political authority was made more effective. He improved to some extent the economic and agricultural life, established various religious and educational institutions on a sound basis, and made several reforms particularly in the education of the clergy.

However, the successors of Charlemagne in each of the various realms of politics, religion and even in his own family, quarreled among themselves for the control of the empire. Furthermore, there were some new invasions which took place from the north. As a result, there was again a breakdown of government, lawlessness reigned, and warfare became very common. Rather than seeking protection in the questionable authority of the king, people sought safety in the political authority of a local strong man in a well-fortified castle who had followers willing to fight for him. The kings continued to exercise merely nominal control, with the actual authority in the hands of these local feudal lords.

In A.D. 962, Otto the First (the Great, 912–973), gained enough strength to conquer Italy and establish himself as the titular head of the

Holy Roman Empire. He liked to think that he had become the successor of Charlemagne and the legitimate heir of his empire.

The "Holy" part of the name indicated that the church was vastly important and the emperor considered himself to be the exclusive head of the secular branch of the great universal Christendom. By the end of the early Middle Ages, this Holy Roman Empire, although changing and nebulous at times, was certainly a power to be reckoned with in European political life.

At this point developments took place in Arabia that had their influence upon Europe. In the early part of the seventh century a man named Mohammed (A.D. 570–632) appeared as political and religious leader of the Arabs. He built a strong following and, with his army, conquered most of Arabia by the time of his death in A.D. 632. When he died, throughout the geographical area under Arab control, strong men known as "caliphs" arose in his place and continued his policy of conquest. At this time the eastern Roman Empire was weak and the caliph rulers were able to conquer most of the Middle East, spreading their empire beyond the borders of Arabia to the Turks to the north, and as far as India in the east. Eventually a group of converted Arabs, known as Saracens and later known as the Moors, crossed northern Africa to Spain and to Italy.

The high-water mark of the Moslem advance in Europe at this time was in Tours, France, where, in A.D. 732, the Moors were defeated and sent back to the borders of Spain where they were to remain for a number of years. The religion Mohammed founded is known as Islam ("submission"), and its followers, of whatever nationality, are called "Moslems" (or "Muslims") which means "faithful ones." The Moslem culture, arising out of the religious intensity of Mohammed's followers, picked up and preserved the Greek (and Persian) culture in the Middle East much more faithfully than did the Europeans during this period. Later on they were to contribute to the European Renaissance by passing on to Europe the preserved manuscripts of Aristotle and other Greek and Roman leaders which had been lost to the European western world.

The long process of the decline of Roman political authority continued after the death of Charlemagne, breaking down into small localized groups. These groups gave rise to the institution called "feudalism," [1] although it was not so named until the Renaissance period. The roots of the feudalistic concept go back to at least two ancient sources. Each of these gave form to two kinds of personal relationships found in feudalism known as feudal tenure and servile tenure.

Technically speaking, feudal tenure is the relationship between two persons, the overlord and his vassal, both of noble birth. This is held by most historians to have had its basis in the custom of the Germanic tribes

[1] An especially good treatment is found in Carl Stephenson, *Medieval Feudalism.* Ithaca, New York, Cornell University Press, 1942.

in which, upon the election of a new leader or king, the freemen would bind themselves to obey him. In theory, as the feudalistic system developed, the king was considered to be the chief overlord, and all the various subordinate nobles owed allegiance to him. But quite often the nobles, because they provided most of their own protection, gave this allegiance only when forced to do so by the king. For a long time in Germany these nobles were able to prevent a strong centralized government by establishing themselves as sovereign rulers over their own estates. The strength of kings to command this loyalty came about much earlier in France and England than it did in Germany. As is well known, Germany did not become completely unified until the late nineteenth century.

Servile tenure, on the other hand, was the relationship between a noble and a peasant or serf who was practically a slave. This had its roots in the latter days of the Roman Empire when the agricultural workers, and to some extent the craftsmen, were ordered by the Roman emperors to remain on the land or at their jobs and work for the owner. The serf, sometimes called a villein, was an unfree tenant who was bound to the land assigned to him. He had to divide the produce of this land with the lord. The serf also had to work part of the time on the lord's land, from which all the produce went to the lord. These serfs, although of higher status than landless persons, had lost their freedom, too. The descendants of the serfs were also bound to the soil and during the early period of feudalism it was difficult to escape from serfdom.

At the lowest level in feudalism was the person who owned no land and who did not have the horse necessary for fighting. In return for the protection given him by the lord, he worked in the fields and on the roads, or he fought as a foot soldier. He was lower than serfs and villeins, miserably poor, and had virtually no status under feudal regime. He worked intermittantly, did "odd" jobs, and owned no land.

The church as an institution was involved very heavily in these feudal relationships. Quite often the monasteries and churches themselves owned land, and sometimes there were persons under servile tenure on this land, or the church officials owed feudal tenure to other lords. It is frequently claimed that at one time in the Middle Ages the church owned almost one-third of the land in Europe.

A set of rigid class distinctions emerged in Europe as a result of these feudal arrangements. It was hard for anyone to change from the class into which he was born. The nobility and the officials of the church made up the aristocratic upper class, later to be called the first and second estates, respectively, and the lower classes were comprised of the rest of the people, most of them being serfs.

In the later Middle Ages, due to the growth of commerce and towns, there began to develop a middle class which had more rights and opportunities than those of the unfree serfs and others subservient to the aristocracy. Thus, the rise of the middle class of merchants, traders, and craftsmen who became what later were called in France the third estate (or the bourgeoisie).

In spite of the fact that feudalism appears from the modern point of view to be a very restricted and undesirable way to live, there were some positive sides to feudal tenure. In the first place, the system was based upon a political contract and the reciprocity of obligations. Although the king could command obedience, he also had certain terms of the contract to fulfill, and quite often there would be struggles between the nobles and kings over whether or not he was fulfilling his contract. On the negative side of feudalism it permitted the development of an entrenched and aristocratic class which was completely privileged over the common people in mode of living and educational opportunities, an entirely different kind of life.

Later Middle Ages (A.D. 1100 to c. A.D. 1300). From the eleventh to the end of the thirteenth centuries, political life in France and England centered around the process of the transferral of political authority into the hands of the kings. Little of this centralization process took place in either Germany or Italy because, in addition to this difficulty between the local rulers, there was also a very complicated struggle between the emperors and the popes. In the eleventh and twelfth centuries, the papacy gained in power in its contest with the emperor. In the thirteenth century, in particular, this was sharpened in the contest between Pope Innocent III (1161–1216) and Emperor Frederick II (1194–1250). Innocent III represented perhaps the peak of papal power in that he probably exerted more secular power than any other pope. Pope Innocent believed that the area encompassed by the Christian religion, i.e., Christendom, should be a great, unified commonwealth in which the pope rather than the secular political authority would be the head. The pope in this respect would be superior to all secular authorities and it would be his job to keep the governments in the "paths of righteousness." The pope was the successor of Peter and, as such, the feudal overlord of kings rather than the reverse. In France and England, however, because the papal power was a little farther away, the monarchies became much more centralized and much more powerful.

William the Conqueror (1027–1086) established Norman rule in England as a result of the invasion of 1066. This rule was a strong, highly centralized government operated in effect by a foreign power. His successor, King John (1167–1216) was forced to sign the Magna Carta (1215), through which the nobility gave notice they were not going to be brought completely under the king's rule without a very intensive struggle. Under a later king, Henry III (1207–1272), the council of nobles was expanded so that the representatives of some of the towns which had now grown to have more power—in particular, financial power—were represented as well as the nobility. This council was not very powerful since its job was primarily to approve the decrees of the kings, but it did constitute one of the preliminary constitutional forms out of which grew the English Parliament, the "mother of all parliaments." Later on, under Edward I (1239–1307), representatives of all the middle classes were admitted to Parliament. The middle class representatives subsequently were to break off and become the House of Commons of the English Parliament. This was the end of a long chain of circumstances which had resulted in the increased power of the middle classes.

Considerable social and cultural change was brought about in the latter Middle Ages by economic forces as shown in the growth of commerce, in the growth of towns, and in the more widespread organization of guilds. Starting back in the early part of the Middle Ages, commerce and economic life had been almost entirely agricultural and rural. There was much local bartering but little long-range commerce. The manor house was the economic unit and, by and large, was fairly self-sufficient. This manor house consisted of the noble family, the serfs and their families, and the artisans. The latter were not bound to the land, but lived close to the manor house. So, in general, during the early part of the Middle Ages, trade and commerce were a local affair, with the bartering being carried on by units which were fairly close to each other.

In the tenth century there was a revival of the east and west trade in which the maritime cities of Italy (Venice, Genoa, and Naples) took the lead. The Crusades, of course, were also a great stimulus for trade because they relied upon a fleet and used the knowledge of the traders. They also stimulated interest in goods found outside of Europe. In the twelfth and thirteenth centuries, there was a great upswing in long-range commerce as the eastern wares were brought into the Italian cities, and then were carried up the rivers and distributed to other places all over Europe.

This expansion of trade had given opportunity to the profession of traders who wandered in bands and sometimes settled on the outskirts of a castle or monastery. However, since they were foreigners and thus outside the feudal system, they were free men and were not bound to the local lord or bishop. As some of these had congregated at various centers, they began to develop a town life. Now some of these centers were on the sites of the old Roman cities. Some of them were near monasteries, river crossings, bridges, or near other likely places where people came to buy their wares. Of course, the local noble or the bishop who owned the land laid claim to the towns; however, since the traders and townspeople had organized themselves into a kind of government, they were eventually able to break the control of the feudal lord and win freedom and autonomy from control under the feudal system.

In the twelfth and thirteenth centuries especially, these towns grew very rapidly in number and in size throughout this part of Europe. One of the results of the growth of town life, of course, was a greater demand for the things which could not be produced in town, particularly agricultural products. Consequently, there was an increase in the amount of land placed under cultivation and new agricultural techniques were developed. These developments in turn permitted an increase in the population of Europe. Some authorities have estimated that by the middle of the fourteenth century the population of Europe was greater than it had been under the Roman Empire.

A tradition evolved which permitted an increase in the amount of freedom. If a serf could escape and go to a town and stay for a year and one day, it was agreed that he had become free. Since there was much opportunity for employment in town, this happened quite frequently. The towns, and later on the cities, thereby became a source of the increasing secularization of western Europe as well as a source of the increasing interest in trade.

Closely related to the development of commerce and economic life was the improvement or strengthening of the guild organizations composed of those persons who had certain common interests and mutual needs of protection and welfare. While there had been such organizations earlier, during the later Middle Ages they expanded greatly. In the eleventh century two different kinds of guilds began to take form, those of merchants and those of craftsmen, and between the two they began to regulate commerce very closely. The merchant guilds were first organized by traders who banded together as they went from market to market. These guilds of merchants would select their own leaders, work out regulations, provide funds for the purchase of goods, extend credit facilities and otherwise help each other. In this way, they began to get a monopoly on foreign trade and obtain the legal right to control their monopolies. Then, they began to exert influence on the town and government and were able to set their own prices. These merchants, because of the strength of their organization, grew in wealth and power. Gradually there evolved the middle class, or the bourgeoisie, which began to be as important as the former privileged class of the nobles and the clergy. The achievement of power by the middle class was a long step forward in the development of democracy.

The craftsman guild was organized by the end of the thirteenth century, somewhat later than the merchants' guild. This guild existed for the making rather than the trading of goods. The artisans or craftsmen organized themselves into groups according to their craft to protect themselves from inferior work and undercut prices and to gain a monopoly of production for themselves. The regulations went so far as to control the working hours, the working conditions, the quality of goods, the wages and prices, the number of tools, and the number of employees in each shop. Through these regulations they exerted very intensive control. However, they were still only quasi-public in nature, since the guilds had no official status, except in some cases where they were chartered by the nobles. The guilds regulated the membership in their craft very carefully. The master craftsmen usually owned their own shops and tools and would employ craftsmen at various levels of skill to produce goods. In addition to their commercial and financial arrangements, the craft guilds also had religious and fraternal aspects. They quite often supported their own priests and helped their own sick and aged. At times they even built roads and schools and organized their own military defenses. The guild educational system, through which the workers were taught and tested in their progress in the various steps in the guild, is discussed later.

The rise of the middle class and the guilds contributed to the development of independent towns and created a drive toward greater freedom, forming the foundation of the movement toward democracy in the early modern period.

The success of democracy as a social institution depends largely upon a strong middle class of individuals capable of able, responsible action in a situation where they are permitted decision-making. This type of situation was developing in the later Middle Ages and during the early modern period. This middle class had sufficient economic power to demand more and more voice in its government, and also to demand a different kind of education.

In spite of the increased emphasis upon economic and secular life, the Christian church still played a strong role in all fields of endeavor during the medieval period. The church had grown very rapidly during the later part of the Roman Empire and during the early Middle Ages. It continued to grow in political and economic power until it reached its probable peak in the thirteenth century. In the area of economic power, it has been shown that the church at one time owned nearly one-third of all the land in Europe.

In the early part of the Middle Ages, the church found its strength largely in the development of monastic institutions. There are two kinds of clergy in the Catholic church, the "regular" and the "secular." The regular clergy were the monks who lived in monasteries according to strict rules or regulations. The secular were those who ministered directly to the people, and the distinction between the two groups became greater during the latter part of the early period of the Middle Ages. The St. Benedict Order, organized in the sixth century at Monte Cassino, was one of the most influential of the regular clergy and developed a very elaborate scheme of regulations. The Benedictine monasteries emphasized the three main principles, obedience, simplicity, and industry.

The monks did not live an idle life. They developed the manual and agricultural arts to a high degree, and the monasteries usually became completely self-supporting. At times when the church hierarchy had become badly disorganized they kept the religious spirit alive. Many of the monks traveled into various outlying parts of Europe serving as missionaries. The monasteries, due in part to the influence of an early Christian scholarly monk, Cassiodorus (A.D. 480 to 575), became centers for much of the literary, artistic, and scholarly aspects of European life. They were famous for their labor in preserving and copying the ancient manuscripts. Since these manuscripts were written originally on perishable materials, this was necessary for their preservation.

After the twelfth century, the monastic orders began to decline. The secular branches of the church began to get stronger because of the rise of the towns, the development of a strong papacy and cathedral leadership, the development of the universities, and the development of the so-called "mendicant" orders. These "mendicant" orders were certain monastic groups that became quite interested in the social problems of their time, leaving their monasteries to wander around helping the poor, to take care of those who were sick, and to preach religion, particularly to the "down-and-outers."

The medieval period has been often described as a time when important theological and philosophical problems were pretty well settled, with universal agreement on the fundamental problems of man and the universe. However, a more careful study by scholars in recent years indicates that there were many differences in points of view in almost all of these periods. Consequently, there was need at every stage for people who tried to reconcile the different lines of thought to keep them always in the line of orthodoxy. There were always those radicals who kept trying to pull off in one direction or another. The church was, by and large, successful in assimilating and controlling these various elements. Sometimes things which were condemned as heresy in one period would become orthodox viewpoints in another period. One of the jobs faced by thinkers of the later Middle Ages (and perhaps this is a perennial job) was to reconcile the religious and spiritual aspects of the church with the secular interests which kept intruding at all times. Because the church itself was engaged in many kinds of economic and political enterprises, this secular interest operated not only outside the church, but within it as well.

Central to all of the religious ideas of the Middle Ages, and perhaps to most orthodox religion, is the hope for some kind of eternal security and salvation beyond this mortal world. Theoretically, this salvation involves the strengthening of the spiritual self rather than risking damnation through too great an involvement with the secular interest of the world. Quite often people have spoken of the Middle Ages as being "other-worldly" in outlook. However, this was not entirely true because men continued to have very strong secular interests. The attempt by the

church to control secular drives and to direct the spiritual energies was
not completely successful. Some of the church leaders themselves were
purely nominal Christians and had a very materialistic point of view.

One of the intellectual problems of the period was to reconcile the
sacred literature of the Bible and the writings of the church fathers with
the secular literature of the classical writers of Greece and Rome. In the
early Christian period there had been an attempt to discount the old
pagan culture. As time went on, there was an effort to try to adapt some
of the thoughts of Plato, Aristotle, and others, to support Christian
teachings.

With the decline in Greek and Roman learning, many of the Greek
books became unknown to the Roman scholars of the later Roman
period. However, with the rise of the Moslem religion, and through the
revival of learning which took place during the period of the ninth, tenth,
and eleventh centuries, some of the Greek classical writings were translated from Greek into Arabic, and eventually into Latin. Particularly
important in this were two Moslem scholars, Avicenna (actually Persian
in background, A.D. 980 to 1037), and Averroes (A.D. 1126 to 1198). Avicenna's influence was left primarily from 1100 to A.D. 1500. Through the
work of these scholars and the Jewish thinker Moses Maimonides, who
reconciled Aristotle with the Jewish religion, the works of Aristotle were
translated into Latin. By the middle of the thirteenth century, Christianity once more had the translations of Aristotle's scientific and philosophical works. The study of his works led to much argument, and the church
became alarmed because the Christian faith seemed to be contradicted by
the results of using Aristotle's methods of scientific investigations through
reason.

These intellectual efforts grappled with the problem of trying to
reconcile the claims of human reason or logic with the claims of the
Christian faith, many times seemingly illogical and paradoxical. Some of
the great, rational arguments of the later Middle Ages which originated
with the "school men" or "scholastics" were involved with this problem.
An attempt was made to strike a balance between faith on one hand and
reason on the other. One of the outstanding thinkers of the late medieval
period whose work actually represented this synthesis of ideas was St.
Thomas Aquinas (1225–1274) perhaps the greatest of all the "reconcilers."

Basically, Thomas Aquinas addressed himself to the problem of
reconciling the pagan Greek thought as represented by Aristotle with
Christian faith. He finally arrived at his synthesis in his Summa Theo-
logica. This doctrine eventually became the official doctrine of the Catholic church, adopted by papal decree in 1879. St. Thomas distinguished
between what he called natural philosophy and supernatural theology.
Philosophy as such deals with the natural world where things come into
existence, go through change, and go out of existence. Thus, philosophy

deals with everything that is open to argument or can be demonstrated by human reason. Theology, however, deals with truth, revealed in one way or the other, involving the supernatural world which is changeless, eternal, and ultimate. These universal truths then make up the content of faith, and they are not open to question by human reason because human reason cannot have any basis for challenging them.

Aquinas asserted that there can be basically no contradiction between theology and philosophy, between truth as revealed and truth as discovered by reason since, in the final analysis, all truth comes from God. Now certain things about faith can be reasoned, but some things are just beyond the possibility of human reason. They are not open to rational demonstration. Divine truth is anchored in some kind of eternal reality which is fixed and unchanging. This truth, divine truth, is not humanly created; it is created by God, and what man tries to do is to discover it by means of his own human reason and intelligence. Man is imperfect and he has to move from ignorance to knowledge through learning. He has been given an intellect in order to help him to do this, but he is not able to achieve all truth through this method of reason, and so sometimes it must be accepted on the basis of faith. God has given man human intellect, therefore, to reach out and grasp truth, but mankind cannot do this without help. Therefore, he must rely on faith, revelation, and grace to rise to the truth of theology and religion. Human reason is the higher or the theoretical intellect which, according to St. Thomas, deals in science, mathematics, and philosophy. The lower or practical intellect has to do with the political economics of everyday affairs of action, conduct, and experience.

Thus Aquinas, like Aristotle, elevated theoretical intellect and theoretical knowledge above practical and experiential knowledge. This characteristic outlook of the Middle Ages has continued throughout modern times, influencing much of contemporary education and philosophical controversy. However, interestingly enough, the scholastic point of view, particularly the thomistic version, was attacked by a number of the scholastics themselves. One of the earlier controversies was carried on by the monk Roger Bacon (1214–1294). Later in the fourteenth century, William of Ockham (1300–1349) and Duns Scotus (1265–1308) attacked the Thomistic philosophical position. Roger Bacon is more pertinent to the present discussion since he dealt with the world of science, preliminary to the scientific revolution of the sixteenth century, whereas the other points of view were motivated through theology and religion per se.

Bacon, a British monk, was very dissatisfied with Aquinas' assumptions. Although he never left the church, he did get in trouble and had to serve some time in jail for his views. He raised his voice a number of times in criticism of the Thomists' reliance on Aristotle for authority in scientific as well as in theological matters. His main argument was against the conclusions of Aristotelian science as accepted by St. Thomas. He argued that the ideas about the operation of the natural world should be verified completely by actual and active experiences. Although he did not state clearly the specific method of experimentation as was done more fully by Francis Bacon (1561–1626) some time later, his ideas of testing things to check on the results of theorizing were certainly a forerunner of some of the scientific notions which came about later.

MEDIEVAL EDUCATION

General Nature of Education in the Middle Ages.   Government in the Middle Ages was a result of compromise between the political institution of feudalism and the organization of the Christian church. Also the intellectual viewpoint was finally worked out as a compromise between the "pagan" philosophy represented by Aristotle and Catholic Christian theology. By the same token, medieval education was a result of the attempt to solve the conflict between the old classical Roman schools built on the Greek pattern and the new emphasis on the other-worldliness of Christianity.

This was an age where there were few books, and those few were held in great reverence. Whenever words were written down, they were held to be authoritative; consequently, education was extremely bookish in nature and the school set out to cultivate the qualities of submissiveness and obedience in the pupils. It was only among a few of the advanced scholars that there were any critical abilities developed or any originality shown and these received no encouragement by the school.

Unfortunately, some of the books most widely used during this period had been written during the period of very poor scholarship of the later Roman Empire. The better books of the past had been lost or were ignored. Many times the books were little more than a compendium of the folklore of the past. All the books were written in Latin, and all education was conducted in Latin; consequently, one of the main aims of education, from a practical standpoint, was the ability to read Latin. The books were the final authority and their memorization was the chief requirement. The process of education was largely one of being certain that the exact subject matter of the textbook was mastered (i.e., memorized) by the student.

There was no concern in any of this for any attempt to use education or books for the purpose of developing the individual or enabling him to better prepare himself to live in the society outside the church. Although such things had been very prominent in the educational theory of the Greeks as well as Cicero and Quintillian, as noted earlier, the religious emphasis of the church began to overshadow these ideas. It wasn't until the Renaissance period that there began to be an interest in the development of the individual and an interest also in secular literature in order to learn more about the delights and beauty of this world.

Elementary and Secondary Schools.   At a time when early Christianity was an underground religion and not in political control, the serious question arose as to whether or not the Christians should send their children to school. Tertullian (A.D. 160?–230?) said that they should, but many parents refused and educated their children in their own homes. This, of course, followed the Jewish tradition. As the church gained in strength, it organized a few schools. One was the catechumenal school. This was a system of training for those who wanted to become members of the church. They were not permitted to become members of the church at once, but had to go through an examination procedure and initiation ceremonies, and then had to spend two years as listeners before they could be baptized and become full members of the church. Some of the ancient writings were used as a basis for this school. Later on, the Christians developed a catechetical school for the purpose of training the children in Christian doctrines so they would be able to resist the influences from the outside. These schools, the catechumenal in particular, developed into various church schools operated by the church to train its own people, and quite often these would be located in the house of the bishop, where they came to be called "cathedral schools."

From the time of the first persecution of the Christians around A.D. 64 through the reign of Diocletian (A.D. 245–313), Christianity suffered periodic persecution. Consequently, the "schools of the martyrs" were founded to train and prepare Christians for the possible persecution. In the schools of martyrs, the Christians were taught self-denial, how to act before judges in that arena, and methods of hardening the body to withstand suffering. Some of this led to fanaticism and exhibitionism. Another outgrowth was asceticism and the rise of monasticism covered earlier in this chapter.

Education as conducted in the monastic and parish schools, which were established by the churches and sometimes called "song schools," and the elementary branches of the cathedral schools was primarily centered on teaching Latin in order to take part in the church service. Only a minimal amount of learning was necessary to be a priest—just enough that he could read Latin and conduct the prayers and chants of the religious ceremonies of the church. Many times the boys and men who became priests did not understand the meaning of the Latin words which were often taught in chants like music. Writing was taught chiefly to those who were going to become copyists. Very likely there were some fundamental mathematical skills taught, but certainly these were very simple in nature.

It seems that the method of teaching was very likely as follows: The teacher of a group of boys would read from his book and dictate the words, the pupils would probably repeat them aloud or perhaps they would copy them down on a wax tablet, and then memorize the words by repeating them over and over again. Then after memorizing the words, they would wipe their slate clean, ready for the next day's lesson. There seems to have been no effort whatsoever to explain the meaning of words or to use pictures or objects. Sometimes, perhaps, a good teacher might explain the words by using the vernacular in order for the pupil to understand it more fully.

As time went on, the elementary instruction in letters (i.e., reading), and the secondary instruction in grammar became distinguished from the more advanced study in the liberal arts. A different group of teachers in the advanced schools soon began to spend their full time teaching the liberal arts. The former schools were not as separate from the church as they were taught by persons who also served as monks or priests during the rest of their time. It should be noted that, although these schools may be criticized for centering on Latin, there was no really good vernacular literature. Latin was also a universal spoken language which enabled one to communicate with persons who might have a different vernacular language. However, Latin was not widely used, except by scholars and priests, and certainly it was completely foreign to the Germanic and Celtic peoples of western Europe. Consequently, to teach boys in a language which they did not understand and which therefore they had to memorize was certainly a difficult task with the limited methods used.

The doctrine of original sin seemed to support the general belief that all youth was stubborn and rebellious. Furthermore, that the punishment of the body physically was good for boys and for their souls. Consequently, this doctrine helped justify the punishment of students in order to get them to learn things which were boring and which they did not want to learn. Hence, there was very little resistance during the period of the Middle Ages—and even on into the middle of the fifteenth century —to severe corporal punishment or to the concept of mental discipline. It was not until the eighteenth and nineteenth centuries that these ideas were seriously challenged. Of course, some of the earlier writers such as Quintilian as earlier noted, had already indicated opposition to the use of corporal punishment.

Chivalric Education.   A complicated system of political and personal relationships called feudalism had grown among the nobility in the early period of the Middle Ages. There had to be methods developed to get the young noble ready to assume his obligations within this organization. Thus the institution of chivalry developed and also became the basis for a set of ideals to guide the education and conduct of the upper or noble class. The patterns of chivalry were based upon the usages which had been worked out as appropriate to the system of warfare, of religion, and of "courtesy" characteristic of the upper classes at this time. Since there was continual warfare among these classes, there needed to be training in the skills of fighting on horseback. The church, however, did contribute certain ideas of honor, of generosity, of protection of the weak, and, of course, of loyalty to the Christian religion itself. In addition, there was the institution of *courtesy* ("courtoisie" or the social graces and manners) which had developed in the court of the nobles. Consequently, the ideal for the knight was a man of action who was a soldier, a courtier (or a courteous man), and a Christian gentleman. He was a man who had reverence for the church as well as loyalty and faithfulness to his feudal obligations.

No special schools developed for the training of the knight, but there did arise a system of training people in the institutions of chivalry. The education of a noble child usually took place at the court of the overlord next above him, and there were three fairly well defined stages of training. The first of these stages was for the younger boy from about the age of seven or eight up to about fourteen or fifteen. During this time, he acted as a page or valet (servant) at the court of the overlord of his father who himself would be lesser noble. As the page of the court, he was more probably attached at this early age to the ladies of the court whom he served and from whom he learned about the life of court. They would require him to practice the courtly graces and courtesies. He would learn how to play a musical instrument, take part in religious ceremonies, and they might even teach him to read and write the vernacular language.

From the age of fourteen or fifteen up to about twenty-one, the boy was transferred to act as a squire or attendant for the overlord himself or one of the knights of the overlord's court. In this capacity he would help care for the horses and the armor and assist his master in war, in tournaments, or in hunting. He probably learned to sing and to dance, to enter into the games and story-telling activity, and to learn all about the institutions of heraldry. At about the age of twenty-one or so, if he had "made the grade," he would be inducted into knighthood by the overlord or the church official after he proved himself worthy of such honor on the field of battle or in a tournament. He would then be dubbed "knight," and would dedicate himself to the overlord. He would take oaths of allegiance, both to his feudal overlord and to the church, and often there was a religious exercise accompanying this procedure.

Now the young knight was ready to enter upon his duties and assume his obligations in return for which he would possibly be given some land or other means of subsistence so that he could exercise his fief to his overlord. He had learned about feudal laws and how to manage an estate, or he had watched others do it, and he knew how to deal with the lower class workmen and serfs. Certainly he had acquired the class consciousness of superiority over the common people, and had the ability to command underlings; therefore, the whole training was a class education for entrance into the aristocracy.

The girl of the noble class was also educated at the same time by being taught the religious faith and ceremonies, learning how to dance and sing, learning courtesy, sewing, weaving and handicraft, and how to manage the household servants. She was possibly taught to read and write so that she could conduct correspondence and keep books. She was trained in these duties at home or she might be sent for a short time to a convent. Later on in her teens, she was assigned to the overlord's court to learn social graces of chivalrous life and act as a lady-in-waiting or tend the mistress of the court until the time of her marriage. Chivalric education, therefore, of the youth of the noble class was a very practical and direct induction into the life which the noble class would have to live. This is quite in contrast to the bookish nature of the other kinds of schools.

Guild Education.   In the early Middle Ages (and this is true of other pre-industrial societies) one method of educating a person for an occupation was simply through the direct imitation of the skills of the father by the son, and thus the handing down of these skills. Later on, this was done through some kind of apprentice system in which the new artisan would be apprenticed to a skilled worker, something like the case of the son learning from the father. When the guild system began to be highly organized in the twelfth and thirteenth centuries, a more systematic basis for the training of the guildsman developed, the system of apprenticeship was further lengthened, and this developed into three stages similar to that of knighthood.

The three stages of development of the craftsmen were apprentice, journeyman, and master craftsman. As an apprentice, the boy would be assigned or bound over to a master craftsman on the basis of some type of contract or indenture which was binding on both parties. The master promised to teach the boy the skills of the trade, to watch over his morals, and to see to it that he was trained in religion. He might pay his keep and give him a small amount of money, and he was supposed to teach him some reading and writing, to the extent necessary to carry on the trade. Probably in most cases, this was very little. In return, the boy had to work very hard and faithfully to learn the skills and secrets of the trade, and to serve his master. This period of apprenticeship varied greatly according to the situation. It could last anywhere from three to ten or eleven years, the apprentice having started at about seven or eight years of age. The similarity is to be noted here between this and the first stage of chivalry, i.e., the page.

The next stage was that of training as a journeyman. During this time the young worker would travel about working as a day laborer for different masters in their shops or he might work in a shop for longer periods of time for a wage set by the guild. After he had proved his work and presented a masterpiece showing that he had mastered the trade, then he would be admitted with ceremony as a full-fledged member of the guild. After that, if he wished, he could set up his own shop, take on apprentices, and become himself an instructor in the arts of the craft.

Higher Education—The Development of the University. During the period of the early Middle Ages the principal agencies for higher education, a term which certainly was not yet clearly defined, was the monastic school and the cathedral school. Higher education was primarily for the purpose of preparing the priests of the church. The monastic schools were the predominant means of higher education until the eleventh century. At this time the cathedral schools found near the see of the bishops began to exceed in importance the monastic schools. The number of students who attended the cathedral schools increased so much that the bishop quite often would actually turn the direct control of the school over to a church officer, called the "chancellor." The authority for the establishment of these schools would come, of course, from the pope to the bishop, and the bishop would then delegate it to the chancellor.

One of the important powers delegated to the chancellor was the right to issue a teaching license to qualify persons to teach within the diocese in which the cathedral school was located. As time went on and certain of these cathedral schools grew to greater prominence, the pope would sometimes give the chancellor, through the bishop, the right to issue the license to teach anywhere (*licentia docendi*). This meant that some of the cathedral schools would have authority beyond their dioceses. It should be noticed that now the schools' purpose includes training for teaching as well as the priesthood. Since almost all persons who were teaching were also clerics, these were not conflicting roles.

As time went on, some of these schools became places of general study, *studium generale*. These were thus named because they tried to attract students from a wide area, and their license to teach was widely recognized beyond the jurisdiction of the particular cathedral. By the beginning of the twelfth century, several of these were quite flourishing. Among these which might be mentioned were: The University of Chartres, which had considerable interest in the study of the classics; Paris, which was interested in the study of theology and logical thinking;

Bologna, which had developed a special interest in law; and Salerno, which had become a center for the teaching of medicine. In most cases these universities had grown out of the free association of scholars, although usually based upon earlier cathedral schools. The study in these schools which was often professional in emphasis, started upon the basis of a three-year study of the liberal arts, plus three to seven years in professional studies. For example, students spent five years in Salerno studying medicine after completing the three years of liberal arts study.

During the twelfth century, there was a considerable increase in the number of teachers and students at some of these schools. They organized themselves into a pattern typical of the Middle Ages, discussed earlier in the case of the merchants and craftsmen, namely, guilds, or in Latin, *universitas*. The university (or *universitas*) was an organization to protect the teachers against the encroachments of the chancellor, the bishop, the king, or anyone else who tried to exert too much control. Often the students would also organize themselves into guilds so they could be protected against the teachers, against the townspeople, and against unruly persons within their own group. Quite often these student "universities" were organized around nationality lines within the university rather than being university-wide.

As time went on the term "universitas" (collective), originally applied to any group of people who were organized for common purposes, began to be applied specifically only to the universities of faculties and students. By this procedure of organizing themselves into guilds and corporate organizations, the cathedral schools became universities. This is actually the first university in its modern sense, since the so-called "university" of Athens earlier was not really the same kind of institution. No exact date can be given for the appearance of the universities, but certainly they were present in the late twelfth and thirteenth centuries.

The teachers were usually organized around the faculties of liberal arts, law, medicine or theology. Not all universities had all these faculties, some being famous for one and some for another. In the later Middle Ages, the greatest university was that of the University of Paris. It is an example of the development in complete form of a university, free as far as power is concerned from the king, the pope, or the chancellor. The University of Paris (or corporate body of the faculty) finally was recognized as the legal body of the university. It had a legal corporate existence, could set its own curriculum issue the license to teach, and confer degrees and appoint its own members. The university, then, in its original form, was the corporate existence of the faculty empowered with a right to run its own affairs without any responsibility to any administrative officers or any kind of board of control outside its own membership.

The situation at Bologna mentioned earlier was the university-type organization developed out of a combination of the old cathedral liberal-arts school, the monastic school devoted to law, and a municipal school of rhetoric which had been in existence for some time. The student guilds or *universitas* began to control the university. The rector of the student guilds (there were actually many guilds working together) was recognized as the head of the university. The professors had to take an oath of allegiance to the student rector and abide by the regulations of the student guilds, which, for example, included the length and content of the lectures and the length of the academic term.

There were numerous other important universities founded during this period, such as those at Rome, Oxford, Cambridge, and Naples. It is said that there were at least seventy-five known universities by the end of the fifteenth century.

The content of the liberal arts portion of higher education prior to the rise of the university had been, in general, the trivium (grammar, rhetoric, and logic) and quadrivium (arithmetic, geometry, astronomy, and music), and beyond these seven liberal arts were the professional studies of law, medicine and theology.

As the university system developed, there was an expansion of the liberal arts curriculum. Since Aristotle's works had been newly re-discovered, including his natural philosophy (a discourse on what is now called the physical sciences), his moral philosophy or ethics and politics, and his mental philosophy which can be labeled as metaphysics, they were added to the curriculum. The University of Paris, the most influential of the universities, was very slow to accept the scientific works of Aristotle, because they did not fit in with the church doctrine, and often elsewhere the papacy exercised pressure to exclude these works. However, in many cases the arts faculties of these many universities became receptive to Aristotle's philosophy and set out to digest and assimilate it. There were a number of persons who began to study Aristotle's works, giving it respectability, as indicated in the case of St. Thomas Aquinas. Another important scholar interested in Aristotle had been Albertus Magnus (1193–1280). So eventually the philosophical and scientific works of Aristotle were included along with the other seven liberal arts in the curriculum.

Why was it that there was a prescription of certain studies for liberal education? This seems to arise out of the manner of licensing teachers to teach in the various schools. All of the teachers in the Middle Ages were actually clerics and, of course, they had to be trained in religious orthodoxy as well as in scholarship. Consequently, the church found it well worthwhile to control very carefully the entrance into the teaching profession. This was done by controlling the granting of the license to teach as indicated earlier (*licentia docendi*). The condition for receiving the license to teach was the completion of the course in the liberal arts. At one time this was granted by the bishop or the chancellor, but as the university organization came into being, it came to be granted by the faculty of the liberal arts. This seems to have been first established as a policy by the University of Paris in 1213, and was soon copied by the other universities.

When the student had finished the study of elementary liberal arts, he was granted a degree, the baccalaureate degree (bachelor of arts, B.A.). This indicated that he was ready to be an assistant teacher and could be given some responsibility as a teacher. He could then go ahead and study the higher liberal arts and particularly the Aristotelian philosophy for three more years. At the end of this period of time, he could be granted the final license to teach and was entitled to become a master teacher (master of arts, or M.A.). In order to win the master's degree, he was required to prepare some type of thesis and defend it against the disputants, as in much the same manner the journeyman in the guild system had to present his masterpiece to the guild members as proof of his qualification to become a master craftsman. It is to be noted, therefore, that the B.A. and M.A. degrees were originally professional degrees opening the way to teaching, and that it was necessary to demonstrate teaching ability by means of the disputation as a workman before fellow students.

The requirements at the English universities, which strongly influenced American universities, were similar. Some of those found in early American colleges were direct transfers from England. For example, at Oxford University in England, a student had a four-year course under a tutor to prepare for his B.A. degree. He had two examinations: one in grammar and arithmetic, and a second on rhetoric, logic and, probably, music. There were three more years of study beyond the B.A. required for the M.A. degree in which he read books on astronomy, geometry, and Aristotelian "philosophy," which really included physical sciences, ethics, and metaphysics. Cambridge similarly had the prescription of the old liberal arts and the "new" philosophical studies. Many of these same courses were prescribed in early American three or four-year colleges.

In the early period of the Middle Ages, some of the monastic and cathedral schools taught law, medicine, and theology along with the liberal arts. Later on, after the twelfth century in particular, the faculty members of law, medicine, and theology became recognized as separate, advanced professional studies, with the liberal arts as preparation for these. Therefore, many of the universities at that time had separate faculties to give the advanced professional degrees.

The methods of instruction which were used at the medieval university were primarily lectures, repetitions and disputations. The lectures consisted largely of oral textbook reading by the masters. The students usually had no text. The master would then comment on the material line by line. The commentaries were sometimes written out, in which case they were called glosses. The lecturing would sometimes become very complicated as one master elaborated on certain passages by referring to the glosses of a whole series of scholars who had commented upon each passage. So the lecture was the oral repeating of the text with accompanying comments. The *repetitions* were basically a review of the lecture materials and the textbook which the students would do by themselves. In the *disputations* the students would, according to certain established rules which had been set up for such argumentation, argue among themselves and defend or attack certain of the ideas set forth.

The information concerning the life of students is very interesting. Even though all of the students who were studying were presumably clerics, they led very exhilarating lives, especially in their out-of-class activities. They were frequently engaged in many kinds of activities that were frowned upon by the university authorities. These authorities made no effort, apparently, to provide for any kind of social activities or for physical exercise for the students. Consequently, there were all kinds of fighting and brawling. There were regulations against cock fights, tennis, gambling, playing a musical instrument, keeping of pets and so forth. However, apparently these practices continued. Students participated in singing, storytelling, and a great deal of drinking.

Control of Education. Many scholars studying medieval education have believed until recently that all of the schools of this period, such as they were, were conducted by the church, since the church did play such an important role in the culture in general and, in particular, in the field of education. However, there is considerable evidence which has recently been brought to light to show that secular schools and lay teachers did continue to function throughout this period and following also.

There was, of course, a decline in education and schools in Italy after the Teutonic invasions and after the acceptance of Christianity, but many of the secular town-operated schools continued. As a matter of fact, after the conditions following the original invasion, some of the kings of Lombardy did reestablish and improve the town schools which had been closed. Evidence has been uncovered of the uninterrupted existence of secular schools in many of the principal towns from the eighth century down to the later Middle Ages.[2] These secular schools, some of which were conducted by a private teacher, and some of which were conducted by a public school teacher supported by the towns, did not give religious instruction, but emphasized the traditional grammar, including the old, classical literature (rhetoric), law or medicine. Some of this instruction, of course, was at a low level. The desire for these schools and the type of instruction given in them did not originate in the religious attitude of the people, but in the desire for the intellectual education and whatever practical advantages that such studies would give them.

2 See Butts, *op. cit.*, pp. 126–7.

There were also a few town schools in northern Europe which continued to exist through the Middle Ages. In the latter part of the Middle Ages, there was a movement again toward the establishment of town schools and, in some cases, the taking over of a school which had already existed. In the northern part this was closely related to the development of commerce and the increase in the importance of the city in the rising middle class. In general, however, these schools were religious in aims although not controlled by the church. They were Latin in content and the emphasis was not so much on secular instruction. They were taken over to establish civil control rather than church control of the schools.

One of the important events in the educational renaissance in the early Middle Ages appeared at the time of Charlemagne. Charlemagne was attempting to establish a strong, centralized government, but he was also interested in extending education. He issued many decrees on religious and educational matters. For example, he decreed that the clergy would have to improve their ability to read and write, and that they would have to be able to write their own letters, and that they would have to have sufficient scholarship to calculate the date of Easter and "know the grounds of their faith." In order to do this, then, he established schools for teaching reading where none had existed before. His decree meant that some of the abbotts and priests who were not literate must now be examined with respect to educational achievements by their bishops. Also, there was an attempt made to correct the manuscripts which had been corrupted by the monks in the monasteries who were not able to read what they were copying.

In addition to Charlemagne's interest in education in general, he also revived a palace school at his court which had been in existence, although not too strong, in the time of Charles Martel. Charlemagne was also responsible for calling the great teacher Alcuin from York in England to head this school. Alcuin was required to teach mature adults the very rudiments of learning. This school was attended, of course, by the king's family and the other nobility of the court, including the adults as well as the children.[3] It is believed that Charlemagne himself did not know how to write when he became king. He was interested in getting the best scholars of that time from all over the world in order to prepare better clergymen and better officials for the church and state. Although Charlemagne was not interested in education for the masses, his efforts, of course, seemed important in contrast to what had happened before and afterwards. He did recognize education as a very important force for tying together the threads of his great empire.

In England, King Alfred the Great was very much interested in learning. Unlike Charlemagne, Alfred the Great was a scholar in his own

[3] See Chapter IV in Harry S. Broudy and John R. Palmer, *Exemplars of Teaching Method*. Chicago, Rand McNally, 1965. Pp. vii + 177.

right. He also established a school at his court for the sons of his nobility, and he decreed that the sons of the wealthy class should attend school until they were fifteen years of age. He, like Charlemagne, brought scholars from all over the world to England. There was also some attempt to improve the learning among the priesthood during the time of Alfred. Later on, in the eleventh century when William the Conqueror took over England, the Norman conquerors became patrons of learning in both the monasteries and cathedral schools, and used this to help them elevate the Norman French institutions and ideals in Norman England.

At the other end of Europe, one of the most outstanding rulers of the later Middle Ages was Frederick II. He set up a court in Sicily where he helped to bring together the streams of three great cultures, Arabic, Greek, and Roman, together with Italian. Sicily therefore became an important center where manuscripts were collected and scholars in liberal arts and medicine were brought together for consultation.

It should be pointed out that although the secular authorities were active in sponsoring education throughout the Middle Ages, with the exception of the town schools before noted, this education was operated through the clergy. When the kings gathered scholars around them, the scholars were all clergy. The schools were all established in the monasteries, the churches, or the cathedrals, with the exception of the palace schools themselves. The kings and emperors quite often provided the stimulation to keep the clergy interested in carrying on better education. The direct control of education, however, stayed in the hands of the clergy and the church. When the powers of the emperors declined in the ninth and tenth centuries, the pope and church councils took their own independent action regarding education.

One of the most important phases of the education of the church was that conducted by the monastic schools. The Benedictine monasteries on the continent of Europe and those operating in Ireland did provide schools as a part of their contributions. These schools not only gave instruction for boys going into the priesthood, but also for nonclerics. As mentioned earlier, it was these monastic schools which dominated the educational scene in Europe from the sixth to the eleventh century.

From time to time the pope and church councils kept asking the various parish and cathedral churches to maintain schools for the general public. For example, a council held in Rome in 853 decreed that elementary instruction should be given to anyone in all parishes, and schools for the liberal arts should be established in all cathedrals. Not only were they to teach boys chosen to become clerics, but also give instruction to less fortunate children who wanted this instruction. However, this instruction was not always carried out, and there is no evidence that these schools were widespread or that they administered to any more than a small fraction of the people of Europe. These schools, where they existed, did provide elementary instruction in reading, writing, and music. Also, the churches and cathedrals provided some instruction in the seven liberal arts as indicated in the earlier discussion of higher education.

One of the developments of the later Middle Ages was the chantry school, usually established by a wealthy person. The chantry foundation was established with a priest to chant masses for the salvation of the soul of some wealthy person after his death. But since the chanting of the masses did not take all of his time, he was supposed to also give some instruction. These became privately endowed and controlled schools rather than operating directly under the church.

Another privately operated school was that established by the guilds themselves for their own children. Sometimes they supported their own priest for their religious services as well. These guild schools for the children of the workers were not the same as the vocational preparation in the apprentice system. These precedents in chantry and guild schools helped establish patterns for private education which are to be important in the later period of the Renaissance and Reformation, especially in England.

Status of the Teaching Profession.   Almost all of the teachers in the elementary schools in the Middle Ages were clerics or minor church officials or, in some cases, the priests themselves. Their status was very similar to that of the lower levels of the clergy. There were some lay teachers, particularly in the towns of Italy, who made their living instructing children by private contract with the parents. However, the great weight of instruction was carried on by monks in monasteries or by priests in their own parishes, sometimes as a part of their regular duties. Many of these monks and clergymen did not live at a very high cultural level. Teaching became a subsidiary part of the priest's duty, and the quality of instruction was certainly not very high.

As discussed earlier, in the later Middle Ages there was increased interest in instruction in liberal arts, medicine and theology. Furthermore, the attempt of more students to get more training helped supply a better quality of teachers, and many students eventually became clergymen to occupy places in the various parishes. Also, there was an improvement in the work of those teachers who associated themselves around the cathedral schools, many of which became universities. Some of these who, although officially clerics, were more noted as scholars than clergymen, and did not participate much in the religious life as such. By the time of the thirteenth century, these university teaching careers became one of the most challenging of all the careers in the church or state for the energies of able young men. Practically all of the important thinkers and writers and the leaders of the universities of the thirteenth century were these university-trained men (or professors). These teachers became the molders of intellectual life more so at that time, perhaps, than at any other time since or before, unless it might have been in the Golden Age of Greece.

The status of the teaching profession in the universities was quite high, and the professors were given all kinds of privileges, exemptions, and immunities. Although they, of course, never attained the wealth of the nobles or high churchmen, they did enjoy a much better than average living standard, and more important, perhaps, they held a very high place in public respect and esteem. At Oxford and Cambridge, they had special representation in Parliament, and quite often as a group they were sought out to decide important questions on political as well as heretical and other theological disputes.

EDUCATION, FREEDOM, AND SECURITY IN THE MIDDLE AGES

While it is true that the medieval society was not basically a free society, still it can be said that there was a growth of freedom during the period of the Middle Ages. The Middle Ages represented, as has been shown in the early part of this chapter, a period which was presumably oriented around the religious nature of man living in this world but destined for another. His main purpose was to prepare himself in this world for the world to come. In this situation, there was one dominant institution, the Catholic Church, which controlled the religious life and determined the way in which man could approach the eternal life. Since the practices and restrictions on life were determined by the church and it did not provide, theoretically, a great deal of freedom in action or thought, this was basically then not a free society. However, one might argue from a particular point of view that this society did do full justice to man's spiritual being and in a sense gave him freedom to become more enlightened with respect to man's "true spiritual nature."

However, one of the great facts in regard to medieval society were the basic incongruities, as Muller has termed it.[4] There was within the church itself great contrast between the hierarchy on one hand and men who were inspired saints such as St. Bernard, St. Francis, and St. Thomas. There were persons who were cruel in their restrictions on their fellow men, as well as those who inspired their fellow men to great heights of spiritual and other types of achievement. Another basic incongruity in the medieval society was the conflict between the institutions of Christianity

[4] Herbert J. Muller, *Freedom in the Western World,* pp. 47–51.

and the institutions of feudalism. Actually in feudalism, which nominally was dedicated to Christianity, man could follow a very reckless and violent life quite inconsistent with the ordinary meaning of the religious life of the Christian. The knight of the Middle Ages could at times be a crude, blood-thirsty, murderous individual and at other times a saint acting for the best interest of the church.

There was also an inconsistency in the fight over the separation of church and state. Since there never has been a complete and lasting interpretation of what the separation of church and state meant, in the fight between the powers of the king and the powers of the pope and, later on, in the fight between the king and the local lords and barons, many times the cause of human freedom for the middle or lower classes was served.

There was also found among Christians of this period such qualities as humor, adventuresomeness, and gusty living which were quite in contrast with the outer facade of saintliness and virtue. Therefore, in these conflicting traditions of religion, classical rationalism, and of the feudal system, the growing power of the bourgeois arising out of the commerce of the latter Middle Ages enabled them to achieve some of the elements of human freedom. This gave rise to new concepts of human freedom during the period of the Scientific Revolution and the Reformation. Certainly there was in the original writings of Christianity a great deal of interest in the individual and the individual's will to do right. In a sense, Christianity was basically a very revolutionary religion, rebelling as it did against the authority of its time. It was almost impossible, therefore, even though Christianity became institutionalized, to completely do away with the revolutionary ideas which were involved in its original form.

SUMMARY

This chapter reviews the changes which took place in the society of medieval Europe roughly from about A.D. 500 to around A.D. 1300. This period was divided into two parts, the early Middle Ages from A.D. 500 to 700 and the later Middle Ages from A.D. 1100 to 1300. In the first part there is the period of the so-called "Dark Ages" in which, due to the confused cultural and political situation, there was a definite decline in learning and culture following the invasions of the teutonic tribes. The fact that the early Christian sects did not wish to accept the old pagan learning, and there was no other learning, led further to the downfall of the education and learning. However, monasteries developed, and with their love of learning, they preserved the great manuscripts, even those sometimes not understood, thereby preventing learning from falling into discard.

In this period of unsettled political life, the institution of feudalism arose by means of which the life of the people was somewhat ordered and a form of law and organization could prevail. A great and powerful figure during this period was Charlemagne. By the end of his reign the feudalist institutions of the Middle Ages had taken form. Through his assumption of the title of emperor, even though the empire dissolved after his death, the feudal institutions were so thoroughly established that they were preserved.

Greek learning had come back into Europe through a group of Moslems, the Moors, and was eventually picked up by Thomas Aquinas and Aristotle and, after being Christianized, became the philosophic base of later medieval Christianity.

In the latter part of the Middle Ages, this rationalization of Christianity and the further breakdown of the civil empire into the smaller subdivisions did occur. It was not until later in the history of Europe that the centralized authority of the kings of the nations such as France and England began to emerge. One might then summarize the cultural history of this period by indicating that it was centered around two poles—the power of the church and the power of government (really the feudal system). Such institutions as the guilds and chivalry and, later on, bourgeois trade or commerce tended to break down the rigidity of this bipolar system.

Likewise did the central theme of the history of education in the Middle Ages fall around two points: first, the decline of schools due to the general disintegration of culture and the early antagonism of the Christian church to "pagan" learning; second, the revival of classical learning after it had been made somewhat consistent with Christianity in the latter part of the period.

It may be noticed that formal education affected only a few persons. Although there was a continuation of town schools, and in a few places there were private schools with emphasis on secular learning, by and large, it was the churches which were important to education. They set up the catechetical classes, the catechumenal schools, cathedral schools, and later on, the monastic schools which dominated the latter part of this period.

In addition to education in the formal schools, there was the chivalric education of the feudalistic system, and the guild education of the craftsman. As in the other periods, the great masses of people had no education other than that which they picked up in their every-day life, this being very minimal in many respects. Perhaps more important in the latter part

of this period was the development of the universities, and the revival of
learning which they brought about, together with the improved status of
the university teachers and professors.

SELECTED BIBLIOGRAPHY

Starred items represent books which most closely parallel chapter content.

General Books

Albright, W. F., *From the Stone Age to Christianity*. 2d ed. Baltimore, Johns
    Hopkins Press, 1940.
Barclay, W., *Educational Ideals of the Ancient World*. London, Collins, 1959.
*Boyd, William, *The History of Western Education*. 7th ed., revised and en-
    larged by Edmund J. King. New York, Barnes and Noble, 1965.
Brockelmann, Carl, *History of the Islamic Peoples*. New York, Putnam, 1947.
Bryce, James, *Holy Roman Empire*, 9th ed. New York, Macmillan, 1880.
Burckhardt, Jacob, *The Age of Constantine the Great*. New York, Pantheon
    Books, 1949. Pp. 400.
*Butts, R. Freeman, *A Cultural History of Western Education: Its Social and
    Intellectual Foundations,* 2d ed. New York, McGraw-Hill, 1955.
Charlton, Kenneth, *Education in Renaissance England*. Toronto, University of
    Toronto Press, 1965.
Change in Medieval Society, Sylvia L. Thrupp, ed. New York, Appleton-Cen-
    tury-Crofts, 1964.
*Cubberley, Ellwood R., *The History of Education*. New York, Houghton-
    Mifflin, 1920.
Davis, J. G., *Daily Life of Early Christians*. New York, Duell, Sloan & Pearce,
    1953.
Documents of the Christian Church, Henry Bettenson, ed., 2d ed. New York,
    Oxford University Press, 1947.
Dodge, Bayard, *Muslim Education in Medieval Times*. Washington, Middle East
    Institute, 1962.
Durant, Will, *The Age of Faith: The History of Medieval Civilization—Chris-
    tian, Islamic, and Judaic—from Constantine to Dante: A.D. 325–1300*.
    New York, Simon and Schuster, 1950.
Frost, S. E., Jr., *Historical and Philosophical Foundations of Western Educa-
    tion*. Columbus, Ohio, Charles E. Merrill, 1966.
Good, H. G., *A History of Western Education*, 2d ed. New York, Macmillan,
    1962.
Heritage of American Education, Richard E. Gross, ed. Boston, Allyn and
    Bacon, 1962.
Jones, A. H. M., *Constantine and the Conversion of Europe*. London, Hodders
    and Houghton, 1948.

Knight, Edgar W., *Twenty Centuries of Education*. New York, Ginn, 1940.

Knowles, David, *Saints and Scholars: Twenty-five Medieval Portraits*. New York, Cambridge University Press, 1962.

Larson, Martin A., *The Religion of the Occident: The Origin and Development of the Essem-Christian Faith*. New York, Philosophical Library, 1959.

Laistner, M. W. L., *Christianity and the Pagan Culture in the Roman Empire, Together With an English Translation of John Chrysostom's Address on Vain-glory and the Right Way for Parents to Bring up Their Children*. Ithaca, New York, Cornell University Press, 1951.

Lot, Ferdinand, *The End of the Ancient World and the Beginning of the Middle Ages*. New York, Knopf, 1931.

Mayer, Frederick, *A History of Educational Thought*. Columbus, Ohio, Merrill, 1966.

Meyer, Adolphe E., *An Educational History of the Western World*. New York, McGraw-Hill, 1965.

McNeill, William H., *Handbook of Western Civilization*. Chicago, University of Chicago Press, 1953.

Mulhern, James, *A History of Education: A Social Interpretation*, 2d ed. New York, Ronald, 1959.

Muller, Herbert J., *Freedom in the Ancient World*. New York, Harper & Row, 1961.

————, *Freedom in the Western World*. New York, Harper & Row, 1963.

Nasr, Seyyed Hossein, *Three Moslem Sages*. Cambridge, Harvard University Press, 1963.

New Perspectives in World History, Shirley Engle, ed. Yearbook of the National Council of the Social Studies. Washington, D.C., National Education Association, 1964.

Painter, Sidney, *Medieval Society*. Ithaca, Cornell University Press, 1951.

*Power, Edward J., *Main Currents in the History of Education*. New York, McGraw-Hill, 1962.

Power, Eileen, *Medieval People*. Garden City, New York, Doubleday, 1924.

Readings in the History of Education, Ellwood P. Cubberley, ed. New York, Houghton-Mifflin, 1920.

Schachner, Nathan, *The Medieval Universities*. New York, F. A. Stokes, 1938.

Shotwell, James T., *The Long Way to Freedom*. New York, Bobbs-Merrill, 1960.

Sources in Western Civilization. The Twentieth Century, 1914–1964, Arthur P. Mendel, ed. New York, Free Press, 1965.

Stephenson, Carl, *Medieval Feudalism*. Ithaca, New York, Cornell University Press, 1942.

Technology and Social Change. Columbia University Seminar on Technology and Social Change, Eli Ginsberg, ed. New York, Columbia University Press, 1964.

The Educated Man: Studies in the History of Educational Thought, Paul J. Nash, and others, eds. New York, Wiley, 1965.

The Middle Ages: 1000–1300, Bryce D. Lyon, ed. New York, Free Press, 1964.

Villehardouin and De Joinville, *Memoirs of the Crusade*. London, Dent, 1908.

Weimer, Hermann, *Concise History of Education.* New York: Philosophical
    Library, 1962.
Wilds, Elmer H. and Lottich, Kenneth V., *The Foundations of Modern Educa-
    tion,* 3d ed. New York, Holt, Rinehart, and Winston, 1961.

Pertinent Paperbound Books

*Beck, Robert H., *A Social History of Education.* Englewood Cliffs, New Jersey,
    Prentice-Hall, 1965.
Broudy, Harry S. and Palmer, John R., *Exemplars of Teaching Method.* Chi-
    cago, Rand-McNally, 1965.
Burrell, Sidney, *The Main Strands of Development from the Beginnings to the
    Eighteenth Century. Elements of Western Civilization,* Vol. 1. San
    Francisco, Chandler, 1959.
*Castle, E. B., *Ancient Education and Today.* Baltimore, Penguin, 1961.
Cheney, L. J., *A History of the Western World: From the Stone Age to the
    Twentieth Century.* New York, New American Library, 1959.
*Cordasco, Francesco, *A Brief History of Education.* Paterson, Littlefield,
    Adams, 1963.
Coulton, G. G., *Medieval Panorama: The English Scene from Conquest to Ref-
    ormation.* New York, Macmillan, 1938.
————, *Medieval Scene: An Informal Introduction to the Middle Ages.* Cam-
    bridge, England, University Press, 1930.
DeWulf, Maurice, *History of Medieval Philosophy,* 3d ed. New York, Longmans,
    Green, 1909.
Frost, S. E., Jr., *Essentials of History of Education.* New York, Barron's, 1947.
*Hatch, Edwin, *The Influence of Greek Ideas and Usages Upon the Christian
    Church.* London, Williams and Norgale, 1904.
Hitti, Philip K., *Islam and the West: A Historical Cultural Society.* Princeton,
    Van Nostrand, 1962.
Hughes, Paul and Fries, Robert F., *Reading in Western Civilization, Units 1,
    2, 3.* Paterson, Littlefield, Adams, 1962.
Hutzinga, J., *The Waning of the Middle Ages: A Study of the Forms of Life,
    Thought and Art in France and the Netherlands in the Fourteenth and
    Fifteen Centuries.* Garden City, New York, Doubleday, 1954.
Kirchner, Walter, *Western Civilization to 1500.* New York, Barnes and Noble,
    1960.
Marrou, H. I., *History of Education in Antiquity.* New York, Mentor Books,
    The New American Library, 1956.
McNeill, William, *History Handbook of Western Civilization.* Chicago, Uni-
    versity of Chicago Press, 1953.
Mundy, John H. and Risenberg, Peter, *The Medieval Town.* Princeton, Van
    Nostrand, 1958.
Painter, Sidney, *Medieval Society.* Ithaca, Cornell Press, 1951.
Pirenne, Henri, *Economic and Social History of Medieval Europe.* New York,
    Harcourt, Brace, 1937.

Poole, R. L., *Illustrations of the History of Medieval Thought and Learning.* New York, Macmillan, 1920.

*Ralph, Philip Lee, *The Story of Our Civilization: 10,000 Years of Western Man.* New York, Dutton, 1959.

Ryan, Patrick J., *Historical Foundations of Public Education.* Dubuque, Iowa, W. C. Brown, 1965.

*Sedillot, Rene, *History of the World in 240 Pages.* New York, New American Library, 1951.

Slater, Robert Lawson, *Can Christians Learn From Other Religions?* New York, Seabury Press, 1963.

The Building of the Human City: A Documentary Record of Western Civilization, Thomas P. Neill, ed. Garden City, New York, Doubleday, Dolphin Masters, 1960.

Thompson, Merritt M., *The History of Education.* College Outline Series. New York, Barnes and Noble, 1958.

Wallbank, Thomas Walter, and others, *Civilization: Past and Present.* Chicago, Scott, Foresman, 1962.

SELECTED FILMS

Art of the Middle Ages (Encyclopaedia Britannica)

Life in a Medieval Town (Coronet)   (16 min.)

A young serf's impression of a medieval town. The film presents a detailed picture of daily life and provides a background for understanding the influence of trade and the role of the merchant in Europe.

Manuscripts   (10 min.)

From the series, *Milestones in Writing.* Illustrates the use of parchment and vellum as writing substances and the creation of illuminated manuscripts in the Middle Ages.

Meaning of Feudalism (Coronet)   (11 min.)

Remnants of feudal life and their contributions to the modern culture of Europe are studied in an area near a French village. Features of the feudal castle, an explanation of the feudal system, the element of the church, and the land organization of the Middle Ages are covered.

Medieval Times: Guilds and Trade (Coronet)   (13½ min.)

Scenes in Germany, Italy, Belgium, England, France, and Spain visualize trade in the medieval world. Shows the rise of the Venetian and Genoan merchant princes and formation and spread of the medieval guilds, or hanses. The economic role of craft guilds in medieval society is illustrated. The subject is related to the present day by parallels drawn to the European Common Market.

Medieval World, The (Coronet)   (11 min.)

Knights and feudalism, Chaucer's Pilgrims, castles and crusades—these words and ideas take on meaning and relationships in this portrayal of medieval times.

Mohammedan World, The: Beginnings and Growth (Coronet)   (11 min.)
    Intercultural influence is the theme which reviews the history of the
Mohammedan way of life and its impact on western culture.

School, The (Gaumont-British)   (15 min.)
    Portrays educational methods of Jews in Palestine at the time of
Christ.

6

The Renaissance and Education
(A.D. 1300–1500)

The period of history which has been called the Renaissance or "rebirth of learning" in two parts. First, we discuss the nature of the European Renaissance itself; next, we describe the changes in education which occurred.

Revival of Classics. Beginning with Petrarch in Italy and continuing throughout the fifteenth and sixteenth centuries in most of the western European world, interest in ancient classical literature increased greatly, and creativity and individuality were emphasized. Some of the men of the Renaissance were called *humanists* because they were interested in the humanities or the great literary classics of the past. Even those Renaissance thinkers who were humanists did not break violently with medievalism or with the religious point of view of the medieval period. As a matter of fact, there were many forces in the Middle Ages which helped to give rise to the development of the Renaissance and the humanist movement. Out of the humanist desire to go to the original sources, i.e., the Latin and Greek classics, for a better understanding of the nature of man and of the joys of this world, they developed an intense love for the classical languages and literature per se, and they tended to scorn all other authority. Strictly speaking, the humanists were no more interested in the investigation of nature itself than were the scholastics. There was merely a change from the theological disputation to pursuit of sculpture, painting, and literature.

A differentiation must be made between the Renaissance movement and the "rebirth of learning" which, in its broadest sense, included a development of the vernacular languages and literature as well as the development of the humanist movement. The latter was largely a new interest in the classics. The scholars of this period found a new interest in human nature and wished to free the individual from those demands which had been imposed upon him by the various authoritative institutions of the medieval period, such as the Church, the guilds, the lords of the manor, and the monasteries.

The humanist group claimed that the best way one could learn in detail about the perfection and the development of human nature was in the classical literature. Therefore, to understand the literature, they attempted to learn more about the classical language (emphasis on grammar). They also began to assume that the people of the classical period (the Golden Age) were examples of perfection to be imitated. Some used the word, humanities, as synonomous with the great classics of literature. Since many of them were interested, primarily, in finding out more about human nature through the revival of classical writings, they called themselves humanists.[1] It should be noted that in the period of the Renaissance, the humanist scholars were liberal or radical in their point of view, whereas in the modern viewpoint, the humanists in the same sense of the word (that is, those interested in the Classics) are a conservative, or reactionary force. The interest in the classical literature civilization came about first in the cities of Italy where there had been a flowering of political and economic life taking place in the fourteenth century.

Francis Petrarch (1304–1374) is considered by most scholars to be the initiator of the revival of the special interest in the Latin classics. Petrarch was very much opposed to the texts used in the medieval period in the schools and universities. Since he was very much interested in reestablishing the glory of the old Roman Empire, he tried to imitate the style of ancient writers. He was particularly interested in Virgil and Cicero, and tried to locate old classical manuscripts. Petrarch did find and edit many of these, using as his only authority pagan sources rather than the more recent Christian authorities.

The work by Petrarch on the classical documents interested a growing number of other humanists in asserting the value of the classical Latin over Medieval Latin. Every effort was made to substitute Classical Latin for Medieval Latin as the medium of discourse of educated men every-

---

[1] There is a contemporary use of the word, "humanism," which is directly in contrast. Its use is in reference to a religious point of view, viz., the study of theology rooted in man as opposed to a theistically-centered theology. It is used here, of course, in the older sense of meaning—those interested in the study of classics—the humanities.

where. Latin had been, of course, the discourse among scholars who used different vernacular languages.

By the fifteenth century, there began to be an interest also in reviving Classical Greek. Greek had almost entirely disappeared in Italy, when a group of Greek scholars headed by Emanuel Chrysoloras (1355–1415) came to Florence from Constantinople and taught Greek from 1396 to 1400. Many Italian scholars also went to Constantinople to study Greek. After the fall of Constantinople (in 1453), more Greek scholars came to Italy and there was a renewed interest in Greek language and literature. It never replaced Latin, however, as the main interest of scholarship, and soon the interest in Greek began to wane.

A scholar by the name of Reuchlin (1455–1522) was interested in the promotion of Hebrew as a scholarly classical language. Because of anti-Semitism, there was much opposition to the study of writings in the Hebrew language, and many persons wanted to burn the books of the Jews as heretical. But Reuchlin's defense of Hebrew writings was a blow against people who would censor books, and a measure in favor of tolerance and freedom in the field of scholarship.

The humanist writers were not interested in making any new contributions to the area of philosophy or man's thinking as such. As indicated earlier, they seemed rather to have the greatest interest in the literature per se and in its style. There was the development of a Platonic Academy in Italy in the fourteenth century, but it was little else than an attempt to restore Plato's original ideas which its founders thought had been polluted by the Christian fathers. In general, the humanists were not so much interested in being critical of religion as they were in reconciling and showing that all religions and philosophy were really identical. They tried to prove by asserting with detailed elaborations that all religions were the same basically, and many of them became quite enthusiastic about this effort. In this way they blurred the distinctions among the philosophies and religions, ignoring practically all the sciences in their attempt to achieve harmony with respect to viewpoints as to the nature of the world.

Among the northern humanists, and certainly above most of the others in terms of his depths of scholarship and creativity, was the great proponent of humanist learning, Erasmus of Rotterdam (1467–1536).[2] He was probably the outstanding scholar of his age. Although most of his scholarly productivity comes after the end of the period under discussion, he represents the embodiment of the best of the humanist and of the renaissance movement. Erasmus taught at universities throughout England and France and travelled widely, talking about the advantages of the

[2] See William H. Woodward, *Desiderius Erasmus Concerning the Aim and Method of Education.* New York, Bureau of Publications, Teachers College, Columbia University, 1964.

humanist point of view. He edited many of the Greek and Latin authors, including the works of the Church Fathers, such as St. Augustine and St. Jerome's Vulgate edition of the New Testament. The latter he translated into a scholarly Greek edition which was later used as the basis for the King James translation into English.

Erasmus, in spite of his emphasis upon scholarly Latin and Greek, denounced Ciceronian formalism and wanted the study of the classics to be used for the purpose of broadening knowledge and taste, and of developing the ability to make decisions. He felt that the interest of boys in the schools should be aroused by the work itself rather than imposed by strong discipline. Like Quintilian and Cicero, he placed emphasis upon gentleness as opposed to physical punishment.

New Literature and Art.   Interestingly enough, in spite of the fact that the humanists were trying to raise the classics to a central place in nearly all the countries of Europe, it was also the period in which the vernacular literature began to have wider appeal to the masses of people, and the early classical writings of the vernacular language began to be established. In Italy, even before this period, Dante had produced the great *Divine Comedy* written not in a classic language, but in his own Italian and, as such, he established his particular dialect as the basis of the Italian language. Dante lived just at the end of the thirteenth century (1265–1321).

Petrarch himself wrote some lyrics in Italian, and another Renaissance writer, Boccaccio, wrote much Italian poetry and prose, as well as being interested in the classics. The most widely known of his writings is the collection of the very earthy tales known as *Decameron*. Dante's *Divine Comedy* is quite in contrast with Boccaccio's *Decameron*. One represents an essentially medieval and religious temper, and the other represents an interest in the "world of the flesh" and in the enjoyment of the pleasures of this world. There was a wide range of interests existing in Italy in the fourteenth century.

In England, it was during this period that Chaucer wrote *Canterbury Tales* (the fourteenth century). Sir Thomas More's *Utopia* came at the end of this period. The work of Rabelais came at the end of this period and the beginning of the sixteenth century with his particular and critical interest in education as shown in his books, *Gargantua* and *Pantagruel*. These were caricatures of the institutions of his day, and appealed very much to the public. The essays of Montaigne (1533–1592), although written after this period, represent the best of the literary tradition of the vernacular writers and of those who wrote scholarly letters for the benefit of the intellectual classes.

There were some prominent humanist historians in Italy in the fourteenth and fifteenth century who tried to do away with the contemporary idea of historical writing as primarily a series of chronicles, and tried to emulate the best of the writings of Livy. They tried to make all events become great events, and tried to describe great battles in phrases of rhetoric like Cicero. Perhaps Machiavelli and Guicciardini, neither of whom were humanists, were more accurate in their writings than were some of the humanist writers who tended to be somewhat emotional and rhetorical. One of the contributions of the Renaissance scholars was their glorification and exaggerated admiration of this period.[3] They felt that the period immediately preceding had been of practically no value. It was they who labelled this preceding period as the "Dark Ages," a term which has prevailed down to the present time.

Although it did not greatly influence education, the development of Renaissance art actually was much more creative than was the literary development. Medieval art had been largely developed for the purpose of teaching a religious lesson as in the Gothic style of the great cathedrals. The Renaissance artist became interested in depicting the human body and the landscapes as realistically as possible, similar to the Greeks.

In the early period of the Renaissance, the artist was interested in depicting nature as it really was, but as time went on, the Renaissance painting and sculpture became much more restrained and dignified, and expressed more sensitivity of feeling. It is in the great masterpieces of the fine arts, painting and sculpture as well as architecture, that the real contribution of the Renaissance is found. However, it was the literary aspect of the Renaissance which has the most influence on formal education.

Scientific Developments.   In the realm of science there was very little progress made in basic conceptions during the Renaissance period. There was some skepticism commencing in the fourteenth century concerning the scholastic notions of natural philosophy (as they then called science). Duns Scotus, who was a great scholastic but opposed to Thomistic philosophy, was interested somewhat in natural science as was Roger Bacon. Scholasticism, which was losing favor—humanism taking its place—was also indifferent at this time to natural science. When the humanists did become interested in the subject of science, they would seek to substantiate their finds back in the ancient texts rather than doing investigation on their own. They were interested in trying to find out more about the language of what was said than in understanding the scientific content. There were some gains made during this period in basic understanding of mathematics, astronomy, and physics, laying the groundwork for the work of Copernicus and Galileo later in the development of the heliocentric theory. Agricola (1494–1595), a humanist scholar, was also interested in the scientific study of mining and metallurgy. Although it was quite slow, there was some scientific progress during this period.

It was really in the development of the practical arts which were basic to later scientific experimentation that the period of the Renaissance did produce tangible results. The further growth of centralized power

[3] Cf. Butts, *op. cit.,* pp. 181–2.

within the national states arising out of the development of gun powder (probably in the twelfth century), and the use of different kinds of military machines were stimulated to this activity. This was also the period of the development of mechanical clocks and watches, with scientific measurement consequently becoming much more accurate. There was also considerable improvement in sailing vessels which laid the basis later on for wider exploration and for expanding commerce.

Finally the development of better paper and ink-making, and the invention of movable type led, of course, to the development of the printing press in the fifteenth century (around 1454) through the efforts of Gutenberg and others.

The implications of the printing press for all aspects of civilization and of education were, of course, enormous. The fact that knowledge could now be made available and easily disseminated by a cheaper method of duplicating books made possible the extension of popular education. Later on when new information became available and was published, people had a necessity to read and education became more important. If there had not been some method for the cheap dissemination of knowledge in print, it would have been quite difficult to support any argument for popular education. Since there were never enough books before that time for everyone to read, no one could have argued for the benefits of teaching the masses to read.

In general, then, the Renaissance period represented a re-awakening of learning as a "bursting out" from restrictions which had kept it in bounds during the medieval period. It, however, did not represent a creative period, except possibly in the field of the arts.[4] It represented largely an attempt to go back and read the ancient classics and to imitate them slavishly. It was not critical of the intellectual point of view of the times, although there was a swing away from other-world ideas to more interest in this world. Furthermore, there was more emphasis upon the classical tradition which became fixed in education for a great number of years, hampering efforts to bring about reform, particularly at the secondary levels.

RENAISSANCE AND EDUCATION

The main developments of schools and education during this period were related to the social and intellectual changes of the times: first, edu-

[4] A number of authorities hold that there were innovations in oil painting, notably by Botticelli, Da Vinci, among others.

cation at the secondary level, and then, vernacular (elementary) schools, and still later, higher education.

Development of Secondary Education.   In general, the only kind of education of interest to most scholars of the Renaissance period was that intended for the youth of the upper classes, now generally termed secondary education. The church was interested, of course, in preparing scholars and clergy thoroughly for the future leadership of the church, and the secular rulers were interested in having well-trained persons around them in the courts who would be gentlemen as well as scholars. The middle class interest was entirely in breaking into one of these two circles—either the church or the nobility. Renaissance education, which had a very great effect on Europe and later on America, was largely for the elite and stressed classical literary humanism and the consequent development of the gentlemanly graces.

One of the Renaissance secondary schools which represented the best of the humanistic influence was that established by Vittorino da Feltre (1378–1446) near Padua in Italy. Vittorino had spent (after a lowly birth) some twenty-five years at the University of Padua, and was a great Latin scholar and also a mathematician. He was invited by the Marquis of Mantua to establish a palace school for the children of wealthy and powerful persons, the sons of some of the scholars, and a few children who were sons of the poor. The children ranged from six to twenty-seven years of age. This school was called La Giocosa.[5] Vittorino's purpose was to educate the complete citizen. He included in his curriculum a wide range of subjects from the classics through mathematics, physics, astronomy, history, ethics, and physical education. The aims of Vittorinos' school was couched in terms of the old Roman ideal of a youth who had good knowledge of reading, a very broad background of manners and social graces, and training in loyalty to Christian principles. This, of course, was the ideal of the educated Christian gentleman. Not all of the humanist schools reached the level of Vittorino's school, and many of them, as indicated later, degenerated to purely form and grammar. There were some provisions for schools for girls at the elementary level in some of the towns of Germany and of the countries along the North Sea and in France.

Vernacular Schools.   The development of the vernacular language and the relative increase in the well-being of the common people lead to some demands for the establishment of vernacular schools. However, these schools definitely were not considered to be on as high level as those of

---

[5] One of the best discussions of Vittorino can be found in a recent publication; William Harrison Woodward, *Vittorino da Feltre and Other Humanist Educators.* Teachers College, Classics in Education Publication No. 18 (New York, Columbia University, 1963).

the classical and the Latin grammar schools. In comparison with the achievements of the humanist education at the secondary level, certainly the vernacular elementary schools during this period made very minor progress. This was partly because the vernacular writers had not yet developed any good literature. It seemed perfectly sufficient to learn to speak without having to study the written language carefully. Then, vernacular literature did begin to develop and the courts of law did begin to use the vernacular in place of Latin for their records. Business papers came to be written in the vernacular language, and the merchants and others began to carry on their business more and more in the vernacular language of the region rather than Latin. It then became much more important to teach the mother tongue.

These vernacular schools which began to develop during this period suffered in comparison to the Renaissance literary humanist schools because of their lack of intellectual content or what was considered to be mental discipline. Later on, it is these vernacular schools (at this time still private and scattered) which became an important basis in the national systems of education. For long periods of time in Europe, even down to the present time, they were considered to be inferior schools for lower classes of people. Only a very few persons could be truly "educated" as defined by the literary humanists.

Higher Education.   By and large, classical learning was not a product of either the church or the university but was sponsored by the nobility and kings and, in some cases, by the municipalities. The older universities, which had become quite conservative and entrenched with medieval and scholastic learning, resisted the entrance of the humanities and, even when they were accepted, they were in somewhat of a subordinate position. Some universities, such as the University of Florence which was strongly humanistic, did not have at this time the reputation of the standing of the older universities which were strongly scholastic and medieval in background.

In France, the kings were the ones who were in favor of the movement toward humanism, and the church and universities were either indifferent or gave it mild opposition. The University of Paris, one of the great universities of the period, kept completely aloof, and at times was antagonistic because they felt that it might destroy Aristotelian philosophy, theology, and the canon law, the main emphasis of this particular university. By and large, during the Renaissance, the University of Paris kept to its scholastic ways of thinking rather than bringing in any of the new humanist ideas with the enthusiasm for beauty and/or Latin style.

Turning to England, however, a different situation can be noted. The Oxford reformers were a group of Orthodox Catholics who tried to reform the church and the society. This group did, in fact, accept the new learning and were able to bring it to the universities of England to a considerable extent at that time and thus influence educational practices. It did also come extensively into secondary education in England.

Where modifications were made in the university curriculum, there was a decline in importance of logic, which would now be called deductive systematic philosophy, and a reemphasis upon the grammar or rhetoric of the Latin language. In some cases, the grammar was expanded to include the literature of languages other than Latin, such as Greek, Hebrew, and some of the oriental languages. There was sometimes a renewed interest in rhetoric which had lapsed considerably since the days of the Romans. The obvious substitution of the ancient classical literature for the medieval and religious literature was the most evident. The classics became the letters for the education of the gentlemen and the aristocratic conception of the liberal education is reaffirmed. This had been strong in the higher education of both the Greeks and Romans.

As indicated earlier, the humanists are in the position of being the liberals or radicals in the educational controversy of their time, whereas the other groups were trying to keep back the changes which the humanists were suggesting. In the eighteenth and nineteenth centuries, when science was trying to get into the school curriculum and into other scholarly bodies, the humanities were then in the position of conservatives attacking the newer points of view. It is likely correct to say that when there was a challenge of the older tradition by the Greek and Roman classicists, there was a stimulating effect upon the individual student. The individual was developed more fully because the ideas found in his culture were being challenged. Later as humanism gave way to the religious humanism of the sixteenth and seventeenth centuries, the scientific curriculum was the factor which challenged the older points of view and caused them to become entrenched or conservative elements.

EDUCATION, FREEDOM, AND RENAISSANCE CULTURE

The Renaissance presents a chapter in the history of freedom although the progress made during this period is not extensive. In the realm of personal freedom, there was probably not much more freedom of the individual with reference to the fleshly pleasures of the world than there was during the medieval period. The difference was that during the medieval period, the people knew that "sin was sin" and could repent and receive absolution. During the Renaissance, the pleasures were open and more flagrant, and were gloried as part of the joys of the human spirit. Even though such conduct was in conflict with the prevailing religion, the Renaissance humanist quite often ignored this.

The areas in which creativity showed itself mostly was in the arts. Here, after having imitated to some extent the Greeks, Renaissance artists and sculptors were free to create in the same general form as the Greek and other classic artists. Many of the artistic objects of the Renaissance represent artistic innovations. The work of the great Renaissance artists represent the creativity of human spirit at its best. The central focus of the humanist "revolution," the literary classics, do not indicate a similar freedom. By becoming subservient to the past to the point of quiescence, the literary classicists blocked any attempt to develop a new literary form or any new ideas concerning the world. As humanism degenerated at a later period into an emphasis on form rather than on meaning of the classics, there was even worse conformity.

The failure of the Renaissance thinkers to come to grips with the basic questions of their time, theological, political, or otherwise, and the lack of any attempt to innovate is the essential failure of the Renaissance. Although the stimulation of the study of the ancient classics did at times lead to a soaring of the human spirit in the creation of literary criticisms among the well-educated people, in the political and social realms there was practically no lessening of the rigid forms into which Europe had become solidified during the Middle Ages.

However, there is hope arising out of this. Due to the contact with ancient pre-Christian classics and other stimulating ideas which come in the fifteenth century, the groundwork was laid for the Reformation and the Scientific Revolution of the next few centuries. These movements were to open the doors to human freedom much wider than they had been at any time in man's previous history.

SUMMARY

The period from A.D. 1300 to 1500, which has been called the Renaissance, saw the revival of the Greek and Latin classics as a means to understanding more about the affairs of this world, concerning man and his works. It was also during this period that a revival of learning based on the use of the vernacular language came about.

The work of Petrarch and others in the field of education gave rise to the educational point of view called humanism which is based upon the study of the classics or the "humanities" (the study of man). There were also some scientific developments in this period, such as better paper and ink and movable type which paved the way for the mass movements in the later period of the Reformation. Secondary education during this time was largely the education of the elite in the Greek and Roman classics.

There was a development of the vernacular schools at the elementary level but these were very few and far between and only a few persons had access to any kind of education. Some of the universities during this period remained aloof from the Renaissance movement, only joining it quite late.

This was not a period of creativity in all areas. There were some in the arts, for though the Greeks were imitated, Renaissance artists did go beyond them somewhat. On the other hand, Renaissance thinkers did not, by and large, challenge the prevailing traditional ideas of their time and their interest in the Classics did fix upon the generations to come an emphasis upon tradition and the use of grammar as such. This was to have a stifling effect upon education later. It should be noted, however, that some groundwork was laid for the Reformation and Scientific Revolution because of the stimulation of minds and contact with the Classics.

SELECTED BIBLIOGRAPHY

Starred items represent books most closely paralleling chapter content.

General Books

*Boyd, William, *The History of Western Education,* 7th ed., revised and enlarged by Edmund J. King. New York, Barnes and Noble, 1965.

Burke, Peter, *The Renaissance.* London, Longmans, Green, 1964.

*Butts, R. Freeman, *A Cultural History of Western Education: Its Social and Intellectual Foundations,* 2d ed. New York, McGraw-Hill, 1955.

Charlton, Kenneth, *Education in Renaissance England.* London, Routledge and Kegan Paul, 1965.

*Cubberly, Ellwood R., *The History of Education.* New York, Houghton-Mifflin, 1920.

———, *Readings in the History of Education.* New York, Houghton-Mifflin, 1920.

*Duggan, Stephen, *A Student's Textbook in the History of Education.* New York, Appleton–Century–Crofts, 1927.

Durant, Will, *The Renaissance: A History of Civilization in Italy from 1304–*

1576 A.D. *The Story of Civilization: Part V.* New York, Simon and Schuster, 1953.

*Eby, Frederick, *The Development of Modern Education: In Theory, Organization and Practice.* New York, Prentice-Hall, 1952.

Ferguson, Wallace K., and others, *Facets of the Renaissance.* New York, Harper Torchbooks, 1963.

Fitzpatrick, Edward A., *LaSalle: Patron of all Teachers.* Milwaukee, Bruce, 1951.

Frost, S. E., Jr., *Historical and Philosophical Foundations of Western Education.* Columbus, Merrill, 1966.

*Good, H. G., *A History of Western Education,* 2d ed. New York, Macmillan, 1962.

Hart, Joseph K., *Creative Moments in Education.* New York, Holt, Rinehart and Winston, 1931.

Heritage of American Education, Richard E. Gross, ed. Boston, Allyn and Bacon, 1962.

Hoy, Deneys, *The Italian Renaissance in its Historical Background.* Cambridge, University Press, 1961.

*Knight, Edgar W., *Twenty Centuries of Education.* New York, Ginn, 1940.

Mazzeo, Joseph Anthony, *Renaissance and Revolution: The Remaking of European Thought.* New York, Random House, 1965.

Mayer, Frederick, *A History of Educational Thought,* 2d ed. Columbus, Ohio, Merrill, 1966.

Meyer, Adolphe E., *An Educational History of the Western World.* New York, McGraw-Hill, 1965.

McNeill, William, *History Handbook of Western Civilization.* Chicago, University of Chicago Press, 1953.

*Mulhern, James, *A History of Education: A Social Interpretation,* 2d ed. New York, Ronald, 1959.

Muller, Herbert J., *Freedom in the Western World.* New York, Harper and Row, 1963.

New Perspectives in World History, Shirley Engle, ed. Thirty-fourth Yearbook of the National Council of the Social Studies. Washington, D.C., NEA, 1964. Pp. xvi + 667.

*Power, Edward J., *Main Currents in the History of Education.* New York, McGraw-Hill, 1962.

Shotwell, James T., *The Long Way to Freedom.* New York, Bobbs-Merrill, 1960.

The Educated Man: Studies in the History of Educational Thought, Paul J. Nash, and others, eds. New York, Wiley, 1965.

von Martin, Alfred, *Sociology of the Renaissance.* New York, Harper and Row, 1963.

Weiss, R., *Humanism in England: During the Fifteenth Century.* Oxford, B. Blackwell, 1941.

Weimer, Hermann, *Concise History of Education.* New York, Philosophical Library, 1962.

*Wilds, Elmer H. and Lottich, Kenneth V., *The Foundations of Modern Education,* 3d ed. New York, Holt, Rinehart and Winston, 1961.

Pertinent Paperbound Books

Baron, Hans, *The Crisis of the Early Italian Renaissance: Civil Humanism and Republican Liberty in Classicism and Liberty*, Volume I. Princeton, Princeton University Press, 1955.

Burckhard, Jacob, *The Civilization of the Renaissance in Italy*. New York, Macmillan, 1909.

Burrell, Sidney, *The Main Strands of Development from the Beginnings to the Eighteenth Century. Elements of Western Civilization*, Vol. I. San Francisco, Chandler, 1959.

Cheney, L. J., *A History of the Western World: From the Stone Age to the Twentieth Century*. New York, New American Library, 1959.

Cheney, Edward P., *The Dawn of a New Era: 1250–1453*, 3d ed. New York, 1936.

Cordesco, Francesco, *A Brief History of Education*, Vol. V. Paterson, New Jersey, Littlefield, Adams, 1963.

Dampier, William C. and Margaret, *Readings in the Literature of Science: Being Extracts from the Writings of Men of Science to Illustrate the Development of Scientific Thought*. New York, Harper and Brothers, 1959.

Ferguson, Wallace K., *The Renaissance: Six Essays*. Boston, Houghton Mifflin, 1948.

Frost, S. E., Jr., *Essentials of History of Education*. New York, Barron's, 1947.

Gilmore, Myron P., *The World of Humanism: 1453–1517*. New York, Hooper, 1952.

Haskins, Charles Homer, *Renaissance of the Twelfth Century*. Cambridge, Harvard, 1927.

Howells, William, *Back of History: The Story of Our Origins*, rev. ed. Garden City, New York, Doubleday, 1963.

Hughes, Paul and Fries, Robert F., *Reading in Western Civilization*, Unit 4. Paterson, New Jersey, Littlefield, Adams, 1962.

Kirchner, Walter, *Western Civilization to 1500*. New York, Barnes and Noble, 1960.

Kristeller, Paul Oscar, *Renaissance Thought: The Classic, Scholastic, and Humanistic Strains*. New York, Harper, 1961.

Machiavelli, Niccolo, *The Prince*. New York, The New American Library, 1952.

Mayer, Frederick, *A History of Educational Thought*. Columbus, Merrill, 1960.

Meinecke, Friedrich, *Machiavellism: The Doctrine of Raison D'Etat and its Place in Modern History*. London, Routledge and Kegan Paul, 1957.

Neale, J. E., *Age of Catherine de Medici*. London, Cape, 1945.

Ralph, Philip Lee, *The Story of Our Civilizations: 10,000 Years of Western Man*. New York, Dutton, 1959.

Renaissance, Edward H. Weatherly, ed. New York, Dell, 1962.

Runciman, Steven, *Byzantine Civilization*. Cleveland, Meridian, 1956.

Sedillot, Rene, *History of the World in 240 Pages*. New York, New American Library, 1951.

Symond, John Addington, *Age of Despots: Renaissance in Italy,* Vol. I. New York, Holt, 1888.

The Building of the Human City: A Documentary Record of Western Civilization, Thomas P. Neill, ed. Garden City, Doubleday Dolphin Books, 1960.

The Renaissance Philosophy of Man, Ernst Cassirer, Paul Kristeller, and John Randall, Jr., eds. Chicago, University of Chicago Press, 1948.

von Martin, Alfred, *Sociology of the Renaissance.* New York, Harper and Row Torchbooks, 1963.

Woodward, William H., *Desiderius Erasmus concerning the Aim and Method of Education.* New York, Bureau of Publications, Teachers College, Columbia University, 1964.

SELECTED FILMS

Art and Life in Italy (Coronet)   (11 min.)

    Two centuries of the art of Italy.

The Renaissance (Coronet)   (11 min.)

    The Renaissance represented a mental attitude and a human spirit. From Galileo's telescope to Leonardo's notebooks, from the Medici Palace in Florence to St. Peter's Cathedral in Rome, students experience the science, the literature, the arts, and the driving spirit of human endeavor that gave us the Renaissance.

7

Education and the Reformation
and the Scientific Revolution
(Sixteenth and Seventeenth Centuries)

In the sixteenth and seventeenth centuries, a number of events greatly affected the entire nature of education. Most historians consider these events the beginning of the modern period. While there were many minor developments during this time, at least two outstanding trends affected culture and education. The first of the two trends was the Reformation movement within the Christian religion which finally resulted in a breakaway of much of the northern part of Europe from the dominant Roman Catholic approach to Christianity. Also, in response to the same problems which had caused the Reformation, there was a Counter-Reformation within the Catholic Church itself.

The second of the important trends was the beginning of what can be truly called the Scientific Revolution. This was characterized mainly by the discovery and use of the scientific method of gaining knowledge. Although this method had been used in a crude form previously and much scientific knowledge had been accumulated, it had not been used with conscious awareness. The impact of the success of the scientific method in amassing factual information concerning the physical world, and the further impact that this information had upon the culture, especially on religions and other fundamental concepts, was tremendous. We examine the effects of these two great trends upon European culture during the sixteenth and seventeenth centuries.

EUROPEAN CULTURE DURING THE PERIOD OF THE REFORMATION AND SCIENTIFIC REVOLUTION (1500–1700)

From 1500 to 1700 there were four cultural forces in competition for the central allegiances of men, and for control of the schools both in their curriculum and in their methods. They were: (1) The social and political forces related to the problems of the growing development of nationalism and of the importance of the new commercial interest. (2) The religious forces related to these institutions and the theological and other value beliefs of both the Catholic and the Protestant churches (with some dissident groups attacking both). (3) The forces related to the new outlooks developed through the scientific method, and to the facts and information uncovered by this method which challenged many of the older conceptions. (4) The continuation of the influence of the classical tradition, humanism, which had become so dominant in the culture during the preceding Renaissance period.

All of these forces had their roots deep in the culture of both the Middle Ages and the Renaissance. Even the third one represented a new approach which had had its roots in a great number of scientific developments occurring prior to the conscious recognition of the scientific method as such at this time. These forces, although starting back in medieval times, had become so interrelated in many significant ways that quite frequently the culture of the sixteenth and seventeenth centuries is called Reformation culture. This term is used even though many aspects of what happened were not directly an effect of the Reformation, but an effect of its causes and the counteracting forces.

The Development of Nationalism. In the periods immediately preceding, the late Medieval and Renaissance, there had been a tendency toward greater political power for the kings. This trend continued during the Reformation to such an extent that often historians call the seventeenth century the "Age of Absolutism." The kings were able to bypass their previous dependence upon their barons and lords and raise money for their armies by working in cooperation with the commercial and banking interests. These groups, the upper wealthy group among the bourgeois class, felt that they could gain by aligning themselves with the kings against the upper class nobility and against the hierarchy of the all-powerful church. During the period of the Reformation itself, many kings were tempted to side with the Reformers since they saw in the

Catholic Church a source for funds which they sorely needed to operate their government and maintain their armies. Consequently, quite often during this period there was a coalition of the monarchy, the commercial class, and the Protestant religious reformer in the break from the military, political, economic, and religious control of the Catholic Christian Church.

The countries which were most successful in being able to break the power of the local lords and centralize it in the hands of the king were Spain, France, and England. Because of accidents of history and because of the very great strength of the local princes, Germany and Italy were delayed for several centuries in achieving any kind of stable national unity. During the early part of the period now under consideration, Spain had emerged as one of the strongest of the national states and had an enormous colonial empire during the sixteenth century. However, gradually during the seventeenth century, she began to lose her place as an international colonial power, but the centralization of power in the absolute authority of the Spanish kings remained unchanged. Also, the Spanish kings had an alliance with the Catholic Church in maintaining such power. In the meantime, the power of the French king became highly centralized and by the end of the seventeenth century France was a major European and world power.

In the Netherlands and in England, the situation was quite different from that in France and Spain. The merchant classes were strong enough to prevent absolutism from being established, as it had been in these latter countries. In England the Petition of Right in 1628, the Bill of Rights, and the Act of Toleration, both in 1689 and based upon the earlier Magna Carta, laid the foundations for the Anglo-Saxon version of civil liberties which have now been written into most of the democratic constitutions of the world.

The centralization of power in the national central government in and about the time of the Reformation caused the growth of a strong spirit of nationalism and an accentuation of national differences. The continual warfare between the various states, the growing official use of their own vernacular languages as opposed to Latin, and a growing sense that somehow or other their national characteristics were different and certainly better than those of the neighboring countries, gave rise to a strong feeling of national importance, patriotism, and love of country. In this process of building up a spirit of nationalism, the schools and education in general have played a very great part.

As the national school systems began to develop some during the Reformation but more fully later during the nineteenth century, one of the primary tasks became that of teaching national loyalty and patriotism. The strength of the national state as it emerged in the Reformation, and many of the developments of education during this time, help to lay the groundwork for later more complete state control of educational organization, purposes, and curriculum—all to take effect so rapidly during the nineteenth century. In many of the states during the Reformation period, the control of education was taken away from the Catholic Church and put into the hands of national churches, but with the supportive authority of the state, a "religio–educational establishment."

A Reformation and Counter-Reformation.   In the year 1500, the Roman Catholic Church was without question the prevailing universal European institution in respect to the theological and other ideologies actually held by the people in fact as well as nominally. Prior to 1500 there had been some attempts to break away from the church and to establish reforms, as noted in the Waldenses, the Albigenses, and the work of John Wyclyffe. These movements had been ruthlessly suppressed by the church and the military authorities, and they were not able to make much of an impact on the prevailing points of view. During the sixteenth and seventeenth centuries, however, a series of additional religious reforms took place. Since these reforms were supported by the military power of some of the national states and by the economic power of the middle classes, they were successful. It is evident that the success of the Reformation was due to many factors other than religious ones. The net result of these revolts was that a number of different national churches were destined to play a very important role on the European and, later, on the American scene.

Although there were very important political and economic factors involved in the forces behind the Reformations and their success, this does not mean that there weren't any changes in man's religious beliefs and attitudes in both the Reformation and the Counter-Reformation. It merely means that they were successful because of the other forces which tended in the same direction. The reforms did represent, at base, a truly religious reaction against the growing worldliness of the Catholic Church, the only Christian church at that time in Europe. They also represented a reaction of the more conservative rural, pious Christian attitude against the secularized interests of the city which had begun to affect the church and the church hierarchy.

The man who is given credit for the first successful break from the church is Martin Luther (1483–1546). He was a monk, a university professor at Wittenberg, and a member of the Catholic clergy. He tried for several years to achieve reform from within the church. In 1517 he is reported to have nailed on the doors of the church at Wittenberg a set of 95 theses denouncing many practices of the church. Such means of communication was a common practice at that time and Luther apparently did not expect to precipitate a break from the church. However, when in 1520 he was threatened with excommunication by the pope if he didn't withdraw his attacks, he finally left the Catholic Church and gradually attempted to set up a completely independent church organization.

Luther was successful in this because he was supported by the German princes of the north. Consequently, Lutheranism, the religious point of view which he established, became closely dependent upon the civil authority of the German rulers which protected him. This principle of a very close alliance between church and state became formally recognized in 1526 as the rival Catholic and Lutheran rulers joined forces to prevent the revolt of the peasants. The peasants had felt that the break in the established religious authority meant more freedom for them and they revolted completely from the authority of the rulers as well. With the support of Luther and other church leaders, both Catholic and Lutheran, the German rulers decided that they would declare an armistice on the religious warfare among themselves. It was agreed that each ruler might decide for himself *and for his subjects* what would be the particular established religion for his own principality. This is the doctrine of *cuius regio, eius religio* (whose rule, his religion). The armistice proved to be temporary and the religious struggle of the Hundred Years' War was yet to come.

Later at the Peace of Augsburg in 1555, the right of the state to determine the religion of its subjects was again accepted at the peace table. This meant that the right of the state to secede from the Catholic Church was now established, but the right of the individual to choose his own religion was still not recognized. The individual could legally be only a Catholic or a Lutheran, and only that if his particular ruler was the same. This meant that there was no real freedom in spite of the fact that the Protestants had maintained that each individual must determine his own beliefs. Each individual was to read the scripture for himself in order to determine his own ideas in religion. During the next hundred years, the strength of Lutheranism went up and down as a result of wars and other social forces. Finally, the so-called Thirty Years' War from 1618 to 1648 left Germany so exhausted that there was no further attempt to recover northern Europe for the Catholic religion.

At the Peace of Westphalia in 1648 far-reaching decisions in regard to the foundation of the present national states of Europe were made. Each state was recognized as completely sovereign (as it is to this day) and the Empire as such became no longer a force to be reckoned with, although it did exist on paper for a number of years. It also reaffirmed the right of each state to decide for itself the establishment of its own form of religion. Consequently, the Peace of Westphalia was an important treaty. Many wars waged since then, including those of the twentieth century, have often been outgrowths of the nationalistic agreements made at this time.

In Switzerland, Huldreich Zwingli (1484–1531), who followed the ideas of Luther and Wycliffe, gained control of the city of Zurich. He led an open revolt against Catholic forces in Switzerland and was killed in the fight that ensued. Then John Calvin became the religious leader of the anti-Catholic forces in this country. He came to exercise very nearly complete power over the people, first in the neighboring province of Basle which had been at one time a part of Germany, and then later on the Swiss canton of Geneva near France. Each ruler in those days was considered the sovereign power. The Calvinist rulers were granted equality along with the Catholics and Lutherans, and given the right to choose the religion for their peoples.

However, the theory back of Calvin's doctrines of those times (to be considerably modified by his followers later) was the subordination of the state to the church. This differed from Luther's reliance upon the state which resulted in the church really becoming an arm of the state. Calvin felt that the state should be considered the political and civil arm of the church in which it would do its bidding or carry out its injunctions. This is the political and theological theory called "theocracy" meaning literally "the rule of God." Since God cannot be present to rule on earth, the church (in this case Calvinism) must rule according to God's laws. In practice, then, theocratic rule meant that the church leaders must exert very strict control over all the affairs of man, economic, political, and social as well as religious. Education, of course, was only one of the many areas of life included in this control. Furthermore, control of the ordinary citizens' behavior and conduct was necessary because the church could not afford to let the powers of the state fall into the hands of the sinners who were outside the pale. People who did not abide by God's rules and regulations had to be put out of the church or "excommunicated" in much the same way that the Roman Catholic Church had acted with respect to theological views. In this case, however, it also meant that an individual's private conduct was kept under strict discipline. The importance of the theocratic concept in the Calvinistic movement can readily be seen because it was the point of view held by most of the Puritans and Pilgrims who came to New England in the seventeenth and eighteenth centuries.

In England the Reformation took place in a different form in that it was from the top down rather than from the grass roots up as in the other countries. Successive kings and queens over a period of years took the initiative in action, at times overthrowing the power of the church or, at other times, restoring it. Furthermore, in England, Parliament had developed, officially representing the middle class. Somtimes it supported the king and sometimes it did not. In 1534 Henry VIII had become able to more or less dominate his Parliament. He forced it to pass the Act of Supremacy. This act recognized the king, rather than the Pope of Rome, as the Head of the Church of England. Actually, from a theological and religious point of view, this first change was more in name than it was in theological ideas or in religious practices. One of the important results was that Henry VIII took over the land and the wealth of the monasteries which, as groups, had remained loyal to the pope. He used this money not only for religious purposes, but primarily to support his work as King of England.

As can be seen, what is involved, in the "English Reformation" when compared to Catholic practices and to changes in many other of the Protestant churches, is much less of change in doctrine, organization, and form. Furthermore, in this case, the religious settlement was initiated and enforced by the authority of the state. As a matter of fact, the groups in England which had Calvinist leanings—later calling themselves the Puritans—felt that the Church of England had not gone far enough in its reforms. They wanted to "purify" it further of the remnants of what they considered to be corruptions of Christianity which had crept in under Catholicism. When James I and, later, Charles I of the Stuart family were on the throne of England, they persecuted the Puritans and other nonconformists. Archbishop Cranmer as the religious head of the Church of England, attacked them vigorously, although they continued to demand religious liberty. Many of them fled to America, and it was from them that most of the strong Calvinistic influence of the early colonial period in America originated, an influence to be felt for some time in American life.

While the dissident groups were beginning to cause trouble for national unity in England, there was also a movement in Germany which was to cause considerable religious unrest there. A group of people—largely followers of Calvin and Zwingli who later called themselves Anabaptists and who lived in the Palatinate region of Germany—felt that the Protestant Reformation had not gone far enough in Germany and Switzerland. They wanted to strip the church of the many accretions over the years and "get back" to primitive Christianity. Originally, they were very much antistate. They believed it was impossible to Christianize a state since it would be always allied with the devil. All Christians must expect persecution throughout all their lives and be willing to die, if need be, for their beliefs. The Anabaptists were very pious, stressing morals and a strict Christian life. Persons who did not live up to their teachings were banned from their church. They did not accede to the use of the power of the state in any way at all and many of them went to the extent of developing communistic ideas in the sharing of their goods. They were opposed to war, they were opposed to capital punishment, and they had what seemed an extreme view of religious liberty.

The Lutherans and the Catholics, as early as 1529 at the Diet of Speyers, united to exterminate them. They accepted martyrdom in great numbers and in Germany a great number of their towns were destroyed.

However, they survived these persecutions. Some of them repudiated their early positions but did maintain the practice of abstinence from worldly affairs and continued to adhere to a strict moral code. Menno Simons, who was the founder of the Mennonites from within this group, gave shape to this viewpoint which was finally to influence a great number of the early American colonists, particularly in Pennsylvania. The Amish, a particularly strict group from within the Mennonites, still have settlements in the Soviet Union, Canada, and the United States.

It may seem from the recounting of the many facets of the Protestant Reformation and the development of the other dissident sects that the Roman Catholic Church had been severely defeated. It was not and remained, by far, the strongest single church in Europe and still to this day enrolls over fifty per cent of the Christians in the world.

At that time, all of southern Europe, France, and southern Germany continued to be loyal to the Catholic doctrine. The Roman church, in addition to the customs and traditions which had become thoroughly ingrained in the people's heritage, also maintained a strong, consistent, highly developed organization. It had a hierarchy of officials with a single head to maintain a consistent policy of discipline. This provided an organization with great stability and security as compared to the chaotic conditions among the various Protestant groups in opposition to each other as well as to Catholics.

During this period of time, the Catholic Church made efforts—inclusive of military ones—to clarify its doctrine, improve its practices, so as to prevent the tide of Protestantism from overwhelming it. In 1537 a group of cardinals was convened to consider the criticisms levelled against the church's practices by the Protestant reformers. Many of the charges were acknowledged and deplored. They admitted that quite often men whose main interests were worldly rather than religious had been admitted to the clergy, that many of the monastic orders were lax, that the giving of dispensations was too easy on a wide variety of aspects of the church canon law, and that the selling of indulgences (which Luther denounced) was too liberal. In a positive way it was urged that better educational facilities be provided by the church to educate the people in its doctrines and to strengthen their resistance to error.

It should be noted that nothing in the 1537 report, nor later in the Council of Trent, was to change the fundamental teachings of the church with respect to its theological positions. The Council of Trent convened in 1543 and met over a period of ten years. It was actually quite reactionary in spirit and made no concessions on matters of theology or in matters of church government. In 1540 the Society of Jesus was founded by Ignatius Loyola as a semimilitary order to combat Luther, "the foulest of monsters." The Jesuits became a strong influence in the Counter-Reformation. In time the Jesuits' influence became so overbearing, even to the Catholic rulers, that they were suppressed by the papal authorities for a period of a hundred years. Later, the organization was revived with a change in organization and purpose. In the modern world, it has become a very important missionary and educational force in the Catholic Church.

As a result of work done in the Catholic Counter-Reformation, by the seventeenth century, the process of the breakaway was halted. No new large segments of population broke with the church. As a matter of fact, as a result of the military actions, Bohemia (which had been Protestant) was won back to the Catholic faith. The church was thus successful in reorganizing and resisting without surrender of its principles and without compromise.

A new interest in education was expressed through the establishment of a great number of new teaching orders. Prominent among these were the Fathers of the Oratory, and the Brothers of the Christian Schools, the latter founded by Jean Baptiste La Salle in 1662. In addition to these, there were numerous other minor orders as well as the earlier Franciscan and Dominican orders which had always played an important part in education and now increased their influence.

The work of these religious orders, teaching and otherwise, was extremely effective in not only promulgating and thoroughly establishing the religious doctrines of Catholicism, but also in strengthening the children and adults in the understanding of their faith. Many of these orders carried their ideas and services to the Americas where their influence has continued to the present time.

Geographical and Commercial Changes.   The period of the European geographical exploration and discovery of the rest of the world began in the late fifteenth and continued on into the sixteenth and seventeenth centuries. This period of expansion, made possible by daring navigators such as De Gama and Columbus and also by new nautical inventions, was stimulated by the desire for economic gain among the merchant classes and among the various state rulers. With the fall of Constantinople in 1453, the ordinary routes to India were cut off and there was an incentive to try to find other routes. The four national states which had become the strongest and most consolidated, Spain, Portugal, France, and England, were the first ones to take over the various trade routes and to discover new lands. Later, in the seventeenth century, when the Netherlands became nearly equal to England and France as a commercial state, it took the place of Spain and Portugal which in the meantime had weakened. The ideas of conquest and enormous wealth which the new world opened up stimulated man's imaginations and, of course, man's economic desires and greed as well. There were all kinds of interlocking ideological motives back of the explorations, among which were religious, nationalistic, and capitalistic. The recent developments in science and the technological advances in navigation, in ship building, and in warfare continued during this period and made the geographical expansion and the conquest of the overseas land possible.

The effects of the advance of the commercial interests which had taken place in the earlier centuries, and which continued during the Reformation period, began to cause changes in the whole economy of Europe. The old agriculture and the economy based upon the feudalistic system began to shake and crumble. Because of the plentiful amount of wealth in the form of money, at that time largely some kind of precious metal such as gold, the prices went up. The possession of land did not necessarily continue to bring wealth. Those persons who possessed access to the merchant economy, or who were the bankers responsible for its expansion, took the place of the feudal nobility as the real powers during this period. The growth of cities, which had started in the previous period, continued and became even more important so that the medieval manor house was no longer the center of economic life. The typical procedures of business capitalism in the form of the stock companies, to play such an important role in nineteenth century America, were developed on a large scale. There also were developed at this time money exchanges, credit procedures, a widespread system of interest charges, insurance protection, and large banking systems.

During the Middle Ages, the economy, which had been based upon the guilds, both merchant and craft, had maintained its position largely by the support of the Catholic Church which had insisted upon fair prices and had outlawed usury, or the charge of high interest rates. The church had actually permitted the loaning of money only when there was a sharing of the risk rather than through interest charges—although apparently this restriction was widely violated. The church also, theoretically at least, supported the idea that persons should own and desire only enough to subsist and that the worldly goods were not nearly as important as getting ready for the world to come. The secular temper, always present but which now became even more sharply into focus because it could be more nearly realized, led the merchant classes again to respect the productive work which would lead to wealth. They had a greater regard for the acquisition of worldly goods just to have them. There was a considerable decline in the respect, so prevalent during the preceding thousand years, accorded by the general lay public for the monastic ideal. This was the period of the "get-rich" spirit which is to ebb and flow during the remaining centuries up to the present time.

The interest of the merchants lay in keeping the trade routes open so that they could reach the source of the raw materials and, furthermore, after having prepared the goods, they wanted them to arrive safely at their destination. During the feudal period, highwaymen and pirates had jeopardized the safe transportation of goods; consequently, the merchant gave his support to the king, hoping that the extension of the king's authority would suppress these hazards. He wanted the rulers to build a large army and navy to protect his trade routes. He wanted rulers who were favorable toward further exploration so as to get more and more lands which would furnish raw materials and also to have greater markets for his goods.

Consequently, with the approval of the middle class, the medieval restraints on the political power of the king were broken. The flow of money in church tithes and taxes even in Catholic parts of Europe was considerably slowed down. Even though the church continued to enjoin persons against building up material wealth, this was ignored and, since in large parts of Europe the yoke of Catholic doctrine and authority had been completely broken, the capitalistic, bourgeois, middle-class spirit was enabled to develop.

It is during this period, that there began a shifting of power among the classes of society: from the first estate (the nobility) to the third estate, the middle classes. These classes were still rigidly defined although there always had been some fluidity between them. The rural gentry and the city-merchant classes became more powerful during the Reformation period than they had ever been before in the recent European history. However, the lower classes were worse off because, as they were moved away from the protection of the manor house and out on their own in an era of rising prices and surplus labor, they were caught in a serious economic pinch. Later, the states had to come to their aid. England, for example, passed a series of "poor" laws.

It has been noted how the principal religious changes of the Reformation affected education. Economic forces also affected education, particularly, its organization and its curriculum. The renewed importance of the gentry class caused the bourgeois to want to create new schools just for their group. This was one of the ways in which they could achieve respectability.

Before the Reformation, only the upper-class nobility had been able to go to school. Now that the merchants had considerable money, they began pouring it into private schools of all kinds. Though they usually gave money to schools which were already established they did found new schools demanding that they be of more use to them than the previous humanistic schools. In addition, in most of the countries and in some of the cities, attempts were made to provide, at least partially, schools at public (or philanthropic) expense for the benefit of all children. This, however, was not widespread until much later.

There were some changes that occurred as a result of these many forces. The nobility instituted schools that were somewhat different from those of the past, in that they wished to train their children in courtly life and manners, not necessarily the Christian-scholar ideal. At the other end of the social scale, due to the contributions of philanthropic agencies, some education was made available to children whose parents could not afford to have their children go to school. Quite often a religious motive was involved. This was more often true of the Protestant churches of Germany and England.

The latter half of the Reformation is the period when life in America —the colonies having been founded early in the seventeenth century— was influenced greatly by events that happened in Europe. In the founding of these colonies, political and religious motives had been closely intertwined; English, Scotch, Dutch, Swedish, German, French colonists and others coming to America out of a complex set of diverse motives.

Some came because of either political or religious persecution. Some came in hope that they might have better fortune. Others came out of a spirit of adventure, out of desperation, or because of some other form of compulsive behavior. Some, even, were sent by their homelands in order to carry out the political and economic purposes of the rulers. In all of this, however, one thing—perhaps somewhat fortunate for the history of America—was that although the colonists came from a Europe which was still feudalistic with a rigid class stratification, feudalism, as a system, was never able to gain a firm foothold in the new American continent. America never developed European feudalism. There were some attempts in the Dutch platoon farms in the Hudson valley; also, there was Southern "feudalism" based upon slavery whose particular problems differed from those of Europe.

There were some who came to America to establish the constitutional-type government which theorists in Europe had been writing about, but which they could not seem to put in operation in their home country. Those people who had come to America so they could worship the way they pleased—the New England Puritans, for example—it turned out, were just as adamant in refusing to permit religious dissent from their way of belief as had been the ruling groups in dealing with them in their own particular country. The idea that people should be free to choose their own point of view was not widely accepted, even in the parts of America to which people had come for religious freedom. In New England, the Calvinistic theocratic state was first set up with the state and church being one. However, very early there was resistance to these absolutistic doctrines. The spirit of constitutionalism and the ideal of civil liberty were expressed more in the principle of separation of church and state than they were in the autocratic spirit of the theocrats, even though they did set up a precedent in some kind of constitution or written charter of government.

Since some of those who came to this country did so because they wanted to have a separate religious body from the established church and, after arriving, found a theocracy in operation which was even more tightly entwined than had been the Catholic or Anglican church, they dissented violently. These "Separatists" in government believed that the state should deal only with the things which people had in common, and the individual should have a great deal of personal freedom in his beliefs. He could join any church that he wished and lived by the discipline of that particular church. The Separatists denied the right of the Puritan churches as well as the Catholic church or the Anglican church to pressure individuals into certain religious beliefs. They argued that the church and state should be separate in order to maintain greater toleration and a greater spirit of civil liberty. Although this separation of church and state did not come about at once, many groups did earn the right to worship by themselves. Some states, such as Massachusetts, set up multiple establishments for a time. However, around the beginning of the nineteenth century, the principle of the right of each individual to worship as he pleased caused the separation of church and state, and the foundation was laid for considerably more freedom in America than existed in European countries at that time.

EDUCATION DURING THE PERIOD OF THE REFORMATION AND SCIENTIFIC REVOLUTION

The Development of the National School Systems. When the actual organization of the educational efforts of the Reformation period are considered, effects of the political, economic, and religious institutional changes can be recognized. The effects of the Reformation wars and the break from the church were at first more harmful than beneficial to the existing educational institutions. Consequently, the middle of the sixteenth century saw education declining. In the first half of the seventeenth century, especially in Germany during the period of the Thirty Years War, there were even worse educational conditions. As peace was achieved in some of the European states, there began to be some organized educational development. The schools and universities which had been destroyed by the war, or taken over by the Protestant groups, were gradually reestablished and reformed along new lines. In the Catholic countries there were changes in the educational institutions as well as in other organizations within the Catholic Church. The outlines of the modern system of European education were being developed, but this time along national lines rather than universal church education.

The Protestant reformers, by and large, directed some of their efforts toward providing more opportunities for education among the common people. The rigid class structure of society was still widespread throughout Europe and would not change for some time. However, people began to suggest that opportunity for education should be given to people in the lower classes as well as the upper classes, though not the same kind. In general, the net result of the Reformation was to make the distinction between elementary education in the vernacular, or common, language of the people for the lower classes, and secondary education in the Classics, primarily Latin and in some cases Greek, for the upper classes.

The demand for common schools for the masses of people did not bring too much response from the upper class and, even though some of the former reformers talked about it, actually very little was done. Luther and Calvin, even though some of their earlier statements did appeal for universal education were, actually, more interested in a classical type of education in order to prepare leaders and prospective clergy for the churches.

Similarly in England under the Anglicans and in France under the Catholics, there was much more willingness to expand and reform secondary education than there was to provide common education for the lower classes. Contributing to this was the lack of money and teachers to do the job of educating everyone. The traditional aristocratic conception of education which prevailed in the medieval and Renaissance periods and, for that matter throughout most of human history, was in terms of the education for the few. This conception still held the predominant position in the ideas of education during most of the Reformation. There were, however, some roots of a more democratic or universal conception of education which were to have an effect in time. This can be noted in illustrations drawn from the works of three of the Protestant leaders. First, in Luther's earlier statements, he urged that all children (including girls), regardless of their wealth, should be educated. Calvin and many of Calvin's followers in the countries of the Netherlands, Scotland, England, and America also talked about and gave reasons for providing universal education. Perhaps the most outstanding and comprehensive proposal was that made by the leader of the Moravian sect, Comenius who is more fully discussed hereafter. He urged that there should be a complete "ladder" system of education reaching from the lower levels to the university. By ladder was meant that when one rung of schooling was completed, the next rung would be available without restriction if the student's ability qualified him to go on. This meant that despite the fact that the aristocratic conception was still widely practiced, the democratic conception was being stated in theory and, in some cases, parts of it were being carried out in the sixteenth and seventeenth centuries. It was to be achieved more fully in the late eighteenth and nineteenth centuries.

A clarification is desirable here. Universal education for all does not necessarily mean democratic education in the sense that equal opportunity is being afforded to all. While in the Reformation period there were great strides made in providing universal education for everyone, the lower classes received one type of education and the upper class another. These two types were quite different in their conceptions. The achievement of democratic education, in which everyone is looked upon as equally entitled to the kind of education for which he is best fitted, is to be a part of the twentieth century and not of the sixteenth or seventeenth centuries—even in theory. In Europe during this period, there were established some state controlled schools for the purpose of providing universal education, although this was not fully achieved. Schools to provide a universal education in the sense of equal opportunity for education of the appropriate kind were achieved first in the United States in the nineteenth century and then, to a lesser degree, in Europe in the early twentieth century.

Some Europeans, Lutherans in particular, had proposed the education of girls. Calvin to a lesser extent had proposed as a part of universal education for both political and religious reasons that girls be educated. Some of the Catholic teaching orders of nuns, particularly the Ursuline sisters, showed that the Catholic Church was concerned with providing additional educational facilities for girls. In particular, Archbishop Fenelon (1651–1715) had made written proposals for education of girls so they would be able to take care of duties in their homes, in the society, and in church. Consequently, the education of girls (to the extent realized) helped to broaden educational opportunity and thus to contribute to its spread.

School Control.   One of the political results of the Reformation was the trend toward a change of the control of education to civil as opposed to the previously largely private and religious control. In the one sense of the word, with the control of education being increasingly civil rather than under the church directly, it can be said that the movement toward public education began in the Reformation period. However, this public education was not necessarily democratic education for all classes. As a matter of fact, public education under civil control can be universal, compulsory, and free (and even supported by taxation) without being democratic. This is the sense in which there are completely different educational systems for different classes, or where the purposes for which education is established may not be democratic. The Prussian educational system of the nineteenth century was in no sense of the word "democratic." Certainly the movement toward public education did provide some of the bases for which later democratic political arrangements could be made, since the people were better educated.

The civil control of education progressed further in the Lutheran and Calvinistic countries of Switzerland, Germany, and Scandinavia than it did in the countries of England, France, Italy, or Spain. In these latter countries, even though there was some civil control, the traditional conception was maintained for some time that education either was the function of the church or should be supported by private philanthropy. The government might require that schools be established in these countries, but it did not play a very important part in comparison with that played by private, religious, and other sources until the late nineteenth century.

When the religious institutions in England were removed from the Catholic Church, and the Anglican Church organization took over with the consequent destruction of most of church education, the state made few provisions to fill the gap. There was some haphazard and unsystematic elementary education. Some parents taught their children. Some hired a tutor. Some of them sent their children to the parish priest if he could teach and had the time to provide a minimal education.

There did develop in England a type of school which was more or less formal and that was given to the neighbor children by a housewife while she did her housework. She did this for a fee. These schools were called "dame" schools. Sometimes the children who had more money were sent to the preparatory department of a grammar school because they were destined later to go to that school. Sometimes this preparatory department was called a "petty" school.

It can be readily seen that education was provided largely only to those children whose parents could afford it. There was an increasing group of the merchant class who were wealthy enough to do so, but for the lower classes. While there were some proposals made for charity schools, they did not participate in any other forms of education.

In all these countries, there was much more interest expressed in the traditional, classic (humanistic) secondary education. Due to the increased wealth, there were many new grammar schools established. Some of the authorities estimate that as many as five hundred schools were founded or reestablished during the period of the Reformation. Funds from the newly rich middle classes poured into endowments for these Latin grammar schools and in England these schools began to be called "public schools." To this day, the word "public schools" in England refers to these kinds of schools. They are really privately operated even though at present they receive some government grants. There were some scholarships given to students at these schools with funds taken from the church or from the government but, on the whole, the students came from the well-to-do classes.

In the Catholic part of Europe, there were some twelve church orders that worked in elementary education. Many of these were concerned about providing free schools for the poor children of the working classes. Not all of the work in extending education was done by the Protestants since considerable progress was made in Catholic southern Europe. In southern Europe the church, rather than the civil authorities, was still carrying on the main part of the work.

At this time, education was starting in America in New England. New England became the example of education for the rest of the colonies and, at first, the Calvinistic practice of religion and education together prevailed. However, the theocratic government founded there did place great emphasis upon education at the local level, namely the towns (not synonymous to the word, villages, but more like the midwest township). The towns took the initiative in establishing the schools rather than the central colonial government. Later, the colonial legislature did add their influence and gave legal authority for the establishment of schools.

When the town meeting convened once a year to select the people who were to run the town, some of these selectmen were designated as the school committee. This meant that the school was run by a lay committee. This lay committee was the forerunner of the American elected lay-school board, not found in the same form in any other school system in the world.

During the early New England period, financial support came from a variety of sources. Tuition was charged, if the parents could afford it, and this was done by the means of rate bills in which the costs were prorated according to the number of children from each family in school and the amount of time spent there. There were some special income for schools from certain town lands and also from special types of taxes and fees. Now and then some money was given out of the property tax, but these schools were in no sense free and fully supported. Run by the local authorities and they were civil in their control. Religion, however, was an important part of the curriculum since the people were quite religious. Usually, there was a similarity of beliefs in each of the towns.

The civil control of the schools took another step forward when the colonial legislatures began to put pressure on the towns which had not established schools on their own initiative. The Massachusetts Bay Colony very early took the lead in this process by two very famous school laws which had a great deal of influence on the other colonies. The Massachusetts Law, passed in 1642, was the first general law in America requiring elementary grade instruction for children. There had been another law of this kind earlier in Holland and there were some other European examples of early laws. None of these early laws were ever carefully enforced. In the 1642 law, the state took upon itself the authority to tell the town officials that they must require the parents to educate their children. This law did not require the town to establish schools nor did the colony undertake to establish schools itself. It did require that the parents must themselves give instruction to their children or hire a tutor. It even indicated what should be taught, how to read English, knowing the "Capital" laws and the Catechism, and the acquisition of a "trade" for each child. The selectmen of the town had authority to enforce this law by fines and even could enforce compulsory apprenticeship for the children.

The principle that education is necessary for the welfare of society was thus made clear very early on the American shores. However, apparently the towns did not respond sufficiently because the General Court, the Massachusetts Legislature, five years later passed the second law which went even further in establishing the authority of the state over the local group in civil control of education. In this law of 1647, the legislature required that every town which contained more than fifty families must provide at least one elementary school teacher and every town of over one hundred families had to establish a Latin grammar school. Another law made it also permissible for the town to levy taxes for the support of these teachers. It also required fines payable to the state for those towns which failed to live up to the provisions of the law.

It can be seen that the two laws together established the authority of state by requiring towns to establish schools and gave to the local civil authorities the right to manage, supervise, and control schools. There was still, however, no compulsory school attendance. The parents could educate their children where they wished. Further, the law appears not to have been well enforced. The state was making it likely that the parents would carry out the provisions of the earlier law by trying to make public instruction more available than it had been.

Educational historians have debated how much effect the legal precedence of these laws had in laying the foundations of the American public school system. Some believe that these were the legal precedents for the nineteenth century establishment of the state system of schools, while others believe that this was merely a case of the Calvinistic church acting through the civil authorities in trying to insure that its doctrines were taught through the catechism in the schools. However, it is certain that the state did establish legal authority over education in the Massachusetts Bay Colony and that other colonies followed later. Thus, when the established churches (the early exclusive establishment soon became multiple establishment in most colonies) were separated from the state as the movement of the separation of church and state came in the late eighteenth and early nineteenth century, the right to control and support the schools remained with the civil authority.

Basic Conceptions of the Reformation and Counter-Reformation Influencing Educational Ideas. During the Reformation, religious creeds played an important role in the lives of people and of governments. These creeds were the foci on which men centered their most ultimate values and loyalties, giving strength and meaning to life and death. The Reformation culture which came to America later, of course, still lies deep in the heart and loyalties of American life. Even, however, at the time of the Reformation, patriotism began to play a larger part in the total group of loyalties. The patriotic sentiment became so overwhelming that persons of different religious faiths were sometimes joined together in a national and patriotic cause against people of their own religious beliefs. In the modern world now, the highest of loyalties, for which disloyalty (i.e., treason) can be punished by death, is in the field of nationalism and patriotism rather than in religion.

In Reformation culture, each of the groups accepted their faith as being authoritative. The people held their faiths confidently because they believed that their leaders had special insight in some way into the supernatural and into an understanding of God. Consequently, there was no appeal from the point of view of their rulers. In the time of the oriental civilizations, a ruler who wished his word to be irrevocably enforceable as law always proclaimed that he ruled by a divine right (or was a god, himself). Also, frequently people felt that good moral conduct was dependent upon a "religious" precept. A man would not be good unless he felt that God had willed that he should live in the way that had been ordained as good. Furthermore, it was felt that if there were different theological (or political) points of view conflicting with one another within a state, a uniform social order could not be maintained.

There, of course, were differences between groups regarding the doctrine and authority of their faiths. For example, the Protestants emphasized the Bible as the rule of faith and the basis of their authority more than did the Catholics. The Protestants also denied the claims of the pope and of the clergy to be the authoritative interpreters of Christian doctrine. In theory, the Protestants argued that the individual had the right to seek salvation directly by the study of the Bible without the mediation of some clergyman. Every man was his own priest. Now this would seem to indicate that the individual or small sect would be allowed to interpret the Bible and believe independently. In many respects this was the theory and, at times, the practice within the Protestant revolt. However, very soon after the revolt, many of the new sects became just as intolerant within their own ranks as the Catholic Church had ever been, and quite often used governmental powers to enforce their convictions and to persecute dissidents. This meant that the Protestant groups did not really break with the fundamental ideas of their age and were as authoritarian as had been the groups prior to their times.

The Protestants objected to the great emphasis on the sacraments and to much of the ritualism of the Catholic Church which insisted that it was necessary to salvation. They also objected to the stress of the Church on the use of the indulgences, pilgrimages, and devotions to relics. The Protestants insisted that the central road to salvation was justification by faith so that the individual soul could come in direct communion with God. Since each individual had to find out the grounds of his belief by reading the Bible for himself, all true believers had to learn how to read, at least enough to read the Bible. This resulted in a widespread demand for education. Since however, the Protestant movement was among the commercial middle class, political and economic motives accompanied the religious ones. When, thus, it finally came from the mixture of all these strands, popular education was something new, since in no period of history had this been tried before.

Protestants and Catholics agreed and continued to believe fundamentally in the medieval conception of God and the nature of the universe. They were opposed to the world view of empirical science which was advancing at that time. They accepted the universe as created by God and believed that man played a role which had been assigned to him by God. They accepted the customary distinction between the supernatural world and the natural world and, of course, as religionists, they believed the supernatural or spiritual world was by far the most important. Also, both the Catholic and Reformation Protestants agreed that the nature of man was dualistic, i.e., composed of an immaterial soul and a material body. The soul was most important since it was everlasting.

The Catholics and the Reformation Protestants both agreed that man's success could not be completely judged by what happens in this world, but rather in the world to come. However, man must be good here and now for the glory of God in order to escape eternal punishment. So both would have joined against the doctrine quite often stressed in the present day that man's ultimate justification comes from the social good that he is able to accomplish in line with the religious and moralistic ethics of his faith. Both the Catholics and the Reformation Protestants believed that knowledge and truth are fixed and are revealed to man from supernatural sources.

The primary aim of the school was to bring the pupil to a knowledge of God's truth, his laws, and his commandments. The Protestants objected to the education of the Catholics not because its main purpose was wrong, but because they felt that the Catholics were teaching things apart from God's truth which had come about by many years of interpretation and changes by Catholic scholars and Catholic tradition. It was not important to either the Catholics or the Reformation Protestants for the student to have much knowledge of the visible world. The purpose of the learning process was conceived by both groups as merely a matter of bringing to light any ideas with which God had endowed each person as explained by the Platonic concept of innate ideas. These ideas were developed by a kind of disciplinary training. The study of language and literature was very important and memorizing was one of the chief methods. It can be readily seen that both Catholics and Protestants in the sixteenth and seventeenth centuries were very much opposed to not only the implications of the new scientific investigations, but also to the concept of the new world view which empirical science was advancing.

The Scientific Revolution and Education.   As previously indicated, the majority of people in this period had strong convictions concerning the authority of religious beliefs. However, it was during the Reformation that there was to arise considerable doubt and skepticism and a very critical inquiry concerning the ideas by which men live. One of the things which encouraged this skepticism was that the leaders of each of the sects believed so strongly in certain things, yet they believed differently. Also, the great wars between the different sects made one wonder whether or not any of the religious doctrines were right. Whether there could be a way to get at truth without basing it upon faith, was also of question since this procedure seemed to have lead in many cases to widely differing, and seemingly arbitrarily based sectarian faiths. Furthermore, the great impact of the geographical explorations of the new lands and knowledge concerning the people of these lands and how they lived raised questions concerning the validity of the belief that European culture was the only possible culture.

Finally, there was the effect of the development of science and the scientific spirit. The growth of rationalism and intellectual liberalism began to develop in a few areas due to a number of the above-mentioned causes. At the end of this period, the scientists, the rationalists, even the skeptics and the heretics were somewhat freer and safer than they had been earlier.

This increase in reliance upon human reason and scientific investigation still has implications for education at all levels. This was the period when the groundwork was laid for the democratic ideas of the rights of men. For the first time men began to use the scientific ideas to solve problems of human existence. These three developments, scientific method, democratic ideas and social philosophy, and the use of technology to solve one's minimal existence problems, formed the major new intellectual forces at this time. Of these, the scientific point of view was, probably, the most basic.

One of the outstanding proponents of science during the Reformation period was Francis Bacon (1561–1626). Actually, Bacon was not a good scientist; however, he was a good essayist and he popularized the value of science. His influential position as an official in England helped to achieve the wide acceptance of the scientific method. In Bacon's writings he set forth the claims of the scientific method eloquently. He lashed out against superstition and tradition, against man's reliance upon Aristotelian philosophies, and against man's concern with words rather than reliance on the testing out of ideas in human experience.

Bacon described the scientific method most fully in his book, *Novum Organum* (New Method). He described the inductive or scientific method through which he insisted that authentic knowledge could be obtained. He suggested that the scientists should first observe the facts of nature, then collect a wide range of facts, generalize from the individual facts to ascertain what they have in common, and then, if possible, express these common factors or likenesses in general formulas. According to today's more modern concept of the scientific method, this method of collecting data before a hypothesis has been formulated is to be criticized. Scientific investigation at the present time requires the collection of specific selected data necessary to verify or prove false a likely hypothesis with respect to the problem at hand. However, Bacon's insistence that knowledge arises completely out of experience rather than through the authority of tradition, and his early recommendations of the use of some kind of a controlled method of investigation, even though crude by modern day standards, is of great importance. Furthermore, he was able to popularize this for the general public so it was more widely accepted not only by investigators, but by the persons who were interested in the results of the investigation and who would then perhaps accept them. Bacon made the scientific method respectable in an age when previously it had been ridiculed in comparison with older authoritarian methods.[1]

Perhaps as important as the method itself were the results of the method, i.e., the factual information concerning the world which gradually emerged from the investigations. It was a long time before the implications of the facts uncovered about the nature of the world began to be realized. When they were, the whole framework of human thought was altered. An example in point was the new conception of a heliocentric universe as compared to the older earth-centered one. In the tradition which had become basic to the Christian religion up to this time, the universe which God had created had been conceived as centering in the earth with the stars, moon, and sun surrounding it. God had created the earth and the other heavenly bodies for his own purposes. When the astronomers of this period, such as Copernicus, Kepler, Galileo, and others, had completed their scientific investigations, this hypothesis of an earth-centered relatively finite universe had vanished. The more likely hypothesis seemed to be one with the sun at the center of the universe, this earth being merely one of several satellites surrounding it. This theory burst upon man's conceptions with a terrific force. Although later

[1] See Catherine D. Bowen, *Francis Bacon: The Temper of a Man.* An excellent biography.

this concept was also found to be inadequate, it did at that time require a complete re-ordering of man's thinking.

All of the churches, both Catholic and Protestant, viewed this new scientific conception with great apprehension. They took steps to combat it because they felt that if the heliocentric theory were established, the idea of the earth as made especially by God for man would become insignificant before the immensity of the universe as it was being revealed. Copernicus was so fearful of publishing his views that he delayed their publication. It was published after his death. Kepler, an astronomer of northern Europe, was treated coldly by Lutheran theologians and was not given any cooperation because of his sympathy for the Copernican view. Galileo Galilei (1564-1642), who did publish before his death a statement in regard to the heliocentric point of view, was actually forced by the Inquisition of the church to deny statements made in his writings even though he had set them forth only as possible hypotheses. Another scientist, Giordano Bruno (1548-1600) was burned at the stake because of his refusal to deny his scientific beliefs, and also because his religious beliefs were considered heretical by the church.

However, in spite of this opposition to certain aspects of scientific development, William Gilbert (1540-1603) studied electricity, actually coining this word. Robert Boyle (1627-1671), also of England, formulated his law of gases, and many others made great strides in studying the laws of light and other mechanical principles. Among the greatest of these was Sir Isaac Newton (1642-1727) who is discussed in a later chapter. Great developments took place including the advances made in mathematics which were necessary to help explain and work with the new science. In the sixteenth and seventeenth centuries the ideas of decimals and logarithms were brought in. These were improvements in algebra, and, as well, there was the development of calculus by both Newton and Leibnitz (1646-1716). The theory of probabilities was advanced, trigonometry was further developed from its earlier Babylonian and Egyptian beginnings, and the beginnings of analytical geometry were set forth by René Descartes (1596-1650).

It was to be expected that the applications of the findings of science to the new conception of the world view would result in the establishment of different philosophical points of view from those which had been predominating. One of these was the development of a philosophy of materialism. Thomas Hobbes (1588-1679) of England and Pierre Gassendi (1592-1695) of France, expounded that the universe was nothing more than a huge machine similar to those which man had constructed but immensely more complicated and that it operated according to purely mechanical laws. Everything in nature was matter in motion. Everything could be explained or reduced to material terms. This represented, of course, a complete reaction against the Platonic idealistic point of view accepted by Christianity which looked upon nonmaterial or spiritual ideas as the fundamental bases for the universe. Both Catholic and Protestant Christians were very violently opposed to this materialistic view and it gained only a very few adherents from the intellectual classes at first. However, in the late eighteenth century, it was more widely held.

What actually was worked out in order to solve this problem during the period of the Reformation, and also later, was a kind of compromise between the Platonic idealism and the extreme materialism. This was done to a great extent by Descartes, the great French philosopher and mathematician. Descartes resolved the difficulties in such a way that, until the development of pragmatism in the later nineteenth and early twentieth centuries, scientists tended to operate in the framework of the dualistic concept which he had laid down in the seventeenth century. Scientific assumptions of this period were upset by the discovery of relativity in the twentieth century, and philosophy was shaken by a great move forward of the pragmatic and positivistic philosophies of the late nineteenth and early twentieth centuries. Descartes had managed to retain the traditional world view of his time as far as possible and reconciled it with the new science. One of his concerns was not to antagonize the prevailing theological conceptions of his time. Although he had some difficulty, at the end of his life he had reconciled himself to the Catholic faith.

In the attempt to reconcile theology with the new science, Descartes divided the world into completely separate and distinct substances, namely mind and matter. Then, neither Plato nor Aristotle had completely separated these substances. To Descartes, mind was the spiritual substance by means of which thinking was possible, and it is completely independent of matter and free of the mechanistic laws. Unlike matter, mind was able to make choices. Matter, on the other hand, was the material substance of the physical world and was made up of objects of time and space which move according to fixed mechanical laws. Mind was, thus, a free agent but matter was a machine. Although both mind and matter were created by God and ultimately controlled by Him, either directly or through His laws, they could not affect each other.

Thus, Descartes left mind, or the spiritual part of the world, to theology (or philosophy), but assigned to science complete supremacy in the realm of matter. This led, of course, to an extreme form of dualism which, although it had been present to some extent in both Platonic idealism and Aristotelian realism, during this period became a concept of the existence of two more widely separate and different substances. Many persons felt that education should concern itself with the mental and spiritual aspects of man's existence rather than the material or practical activity. This separation would cause education not to be concerned about the scientific and the material aspect of man's existence, or at least to minimize these as compared to the mental and the spiritual.

Certain implications with regard to how learning occurred were derived from the scientific development of this time. The materialists such as Hobbes seemed to imply that all that man could learn about the external world came through the senses, ordinarily conceived of as five— seeing, hearing, tasting, touching, and smelling. Knowledge was built up therefore through situations which the body experiences by means of the senses. This doctrine, quite often labelled as empiricism, came out of the scientific methods of observing and testing the natural phenomena of the external world. In empiricism the only test of the truth of a statement lies in its being capable of sensory verification.

The idealists placed their emphasis upon learning through the mind, particularly that faculty of the mind which enabled it to reason. To them, sense perception limited one to the knowledge of physical objects, a very small part of the total world, but reason enabled one to obtain knowledge of the unchanging world and of truth in an absolute sense. This conception came to be known as rationalism because of the heavy emphasis on reason as compared to the senses.

Descartes tended to support the rationalist point of view, even though he was strongly influenced by the scientific method. Also, he felt that mathematics was a good example of a system of the permanent truth and rationalism seemed to fit in well with this. Furthermore, other modern-thinking philosophers such as Benedict Spinoza (1632–1671) and Leibnitz relied on reason even though they were strongly influenced by scientific knowledge. These latter two were not strongly religious. The persons who were religious in their thinking inclined toward rationalism as a basis for buttressing their faith. They did subordinate human reason to their religious faith, but it seemed to them that reason provided a more acceptable way to learn about religious truth than did sensory experience. The later pious ideas of direct religious experiences had not yet permeated very deeply into the religious groups.

The important stress in education at this time, and continuing on through the enlightenment period, was an emphasis upon the rationalistic aspect both in its purposes and its content. Rationalism fitted in with the old humanistic tradition and, although mathematics and to some extent modern languages were taught, the continued emphasis upon classic literature was deemed to be more important in developing reason than science which depended on sense experience.

Up to the end of the seventeenth century, most of the rationalists were still closely allied with theology. Before that time such thinkers as Hobbes and Bacon had developed a rationalism with respect to empiricism and did not fully support religious or theological concepts. Later, they were joined by Locke, Hume, and other eighteenth-century enlightenment thinkers. One of the by-products of their emphasis upon human reason, was that it began, even during the Reformation, to take precedence over the claims of religious faith, revelation, mysticism, authority, and the ancient tradition. In the enlightenment period which was to follow, the rationalists found themselves in direct opposition to the authority and tradition of the past.

Some of the other scientific inventions and technological developments of that time were as important as the ideological consequences of science. For example, the invention of successful movable type and its improvement some time in the fifteenth century brought about a greater volume of cheaper printed material so that for the first time a wider literacy and more extensive dissemination of knowledge were possible. Furthermore, the growth of the middle class which was interested in reading led to the demand for the publication of books on a wide range of topics. It would be almost impossible to think of mass education without the mass production of reading materials.

Incidentally, the universities were slow to take up the ideas of the new science. Most of the interest in scientific knowledge and its dissemination took place in scientific societies outside of the universities and was promulgated through the expanding publication by printing press.

General Development of Education. When students of the history of education state that sixteenth and seventeenth century education was primarily religious in its fundamental goals, this is in part true. However, this statement has to be considerably qualified. The main impetus for education did come from religious leadership, Reformation, or Counter-Reformation. But the effects of all the other forces must be taken into account.

The aims of the Catholic teaching orders mainly in France, Spain, and Italy, of course, were principally religious. Their central purpose was to prepare boys and girls to be good Christians and devout adherents of their Catholic faith. This same aim of developing sound religious faith was present in the Protestant reformers, but they permitted other goals to influence education. Luther had always insisted in his conception of the relationship between church and state that one of the purposes of the school was to educate for the good of the state as well as the church. Although he originally felt that all should read the Bible, later on he questioned whether people would always read the Bible correctly and considered that probably the study of the Lutheran catechism would be sufficient. In the case of the Calvinists, where church and state were one, the education for the glory of God included all aspects of the theocratic state. John Milton (1608–1674), the Puritan of England, had held as the primary aim that all learning and life itself was to know God, to love him, and to follow him in actions with the purpose of gaining eternal salvation. Milton also formulated, later, a definition of education which did not necessarily include any kind of religious reference, but one which would fit "a man to perform justly, skillfully, and magnaminously all the offices, both public and private, of peace and war."

John Amos Comenius (1592–1670), the bishop of Moravia—now a part of the country of Czechoslovakia, was extremely religious and felt that in the end all knowledge was revealed in the scriptures. He insisted, similarly to the modern anthropologists, that children are not born human but become so through their experiences and education as they grow up in the culture. He had heard reports from travelers of children who had lived apart from society and who had not become human in the same respect as those in society. These observations led Comenius to arrive at certain conclusions about the nature of education which are so similar to those of modern educators that quite often historians have justifiably hailed him as being the first of the modern educators. He viewed the school as the special instrument of society for the purpose of shaping children into human beings. One of the central purposes of education is the reconstruction of society and, thus, the school would play a large part in the improvement of society, a kind of early reconstructionist philosophy.[2] Aims of education to Comenius were therefore much wider than merely religious because the pupil must be taught to live life for many purposes, not merely religious. He was one of the first to advocate the same school for everyone, the democratic ideal in his concept of the Christian or religious republic. Comenius's viewpoints are discussed more fully later.

Some of the other influences which tended to widen the aims of education are now looked at. The economic and political influences were seen in some new provisions for vocational education, particularly in teaching a trade to the lower-class children. The attempts of the middle classes to have more education in the vernacular languages in order to meet commercial needs is another example of an economic factor at work. Even the moving ahead of the humanist tradition into the Reformation schools tended to widen to some extent their rather narrow theological outlook because it brought them in contact with the secular cultures of ancient Greece and Rome. Reformation secondary schools thus remained strongly classic. The courtly classes wanted to establish new academies which met their needs from the standpoint of military demands and for accomplishment in the social graces. The final impact on the widening of school curriculum was the scientific influence which became only partially an effective influence on schools at this time, but which was to have such a tremendous influence in later times, both on the content of the schools and on the methods of teaching.

The idea of educating people in their own language met with considerable success in the Lutheran states of Germany and later in Scan-

---

2 Compare with the position of the modern reconstructionist philosophy to that held by a group of Comenius's followers.

dinavia. The German curriculum in the vernacular included reading the German Bible, learning Luther's catechism, and also learning how to read, in German, *Aesop's Fables* as translated by Luther. In most of the elementary schools in Lutheran territories the singing of hymns, a little history, and some physical activity was also included. Certainly what was taught in arithmetic was very minimal. This meant that the curriculum consisted basically of reading, writing, some arithmetic and religion, along with a few rudiments of history, music, and physical education.

Calvin, like Luther, was also strongly interested in and did start some vernacular schools in which the children could learn catechism in the Calvinist fashion, how to read, write, and compute in their own languages and to sing the hymns of the Calvinist Church. Some of the teaching orders of the Catholic Church also developed vernacular schools for the common people, perhaps because of the competition of the Protestant gains in the adjoining lands. For example, two of the orders, the Port Royalists and the Institute of the Brothers of the Christian Schools, taught their elementary classes in French as did some of the teaching orders for women. The Fathers of the Oratory, although interested basically in secondary education, did do much of their preliminary teaching for the presecondary years in the language of the people. These schools were similar in their emphasis to the Protestant schools except that they emphasized Catholic theology. There was also an increased emphasis in the parish schools taught by local priests in response to the recommendations of the Council of Trent. Many of these began to turn their attention to teaching in the vernacular of the particular country in which they were located.

Of course, in the English Reformation, the liturgical language of the Anglican Church became English so that the parish schools taught by the priests of the Anglican Church were also taught in English.

Among the Puritans and some of the other dissenters in both England and Germany, the vernacular language was important. The Puritans had started schools of their own, but were driven underground when the British passed the Act of Uniformity; however, they continued to operate these underground schools in the vernacular. Later, as more toleration was granted the dissenter in the seventeenth century, there were several test cases concerning these schools which came before the British courts. It was finally decided that elementary school teachers need not be licensed by the (Anglican) bishop, although the license was still a requirement for the secondary teachers. Consequently, this encouraged the continuation and starting of new dissenter elementary schools on into the eighteenth century.

At the secondary level, most of the dissenter's academies taught in the vernacular. They emphasized the classics, but often they did expand their curriculum due to pressures for mathematics and scientific content.

Some of these dissenters' academies (probably because they were established without as much educational precedent) had the broadest curriculum of any of the secondary schools of the seventeenth century. They quite often added courses in geography, surveying, navigation, economics, politics, natural science, anatomy, and modern languages to the ancient content of the secondary school curriculum. Not all these subjects were given in any one school, but this range of studies could be found in examining all of the schools of the dissenters in England at this time. It is usually felt that these schools whose influence was felt largely in the eighteenth century did have an effect upon the academies of America.

There was some emphasis during this period in trying to provide minimal vocational training for the masses, particularly if the families were extremely poor. Luther had stressed the importance of teaching all children a trade, but he had indicated that this should be done in the home. Some of the writing and "reckoning" schools which grew up in the fifteenth century in Germany, and which continued to exist during the Reformation period, had taught largely writing, commercial arithmetic, and bookkeeping, i.e., practical, vocational subjects. In the Netherlands, there was considerable attention given to commercial and trade education for certain persons. In the Netherlands, in 1531, a law had been passed which required that a child either go to school or be apprenticed, and the municipal governments were directed to establish schools to give vocational training. This took place almost a century before similar laws in the American colonies. Vocational education was to get its most effective start, although certainly not in any widespread or completely effective way, in those countries which had the most commercial interests during this time, Germany, the Netherlands, and England.

In the Elizabethan period of England, steps were taken as a part of the poor laws to provide compulsory apprenticeship and work houses for poor children. The "work houses" of this period were not prisons but places to train people to work. There was some attempt during the seventeenth century by Puritan reformers to try to get more vocational education into the private academies to train for tradesmen, but this was not too successful because of the classical tradition in education. Some of the dissenter's academies, however, did place some emphasis upon these practical subjects.

Later on in the eighteenth and nineteenth century, when there was even still greater pressure, the vocational subjects began to be taught in the schools as well as through apprenticeships. It may well be that the teaching of the vocational subjects through the schools (still a controversial issue in education in most of the developed countries) is an extremely important event in the development of modern education and in creating the basis for a modern technological society. It does raise a question as to the role of liberal as opposed to vocational studies. In many cases in Europe it was usually either one or the other—a student either took a "liberal" education with no practical training, or a vocational one with few general "liberal" subjects.

It is now important that a more careful look be given at the educational ideas of Johann Amos Comenius, the bishop of Moravia. He probably was the outstanding writer in educational theory during the Reformation period and certainly he paved the way for the application of the "sense-realist" approach to education which came about more fully in the eighteenth and nineteenth centuries. Comenius tried to apply the methods of science to educational theory and to his ideas concerning curriculum and the methods of teaching. Comenius felt that all instruction should be arranged to follow the order of the development of the child as it was shown in nature. He felt that this meant, by and large, the materials of instruction should be arranged from the simple to the complex and from the known to the unknown. Throughout all teaching he felt that the motivation should be to appeal to the child through his sense experiences. He preferred the child to have direct contact with actual objects wherever possible, or at least through pictures or other representations of things (models, and so on). The many textbooks he wrote were illustrated with pictures in order to provide this contact and he is generally given the credit for being the originator of the picture textbook. Comenius set forth his educational ideas and plans in his work, *Didactica Magna*. In this he proposed a complete plan for reforming the curriculum and a complete organization of the schools from the preschool period through the university. In general, he approached the possibilities of social reform through what he called "Pansophism," that is, the teaching of all knowledge to all persons.

Education would start in the schooling of the infant up to the age of six, which he called the "School of The Mother's Knee." Comenius would train the senses and would bring about a well-rounded moral, spiritual, and bodily development through the use of games, through fairy tales, through the learning of rhymes, music, and hand activity. Following the School of The Mother's Knee, he would have a school in the child's own language from age six to twelve in which he would teach singing, religion, morals, economics and political science, history, and the manual arts. Then, this would be followed by the classical school, from ages twelve to eighteen, where the child would be taught the classical languages of Latin, Greek, Hebrew, and German (not the native language of his country), and rhetoric, logic, mathematics, science, and art. This would be followed by the university, the top rung of what is now called a "ladder system." The "ladder system" means that all children would take the same route and would merely stop at different levels. Subject matter would be carefully organized in the classes and graded according to the pupil's ability. The school year and all the activities for the school day would be carefully planned ahead. He felt that group instruction was much more important than individual instruction in order to gain advantages for social reform. Furthermore, he talked about the idea of correlating the various subject matters. These points were to influence strongly Froebel, Pestalozzi, and Herbart. The main purpose in all the activities was to make education practical for life as well as to make it relate to an upright, religious life.

It can be readily seen that Comenius was far in advance of his time and his ideas probably had very little effect upon contemporary education. He was not permitted to apply his ideas in his own country from which he fled due to religious persecution. Eventually his country was brought back into the Catholic faith. Comenius then travelled to many other countries, Poland, Sweden, Hungary, and England. There is some evidence that plans were made to bring him to the United States to become president of Harvard University. This did not materialize, however.

His influence was not as great as it might have been due to the persecution of his particular religious sect. His books were published late in his life and had wide circulation largely after his time. His influence was mainly through the effect it had upon those who read him, such as Rousseau and others in the countries he had visited.

Despite the fact that the different religious sects disagreed on many things, there was one thing on which they seemed to be agreed. They agreed that the traditional classical curriculum provided the best type of secondary education for training leaders for church and state. The purpose of secondary education of this time was almost entirely for such leadership. It should be remembered in appraising this type of curriculum that the sacred literature of the Christian Church was written in Latin and Greek and that, furthermore, the Renaissance had established the classics so firmly as a basis for education that very few people would even question their validity. Thus, their wholehearted acceptance by both Protestants and Catholics, during this period helped them to maintain their central position in secondary and higher education much longer than would have been the case otherwise.

It must be remembered that the educational system at this time was a completely two-track system. The secondary school was not as extensive as the elementary, but was a completely separate school system. Youngsters who were going on to secondary education usually took their preliminary work either with a tutor or in a preparatory school attached to the secondary school. The classical education then became a mark of scholarship, religious knowledge, and also a mark of superiority in manners for the upper class. This was a kind of gentility which could not be completely accomplished by pure financial success, but needed to be embellished by a classical education. Some of the educational reformers were interested in further developing the vernacular language and also in including science in the elementary school. However, this interest did not affect their reliance upon the basic classical ideal for secondary education. It is this viewpoint in the Reformation and Counter-Reformation which dominated secondary education for the next two centuries of the gymnasium in Germany, the lycée in France, and the grammar school in England.

The secondary school of the Reformation became more carefully graded (divided up into classes) with regularly prescribed books in the curriculum to be read each year. This standardization of the curriculum lead to greater rigidity as opposed to the flexibility in earlier periods. Quite often in earlier periods a student would wander around from one school to another, particularly in the universities, and there was no generally prescribed curriculum or standardized procedure. This was now to give way to order, regular attendance, and prescription. Consequently, there were numerous attempts to make the student conform to the rules which were now laid down in the secondary schools and in the universities. Severe punishments began to be meted out in an attempt to have conformity to the rules of discipline. This discipline seemed to be necessary because the secondary schools took over many of the subjects of traditional liberal arts which had been taught at the university. These subjects were quite difficult and since the pupils, often, would finish their secondary work as early as age fourteen up to age seventeen, the schoolmasters found it necessary to use severe discipline in order to enforce the learning.

The attitude of some of the highest of the social classes, particularly among the nobility, during the Reformation, was dissatisfaction to some extent with this classical curriculum. They felt that, since their sons were training for a life to be centered around the courts, the social graces and the ability to carry on duelling or horsemanship or other graces, which could best be described as those of a gentleman–scholar, were the important aims of education rather than the classics, per se. They felt that their boys needed a more practical kind of education to prepare them for this courtly social life. Therefore, some academies were set up to fulfill the needs of this special group. It has been estimated that at mid-seventeenth century there were around forty of these academies for the nobility which had heavy emphasis upon court manners and the military skills. One example of this emphasis can be found in the *Ritteracademie* (knight academies) of Germany. These academies quite often taught how to duel with either a sword or a pistol and how to ride a horse. The students were taught military skills, some geography, history, mathematics and science, and other vernacular languages, usually including French.

The most conservative of all levels of education at this time were the universities. These universities almost completely ignored the new science and the new philosophy growing out of it in favor of a continued and detailed study of theology and of all kinds of religious disputations. Universities were not yet centers of free inquiry, investigation, or research. They lagged considerably behind other cultural developments and gave practically no attention to new sciences.

At the time of the colonization of America, the liberal arts course in the European university consisted of the medieval seven liberal arts, plus a study of Aristotle's philosophy and some of the Renaissance humanistic classics. The Reformation and Counter-Reformation made these subservient to religious and sectarian interests and, in the north, in addition they were made subservient to the demands of the political state, closely associated with the church.

The historic ideal of liberal education emphasized primarily linguistic and literary studies. It was felt that one could develop a man of action best through such study. (An exception to this was in the Ritter Academies for the nobility.) It was believed that only a few men were really capable of higher education in literary matters and, for that matter, only a few were capable of leadership. Consequently, liberal education of the Reformation was based on an aristocratic conception of society, and degrees in academic and liberal education were to be valued more highly because very few could attain them—a "scarcity" theory. Liberal education meant that the student was more or less conversant with the Latin or Greek classics, mathematics, and philosophy.

Some of the Reformation leaders began to emphasize the importance of the teacher and of having teachers who were well prepared. Actual improvement in this was quite slow, however. In German states there was some setting up of standards for the teaching profession and there was the beginning of some certification of the teachers by the state churches. In writing, Luther had talked about teachers who would be well trained, would be respected, and would be licensed by the government. Teachers had to obey very strict laws which had prescriptions for curriculum, for methods of disciplining, and for their religious views. It is interesting that even in this relatively early period, in order to attract people into teaching, there was provided services which we would now call social security, old age pensions, and sickness pay. At that time this was not in the form of insurance, but in the form of pensions (gifts) to the teacher as a part of their profession.

To insure that teachers were orthodox in their religious teaching, there was some supervision of instruction. Although there was a growing respect for the potentialities and for the importance of education in the national interest, there was still some fear that unsatisfactory teachers might not do justice to the religious teaching.

In connection with the training of better teachers, the work of St. Jean Baptiste de La Salle (1651–1719) [3] was important in changing the occupation of teaching in the lower schools (elementary) into more of a profession. As indicated earlier, he established the Institute of the

3 See Fitzpatrick, Edward A., *La Salle, Patron of Teachers.*

Brothers of the Christian Schools. In this, La Salle demonstrated the value of training for elementary teaching and worked out better methods of instruction.

In the past, elementary teachers had received practically no special preparation. La Salle felt that it was necessary to raise the professional status of those who taught elementary school. He felt that free education of poor children was of value to society and to religion and that elementary education was as important as teaching in the secondary school. To this end he established the *Institute,* the first of the normal schools, for the purpose of training elementary teachers. His normal schools, of course, were centered on religion as the core of the educational process and of the preparation of teachers; still, he did give attention to the teaching of the essentials and to the practical and vocational training for young children. He was interested, also, in teaching socially maladjusted (or delinquent) children.

As indicated earlier, La Salle advocated the teaching of vernacular language rather than Latin. He was also interested in the use of more humane methods in teaching. Stressing his concern for the individual child, he felt that there should be created an orderly and effective school atmosphere. Children were to be taught in graded classes rather than by individual instruction (tutoring). He even proposed and set into operation a few vernacular secondary schools in order to meet the needs of the new middle classes. One of the first to recommend education on Sundays for those who worked throughout the other days of the week—the "Sunday School," La Salle's ideas and innovations represent the importance of continued effort for the improvement of education.

There was some attempt during this period to apply the principles of the new science to educational methods. Some of the sense realists and humanistic realists gave attention to this problem, but actually very little was done until after the period of the Reformation.

FREEDOM IN THE PERIOD OF THE REFORMATION AND SCIENTIFIC REVOLUTION

When one considers the development of freedom of man during the period of the Reformation and the Counter-Reformation, one must take into account the long-range consequences as well as some of the short-range results of this period. The Protestant revolution, of course, began as a revolt against authority and this was successful. It set forth the theory that the individual had a right to go against authority. Very quickly, however, both the Calvinists and the Lutherans began to restrict the authority of every individual to decide for himself. In Europe, religion was a political matter and each individual had to adopt the religion of his particular ruler or state. The details of the religious creed had to conform with that which was considered to be right as determined by the leaders of his church. Dissident sects soon learned that there was no freedom except for the religious majority. However, the example of the breakaway from the church did lead others to continue with the struggle for religious freedom until this right was eventually won in most of nineteenth century Europe.

Closely allied in point of time to the freedom which came about as a result of the Reformation was the challenge of authority by the scientific groups. The scientific view, however, affected only a relatively few persons until a later age. The fact that scientific inquiry did challenge the traditional learning of the past led a great number of scholars to reject authority, both the authority of the time as well as the traditional authority as found in the classical literature. It should, nevertheless, be pointed out that at this time the number of people who felt themselves emancipated from the past or from political authority were very, very few. It is not until the period of enlightenment (next to follow) that a larger number of intellectuals felt somewhat freed from the past tradition. It can be shown, of course, that even in this later period they were not entirely free but were still considerably bound by the tradition of the past.

The Counter-Reformation of the Catholic Church possibly had the effect of reducing freedom more than if there had not been the break of the Protestants from the church. Even though the Council of Trent did admit to some of the weaknesses of the church which Martin Luther had proclaimed, there was no compromise at all with respect to Catholic dogma. The rigorous adherence of the church to dogma was much stronger in the period which was to follow than it had been in the relatively easy-going tolerance of the earlier period. It remains, of course, for the Vatican Council in the 1960's to continue the Reformation to the extent that the Church does now permit much more freedom and encourages dialogue with persons of other points of view.

SUMMARY

The main social development of the time consisted of the Reformation movement of the Christian church which resulted in the breakaway of the Protestants and other dissidents from the dominant Roman Catholic form and the Counter-Reformation within the church itself. Another development was the discovery and use of the scientific method and its impact of this method upon the world of its time.

This same period saw the development of nationalism in most of the major countries of Europe and the accentuation of national differences. It saw the development of the right of the state to determine religion over individual conscience. It saw the development of differing religious points of view in separate parts of Europe and consequent flight of many persons to the new world in order to gain religious freedom. It saw, also, the development of the commercial and merchant class interests which in the end strengthened the hands of the king.

In the field of education, the advance of methods in teaching and the over-all achievement of this period were not much greater than those of the period before. Although there was some talk and uneasiness about bookish education on the part of a few of the promoters of the vernacular schools and academies, in general, the accomplishments of the period fell far short of what some of the leaders and writers were talking about, e.g., Comenius.

Success in school was still largely determined by the ability to memorize large quantities of material and to recite it. This had been true, of course, ever since the use of the written language as a cultural tool. As soon as someone had made a study of language and organized a body of rules, then a study of that body of rules (or grammar) had to include the memorization of the rules. In the case of the English language, the grammar followed that of Latin, the language of the scholarly people of the time, even though this grammar did not apply to English. The study of the rules of logic and rhetoric led to the use of disputation in which students argued according to the rules of formal logic. The declamation methods used by many of the schools required students to speak by using classic examples or they prepared their own composition in accordance with the formal classic rules. These methods of bookish learning arose in consistency with an adherence to the concept of the rationalist mind. Sometimes the classical authors were so much imitated that this method was called "Ciceronianism," basing Latin upon the form used by Cicero, the "perfect master" of Latin.

Previous to this time, school masters had to teach pupils of a wide range of ages grouped together somewhat as in the one-room school, later, in America. There was an attempt made during the Reformation period to classify pupils according to age and grade. Discipline became very severe during the Reformation period, particularly in the Protestant and, even more particularly, in the Calvinistic parts of Europe. Whipping and ridicule were very prominent among the methods used.

The development of the empirical point of view was expressed in the doctrines of sense realism. A few educators began to react against the formalism and the excesses of physical discipline. They argued that education ought to be learned by the senses and that this is much more effective than by learning words in books. They reasoned from the inductive method of science whereby the learner finds out about things by actual observation. Several thinkers during this period argued that one should go from the real and the simple to the complex and abstract. There was an attempt to develop interest in the pupils for learning so as to help them go farther. These persons were mostly theorists, and their ideas did not affect a great deal of what was happening in the schools. They were, however, to influence greatly some persons such as Pestalozzi and Froebel in the period to follow.

The Reformation increased respect for the state as a source of authority, as compared to previous religious authority. That there was, also, an increase in respect for material wealth is seen in more favorable attitudes toward the upper middle classes.

Protestant reformers had emphasized the importance of the family as an educational institution. Luther felt that the family should take the responsibility for teaching the child the catechism as well as teaching him a trade. Calvinists had done likewise and called for extensive Bible reading and prayer within the family circle, emphasizing to the children the possibility of eternal punishment. Even Comenius, among modern educators, had urged that there be a school at the mother's knee. Calvinistic emphasis upon family and devotions, of course, had great influence in America during its formative colonial period.

The increased availability of printed books and the fact that more people now knew how to read was in itself an enormous educative force. As people acquired books and there were private libraries, individuals were able to become better educated by their own reading. Some persons, particularly religious groups, did quite a bit of pamphleteering. This was done, sometimes, by scientific groups who would publish small pamphlets on their new scientific discoveries. All these nonschool educational influences stimulated organized education.

Paralleling these influences was an increase in the number of people, although small, who took part in elementary and secondary education.

In summary, then, the following emphases began in this period, although they were not carried very far:

1. Mass education. Motivation, however, is still religious.

2. Recognition of individual differences in children with an effort to group them for better instruction.

3. Educational methods in line with scientific study.

4. Improvement of teacher training.

In spite of these small trends toward what could be considered now as "modern," education there still continued to be throughout the schools a heavy emphasis upon memory; on grammar, rather than on meaning;

and on the Classics, rather than on science and social studies. There continued widespread use of corporal punishment as the main enforcement of an ill-adapted curriculum taught with poor methods upon unhappy children.

SELECTED BIBLIOGRAPHY

Starred items represent books most closely parallel to chapter contents.

Bainton, Roland H., *Here I Stand: A Life of Martin Luther.* New York, Abingdon-Cokesbury Press, 1950.

Berkner, L. V., *The Scientific Age.* New Haven, Yale University Press, 1964.

Bowen, Catherine Drinker, *Francis Bacon: The Temper of a Man.* Boston, Little, Brown, 1963.

*Boyd, William, *The History of Western Education,* 7th ed., revised and enlarged by Edmund J. King. New York, Barnes and Noble, 1965.

*Butts, R. Freeman, *A Cultural History of Western Education: Its Social and Intellectual Foundations,* 2 ed. New York, McGraw-Hill, 1965.

Dampier, William Cecil, *A History of Science: And its Relation with Philosophy and Religion,* 3d ed. New York, Macmillan, 1942.

*Duggan, Stephen, *A Student's Textbook in the History of Education.* New York, Appleton–Century–Crofts, 1927.

Durant, Will, *The Reformation: The Story of Civilization.* New York, Simon and Schuster, 1957.

*Eby, Frederick, *The Development of Modern Education: In Theory, Organization and Practice,* 2d ed. New York, Prentice-Hall, 1952.

Eiseley, Loren, *Francis Bacon and the Modern Dilemma.* Lincoln, University of Nebraska, 1962.

Fife, Robert H., *The Revolt of Martin Luther.* New York, Columbia University Press, 1957.

Fitzpatrick, Edward A., *LaSalle, Patron of All Teachers.* Milwaukee, Bruce, 1951.

Frost, S. E., Jr., *Historical and Philosophical Foundations of Western Education.* Columbus, Merrill, 1966.

*Good, H. G., *A History of Western Education,* 2d ed. New York, Macmillan, 1960.

Hall, A. Rupert, *From Galileo to Newton: 1630–1720.* London, Collins, 1963.

Harbison, E. Harris, *The Age of Reformation.* Ithaca, New York, Cornell, 1955.

Hart, Joseph K., *Creative Moments in Education.* New York, Holt, Rinehart and Winston, 1931.

Heritage of American Education, Richard E. Gross, ed. Boston, Allyn-Bacon, 1962.

Holton, G., and Roller, D. H. D., *Foundations of Modern Physical Science.* Reading, Massachusetts, Addison-Wesley, 1958.

*Knight, Edgar W., *Twenty Centuries of Education.* New York, Ginn, 1940.

Mayer, Frederick, *A History of Educational Thought.* Columbus, Merrill, 1960.

McNeill, William, *History Handbook of Western Civilization.* Chicago, University of Chicago Press, 1953.

*Meyer, Adolphe E., *An Educational History of the Western World.* New York, McGraw-Hill, 1965.

Muller, Herbert J., *Freedom in the Western World.* New York, Harper & Row, 1963.

Main Currents in the History of Education, Edward J. Power. New York, McGraw-Hill, 1962.

New Perspectives in World History, Shirley Engle, ed. Thirty-fourth Yearbook of the National Council of the Social Studies. Washington, D.C., National Education Association, 1964.

Rusk, Robert R., *The Doctrines of the Great Educators.* New York, St. Martins', 1965.

Shotwell, James T., *The Long Way to Freedom.* New York, Bobbs-Merrill, 1960.

Singer, C., *A Short History of Scientific Ideas to 1900.* Oxford, Clarendon Press, 1959.

The Present-day Relevance of Eighteenth Century Thought, Roger Philip McCutcheon, ed. Washington, D.C., American Council of Learned Societies, 1956.

Sources of Western Civilization, Daniel D. McGarry, and Clarence L. Huhl, eds. Houghton-Mifflin, 1962.

Walker, Williston, *John Calvin: The Organizer of Reformed Protestantism, 1509–1564.* New York, G. P. Putman's, 1906.

Weiss, R., *Humanism in England During the Fifteenth Century.* Oxford, B. Blackwell, 1941.

Wilds, Elmer H. and Lottich, Kenneth V., *The Foundations of Modern Education,* 3d ed. New York, Holt, Rinehart and Winston, 1961.

The Educated Man: Studies in the History of Educational Thought, Paul J. Nash, and others, eds. New York, Wiley, 1965.

Pertinent Paperbound Books

Bainton, Roland H., *Reformation of the Sixteenth Century.* Boston, Beacon, 1952.

Beck, Robert H., *A Social History of Education.* Englewood Cliffs, New Jersey, Prentice-Hall, 1965.

Beloff, Max, *Age of Absolutism, 1660–1815.* London, Hutchinson, 1954.

Blitzer, Charles and Friedrich, Carl J., *Age of Power.* Ithaca, Cornell University Press, 1957.

Broudy, Harry S. and Palmer, John R., *Exemplars of the Teaching Method.* Chicago, Rand McNally, 1965.

Burrell, Sidney, *The Main Strands of Development from the Beginnings to the Eighteenth Century. Elements of Western Civilization,* Vol I. San Francisco, Chandler, 1959.

Butterfield, Herbert, *The Origins of Modern Science: 1300–1800,* rev. ed. New York, Collier Books, 1962.

Cheney, L. J., *A History of the Western World: From the Stone Age to the Twentieth Century*. New York, New American Library, 1959.

Cheyney, Edward, *The Dawn of a New Era: 1250–1453*, 3d ed. New York, Harper, 1936.

Cordesco, Francesco, *A Brief History of Education*. Paterson, New Jersey, Littlefield, Adams, 1963.

Dampier, William C. and Margaret, *Readings in the Literature of Science: Being Extracts from the Writings of Men of Science to Illustrate the Development of Scientific Thought*. New York, Harper, 1959.

Friedrich, Carl J., *Age of Baroque: 1610–1660*. New York, Harper & Row, 1952.

Frost, S. E., Jr., *Essentials of History of Education*. New York, Barron's, 1947.

Hall, A. R., *The Scientific Revolution, 1500–1800: The Formation of the Modern Scientific Attitude*. New York, Longmans, Green, 1954.

Harbison, E. Harris, *Age of Reformation*. Ithaca, New York, Cornell, 1955.

Howells, William, *Back of History: The Story of Our Origins*, rev. ed. Garden City, Doubleday, 1963.

Hughes, Paul and Fries, Robert F., *Reading in Western Civilization*, Unit 5. Paterson, New Jersey, Littlefield, Adams, 1962.

Janelle, Pierre, *The Catholic Reformation*. Milwaukee, Bruce, 1949.

Kirchner, Walter, *Western Civilization Since 1500*. New York, Barnes and Noble, 1958.

Mayer, Frederick, *A History of Educational Thought*. Columbus, Merrill, 1960.

Nussbaum, Frederick L., *The Triumph of Science and Reason, 1660–1685*. New York, Harper & Row, 1963.

Pledge, H. T., *Science Since 1500: A Short History of Mathematics, Physics, Chemistry and Biology*. New York, Philosophical Library, 1947.

Ralph, Phillip Lee, *The Story of Our Civilization: 10,000 Years of Western Man*. New York, Dutton, 1959.

Ryan, Patrick J., *Historical Foundations of Public Education in America*. Dubuque, William C. Brown, 1965.

Sedillot, Rene, *History of the World in 240 Pages*. New York, New American Library, 1951.

Smith, Preserved, *The Age of Reformation*. New York, Holt, Rinehart and Winston.

———, *Origins of Modern Culture: 1543–1687*. New York, Collier Books, 1962.

Symond, John Addington, *Age of Despots: Renaissance in Italy*. New York, Holt, 1888.

Thompson, Merritt M., *The History of Education*, College Outline Series. New York, Barnes and Noble, 1958.

SELECTED FILMS

Rise of Nations in Europe (Coronet)   (13½ min.)
     Traces the rise of nations from feudal beginnings to highly centralized states of the seventeenth century.

The Reformation (Coronet)   (13½ min.)

Discusses the Reformation in terms of the Church, the cultural rebirth brought about by the Renaissance, the emergence of national states, and new interpretations of the Scriptures.

8

Education and the Enlightenment (A.D. 1700–A.D. 1830)

The nineteenth century can be identified by the continued rise and consolidation of the national states, as well, the founding of national systems of education. In this chapter the period up to 1830 is included, the whole being considered as the period of "The Enlightenment."

The word, "enlightenment," in the literature of historians, refers to the set of ideas held by many of the leading scholars and thinkers of the eighteenth century. The Enlightenment was a reaction against the absolutistic and the authoritarian systems of the previous Reformation period. The Enlightenment was in opposition to the absolute monarchy, to "closed" economic systems such as mercantilism, to rigid social classes, to religious authoritarianism, to superstitious and unscientific views of the world, and to the doctrine of "original sin" with respect to human nature as set forth by the Calvinists. It was also against the domination of those ideas buttressed by the ancient and medieval conceptions of the way in which truth and knowledge were to be verified. Basically, then, the Enlightenment was a protest. Underlying it was a growing faith in the worthwhileness of the common man, in science as the important method of arriving at knowledge, and in human reason, per se. This period has also been called the "Age of Reason." The term implies the belief that had developed that man could by his own reason improve his own institutions and thus bring about much better general welfare for all men. This movement toward faith in the common man, science, and human reason was the one upon which was built the liberal and democratic spirit of modern Europe and America.

The Enlightenment reformers sought to justify their revolt against the various forms of privilege by trying to formulate a concept of natural law as a basis from which to attack the power interests of the past. Natural law used in a different sense had, of course, been formulated by the scholastics of the twelfth century and even earlier,) perhaps (by one interpretation, at least), by Aristotle. The Enlightenment scholars, however, appealed to nature directly and held that the natural rights of man rose directly out of man's own nature and his natural history. It was felt that these rights were superior to the rights held by the privileged groups because these groups had retained their rights long after they continued to merit them. The great masses of people were excluded from having, or even seeking, access to these benefits. The new "natural law" had presumably been developed as an extension of the scientific concepts of the world and, by analogy, it was held to apply to social conceptions as well. By and large, the scholars of the Enlightenment represented the interests of the middle class and the attempt to formulate these natural rights was very helpful in the great progress made toward more freedom and democracy.

THE ENLIGHTENMENT AND THE SOCIAL IDEAS OF THE EIGHTEENTH CENTURY

The development of eighteenth century enlightenment was accentuated by the ideas of political liberty and of laissez-faire capitalism and partly characterized on the one hand by the so-called "great awakening" in religion and in a quite different vein by the further development of such philosophies as materialism and deistic conceptions of God. There were numerous European political and governmental changes, including the American revolution, and there were new ideas developed such as the enlightenment concept of natural law and a new total world view.

Political Liberalism. Near the beginning of the eighteenth century, the doctrines of one version of "political liberalism" were set forth forcefully and clearly by the Englishman, John Locke (1632–1704). Locke's most basic book on government was written in 1690. He formulated the so-called "contract theory" in order to justify taking away the absolute powers of the English king by the Parliament which had come to represent the interests of the middle class. He had argued the existence of the "social contract," an agreement by which, at some time in human history, the people had delegated their authority to the government and in return the government had agreed to protect the basic rights of all the citizens. John Locke held these basic rights to be life, liberty, and property. This means that, whether or not there is still in existence a *written* instrument or "contract," there is a general agreement implicit in the relationship between a government and its citizens in which there are mutual rights for each to respect. This is the concept underlying constitutionalism, a principle that conceived of government as resting only upon the consent of the citizens and exercising its authority through their representatives. Locke insisted that the civil liberties are a necessary and proper right of all citizens and the government must protect them.

In his presentation of the "proper form of government," he held that there were actually three necessary agencies of government. Locke's influence in the formation of the American government can be very readily seen here. These three agencies were the legislative, the judiciary, and the executive. Locke felt that the legislative would represent the property owners and its purpose was to define the crimes which might be committed against the natural rights which he listed as life, liberty, and property. It would be the role of the judiciary to direct the punishment for these crimes and it should do so impartially without respect to the class status or position of the guilty person. The executive branch of the government should, according to Locke, administer the laws of the legislature and see to it that the decisions of the judiciary were executed. In the case of conflict between these balanced powers of government, Locke felt that the legislative agency must be supreme since it represents the citizens directly. If the legislative body itself would ignore the interests of its people, then a revolution would be justified in order to overthrow it. The basic cornerstones of Locke's doctrine, from which the American constitution developed, leaned heavily on liberalism, constitutionalism, and property ownership.

Another thinker of the Enlightenment who strongly influenced democratic governments, including that of America, was Montesquieu (1689–1755). Montesquieu also held that the laws should rest on the sovereign will of the people (similar to Rousseau) and, therefore, the laws would differ according to the nature of the group for whom they were made (a kind of legal relativity). Montesquieu also advocated an elaborate theory of checks and balances among the three branches of government, some aspects of which were adopted by the American constitution. Both of these men (Locke and Montesquieu) were relatively conservative in their points of view. Rousseau, however, at least in the early period of his life, was considerably more radical in his political and social philosophies. Jean Jacques Rousseau (1712–1778) had argued not only for the natural rights of life, liberty, and property, but also for the pursuit of happiness and for attention to the welfare of all the people. This would eliminate the primacy of property rights. Rousseau like Locke felt that the central purpose of the government was to promote the general welfare; consequently representation in government should be based ultimately on all the people (not just the property owners).

This quite radical, democratic conception was used as a rallying cry by the peoples of France and the rest of Europe during an age of heavy absolutism and affected the American Revolution and, later, the French Revolution. In America, for example, the constitutionalism of Locke and Montesquieu, largely middle class in emphasis, was taken up by Hamilton and the more radical, democratic humanitarianism of Rousseau was espoused by Jefferson. In the matter of the development of free, public, democratic education, as Butts has shown,[1] the two strands of the social humanitarianism, French liberalism on the one hand and the individual constitutionalism of English liberalism on the other, played important roles. Possibly the social humanitarianism is the more prominent of the forces which finally determined the nature of American free public education.

Laissez-Faire Capitalism. French liberalism was based upon the idea of men working together to improve their existence. On the other hand, English liberalism tended to emphasize individualism much more. This rugged individualism of English liberalism came about because the British thinkers placed more attention on the material aspects. Certain ideas were developed out of economic experiences and were brought together in the book by Adam Smith, *Wealth of Nations* (1776). In this book a theory was formulated. Smith held that individual effort will result in increased productivity both in the amount and quality if it is not restricted by governmental action. Each individual will act in his own self interest—which is good for himself. What is "good for himself" will work out to be also what is "good for society." The laws relating to economic matters are really "natural laws" and they should not be interfered with and, thus, they would work out automatically for the good of the total group.

This is an appeal again to "natural" law, but on a different basis than the natural law of the Thomistic or even that of the early Newtonian periods. It posits an "economic man," primarily motivated by a desire for profit. The urge to acquire wealth or property provides the motive power for every man. The profit motive, for example the desire of man to acquire his own consumer goods, makes it possible for goods to be produced. This conception of economic man was thus tied to certain "natural laws" of economics as, for example, the "law of supply and demand," which is to replace the "just" price concept of the guild and church in the Middle Ages. According to the supply and demand theory, prices would always reach their natural level in a free market in which goods

1 Butts, *op. cit.,* p. 270.

can be bought and sold without restrictions. If a seller tries to get a higher price than it is proper for him to get, then the buyer will go elsewhere. If the buyer will not pay the price that is offered on the market, he will either not get the goods or eventually, if there is a surplus, the prices will be lowered. But in order for this natural process to operate, the government must let business alone; hence, the words, "laissez-faire" capitalism from the French, meaning "to let alone."

It can be seen, then, that there were in eighteenth century liberalism two major strands—the individualistic or laissez-faire liberalism and the social or humanitarian liberalism. In the history of America it can be seen how these two views have interacted. The pendulum has swung back and forth between them. The industrial interests of the nineteenth and early twentieth century had tended to exalt personal and individualistic concepts and to place less emphasis upon humanitarianism. Public interest demands the unrestricted "free enterprise," by which was meant, private enterprise. On the other hand, the social reformers in various areas of economics and of education have tended to stress the social ideals —human rights.

European Political and Governmental Changes.   The periods of the eighteenth and early nineteenth century continued to represent a period of mingled war and political struggle. Eventually there came revolutions and attempted revolutions. France had developed into an absolutistic state under the despotism of the Louis' and then the French Revolution came belatedly (1791) with its extremes. Its very great violence finally ended in the absolutistic Napoleonic regime. After Napoleon's defeat, France was weakened for many decades. Gradually many of the gains of the French Revolution were lost in the reaction which followed; however, liberty, equality, and fraternity were to be the cries which the various reformers were to echo for some time to come. In addition to France, the other great powers of this period of the eighteenth and early nineteenth century were England, Prussia, Russia, and Austria. These countries fought many wars in different combinations between themselves. The Holy Roman Empire had become just the name of a geographical territory in central and southern Europe.

In America, the thirteen colonies did revolt, finally, and establish a federal, republican type of government which drew very heavily upon the ideas of Locke, Rousseau, and others of the enlightenment thinkers. The American Constitution probably represented at the time of its adoption (1789) one of the most democratic governments in existence. America was relatively free of the established traditions of Europe, and, therefore, over the years, Democracy was able to evolve even more. Democratic practices came about which, eventually, placed decision-making, through their elected representatives, completely in the hands of the people.

The Great Awakening. Along with the Enlightenment, there occurred an extensive and dramatic religious "awakening" within Christianity. This was occasioned by the starting of many new religious organizations. A reform movement started within many of the established churches in order to improve them. For example, the Wesleyan movement was, at first, a revivalistic effort within the Church of England. Actually, the leaders of the Wesleyan movement, John and Charles Wesley, never left the Anglican church even though their followers did start the new denomination, the Methodists. The Methodists tried to do away with the formalism and ritualism of the church and to put into it more emotional enthusiasm along with a greater emphasis upon faith. The Baptists and the Quakers protested even more completely against the rigid practices of most of existing churches of the time.

One reason why these religious groups could grow and develop was because the liberal attitudes of the eighteenth century Enlightenment permitted greater freedom of speaking and agitation. Many of these groups developed with such great enthusiasm that they almost bordered on the hysterical at times. This period was reminiscent of the Biblical Pentecost period and has been called the "Great Awakening" by historians. Hundreds of thousands of people who, before, had been merely nominal members of established and traditional religions, joined these new religious institutions and became religiously active.

This movement was to affect education especially in England, Germany, and America. It also stimulated both the missionary movement and educational philanthropy among the poor. In spite of the fact that the Great Awakening occurred during the period of Enlightenment, it was in conflict, in many ways, with the rationalism of the Enlightenment because it stressed faith and emotion as opposed to logic and reason.

New Ideas in World Views and in Natural Law. Enlightenment scholars drew heavily on the new interpretation of the universe as based upon the new scientific ideas. A typical scholar of the new scientific world view was Sir Isaac Newton. Quite often the scientific period up to the time of Einstein is called "Newtonian" science, replacing "Aristotelian" science of the earlier period. Newton (1642–1727) had developed the "Laws of Nature" which became the basis for all scientific thinking at least until the late nineteenth century. He developed the Law of Gravitation, the Law of Cause and Effect, and other laws of energy and motion. The universe as described by Newton was an orderly system moving about in unlimited, absolute space and time, simple in its basic structure, and obeying a certain number of finite and fixed laws in uniform causal relationships.

The universe was a great machine, not subject to novelty or even to divine intervention, operating in accord with mathematical laws. The declaration of the existence of such relatively simple, universal scientific laws influenced all thought and these laws became the models for naturalistic and scientific explanations in many other fields of thought.

One of the new world views arising out of science was a quite radical one, materialism. The materialists postulated that, because of the great importance of motion and matter in the new scientific laws, everything that existed were combinations of atoms forming matter operating according to natural, mechanical laws. Some of these materialists went to the extreme of eliminating all necessity for the existence of a spiritual (or idea) world, of the soul, or of any kind of mental substances.

But there were persons who went to the other extreme. One of these was Bishop George Berkeley (1685–1753) of the Church of England, an extreme, subjective idealist. Berkeley attacked vigorously, both science and materialism, insisting that the world was basically and ultimately spiritual and mental. He felt that theological beliefs could be supported and that God's existence could be proved. Berkeley maintained that all material objects are only *apparently* "material" but they are really perceptions in the mind of God. Since God's mind does exist throughout all space and time, they do appear to exist in space and time. But these material substances "really" exist only in our imagination and our ability to recognize them stems from the similarity between our minds and God's mind. Furthermore, these material substances do not have any qualities of their own; they only change their apparent qualities as our perceptions of them change.

Some of the enlightened intellectuals broke with the traditional Christian theism; but most did not wish to go as far as these materialists who eliminated any kind of a god or creator of the universe. There was a middle-of-the-road conception known as deism which was very popular among scholars of the Enlightenment period. According to them, while the world is a great machine and operates according to natural laws, these laws have been set up by God who is the designer and creator (first cause). This conception of God is different than that of the theists. In the deist's view, God is not the person who created the world in a limited period of time, but he is the spirit or principle which lies behind the material universe. Once the universe has been set into operation, even God (the spirit which lies behind) cannot interfere with the laws of the universe. Furthermore, many of the deists argued that to imply that God needed to interfere with his handiwork would be a reflection upon his omnipotence and omniscience. Many of the deists went on to attack the orthodox religions for their alleged superstitions, their reliance upon miracles, upon the necessity for God to reveal himself supernaturally, upon the necessity for any interference by God in His own world or, again, through man's intercessory prayer.

They tend to accept only those facts which scientific investigation or human reason could describe and comprehend. Many of the founders of the early American Constitution were Enlightenment thinkers and also, deists. Two such were Franklin, and Jefferson. A third, probably, was Washington.

In his attempt to get at basic ideas underlying the social philosophies of the Enlightenment—such as a conception of how human nature is constituted or how one can obtain knowledge—John Locke [2] was perhaps the most penetrating of the Enlightenment thinkers. He started out by assuming that the Newtonian conceptions of the world were correct and he wanted to elaborate the laws of human nature in the same way in which the laws of science had been elaborated. Consequently, Locke developed ideas about how the mind was formed, about the philosophy of being (ontology), and of human existence. He assumed, at the start, that human nature is not pre-formed at birth but is the result of the effect of environment upon the raw material of the human mind. This has been called the blank tablet (tabula rasa) theory of the mind. In this theory, the mind is like a blank tablet upon which the perceptions which the organism has of the outside world are imprinted. Man's mind becomes what he has perceived. Locke did not go to the extent of becoming a complete materialist. He still believed in the existence of a soul and that the mind has certain qualities which were quite independent of any material basis. Consequently, Locke can be thought of as an intermediator between materialism and idealism (in other words, a dualist), doing in the eighteenth century what Descartes had attempted to do in the seventeenth. Locke, however, did not accept the traditional religious conceptions which Descartes finally did. Locke, however, did try to fit the old moral values systems into his new conceptions without the necessity for a revealed religion.

Locke was one of the first to formulate clearly ideas dealing with the verification of knowledge through experience. Empiricism lays stress upon experience and environment as the source of learning. The empirical thinkers attacked the concept of innate ideas existing at birth, which had been held by Plato and many earlier religious and philosophical thinkers. The concept of innate ideas has now been almost completely eliminated—even from idealistic philosophies. Locke attempted to discuss the "natural laws" of learning, and argued that the child is not born with innate ideas concerning God, or justice (as Plato argued) or any other values. These ideas and values have their origin in his experience with the outside world including the people with whom he associates. In this respect, although his theory of mind is different, Locke is in agreement with the prevailing conceptions of the mid-twentieth century.

There were extremists who came after Locke just as there had been

[2] Two recent books on John Locke would be helpful to students here:

Aaron, R. I. *John Locke*. Cambridge: Oxford University Press, 1965. Pp. 326.

Gay, Peter. (ed.). *John Locke on Education*. (Classics in Education No. 20). New York: Bureau of Publications, Teachers College, Columbia University, 1964. Pp. vi + 177.

extremists who followed Descartes earlier. At the one pole, there were the materialists holding there was no such thing as soul and mind existing apart from the movements of the physical body. Some materialists did not go so far as to do away with the soul but they said that the soul is one form of material differing only in kind from that of the physical body.

The opposite view, held by Berkeley, was that the soul (the "perceiving mind") was the essence of human nature. Even the body is dependent upon the existence of the spiritual soul. This is a kind of monistic idealism in which everything is reduced to the subjective perception of each individual. Interestingly enough, Hume, the great English skeptic, carried this position still further than Berkeley who had presented his point of view as a defense of religion. David Hume (1711–1766) argued that all that exists is the flow of perceptions of experiences, and consequently, he argued that man is thus not able to come to any solid knowledge. He was skeptical about all claims for truth other than those representing the subjective views of each individual. Hume was not arguing that either mind or matter is the true nature of the universe, but that we can never know concerning these and many other questions.

One of the arguments that almost always arises in the study of human nature is the question of the nature of good and evil. Is human nature prone to good or is it prone to evil? Rousseau [3] held that human nature is essentially good and becomes evil through contact with society. He felt that through this use of the natural laws of human nature, social and educational practices could be developed which would prevent the child from becoming evil. Out of Rousseau's doctrine and other concepts of the Enlightenment period there came the idea that human nature was perfectible and therefore made better through attention to the nature of our social institutions. This belief in human perfectibility became one of the great bulwarks of the liberal tradition of Europe and of America. When this belief was coupled with belief in the essential equality and dignity of man (one basis of American democratic ideas), it gave strong support to the development of belief in the rights of the individual in a democratic society.

EDUCATION AND EIGHTEENTH CENTURY ENLIGHTENMENT

Forces and ideas of enlightenment affected educational ideas and the educational institutions and practices of this period and those that followed.

[3] See later section in this chapter for fuller discussion of Rousseau's views.

New Ideas in Education. The changes which came about in education during the eighteenth century were primarily the result of the changing social and intellectual ideas. Particularly, there was a marked change in the conception of the nature of the world and of man. Stemming from the impact of science upon the thinking of enlightenment scholars, these ideas also influenced man's judgment concerning the purposes of education as well as the methods by which education could best be carried on.

One result of the Enlightenment social philosophy of Locke and others was the increased emphasis upon education for citizenship. In the Reformation period there had also been this stress. The northern reformers, in particular, wanted to produce a citizen who would take his place in the state as well as in the life of the church. Most of the Enlightenment reformers were favorable toward the separation of church and state and, therefore, they defined citizenship almost completely in secular terms. This emphasis was strongest among the French Enlightenment thinkers.

In the period of overwhelming church sponsorship of education, French Enlightenment reformers advocated that education be placed in the hands of lay teachers who would be responsible to state government. Education would be a civil affair in which the schools would educate the people to serve the state as good citizens. They advocated a state system which would be completely secular. The ideal of a free, universal, and compulsory education for everyone, regardless of wealth, was advocated by a number of the enlightenment scholars. However, this viewpoint did not get into practice until well after the period of Enlightenment.

The aims that really dominated at this time were the religious and humanistic aims of the Reformation movement. The secondary schools of all countries maintained, in general, a combination of religious and humanistic aims. The controversy in education at this time was between those who wished to introduce science and to undertake a study of nature. At this particular time the classical study won out especially in the secondary schools and in the universities.

There were some people who emphasized education for social status. Even John Locke in his book, *Some Thoughts Concerning Education,* had emphasized the education of the gentleman's son as consisting of fulfillment of aims such as virtue, wisdom, breeding, and learning. These terms had particular meaning at that time and Locke's use of the terms are somewhat different than their meanings in the present day. Locke's ideas are important because of their influence in shaping the liberal education of American colonies. Therefore, the meaning of these terms should probably be translated by the modern reader. "Virtue" probably can be equated with the idea of good character achieved in schools through practice in good moral habits. By "wisdom" apparently was meant being careful and skillful in the handling of one's own personal affairs. "Breeding" seemed to be one's social graces, the appropriateness of one's behavior. "Learning" was probably the equivalent to the intellect developed through intellectual training as opposed to the quite common concept of the time of the mere acquisition of facts or knowledge. Though Locke's ideals in this respect reflected the English upper-class values, they did have considerable influence on America.[4]

However, in addition to the upper-class influence of John Locke and others, some of the middle class also tried to bring in subjects which could be more useful to prepare youth for trade or other vocations. One example of this was the development of the private academies, such as Franklin's academy in America. Some of the middle class believed that education should give attention to the "useful" arts for people who were going to enter into commercial or industrial occupations.

The main struggle in education during the nineteenth century was between those favoring the aristocratic, conservative tradition of education, bulwarked by nationalism, capitalism, and conservative religion, and the forces of liberalism, both individualistic and humanitarian, coupled with the movement toward socialism. The developments in France, Germany, and England had the most influence during the nineteenth century on American education. In the later sections on elementary, secondary, and higher education, the influences of the conflicting social philosophies on education is more fully discussed.

Educational Theories of Influential Men.   There were four educational theorists in the eighteenth and early nineteenth centuries who represented the new ideas which were coming into education during the age of Enlightenment. Their ideas were, however, to influence education more in the twentieth century. As a matter of fact, the influence of these men was felt earlier and more strongly in America than in Europe because in America the climate was more favorable to the acceptance of new ideas, whereas in Europe the institutions were resistant to change.

Jean Jacques Rousseau (1712–1778).[5] The views of the main Enlightenment scholars, who were primarily rationalistic in their approach, were strongly challenged during the period of Enlightenment by the doctrine of naturalism set forth most fully and most radically by Rousseau, in his famous book, *Emile*. Rousseau took the point of view that man, as he comes from nature, is good but that he becomes evil by contact with society. Consequently, in developing his theory of learning, he emphasized the necessity for the child to be free to develop according to his own natural impulses. Practically all restrictions and discipline should be withheld and the child should be able to grow up in a setting in which he could engage in the

---

[4] Cf. Butts, *op. cit.*, p. 292.
[5] An excellent edited translation of Emile is William Boyd (ed.). *The Emile of Jean Jacques Rousseau:* Selections. Teachers College, Columbia University, 1956. See also, William Boyd (ed.). *The Minor Writings of Jean Jacques Rousseau.*

activities which interest him. In the case of Emile, this was in a forest or wood. Rousseau's psychological ideas were also related to the doctrine of empiricism with its emphasis upon active contact with the real object, and upon dealing with persons in a face-to-face relationship rather than through books. Rousseau was very much against the use of the scholarly tools of the rationalist movement, mathematics, the languages, and the unquestioning use of books. The key words of Rousseau's educational aims were freedom, growth, interest, and activity. These were all very similar to many of the aspects of the more liberal wing of modern ("progressive") education of the early nineteenth century in America.

Rousseau developed by his own arm-chair, "rational" methods what he called the "natural stages of development" by which the child grows to maturity. These stages were infancy, childhood, the age of reason, and the social stage. Each of these four stages had its own characteristics, and Rousseau implied that the changes from one stage to the other occurred rather suddenly. During the infancy stage, from birth to five, the child was basically involved in the growth of his body, in motor activities, and in the beginnings of some sense perception and feeling. Consequently, the methods of nature must be followed very carefully. The child must be freed from restraint. The body must be hardened by actual participation in nature. The child must become self-dependent. He should act naturally and experience directly the result of his actions. This would enable him to find out for himself that there are some things he can do, some he cannot do. This growth process was not to be accomplished through external compulsion.

In the period of childhood, from ages five to twelve, Rousseau would still continue to avoid books and would expose the child to "real" things. He took a negative, laissez-faire approach to education, "do nothing and allow nothing to be done." Let the child develop as the inner nature demands. Let experience be the only teacher. There should be an emphasis upon games and work with his hands to assist his physical growth—his organs, senses, and other natural powers.

The big change, occurring about age twelve through fifteen, Rousseau called the age of reason. Now education by human agencies should begin. The child must be helped to develop his reason. There should develop the natural desire to learn and the pupil would then recognize the usefulness of knowledge. He recommended the use of the great naturalistic novel, *Robinson Crusoe,* and also the study of such sciences of nature as geography, astronomy, the physical sciences and agriculture, and manual arts and crafts. The factual materials of science was not nearly as important to Rousseau as was its use as an example of the correct way of getting clear and accurate knowledge. The child should really construct his own materials for use in his study.

Finally, in the social stage—from fifteen to twenty—the period of perception of human relations arises. Rousseau held that the sex impulse appears at this time. Reason must check the desires of sex and mold them into socially desirable channels. At this time the child is ready to study the subjects of psychology, sociology, ethics, and natural religion. He should develop an ethical point of view, should strive for spiritual inspiration, and should cultivate the esthetic side of his life. Sex would demand a companion. One of the results of his development from fifteen to twenty would be eventual marriage. Rousseau had quite a different idea for the education of girls. He had a rather low opinion of the feminine sex and thought that women should be educated only to please man and to be subservient to man's demands. In this respect he was not much different from others of his time.

Rousseau's influence on education was certainly constructive in its emphasis on the necessity for studying the child in order to develop an education better adapted to his needs. He was talking, of course, in a period when heavy-handed authority was prevalent in most of man's institutions and absolutism predominated in government. However, from the viewpoint of psychological and other studies of recent times, it is well to recognize that he completely over-emphasizes the role of the individual experience in human development, and almost completely ignored the importance of the culture in which the child lives in developing the quality of "humanness."

Johann Heinrich Pestalozzi (1746–1827). Pestalozzi, unlike Rousseau, was actually a practicing schoolmaster who wrote of his ideas only after he had tried them out. Pestalozzi, though grew up in Switzerland, was descended from Italian ancestors. Most of his work, however, was done in Prussia and France, and his influence was felt strongly in normal schools in the United States in the latter half of the nineteenth century. Pestalozzi worked with a boarding school for boys in which he created an atmosphere similar to that of a home. He maintained a very mild system of discipline and used little coercion to force the boys to learn. However, because of his personality and methods of operating, the school was a success educationally, although a failure financially. He was a very poor business man.

Although Pestalozzi built his learning conceptions upon the basis of empiricism and naturalism, he still retained belief in faculty psychology. In accord with the general attitude of his times, he was quite religious. He felt the child was made up of at least three separate faculties: intellectual, physical, and moral—or what he called the head, the hand, and the heart. Since Pestalozzi felt that religion was primarily emotional, he would talk about morals and religion with respect to the development of the heart, but he intended that educational practices should permit the harmonious development of all these faculties into a well-developed whole personality.

Pestalozzi revealed himself as belonging to the school of naturalism and indicated that the natural instincts of the child should be the basis for motivating learning rather than compulsion from without. He felt that discipline could best be achieved by cooperation and sympathy; thus he did not employ physical punishment, the common method of that day. If physical punishment were not used, he felt the child could develop and could express himself more freely and naturally.

Pestalozzi believed that nature was the basic driving force in all of life; therefore, the teacher should adapt his instruction to the child so that the child's own nature could freely "unfold." As Rousseau, he felt the teacher should use the various stages of the child's own natural development in his educational plans. He believed that knowledge comes through sense impressions, along with the other empirical naturalists of his day. The mind is active and must deal with the sense impressions and build concepts from them. On this basis Pestalozzi set up his object lessons to give full play to the child's natural desire to develop his senses. All instruction, then, began with form, number, and languages. These became the fundamental basis of the child's curriculum.

Intellectual instruction, by and large, proceeds from the known to the unknown, and from the concrete to the abstract. Pestalozzi believed this to be a logical (as well as natural) development but, of course, he failed to realize what many modern psychologists have demonstrated, *i.e.,* that the child learns better by using a "psychological" order rather than by the purely logical structure of the finished scholar.

Friedrich Froebel (1782–1852). Froebel, one of the other great leaders of this time, like Pestalozzi was a practicing teacher. He actually taught with Pestalozzi and later conducted his own schools in Switzerland and in Germany. Froebel was attracted by the sense realism of Pestalozzi, but he expressed himself largely in idealistic philosophy still present in his day. He tended to move away from the concrete toward the development of the whole philosophy of what might be called absolute idealism. In his philosophy, then, he had a definite place for education, and the development of individuals in the world of the absolute.

Froebel thought of the world as being in the process of a kind of conscious cosmic evolution. God is the original, active source of all things and everyone and everything comes from this source. Man rises from nature to his present stage and goes on to develop into a self-conscious adulthood, and eventually into a sensing of oneness with this God or Absolute. The Absolute appears in all nature as a kind of an over-arching spirit on one hand and on the other it is the ultimate goal of all existence. The essence of all things is found in God as his will is carried out on earth. Froebel developed a theory of unity in which everything is a unity in and of itself, but is also a part of a greater unity. This is a kind of a "part–whole" theory. The unity of God's universe is best when all its parts function together, but none of the parts would lose its identity within the larger whole. Froebel's theological theory implied by his absolute idealism is sometimes labeled panentheism (nature as part of God) as compared with pantheism (God is identical with nature).

Froebel was interested in starting education with the small child of three or four years of age. This institution developed for young children he called the kindergarten, taken directly from the German and widely used in English-speaking countries—a "child's garden." The methods by which young children grow and learn are the play activities which are the same for small children as would be occupational activities for adults. Froebel worked out a very systematic variety of play activities which would develop the whole child. Many kinds of objects were designed especially by Froebel for this purpose and all kinds of activities were planned. Each were given a certain kind of symbolic interpretation related to Froebel's idealistic philosophy.

These symbolisms soon began to be lost in the world of American pragmatic realism in which Froebelianism was introduced. Some of the ideas of Froebel did remain and became influential in American education, particularly for preschool and kindergarten education. The things accepted from Froebel were a respect for the uniqueness of each child and the active energies found in his nature. This meant a lessening of the rigid discipline and making the school classroom much less formal. There was emphasis upon actual manipulation of objects and more freedom of action in the classroom. There was group activity in which the child would learn to express himself within the group as a part of the preparation for good social relationships in the school as well as for his later participation in community life.

Froebel, like Rousseau, viewed the child as inherently good and believed that the study of child nature would be a guide to the educative process. Throughout the Froebelian educational philosophy, the words, creativity, activity, growth, freedom, and cooperation are frequent. Through Froebel's influence, the teaching of young children became an important function of the school and the first stage in the well-rounded development of the child's personality in its own right. He was also responsible for some aspects of the "child-centered school," finding expression in the more extreme forms of the progressive movement in the U.S.

Johann Friedrich Herbart (1776–1841). The third important European influence on American education in the nineteenth century was that of the German professor who was both a philosopher and a psychologist, Johann Friedrich Herbart. Whereas both Pestalozzi and Froebel had been active teachers and interested in the elementary school, Herbart was a university professor and was not experienced in teaching other than in universities. His acceptance was found largely among the secondary and university teachers. Herbart made perhaps his most important contribution in his insistence upon the idea of the formative nature of education, especially on the development of morality. Each pupil would come to have a dependable moral character. His second contribution was a very systematic formulation of methods of teaching based upon his idea of how one learns.

Herbart's concept of morality and sound character was not necessarily a religious conception but was related to the question of the "social adjustment" of the individual. Thus, his main stress in the curriculum was on history and literature in order to develop desirable social attitudes. There was even some emphasis toward making the historical and literary subjects the core of the curriculum and to have all other studies correlated with these. In Herbart is found one of the first references to *concentration* and to *correlation*. These terms later on are given emphasis in the introduction of social studies into the American schools. This occurred at a time when Europe was still trying to decide between classics and mathematics on the one hand and sciences on the other. Although Herbart did stress the moral and social aims of education, his analysis of the way in which the aims of education were to be achieved indicated a highly intellectualistic conception. His psychology, developed through arm-chair contemplation rather than through experimentation, is sometimes called associationism.

Herbart stressed the sharpening of the ideas in the student's mind. He even held that emotion and feeling are reducible to ideas in the mind. Herbart had a peculiar picture of the mind based upon an idealistic, dualistic philosophy which would not be acceptable to most modern psychologists. His concept of learning was therefore based upon the processes by which ideas are formed from the sensations and the perceptions of the body and of the mind.

Herbart had a doctrine of interest. One would be interested in a newly perceived idea if he could clearly associate it with ideas which were already a part of his experience. Therefore, in teaching a lesson, the teacher should show clearly the connection between the new idea and the organization of old ideas which had been built up in the learner's mind. This organization of ideas is what Herbart termed the "apperceptive mass."

Although in Herbart's theory there were only four steps to this process of idea formation, in the hands of Herbart's followers they became five steps. These "Herbartian five steps" are as follows:

1. Preparation. The ideas which are found in the conscious or the subconscious are recalled to the student's attention and thus the proper "apperceptive mass" is made ready to receive the new material.

2. Presentation. The new material is presented in concrete form so that there is, first, a sensation and then a perception.

3. Association. The new material is now to be assimilated with the

old. The teacher helps by pointing out the differences and likenesses, connections, and other relationships between the old and new so that the learner can properly relate them.

4. Generalization (or abstraction). The experiences or percepts related to the sense impressions are analyzed and general concepts are formed under the guidance of the teacher so that the individual can move from a low level of perception up to a much higher level of judgment or general principles.

5. Application. Now the general principles are given meaning as a part of life as they are tested out in interpreting specific examples in practical life situations.

All of these steps must be carried out in each day's lesson in contrast with the longer period of "unit teaching" used in the U.S. in the twentieth century.

Although the Herbartian approach may seem to the modern-day student as being very *un*psychological and *un*scientific, at the time when merely reading, memorizing, and reciting were the main methods of teaching, the "scientific," systematic methods of Herbart became popular. They spread, particularly, in the teacher education institutions in the Untied States; and since they provided something which could be taught specifically to teachers, they helped to stimulate the whole process of the development of teacher education. What happened was that in fact the new method did actually revitalize teaching and make it more professional. However, in the hands of some it became extremely formalized and many teachers felt compelled to formulate rigid lesson plans from which they could not deviate.

In the United States, Herbartianism became so prevalent that the National Herbart Society was organized in 1892. However, by 1902 there was sufficient criticism of Herbartianism that the name of the organization was changed in that year to the National Society for the Study of Education (still in existence) and many American educators turned away from adherence to Herbartianism, per se.

Changes in Elementary and Secondary Education. In spite of the fact that during this period of the eighteenth and early nineteenth centuries there were many new formulations of educational aims, and despite the fact that they were quite effectively stated, the elementary schools of Europe remained essentially unchanged. There are some exceptions but, by and large, the schools conceived their basic task to be that of teaching pupils how to read. There was some new interest in teaching students how to write and, in a few cases, how to use numbers as this skill became of greater importance to commercial interests. There was, also, sporadic interest in singing and music. This was partly the result of religious revivalism. Revivalism had stimulated hymn singing, a practice which had not been found in the more formal churches. In some cases, the nationalistic spirit had brought about the singing of patriotic songs in school. However, mathematics and music were still the exception, and the elementary curriculum remained largely unchanged.

Contrary to the fact that throughout the history of education elementary schools usually changed more readily than the secondary, in this period it was secondary education that was a little more responsible to the new trends. In the secondary schools, some progress was made toward introducing studies based upon science and to a lesser extent "practical" studies. In the older, traditional schools, the classical emphases remained quite strong, and the regular elementary school did not accept the new trends.

Some of the rigidly traditional grammar schools had become quite remote from the interests of the students. In some cases, this resulted in considerable rioting among the students or a loss of enrollment. In the latter part of the eighteenth century some reform in English secondary school were instigated. For example, some of Locke's ideas about the education proper to that of a gentleman also began to affect the reform. Some of the upper classes had become more interested in a school which placed more attention upon manners and less upon learning, per se. Consequently, there had to be new schools—such as the academies of England and America and the newer *Realschulen* in Germany—to implement the new science and practical studies.

The great, modern "public" schools (private in the American sense but "publicly" endowed) of England began to take on their present form in the latter half of the eighteenth century. In the academies which had been started by the dissident clergy for their own congregations there began to be some attention paid to "realistic" studies. (Such studies appealed to the middle classes who largely supported these nonconformist schools.) As for those academies which, at the beginning of the eighteenth century, were teaching English language and literature, modern foreign languages, some mathematics, some science, and philosophy along with the classics, by the middle of the century, were teaching science and mathematics. As commercial subjects began to gain prominence, this was the time (1751) that Franklin proposed the academy to replace the Latin grammar school in America.

The secondary schools of Europe existed largely for the upper classes as preparation for entrance to the university or for leadership training. In the nineteenth century the strong hand of classical humanism began to be evident in the secondary schools again. There was a great fight against the idea of introducing scientific or modern subjects. The "best" schools still remained heavily classical. The only country during this period which was able to eliminate the two-track system of parallel elementary and secondary schools was in America where the ladder system was established in mid-nineteenth century.

Status of the Teaching Profession in America. Since the status of teaching in Europe did not change much during this period, the discussion is confined to the status of the profession in the America of the eighteenth century. Because the American schools in the eighteenth century had a strong religious character, the most common qualification among the varying qualifications of different areas was that of religious orthodoxy as defined by the community. The educational qualification would range from mere ability to read to (a few who had) a college education. Usually, those who taught in the secondary schools, the Latin grammar schools or later the academies, were considerably more highly educated than those in the elementary schools. Some of the colonies at times demanded that the teachers be loyal to whatever government was in existence at that particular time. In general, the teachers had to be of good moral character and had to lead a type of strictly moral personal life to be an example for their pupils.

In the early part of this period, in places where the religious control of the school was still important, quite often the church officials were charged with the appointment and, in some cases, the supervision of the teachers. In New England, after the brief period of the theocratic state had passed, civil control without a religious context was predominant. The selectmen from the local town meeting or the school committee took the responsibility for examining, appointing, and supervising the teachers. Sometimes the local minister had the power of veto on the question of orthodoxy. Quite often the citizens would visit the schools and act as judges over the achievements of the pupils on special ceremonies of various kinds. This interest by the patrons of the schools in what was happening in the schools set a precedence for America which manifests itself today in the local operation and control of the schools by the local boards of education (as they are now most commonly called). Such question soon arises when there is strong citizen interest and control in the schools as to what extent the profession itself, eventually much better prepared, has responsibility for the conduct of the schools. It is a question still at issue in modern America.

The pay of teachers during the eighteenth century was quite low because of the difficulty of getting funds for the schools. Although teachers were sometimes paid partly in money, regular pay days were rare and they were often paid in services, such as the so-called "boarding around," in which different families would take turns in providing free board and room. Sometimes they were paid directly with gifts and produce, in lieu of tuition, and some of the communities did exempt them from some of the taxes. It is likely that they were higher in social regard than in their salaries, although the social respect for teachers may have fluctuated a great deal from time to time and place to place. Quite often during this period, both in America and in Europe, teaching school was a part-time job which was performed along with other duties, or as a preliminary to earn some money that would be used later to go to college to get into some other profession that would provide a better income.

Education, Enlightenment, and Freedom. The political and intellectual events which occurred during this period were such that most of the ground work for modern political and intellectual freedom was laid during this period. Even though in France there was not much actual freedom until after the French Revolution, the writings of the *philosophes* such as Diderot, Voltaire, and others were directed toward the idea of freedom of thinking (and teaching).

One of the most important developments of political freedom was the emergence of Parliament in England as the mother of all parliaments. Even when Norman the Conqueror had come to England he was very careful to maintain himself as the king of the Anglo-Saxons without setting up a hereditary monarchy. It was necessary for each new king to receive the approval of the Anglo-Saxon lords. Consequently, from time to time, the ruling kings of England—such as Prince John in the Magna Carta—had to compromise in order to secure the support of the ruling nobles. Great documents of human history, such as the Magna Carta and the Bill of Rights, were gradually extended and, as the middle class became more important, these documents became charters of freedom for them as well as the nobles. Gradually through the Puritan Revolution, the Age of Cromwell, and the Age of the Glorious Revolution (William and Mary), responsibility for making decisions in England came to be placed more and more upon Parliament than on the monarchy. Because of considerable turmoil with the Catholic, the Puritan, and the Anglican factions, finally, in practice, there developed the beginnings of the idea of tolerance or religious freedom even though the laws did not give complete political rights to persons of all religious beliefs for some time to come. There was much more freedom, in general, in terms of the publishing of writings even though, sporadically, there were prosecutions—as in the case of the publisher of Thomas Paine's works.

With the possible exception of the conservative but influential political and social thinker, John Locke, most of the ideas of freedom—which later were to eventuate in our Declaration of Independence, the American Constitution, and the accompanying concepts of American social humanitarianism—came from French thinkers such as Montesquieu and Rousseau. Because of the lack of restrictive institutional precedents, their ideas could be tested here.

Later, these ideas gradually were adopted in England—as its democracy was extended from the middle class to all persons. In France, after the French Revolution, in between the swings of the pendulum, there was also much progress in liberty and democracy. The net result was that by 1830 most of the ground work for later European freedom had been laid, although in many practical instances it had not yet been achieved. The ground work for the Parliament of England—which eventually is to rule England through the Prime Minister and his cabinet—and the ground work for the various French constitutional monarchies and republics over a period of years have been made and have become the example for many other European nations. However, in Germany, after 1871, one of the most rigid of autocracies is to spread from the country of Prussia to all of Germany.

SUMMARY

The eighteenth and early nineteenth centuries represent periods of far-reaching changes throughout all of the western world. Ideas of enlightenment and many of the events which occurred at this time were to affect political and social ideas and result in a tremendous extension of democracy in all of the countries of Europe except Germany. The ideas of enlightenment were to affect education and also change the social ideas which in turn, still later, effect many educational ideas. The sciences continued to develop and created a new educational emphasis which, although slow to be felt did influence the thinking of such men as Rousseau, Pestalozzi, and Froebel.

The forces which were unleashed by Enlightenment had greater effects upon the political climate of the times than on the schools. They were very slow to make themselves felt in educational ideas and practices. Changes in schools were not marked in Europe until the twentieth century. In America, where the institutions of the past had not been so thoroughly established and where democracy was achieved more thoroughly earlier, they were more strongly felt. Even here, however, the methods and general climate of much of the teaching was not affected until late in the nineteenth century.

The development of national states with the accompanying consciousness of national destiny stimulated the countries to set up national school systems. Most of this development was to affect the education in the period which is to follow, but some of the ideas and precedents are laid during this period. With men such as Locke with his "blank tablet" theory and Herbart with his systematic ideas about educational methods, there is a start of systematic theorizing about how educational curriculum and methods should be implemented. These influences are to hold full sway until the experimental psychology of the twentieth century began to react back upon educational thinking and practice. Later, the developing social changes begin to influence education, making additional inroads upon the traditional educational ideas.

SELECTED BIBLIOGRAPHY

Starred items represent books most closely paralleling chapter content.

General Books

Archer, Francis, *Essays and New Atlantis.* New York, Walter J. Black, 1942.

Bowen, Catherine D., *Francis Bacon: The Temper of a Man.* Boston, Little, Brown, 1963.

*Boyd, William, *The History of Western Education,* 7th ed., revised and enlarged by Edmund J. King. New York, Barnes and Noble, 1965.

Butts, R. Freeman, *A Cultural History of Western Education: Its Social and Intellectual Foundations,* 2d ed. New York, McGraw-Hill, 1955.

Crocker, Lester G., *Nature and Cultures Ethical Thought in the French Enlightenment.* Baltimore, Johns Hopkins, 1963.

*Cubberly, Ellwood R., *The History of Education.* New York, Houghton Mifflin, 1920.

*Duggan, Stephen, *A Student's Textbook in the History of Education.* New York, Appleton–Century–Crofts, 1927.

Durant, Will and Ariel, *The Age of Louis XIV: The Story of Civilization.* Vol. 8. New York, Simon and Schuster, 1963.

Durant, Will and Ariel, *The Age of Reason Begins. The Story of Civilization,* Vol. 7. New York, Simon and Schuster, 1961.

Durant, Will and Ariel, *The Age of Voltaire. The Study of Civilization,* Vol. 9. New York, Simon and Schuster, 1965.

*Eby, Frederick, *The Development of Modern Education. In Theory, Organization and Practice,* 2d ed., New York, Prentice-Hall, 1952.

Educational Theories Selected from Emile, Julie, and other writings by Jean Jacques Rousseau. R. L. Archer, ed. Great Neck, New York, Barron's Educational Series, 1864.

Friedrich Froebel and English Education. Evelyn Lawrence, ed. New York, Philosophical Library, 1953.

Frost, S. E. Jr., *Historical and Philosophical Foundations of Western Education.* Columbus, Ohio, Merrill, 1966.

Good, H. G., *A History of Western Education*, 2d ed. New York, Macmillan, 1962.

Heritage of American Education, Richard E. Gross, ed. Boston, Allyn and Bacon, 1962.

John Locke on Education, Peter Gay, ed. New York, Bureau of Publications, Columbia University, 1964.

Krug, Edward A., *Salient Dates in American Education*. New York, Harper & Row, 1966.

Mayer, Frederick, *A History of Educational Thought*, 2d ed. Columbus: Merrill, 1960. Pp. x + 561.

*McNeill, William, *History Handbook of Civilization*. Chicago, University of Chicago Press, 1953.

Meyer, Adolphe E., *An Educational History of the Western World*. New York, McGraw-Hill, 1965.

Middlekauff, Robert, *Ancients and Axioms: Secondary Education in Eighteenth Century New England*. New Haven, Yale University Press, 1963.

*Mulhern, James, *A History of Education: A Social Interpretation*. New York, Ronald, 1959.

Muller, Herbert J., *Freedom in the Western World*. New York, Harper & Row, 1963.

Palmer, Robert R., *The Age of the Democratic Revolution: A Political History of Europe and America, 1760–1800. The Challenge*. Princeton, Princeton University Press, 1959.

*Power, Edward J., *Main Currents in the History of Education*. New York, McGraw-Hill, 1962.

Readings in the History of Education, Ellwood P. Cubberley, ed. New York, Houghton-Mifflin, 1920.

Rousseau, Jean Jacques, *Emile*. New York, Dutton, 1938.

Rusk, Robert R., *The Doctrines of the Great Great Educators*. New York, St. Martin's, 1965.

*Ryan, Patrick J., *Historical Foundations of Public Education in America*. Dubuque, Iowa, William C. Brown, 1965.

Sampson, R. V., *Progress in the Age of Reason: The Seventeenth Century to the Present Day*. Cambridge, Harvard University Press, 1956.

Singer, C., *A Short History of Scientific Ideas to 1900*. Oxford, Clarendon Press, 1959.

Stephen, Sir Leslie, *History of English Thought in the Eighteenth Century*, 3rd ed. New York, Putnam, 1927. Vols. 1 and 2.

The American Enlightenment. The Shaping of the American Experiment and a Free Society, Adrienne Koch, ed. New York, Braziller, 1965.

The Educated Man: Studies in the History of Educational Thought, Paul J. Nash, and others, eds. New York, Wiley, 1965.

Watkins, Frederick, *The Political Tradition of the West: A Study in the Development of Modern Liberalism*. Cambridge, Harvard Press, 1948.

*Weimer, Hermann, *Concise History of Education*. New York, Philosophical Library, 1962.

Wilds, Elmer H. and Lottich, Kenneth V., *The Foundations of Modern Education*, 3d ed. New York, Holt, Rinehart and Winston, 1961.

Pertinent Paperbound Books

Benjamin Franklin on Education, John Hardin Best, ed. Classics in Education, No. 14. New York, Teachers College, Columbia University, 1962.

Burrell, Sidney, *The Main Strands of Development from the Beginnings to the Eighteenth Century. Elements of Western Civilization.* San Francisco, Chandler, 1959.

Cahiers d'histoire Mondiale. The Nineteenth Century World, Guy S. Metroux, and Francais Cronzel, eds. New York, New American Library, 1963.

*Cordasco, Francesco, *A Brief History of Education: A Handbook of Information on Roman, Greek, Medieval, Renaissance, and Modern Educational Practice.* Paterson, New Jersey, Littlefield, Adams, 1963.

Fifty Major Documents of the Nineteenth Century, Louis Leo Snyder, ed. Princeton, Van Nostrand, 1955.

Friedrich Froebel and English Education, Evelyn Lawrence, ed. New York, Philosophical Library, 1953.

*Frost, S. E., Jr., *Essentials of History of Education.* New York, Barron's, 1947.

*Havens, George R., *Age of Ideas: From Reaction to Revolution in Eighteenth Century France.* New York, Holt, 1955.

Hughes, Paul and Fries, Robert F., *Readings in Western Civilization,* Unit 8. Paterson, New Jersey, Littlefield, Adams, 1962.

Kirchner, Walter, *Western Civilization since 1500.* New York, Barnes and Noble, 1958.

The Present Day Relevance of Eighteenth Century Thought, Roger Philip McCutcheon, ed. Washington, D.C., American Council of Learned Societies, 1956.

Ralph, Philip Lee, *The Story of Our Civilization: 10,000 Years of Western Man.* New York, Dutton, 1959.

*Sedillot, Rene, *History of the World in 240 Pages.* New York, New American Library, 1951.

Smith, Preserved, *The Enlightenment: 1687–1776.* New York, Collier Books, 1962.

The Emile of Jean Jacques Rousseau: Selections, William Boyd, ed. Classics in Education, No. 10. New York, Teachers College, Columbia University, 1962.

The Minor Educational Writings of Jean Jacques Rousseau, William Boyd, ed. New York, Columbia Teachers College, 1962.

The New England Primer, Paul Leicester Ford, ed. Classics in Education, No. 13. New York, Teachers College, Columbia University, 1962.

SELECTED FILMS

Age of Absolute Monarchs in Europe, The (Coronet)   (13½ min.)
   After a brief review of absolute rule by ancient kings and emperors, this film sets forth the concepts of absolute rule by divine right in the

words of James I of England and by re-enactments of the court of Louis XIV. The seventy-two year reign of the "Great Monarch" amid the splendor of Versailles carried to its heights the political philosophy that shaped Europe's destiny in the late sixteenth and seventeenth centuries.

Age of Enlightenment in Europe, The (Coronet)   (13½ min.)

Applying science to the physical world, Copernicus, Kepler, Galileo, and Newton demonstrated that the universe operates according to natural laws which could be discovered by reason. Applying reason to the affairs of man, Locke, Montesquieu, Voltaire, Rousseau, and Diderot put forth ideas of democracy, freedom, and equality. These ideas were translated into action as the American and French Revolutions.

French Revolution, The (Coronet)   (16 min.)

The controversial issues, great personalities, and turbulent events leading to and through the French Revolution.

Napoleonic Era, The (Coronet)   (13½ min.)

A retired army officer who served with Napoleon recalls the momentous Napoleonic Era of 1796–1815 and its effects upon France and Europe.

9

Development of the National System of Education (*c.* 1830–*c.* 1930)

In the period from 1830 to roughly 1930, the development of most of the national systems of education in the Western world took place. In the first part of this chapter, the social and political changes that were taking place in western Europe and in the United States during this period are discussed. First, the further development of nationalism is described; second, the extension of American democracy with some look also at the development of democracy in western Europe; and third, the impact of the industrial revolution and the rise of capitalism, and the effects of these on society and thus on the educational systems. In the second part of this chapter, the details of the development of the national systems are set forth.

Development of Nationalism in Europe and America. As has been discussed, there had been some trend toward nationalism, particularly during the Reformation and Enlightenment periods. This trend moved rapidly toward an even greater development of nationalism in the nineteenth century. The nation–state became without question the supreme unit of the political authority in the modern Western world. This is in contrast with the situation prevailing in the medieval and the feudal world. Central to the ideology of nationalism was the concept of national sovereignty, recognized in the Treaty of Westphalia. This became even stronger during the period of the nineteenth century. The sovereign state was assumed to be completely independent of any kind of authority that originated anywhere outside of its own borders. This state was held to be sovereign regardless of its internal nature otherwise. It might be an absolute monarchy, it might be a constitutional monarchy with a parliament, or it might be a republic. In any case, the nation–state was conceived to be a completely supreme power which had its right to determine its own internal arrangements, its own form of government, and its own boundaries (if it could get by with it), and to treat its people as it chose as long as it did not oppress the national minorities of another country.

With the rise of political nationalism, the national states tried to develop, in many cases appropriately, the idea of a national culture. Not only did the Frenchman belong to the French political state, but it was felt that there was something unique about being a Frenchman and, therefore, definitely being superior to other nationalities. Each of the other nationalities, such as the English, the Germans, the Italians, the Dutch, or the Czechs, felt the same way about their own culture. In every case, the nationality laid claim to having a common history, in most cases a common language and common customs and, in quite a number of cases, unique religious, artistic, and other institutional forms of life. Religious commonality of culture was often shared by the several differing religious beliefs within the state—at least by the end of the nineteenth century.

In cases where the political boundary of the state did not coincide with the lines of cultural nationality, every effort was made to achieve this. This course led to a great number of disputes concerning the location of such cultural boundaries. Appeal was frequently made to history as to which nationality this cultural history had belonged. In many cases cultural history depended on how far back history was considered. Though these contentions were a source of much friction between the nation–states, one of the results was to foster within people a strong sense of love for their state and to build pride in their own particular national culture.

During much of the period of the nineteenth century, nationalistic development was somewhat liberal. It enabled some people who had been oppressed to gain their freedom from foreign groups and to achieve their own political self-determination. In fact, some of the revolutions which occurred during this period were undertaken by groups who were trying to turn their cultural unity into a political unity among themselves or with similar cultural groups outside of their current political status.

The Development of Democracy in the United States and Europe.   In the nineteenth century, the social aspects (as shown particularly in the political and economic phases) began to overshadow other elements—such as religion—and became the center of the energies and the source of dynamic for the people of the United States and, to a lesser extent, of Europe. During the nineteenth century, the United States became largely a secular society. Religious institutions still played a strong part, particularly in the private lives of people, but no longer did they play the leading role with regard to motives and goals. These became much more secular. There was, however, still a struggle between the religious-centered and the secular aspect of man's thinking. Illustrative of this was the conflict among the various political and religious authorities for the political and religious control of schools and colleges and, thus, the means of education. Nevertheless, the main trends in America, during this period, were the growth of political democracy, the expanding role of government (even in the nineteenth century), and the growth of nationalistic patriotism. These contributed to a growing acceptance of the idea of public education and universal schooling despite opposition to public education from some groups.

The Extension of American Democracy. Even though the American constitution and the spirit of the Declaration of Independence had been favorable toward democracy, in many respects this concept had not yet matured in the early periods of the American republic. Around 1830 with the development of Jacksonian democracy and the extension of the ballot to more and more elements of the population, that is, universal manhood suffrage, a great step forward in democratic practices was gained. This extension was not only in the pure machinery of voting participation, it was also a point of view, or set of values, which transferred to other institutions and social customs. The distinction of dress between the classes had been eliminated between 1820 and 1830. The Jacksonian concept of the worthwhileness of the common man and the extreme emphasis toward equalitarianism became quite prevalent in the period just before the Civil War and has influenced American thinking, even to the present day.

Although America was to remain predominantly a Protestant society during the nineteenth century, the influence of Protestantism in our government and public affairs was considerably less important at the end of the century than it had been at the beginning. The principle of liberty of conscience and the separation of state had been achieved by the late eighteenth and early nineteenth centuries. However, it is well to note that a conservative, philosophical outlook was relatively predominant in the United States during the nineteenth century and went hand-in-hand with conservative political-economic ideas. Consequently, there was not so much a conflict involved here as there was a change of emphasis and a recentering of the value systems of the people.

This was a period of gradual growth in the strength and vitality of the churches in America. Most modern-day Americans feel, regardless of their religious backgrounds, that the principles of religious freedom and the separation of the church and state as embodied in the first amendment of the American Constitution and in the Bill of Rights of many state constitutions as they evolved, was largely responsible for this growth. As new states came into the Union during the nineteenth century, the principles of the freedom of religious conscience and the separation of church and state were adopted. In particular, this involved denying the use of public funds to support one or any number of churches (multiple establishment) and forbidding sectarian instruction in public schools. Up to 1876, this was done voluntarily in line with the leadership which had been established by some of the early colonies, notably Pennsylvania, New Jersey, and North Carolina. After 1876, in the Enabling Act by which new states were admitted, Congress began to stipulate that the states must adopt irrevocable ordinances implementing a policy of separation of church and state. By the end of the century Americans, by and large, had come closer to an agreement on these principles than at any time earlier in their history. This was quite in contrast to European developments where education was becoming affiliated (for example, in Germany and Italy) more closely with the established churches. (It is true that there was a secularization of the school system in France and perhaps no great change occurred during this time in England.) These principles of separation of church and state and of religious freedom in the United States have been reiterated by law and by court decisions time and time again. These issues are, of course, to be raised again at numerous times throughout the twentieth century with the United States Supreme Court finally having to make certain decisions clarifying the issues.

The Industrial Revolution and the Rise of Capitalism.   After the American Revolution and particularly after the War of 1812, there was a considerable change in the economic system basic to America. The frontier was still largely an agricultural economy. However, along the eastern seaboard there were changes from an agrarian to a commercial society and, later on, to finance-controlled capitalistic enterprises. The industrial revolution which had started in England in the latter part of the eighteenth century moved to America by the 1830's, particularly in the New England textile mills. A conflict between the agricultural (which did dominate the nation for some time) and the industrial interests played a very important part in the political and economic life of the American nation. Paralleling the industrial changes was the growth of city life as the people came in to live close to the factories. There was an increase in the amount and rapidity of communication and transportation. The development of railroads and an extensive canal system occurred at about the same time, 1828.

In the early part of the nineteenth century the prevailing economic system was laissez-faire capitalism involving mostly small business enterprises. Adam Smith had published his *Wealth of Nations* in 1776. The concept of economic laissez-faire set forth in his book came at a time when the American people had few precedents to guide them. Consequently, the new country probably more nearly achieved a laissez-faire economy than was ever achieved at any other time in the world's history. The basic principles of laissez-faire economics were: private property, profit motive, free competition, flexible prices, and little or no government interference with business. Under this system businesses would compete freely with each other. This would keep the quality up and the prices down. The cost of labor would be kept down since there would be competition for the available jobs. But on the other hand, payment of wages for labor would have to be high enough to enable the industrial plants to get sufficient labor. In other words, the system would be self-regulating.

Many things happened very quickly to break down the laissez-faire system to some extent even early in the nineteenth century. Protective tariff laws were established and the free lands of the west were opened to homesteading. In the meantime, however, the development of technology caused the industrial strength in America to increase greatly, even before the Civil War. Further, the idea of corporation capitalism enabled American business, now successful, to expand. The United States became more and more highly industrialized in the period from the Civil War up to 1929. Problems began to develop when these enterprises became successively larger corporations, many of them combining into large monopolies or trusts. These large monopolistic trusts caused a breakdown in the economic laissez-faire since free competition was no longer possible. Thus, the first important break in the laissez-faire economic system came out of the success of the system itself, resulting from the expansion of big business into monopolies dominated by a few large companies. Continuing situations, moreover, arose in such areas as the gas, electric, and telephone industries which led to "natural" monopolies. For example, it is not economically feasible to have competing gas lines supply the houses down the same street. Consequently, the state had to step in to set up public utilities boards to set rates, and these natural monopolies were taken out from under the ordinary laws of competition. Furthermore, some other private enterprises, such as railroads in many towns without competition, had to have their rates set by the Interstate Commerce Commission. Otherwise, there would be no limit as to what rates they could charge in towns in which there were no competing railroad lines. All this led to an increase in the participation of government in the economic system and, thus, to a further partial breakdown of the laissez-faire system.

The industrialization process and other resulting changes did not greatly affect the educational system until World War I. By this time there was a beginning of interest in the teaching of vocational skills.

With the development of the strength of capitalistic enterprises, there was the growth of organized labor. With the increase of population and the influx of immigrants there was an urgent need to expand the schools and, particularly, to develop schools to train for citizenship and patriotism in the areas of the city into which large numbers of immigrants were moving.

In 1893 the government announced that there was no longer a frontier. The frontier was defined as an area in which there were more than two but less than six persons per square mile. The frontier is shown by Turner in his "frontier thesis" to have had a great effect upon the American ideas and ideals of this period. It had stimulated the ideals of individualism and equality to a greater degree in the United States than in any other country in the world because it always gave the person who might be crowded out of the economic system a place to go—i.e., to the frontier where he could find free land. It helped to make these ideals a part of the American dream of opportunity for all, so that everyone could rise as high as he wished. But as we have seen, even before the end of the century, this was no longer true in fact, and soon people began to realize that this dream of unlimited opportunity was not as likely to be achieved as once it had been. The spread of monopoly, the mass-production factory system, the growing concentration of wealth and, eventually, the virtual control of the government during the last decade of the nineteenth century by wealthy interests, led to a lack of realization of the ideal of equality.

Because of the bad conditions (low wages, long hours, and unsatisfactory living arrangements) that arose in industrial towns, labor was beginning to organize in order to defend itself. It was here as elsewhere a protest and reaction against the widespread, uncritical acceptance of capitalism. Even at the beginning of the nineteenth century, the workers and craftsmen, who before this time had been more or less independent workers, lost their status as they were forced to compete for jobs. Wages were forced down and craftsmen lost their independence. Soon they began to organize into trade and craft unions in order to improve their bargaining power with employers. These unions were in contrast to the guilds, which had been organizations of master craftsmen who controlled, by and large, their own shops.

There was at this time a combination of the social humanitarianism arising out of France, the transcendentalism of Germany, and the romantic ideals of England into which was forged a kind of new humanitarianism that wanted to strike out to improve social conditions. During the period of the nineteenth century, a great number of humanitarian societies were established for a wide variety of purposes, among them, the prevention of poverty, the abolition of slavery, the softening of criminal codes, and the improvement of conditions in prisons. Some other aims were served that were not so closely related to economics, such as women's rights, temperance, and help to handicapped persons.

Shortly after 1920, America had, as far as her technology and economic systems were concerned, entered an age of abundance. There was a surplus of food and goods in almost all areas. The economic system, of course, was to reach a height in 1929 and then to suffer a serious depression.

While all of the industrial and political changes were taking place in America, changes were taking place in Europe as well. It was a period largely of conservatism and moderation. Although in some of the countries steady progress toward democracy was made, in others the tendency was in the opposite direction. The early period from 1830 to 1848 is sometimes called the bourgeois era. During this period there were revolutions, bloody and otherwise. One such revolution came in 1848 in Germany and resulted in the repression of liberty. After the Franco-Prussian War in 1870 an even more severe repression of democratic liberties in Prussia came about. In order to prevent further uprising, the German states developed paternalistic care for their citizens that was more like that of a socialized state, for example, unemployment insurance and pensions.

In England there was steady progress under the reign of Queen Victoria toward the development of the Parliament as an important source of government. Prime ministers became responsible to Parliament although the Queen continued to play an important role until her death. Following the death of Queen Victoria, the British Prime Minister, chosen by the parliamentary majority, became supreme in the constitutional monarchy of England. The Parliament, however, at the turn of the century was still largely representative of the middle class. It wasn't until around World War I that the lower classes became enfranchised and able to exercise influence. Eventually a labor (or socialist) government was set up under Ramsey McDonald.

In the latter part of this period the unrest under the Russian Czar and the chaos of World War I lead in 1918 to a communist revolution in Russia. This event was to have many repercussions and cause many political power struggles in the world even down to the present time. It had little effect, however, on western Europe until after the period 1930.

By and large, keeping in mind that the action was not always equal to the thought, the period of the nineteenth century in western Europe and in America was a period of political liberalism. Liberalism was to reach its height in the period before World War I and then to enter a twilight period after 1930. Reaction against democracy, out of conditions resulting from World War I, came to Italy first and later in an even more repressive form in Germany. From the ideas of Karl Marx—developed with respect to economic conditions among the laboring people of France, Germany, and England in the middle of the nineteenth century— came the twentieth century revolutionary ideas that were to cause the reactions against democracy which occurred in the Communist countries after 1919.

Looking back, it was a period of rather steady but unspectacular progress toward greater democracy in most of the countries, except Russia, Italy, and Germany, although there were swings of pendulum back and forth during this period. It was a period of rapid industrialization in most of the countries of the Western world, a period of the growth of cities, a period of great increase in technology and in the quantity of manufactured goods. It was a period when, due to increased population, education, and the printing presses, a greater proportion of the people were able to read, to think, and to agitate. It was a period of the development of large businesses, a great extension and improvement in the size of government (even by 1929 the government in Washington had expanded greatly over any previous time), and a period of increase in the size and influence of the labor movement. The world had entered into the age of abundance, or at least was close to the threshold of it, but it was not yet able to fully utilize this potential. Therefore, it was to fall into the extremely difficult economic situation, the Depression of 1929–1933.

EDUCATION IN THE NINETEENTH CENTURY

In the vast majority of schools in Europe during the nineteenth century, the changes were very minor in spite of the work of the reformers mentioned in an earlier section. Most teachers did not hear about these reforms during—let alone for some time after—their life-times and, if they did, they did not usually take seriously any of their suggestions. Most of the changes in European education were to come largely in the twentieth century, perhaps more during the third and fourth decades than any other time up to the most recent current decade. Even in the United States the influence of these reformers was not widely felt until the latter part of the nineteenth century. However, there were other forces in America, such as the extension of democracy and of the ideas of Jacksonian equalitarianism, which were influential in changing the school to some extent—perhaps more influential than any theorists were at this time or would be later.

Development of the American Common Schools. The school system in the United States has been developed by each state separately and there are wide variations among the different states. The nineteenth century was the formative period for the American concept of education to the extent that it differed considerably from that of Europe of the same period. The distinctive difference began to appear in fairly clear outlines in the mid-nineteenth century. In most of the European countries during this period, a "dual" system of schools was maintained to continue the separation between the upper and lower classes. However, the United States, which had abolished its class system in theory (although not completely in practice), had launched a system of education, by design at least, to make available equality of opportunity. One could go as far as his talents could take him. This opportunity was to be provided through free education made available to all and even a compulsory attendance law to see to it that everyone could take advantage of it. This educational system was to be extended eventually from the lowest levels on through the university.

This concept is sometimes called the "ladder" system of education. By this it is meant (as it did also to Comenius) that the next rung of each educational institution would be available without restrictions or handicaps except the limitations in the desire and ability of the student to continue. This was the conception of a universal, free, public, compulsory and, largely, co-educational school system contrasted with a restrictive European system where there were still separate schools for the upper classes. Education became free for the lower classes in the elementary school but there was tuition for the upper classes in their private schools. Furthermore, the practice of separate schools for boys and girls was widespread throughout Europe.

Another important contrast between American and European education lay with respect to the teaching of religion. Since America had set about to disestablish the church in order to insure religious freedom, the American ideal of nonsectarian education emerged quite rapidly during the early part of this period. This is quite in contrast to the European practice which still permitted the state church, or at least the established religion, to exercise a very important control over the schools, even those operated directly by the state.

The American principle of a neutral school system which could not teach sectarian doctrines, of course, entailed a very bitter struggle. In the early part of the nineteenth century, there were many cases in which public funds had been alloted to private religious schools. However, some people saw a potential danger in this system with respect to religious freedom and an inconsistency with the doctrine of separation of church and state (first amendment). Eventually, however, the policy of not permitting money from taxes to be used for privately owned schools and not permitting sectarian religious doctrines to be taught to youngsters in the public schools won out, although it was not consistently practiced.

The battle to make the public schools available and free to all children was bitterly fought. Going back to the period of the seventeenth century in Massachusetts, many laws had been passed requiring the political districts, townships, or the school district to set up schools adequate to take care of children. However, during this early period, tuition was charged or other means were used to raise the money needed. In order to get all children to attend schools, laws were eventually passed which permitted the "pauper" children (charity cases) to attend schools. There were other boys and girls who were not "paupers" but who could not afford to pay the tuition rates required by the school and therefore attended very little.

This battle to pass laws to require each county or school district to set up tax-supported, free schools was long and bitter. There were cries of socialism (and even atheism) against those people who would use one man's money to educate other people's children. However, gradually and slowly the principle of permitting (or even requiring) local districts to tax themselves for the purposes of providing free education to all children, wealthy or poor, began to win out. It is true that laws did establish free education in theory, if not actually in practice in some states, but they were not completely enforced or carried out in all districts even in the twentieth century.

It was not sufficient to provide a public school and provide the funds for boys and girls to attend free. It was not sufficient to present sectarian religious instruction so that there would be no reason why boys and girls of all kinds of faith could not attend. There still had to be provisions made to see that the boys and girls did take advantage of it, or to require their parents to see that they took advantage of it. Furthermore, there was a great influx of immigrants from nearly every country of the world in the nineteenth century, and it was necessary to help assimilate them into our culture. Furthermore, they tended to congregate in isolated groups in the large cities, and were not too willing to go to the schools provided because of the language handicap. The schools by law were required to provide the classrooms and teachers in order to take care of this group but the problem was to get them into the schools.

The voluntary measures of trying to get the youngsters into the schools did not work well. Some of the parents were old-world-oriented enough to send their children to work at an early age. Consequently, as a part of the movement to abolish child labor and for other sound reasons, compulsory school attendance legislation began to appear in the state legislatures. The first such compulsory attendance law was passed in Massachusetts in 1852 (in contradistinction with compulsory education laws of 1647), and most other states had passed some laws by 1900. Some of these early laws were not very restrictive, only permitting or requiring attendance for two or three years and for a few months each year. But, as time went on, these laws required a more lengthy attendance and enforcement was more strict. By 1918 every state in the union had some form of compulsory attendance law.

One of the problems which emerged even more sharply as soon as there was compulsory attendance was the problem of whether any kind of religious instruction could be given. Because of the problem of the freedom to attend private, religious schools, it became necessary to permit compliance to the law to be taken care of by attendance at private schools as well as public ones (Oregon case, 1925). It was not until around 1850 that more students were enrolled in public schools than in private or religious ones. After this date, the public schools continued to expand very rapidly. Situations arose as to whether or not money should be given to the private schools and as to whether or not there was any attempt to restrict the activities of the private schools for those who chose them. In each case the answer was that the public schools were to remain completely secular, that is, nonsectarian, and the private and religious schools were to receive no public money.

The main purposes of the elementary schools of the nineteenth century was to teach patriotism and citizenship, to develop good moral character, and to teach the three "R's." These aims loomed more important than any others which were set forth during this time, although some of the other newer aims were beginning to be considered. During the nineteenth century, in spite of the great progress which was made toward democracy and toward humanitarianism outside the school, it was still a period of very strong emphasis upon corporal discipline, that is, frequent recourse to whipping the child and punishing him by other physical means to keep him in line. The democratic idea of teaching the child to think for himself had not permeated the school. Such ideas were quite prevalent socially in the country but not in the schools.

Some of the newer ideas which had been fostered by Pestalozzi, Froebel, and Herbart did eventually arrive on the American shores. Pestalozzianism invaded the normal schools which were started around 1830, but it did not get very far into the school systems themselves. The ideas of Froebel came here with the kindergarten largely through the German immigrants of Milwaukee, St. Louis, and Cincinnati. Through this new institution his ideas did permeate perhaps more so than any others at this early period. The ideas of Herbart came to America with those Americans who went to Germany to study for their Ph.D. degrees in the latter half of the nineteenth century and were largely applied with some adaptations to secondary school teaching. The work of the McMurry brothers who first brought Herbart's ideas to American schools, and the further adaptation of the Herbartism ideas by Morrison of Chicago, did bring about some improvement in the organization of the teaching materials at the secondary level.

There were some new methods that were developed to improve the teaching of the three "R's." There was some attention to nature study and the use of concrete objects which arose partly out of the influx of the ideas of Pestalozzi and Froebel. There were some "practical" subjects introduced into the schools such as geography, drawing, music, home economics, and the industrial arts. There were some teachers who began to try to organize their subject matter on a psychological rather than logical basis in order to meet the learning needs of the students. There were some teachers who were enthusiastic and well trained in normal schools and who thereby brought about better learning. There were other teachers who, even with these new ideas, still carried on their classes in a very formal way. The vast majority of teachers in America, just as in Europe, only dimly knew about the work of Pestalozzi, Froebel, and Herbart. It was not until after 1900 that there was a decided improvement in the teacher education programs in the various states and even then the changes in teaching methods were very slow to trickle down to the classroom of the ordinary teacher.

The way in which the elementary school during this period actually did change was as follows. There was an expansion in the kinds of subject matter taught. At first, there had been the rather narrow three "R's" of the dame schools and of the reading and writing schools. These were later expanded to include some of the subjects which had been taught previously in academies and in the early high schools. One of these was an insistance upon the study of the English language more fully as a language skill in addition to the ability to read and write. Included, of course, in the language study was the emphasis on spelling and on the rules of grammar.

The work in arithmetic came into the elementary school later and became even more prominent because many teachers began to believe that it did have a strong disciplinary as well as a practical purpose. By and large the teachers gave the students difficult problems and told them how to solve them by following the appropriate rules. If the student made a mistake the teacher corrected the answer. There was very little effort made to teach the boys and girls the reason or rationale behind the rules. Nature study was somewhat developed because of the influence of the object lessons of Pestalozzi. But nature study or science skills played a very small part in this period, even though the latter part of the nineteenth century was a period of tremendous scientific development following the publication of Darwin's theory of evolution.

There were, of course, some social studies: largely, geography and American history. The study of government, civics, and political problems in some states came in as early as 1830, although they did not play a very important role until the nineteenth century. Some of the elementary schools did give attention to drawing, music, and physical education, but this work was sporadic and again did not play an important role until the nineteenth century.

Such is the story of the common school, the elementary school, to roughly around 1930.

The Development of American Secondary Education. The colonial Latin grammar schools had been patterned after the secondary schools of Europe and had become the predominant secondary school in America until about the end of the eighteenth century. Then at the beginning of the nineteenth century the academy founded by Franklin (as indicated in the preceding chapter) became the most common of the secondary schools. Academies were almost entirely private and many of them were sectarian. There were still some Latin grammar schools in New England, sponsored largely by the towns.

The secondary schools took boys and girls around 10 to 12 years of age and the course was around 4 to 6 years in length. The academies stressed English as well as foreign languages and most of them had a preparatory department, much like their counterparts in Europe, to give the children a foundation upon which to predicate their entry of the academy proper. Thus, there was in this start, a strong possibility that there might have developed in America a dual school system similar to that in European countries.

As noted earlier, however, around the 1820's there were forces in the United States, possibly the same forces involved in the Jacksonian political democracy, that began to demand a type of secondary school which would give at public expense the kind of education helpful to youngsters who had finished the elementary schools. It was the public high school that was designed to meet this demand and eventually it was to overcome the undemocratic class character of the academies. The laboring classes did not wish to go on to college and could not afford to do so. Consequently, they did not want the college preparatory kind of high school which the Latin Grammar School had been, and which even the academy came to be.

Therefore, in Boston in 1821 a school called the English Classical School was established which admitted boys 12 years of age or over who had finished the elementary school and did not plan to go to college. This school was at first a school which stressed English, mathematics, and other studies of a more practical nature. In 1824, its name was changed to the English High School. It eventually became a four-year institution. It is not known where the word "high school" came from, although it is thought by some authorities to have come from the words used in Scotland to refer to the secondary schools in that country. In 1827, Massachusetts became the first state to pass a law requiring the towns to establish high schools for their boys and girls. However, at this time these high schools were not free of tuition and the law was not implemented completely at this time.

These high schools began to grow rapidly and by 1860 there were probably over three hundred of them. Most of them were in the three states of Massachusetts, New York, and Ohio. After 1860 the number of high schools expanded even more rapidly. By 1900 there were probably

6,000 public high schools and these enrolled over 80 percent of all secondary age students. The high school, originally conceived as a non-college preparatory institution, now became a 4-year coeducational institution and it did prepare students for college as well as directly for business or commerce. As a matter of fact, in the period after the Civil War and up to the early part of the twentieth century, its curriculum had gradually become strongly college preparatory.[1] Before 1870 it had not been clearly established as to whether or not the public high school was legally part of the common school system or not. It had been established by the school systems or in some cases by different boards or under different auspices than the elementary schools. Many taxpayer groups opposed them very strongly; furthermore, the groups that had a vested interest in the private academies also opposed them. In the great depression of 1873 the industrialists attacked the idea of public secondary education because of the potentially great expense involved. They felt that all the tax would eventually fall upon them. These industrialists, who wielded a great deal of power in the state and national governments at this time, wanted the school boards to retrench in their educational budget. Furthermore, they were particularly opposed to the free public high schools.

The school boards were uncertain whether or not they had the right to levy taxes to support public high schools. Levying taxes for the common elementary schools was clearly legal but they did not know whether it was legal to do so for high schools. Therefore, a number of law suits were started in order to try to determine the legality of spending common school money for the public high schools.

The most famous of these decisions was the Kalamazoo case which became a precedent for other cases. This case was decided by the Supreme Court of Michigan in 1874, with Justice Cooley giving the decision. The right of the school board to levy taxes for the public high school was affirmed. The reasoning involved was as follows: The common schools had been provided through local taxes. Many states had already set up the free or nominal charges for tuition in the large state universities. It seems reasonably clear then that there ought to be an authority for establishing a free high school and for levying taxes for its support. Otherwise, there would be no way for graduates of the elementary schools to prepare for the state universities.

With the clearing up of the legal basis, local boards were then free to establish high schools when demands arose. State legislatures now passed laws encouraging local boards to proceed and, in some cases, they even offered state aid to the areas that established high schools. Finally state laws were passed, as had happened in the case of the elementary

[1] Compare with Theodore R. Sizer. *Secondary Schools at the Turn of the Century* (New Haven, Yale University Press, 1964).

schools, requiring local districts to establish high schools. By 1900 high schools were so widely established that they were available to practically every youngster in the United States as a continuation of the elementary school and as a part of the "ladder" system of education.

Let us, now, examine some of the shifting aims and purposes and the curriculum of secondary education. At the beginning of the nineteenth century the academy still was the predominate secondary school and offered (at least) a classical course for college preparation and an English course of study for noncollege purposes. But as time went on the academies put greater and greater stress upon the classical division and very little emphasis upon the practical curriculum.

The original intention of the high school had been to offer the practical nonpreparatory studies. Because it was free, however, and because it began to expand rapidly, it also began to include the college preparatory courses for those youngsters who wanted to continue on to college. Therefore, the high schools contained several types of parallel courses—the classical courses for college preparation, English-historical courses, scientific courses, business courses, technical courses, and home economic courses. All of these courses were for certain distinct practical purposes and in a sense were in conflict with the religious–humanistic aims which had dominated secondary education in Europe and the Latin grammar schools and the academies in the United States.

These changes in the secondary schools reflected the changes arising in society at that same time. American society was becoming much more secular. Nationalism, technology, the development of science and industry, and the expansion of the capitalistic system were taking more and more of our energies as opposed to the prior emphasis on the religious or other-worldly traditions. Along with these secular forces was the development of the democratic trends, which implied that all American youth ought to have an opportunity to succeed. These opportunities being for girls, as well as boys, thus opened up education to girls, still a very limited practice in other countries of the world at this time. Although the opening of all occupations to women was to come later, there was an increase in the mid-nineteenth century toward accepting women in some types of work, particularly in teaching. When the girls were admitted to the American elementary and high schools, it was on a coeducational basis. Surprisingly enough, some of the objections to having girls in school resembled those objections, at a later period, to the giving of education to certain minority groups. The girls, when they were given the opportunity, did go to school in large numbers and tended to excel over the boys in respect to their scholastic achievements. In recent years the percentage of retention of girls in school and the level of achievement of girls in school have both tended to exceed those of boys.

Not only was there an expansion in the emphasis of the secondary school, there was also a rapid increase in the number of courses available. This raised the question as to how the curriculum could be set up. There were too many courses to take all of them. The child at first could choose from the many different curricula of studies but he could not choose subjects within this chosen curricula. This is still true largely in the European secondary school. But as time went on, starting about 1890 with the elective system in college, there began to develop the principle of permititng some electives in high school until finally the "constants with electives" system was provided. This permitted a great deal of flexibility with respect to courses which boys and girls could pursue. Their program could be worked out with relation to their particular needs and abilities much more readily than when there was a closely prescribed course of studies.

European Developments. As these things were happening in the United States there were changes occurring in the educational systems of Europe. Although these changes were not as great as those that occurred in the United States during this period, they were still significant.

There had existed in America and in some of the English communities philanthropic, or charity, schools for the people of the lower classes. The idea that the education of the poor is a form of charity rather than a public service was prevalent in America until after the so-called free education of "pauper" children was done away with and laws for universal free education were passed in the various states around the 1830's. But this belief persisted in England until the passage of the first public school law in 1870. It is true that the British government did appropriate some money in 1833 to be given to those private groups that had been already operating schools for elementary education. These private schools were open to all persons although there was some cost to the pupils. It was not free education. Also starting in the late eighteenth century and continuing through the nineteenth was the Sunday School movement which had started as a one-day school for working children to teach them the fundamentals. Also, the so-called infant schools, that is, education between the ages of three and seven, started at this time. These eventually developed into the present nursery school. These schools started in England and in Scotland and eventually spread to the United States. There was some development of industrial education and manual training classes in England during this time but this movement, like the so-called manual training movement in America, never really caught on.

One of the most significant of the European developments occurred in the country of Prussia. With the unification of Germany in 1871, the Prussian system became the basis for the German educational system. Prussian education was completely under the centralized control of the state but it did provide for religious education in cooperation with the church. It was entirely a class education with two kinds of schools, the so-called *Volkschule,* or folk school, for the masses, and secondary education for the upper class. In the secondary schools of Prussia there were two types: first, the *Gymnasium,* or classical schools, named from the similar schools in ancient Greece which had developed out of the gymnasia, originally places of physical exercise; second, was the *Realschule* which emphasized the study of modern languages. Since it was impossible for the new subjects to break into the classical schools (*Gymnasium*) in Germany, the Germans found it necessary to set up completely new schools each time there was a reason for trying to modify the secondary school curriculum. Not until quite recently has there been any attempt in Germany to bring all the curricula into one school, the *Einheitschule.* This movement toward comprehensive schools enrolling all pupils has become characteristic of the mid-twentieth century in France, Germany, and Italy as it had in the United States much earlier.

After the French Revolution, there were some reforms made in the French system of education. It had been Napoleon's purpose to try to indoctrinate his subjects in French citizenship and culture. For this purpose he established strong centralized control over the schools. The elementary schools were placed under the central authority which he called Imperial University. He established two kinds of secondary schools, one directly run by the state called the *lycées* and the municipal schools, the *collèges.* These two types existed down to the French school reforms in the early 1900's. In 1833 a law was passed to establish a national system of elementary education. This required each commune, the smallest political subdivision, to support a lower primary school and every department (province) to support a normal school. The elementary teachers did not have much status or freedom. They were directly under the school of the Ministry of Education. The elementary education curriculum was highly controlled from the central ministry. The church thus lost control of any part of the educational system and it became almost completely secular. Although the amount of control by the church in France has varied somewhat over the years, at the present time the national schools do not have any religious teaching. However, there has been at times some recognition and occasionally some money given to the schools. In France as in the case of the other countries there were, up to World War I, really two educational systems, elementary education for one set of children and secondary education for another. After World War I, France established *l'école unique.* This was universal elementary schooling and all pupils were required to attend this same school. Then, only a few people would be admitted to the secondary school upon the passing of an intensive examination at about age eleven or twelve. Students admitted to the secondary school were not given free tuition until after 1930. Before that time the children of poor people could not afford to attend the secondary schools even though they might have been able to pass the examination. Those pupils not admitted to secondary schools could continue in elementary school until they dropped out. This school led nowhere and instruction was very inferior after the selected secondary pupils left. There were some advances in vocational and technical education but this was still very much de-emphasized. The main emphasis of the French schools was upon the French culture. Culture was taught independently of theology. It was entirely intellectual in content.

Those French students who were admitted to secondary schools could go on and could eventually take the *baccalauréat*. The *baccalauréat* was a very rigorous examination given at about age sixteen or seventeen which opened the way to many privileges including admission to government or civil service. However, to get into the universities, a student must still take some additional work and pass a university admission examination.

In England after 1902 an education act required that the voluntary schools could share in the money raised by local taxes and school boards could establish both higher elementary and secondary schools. This meant, of course, there now was the possibility of public elementary schools either free of tuition or very cheap. During the time when the child was about age eleven, he took an examination called the "eleven plus" examination which, if passed, would admit him to the secondary system. He could go to one of the "public" schools that, with the exception of a few who received scholarships, required the student to pay high tuition fees. These schools had difficult admission requirements in addition to that of passing the "eleven plus" examination. He could go to other private schools or governmentally established schools which were of the "grammar school" type. Those not passing the eleven plus continued in the elementary school or dropped out. There began to develop over the years some technical or vocational schools and some "modern" schools for those pupils who did not pass the examination for admission to the grammar school. However, these three schools were quite separate and quite independent of each other. It was not until in the late 1950's and the 1960's that they began to develop a comprehensive school system for enrolling all children of secondary school age in one school.

Role of Educational Leaders and Theorists.   The recommendations of the educational theorists of the Enlightenment period have been set forth earlier. Their influence is not to be greatly felt in Europe until much later. However, America was to feel the influence of Froebel through the development of the kindergarten movement in the 1850's through German immigrants. The influence in this movement was much more than might have been expected since the German kindergarten had not been universally accepted in Germany. The people who migrated to this country, however, were the liberals fleeing persecution and they brought the liberal ideas of the kindergarten with them. Herbartianism was brought to this country in the latter part of the twentieth century by persons who had studied in Germany. It showed its influence on educational methodology through such educators as the McMurry brothers and, later on, Morrison of the University of Chicago. Morrison worked out his ideas on the teaching unit as much on the theory of biological adaptation as on Herbartianism. However, the Morrison steps did closely resemble Herbartian steps.

In the formative period of the American public school system such state leaders as Horace Mann (Massachusetts), Henry Barnard (Connecticut and the United States Office), and Calvin Stowe (Ohio), played important leadership roles in developing the state school system. These men were not so much theorists as they were publicists for the great public school movement. Horace Mann gave effective leadership in helping to solve the problems as to whether the public schools should be sectarian or nonsectarian. He felt very definitely that the public school, because it was serving all the youngsters, must of necessity be a nonsectarian institution.

Other persons influenced education in this country during this period. The first of these was the British thinker and writer, Herbert Spencer (1820–1902). Spencer was greatly influenced by the concept of evolution. Darwin had published his *Origin of the Species* in 1869 and England and America were convulsed with the arguments growing out of it. Spencer completely accepted the Darwinian concept of evolution and held that not only did it operate in the biological evolution of the species but also there was an evolution of society or culture. Consequently, he began to think through what would be the role of education in such an evolving society. In the book, *What Knowledge is the Most Worth,* Spencer analyzed man's activities and then held that it was the job of education to help men do better these things he did as they had evolved in the culture. This was a strongly realistic movement which has found its modern counterpart in the social realists who place their whole attention on helping individuals to adjust to the contemporary society.

Also strongly influenced by the theory of evolution and other factors which were emerging, was John Dewey (1859–1952).[2] Dewey, born and reared in Vermont, received his doctor's degree from Johns Hopkins, one of the first American universities to offer such a degree. He had become interested in Hegel's philosophy and after leaving Johns Hopkins he went into university teaching in the area of philosophy. He became dis-

[2] An excellent brief outline of Dewey's contributions can be found in Howard A. Ozmon, Jr., *An Outline of Dewey's Philosophy* (Boston, Massachusetts, Student Outlines, 1964).

illusioned with Hegel, however, and interested in some of the implications of the Darwinian evolutionary hypothesis, in the values of a democratic social order, and in the scientific method. In 1894 he became head of the Department of Philosophy and Education at the University of Chicago. The university had established a demonstration elementary school and the experiences in this school greatly influenced Dewey. He left in 1904 to go to Columbia University and, although while there he was a member of the Columbia University faculty (and not of the Columbia Teachers College), he continued his great interest in education. He felt that philosophy was a "general theory of education." Dewey was a prolific writer with some publications before 1900. Some of his most famous later books were *Democracy and Education* in 1916 and *How We Think* in 1913, revised in 1933. He wrote *Experience and Education* in 1938 as an answer to those who were suggesting that progressive education in its extreme form was in line with his ideas.

Dewey developed his philosophy out of the strains of thinking which arose from the scientific method of obtaining knowledge as his epistemology and out of a social philosophy based on democracy. He combined these together into a well-worked out philosophical point of view. He adopted the point of view called pragmatism. It had been originated by Charles Peirce, a mathematician who had been concerned with the problem of the verification of the truthfulness of a statement. The so-called "pragmatic" test of the validity of a statement is a central principle of the pragmatic philosophy. This means the truthfulness of a statement lies in whether or not action based upon it does in fact work out in terms of the consequences of the statement.

William James, a medical doctor and a teacher of physiology at Harvard University, also took up the pragmatic philosophy and developed it further but it remained for Dewey to develop it even more systematically. He took a more rigorous, logical, analytical approach to pragmatism. In its modern version, as used in education, it is quite frequently called "experimentalism," somewhat of a misnomer. The meaning here would have been clearer if the word had been "experientialism." Dewey placed his main emphasis on the reality of human experience. In this way he tried to avoid the age-old dualisms and irreconcilable ontological controversies. By saying that all we know or hope to know is that which is found in our experience, he felt that he had avoided the impossible, irreconcilable difficulties of the older ontological answers to such questions. The verification of all knowledge was through the use of the scientific method. He did approach this through what he called the reflective thinking which was basically a method which he described by enumerating the steps. Basic to this as (1) a recognition of the problem, (2) the proposing of hypotheses, and (3) the testing of these hypotheses out until one is found which works out in consequences for action. The last is the "pragmatic" test.

Education itself is defined as the process of the reconstruction, or reconstitution, of experiences which would give it more value through the medium of increased individual effectiveness in solving his problems. As the individual faces a changing environment and makes adjustment to it, he reconstructs his experiences. In other words, he learns. The end or aim of education then is more growth or more learning. This aim is within the process of education, not something that is peripheral to it. The school is a social institution and it must be a place where the child has "real" experience not something remote from the reality the child faces outside of the school.

It is questionable to what extent Dewey has actually influenced modern education. His views did develop at about the same time as the "progressive" movement that took some things from Dewey, in many instances going far beyond Dewey's point of view. Dewey from time to time even as early as 1899 and finally in his book, *Experience and Education,* in no unmistakable terms disassociated himself from the extreme elements of progressive education. The Progressive Education Association was founded in 1918 and composed of those who were dissatisfied with traditional education. It contained many points of view differing among themselves, some radical, some conservative. Dewey was himself a member of the group. At times there were some extremists who seemed to propose to let children do as they please and thus "run wild." It is doubtful this view was held by any large number of persons in the group. In 1941 the Progressive Education Association (or what was left of it) officially adopted the pragmatic philosophy as its point of view. However, still in the mind of most persons when progressive education is mentioned is the spectacular exception of the teacher who permitted the youngsters to choose their own curriculum and to "do as they please" in some of the more extreme schools of the 1920's and 1930's. Actually this point of view partakes more of Rousseau than it does of Dewey. There are many other psychiatric and other psychological views which influenced "extreme" progressive education but many of these are quite in contrast with Dewey's point of view.

Dewey himself was a mild-mannered, soft-spoken individual who was not an effective speaker. His writings are very difficult to understand; consequently, many of Dewey's ideas have been interpreted and extended through his followers. Some of these disciples did go at different tangents. Boyd Bode of Ohio State University stressed Dewey's ideas of democracy as a "way of life." John Childs of Teachers College, Columbia, was considerably interested in social philosophy and in political applications of the pragmatic philosophy. William H. Kilpatrick who also taught for a number of years in the Teachers College, Columbia, was very strongly interested in the "project" method and it is likely that certain extreme interpretations of Kilpatrick may have been more influenced in the progressive education movement than the direct interpretation of Dewey's own writing and thinking.

What influenced education after the twenties and into the thirties was more the pressure of mass education, the effect of cultural change and the shift in education of purposes than was the direct application of the Dewey point of view. These trends are discussed more fully in Chapter 11.

Out-of-School Education. It is well to remember that not all education takes place inside of the school and university systems. One of the things which affected the development of the United States greatly during the nineteenth century was the education which took place out of school. Knowledge was spread by philanthropic and humanitarian agencies as, in some cases, through commercial ventures. Some of these were organized movements which affected various classes of the population, such as the laboring class or the white-collar groups. For example, there were many mechanic's institutes founded. There was the development of the working man's and merchant's libraries. There were lecture series designed for industrial and commercial workers because the people felt that knowledge gave power and they thus wanted more knowledge. There were whole series of lectures, discussion–debates, and public events of many kinds.

Some of these were on a very large scale and even went out into the rural areas. One of these was the Lyceum movement. This became a very important agency for rural education sometime early in the nineteenth century and it continued until the 1920's. Another was the Chautauqua movement which included lectures, public discussion, reading, and other features. This movement was very popular in not only providing a place where people could go for vacation trips, but also its members traveled throughout the country with tents and put on plays, entertainment, and public lectures for the enlightenment of the people. This movement had also reached its peak and started to decline by the 1920's.

There was also the growth of the public libraries, which had appeared early in the nineteenth century in New England. Later, Enoch Pratt and Andrew Carnegie began to give money for the founding of public libraries.

With the development of high-speed printing processes, it was now possible to fulfill the increased public demand for reading material since more could be made available. Newspapers began to be published for a penny. There were many cheaply printed magazines and books that were put out in great numbers. This "self-improvement" urge went on among the women also and they established women's clubs and literary circles. Finally, the General Federation of Women's Clubs was founded in 1889.

Later, settlement houses for the underprivileged were established. Various museums, such as in natural history, or in industries and sciences, were established. The county and state fairs throughout the country were also a kind of education that helped people to learn about new things. It is possible to underestimate the effect of the mass circulation of newspapers and magazines and other publications upon keeping the populace up to date with new information and knowledge coming out.

Status of the Teaching Profession in the Nineteenth Century. Because of the great demand for teachers that resulted from the expansion of education in the developing national systems, sometimes on a mass basis (at least in the United States and Prussia), in a relatively short period of time teaching became a widely recognized profession. There began to be developed a specific institution for teacher training, the "normal" school. As soon as these were developed the importance of education began to be noted. Reactionaries in most countries spoke against the normal schools and the type of education the teachers received because they were afraid the teacher might help overthrow the established order.

Views of teacher training in France, Germany, and England were similar with regard to the notion that the elementary teacher should receive preparation different from that of the secondary teacher. These views held that the jobs were different because of the different type of people to be taught, i.e., those dividing for the two-track system of schools. Secondary school teachers were allied with the universities and the universities prepared them to teach in the secondary schools. Elementary teachers could be prepared by some kind of lesser grade training institutions. These were called *L'écoles Normales* of France and, later, they were to be called "normal schools" in the United States. In the early years of the United States whatever higher training was available was done through the colleges or universities, but there was no training specifically for teaching. Most of the elementary teachers had not even completed secondary school, let alone gone on to the college or university. For the elemestary school teacher, religious orthodoxy, and good moral character were much more important than knowledge of subject matter and skills, not even considering the ability to teach.

Starting in the 1820's some action was taken toward doing a better job of training their teachers. They began to establish the normal school, designed to give teachers rules or examples for teaching. These normal schools often admitted students directly from the elementary schools. They certainly did not require high-school graduation. This was true in many cases even as late as 1900. The course of study varied in length but it was usually about two years. It was decided that the normal school would devote its time not to raising the educational level of teachers but to mastering the elementary school subjects and to improving the methods of teaching. This gave a certain cast to teacher-training in the United States that it has not yet been able to live down.

However, there was soon another development. Some of the liberal arts colleges began to give lectures on the art of teaching and pedagogy. New York University had its first course of this kind as early as 1832, Brown in 1850, and Michigan in 1860. These courses, however, were very minimal. It was not until near the end of the nineteenth century that teaching began to be looked upon as a profession, thereby requiring special kind of preparation in professional education courses. Education courses began to come into the liberal arts colleges and specialized "colleges of education" on the university level began to be set up. There also began the development of graduate study in "education." This helped to contribute research and ideas concerning better elementary and secondary schools, curriculum, teachers and administrators.

Closely related to the development of teaching as a profession from the standpoint of preparation and certification was the development of teacher associations, locally, statewide, and nationally. Springing up widely in the nineteenth century, they held meetings and quite often set up institutes. They, also, published magazines for teachers, and tried to get legislation passed that was favorable to education. These associations tried to obtain better salaries, better working conditions, and better schools.

Although their action during the early period was not too effective, there were some cases where, allied with other groups, they did bring about some better conditions for education. By the end of the century, salaries paid to school teachers were a little bit above the common laborer —somewhat below that of skilled laborers. At that time there was a very strong differential between those that taught in the city and in rural areas. Part of this may well have been due to the fact it became a profession which women could get into fairly easily and women's salaries in general were lower in those professions in which they competed with men. Gradually, however, the qualifications for teachers were raised. Longer years of college study were required. Systems of licensing and certificates were established for the purpose of raising the standards of teaching. About the time of World War I, most of the states began to develop some sort of pension or teacher retirement system. With the exception of railroad employees, it was one of the first of the occupations for which a worthwhile pension or retirement system was provided.

One aspect of the teaching profession was that its candidates tended to be drawn from the lower middle classes—it was one of the first occupations in the mobile-upward trend. Until quite recently teachers were restricted very heavily in their personal lives. They were to maintain a good example for the pupils of their community. In many cases, freedom of speech which was widely accepted by the other people of the community was not permitted to them, nor were most married women permitted to teach in the United States until after World War II. Teaching, consequently, for women was something one did until one was married or it was a career only for those who did not wish to marry (the "old maids"). The result was that those women who were probably the least able and the least competent, at least from the standpoint of personality, engaged in teaching as a life career. Even though some changes had been made in teaching as a profession by 1930, there was still a long distance to go before it became a genuine profession and, of course, to this day there are several respects in which teaching still has to achieve some of the attributes of other professions.

EDUCATION AND FREEDOM IN THE PERIOD OF THE DEVELOPMENT OF NATIONAL SYSTEMS OF EDUCATION

This period from 1830 to 1930 represents a significant period in the development of democracy and freedom, although at the end of this period (1930) democracy seemed to be somewhat demoralized. The Fascist movement in Italy and the Nazi movement in Germany seemed to herald a trend away from democracy. This proved to be, however, only a temporary setback.

Following the French Revolution, the countries of Europe had been subjected to movements for greater freedom and greater democracy and periods of repression of such movements. In England, progress was fairly straightforward toward the development of a parliamentary system based upon the extension of universal suffrage to all. Until the twentieth century, this meant manhood suffrage only. During all this period the possibility that the peoples of Europe who were subject to the persecution could migrate to the New World enabled many to seek freedom if it were not possible in their own country. The general reputation of the success of the democracy and freedom in America did undoubtedly lead to the eventual triumph of democratic ideas also in Europe. There was to be, however, a period of disillusionment following the close of World War I.

Looking again to America, the influence of the Western frontier meant that an individual for whom the state of life was not satisfactory could move on to a place where there was relative freedom and great opportunity. The frontier, along with the intellectual and idealogical traditions toward liberalism among those persons who came to this country for freedom, caused a movement toward greater and greater democracy. Although there is debate among American historians as to the relative effect of the frontier and of the democratic and humanitarian ideals of the enlightenment, certainly both influences would seem to have been important.

The framers of the American Constitution were certainly not completely willing to turn the government over to a completely popular democracy. They arranged for the President of the United States to be chosen by a group of selected persons, the Electoral College. They also arranged for the indirect election of the Senators, the members of the upper body of Congress. As time went on, however, and there was more and more movement toward equalitarianism, universal suffrage, and other democratic practices, democracy was widely extended. Although the success of the rapidly growing development of our industrial system gave political support to those elements of our society that were in sympathy with business interests, there was widespread popular support for this. At the latter part of this period, there began to be some movement against such support of the business interests, starting with the Populist movement and continuing with the development of the strong labor unions and the progressive movement of the early decades of the twentieth century.

The abolition of slavery as a result of the Civil War and the extension of suffrage to women in 1920 were also movements toward a greater democratization of the American scene. Virtually all the nations of the world now have universal suffrage.

Students of the development of increased governmental interest and involvement in the solution of social problems point out that it is in the period from 1930 on that there is conscious attention given to the direct role of government toward controlling these conditions that at times have hampered the practical enjoyment of freedom by the individual as limited by unemployment, bad housing, poverty, and so on. However, the groundwork for this extension of the rule of government had been laid in the democratic structure and ideology of the American system. As we moved into the latter part of the twentieth century, it became necessary for the American people, finally, to put into practice actions in line with what they had preached as far as their statements of goals found in their traditional documents (such as the Declaration of Independence) as well as their legal actions of the earlier periods.

SUMMARY

The period from 1830 to 1930 is characterized by the further development of nation–states in Europe and America. There was also the development of political democracy to the point at which it can be said that most of the countries were practicing some form of democracy. Exceptions were the German Empire up to World War II and Fascist Italy in the late twenties. The breakaway of Germany (after 1933) and of Italy from democratic development and the rise of Communism in the Soviet Union represent trends which are opposite to the main trends occurring in the Western world but they are to be temporary ones in all except the Soviet Union (and possibly Spain).

This was also the period in which the effect of the Industrial Revolution was felt and the capitalistic system was developed. There developed in America at this time the economic laissez-faire system which was to become successful, and because of its success, was to grow and develop until many industries became quite large and industry as a group became very powerful in this society. In large part as a result of the success of the system, economic laissez-faire broke down the monopolies developed which partially offset laissez-faire policies. Because the laissez-faire system did not seem to always protect the workers, there began to be laws passed on social humanitarianism, to reduce the work week, to prevent child labor, and to improve otherwise the conditions of work. In the early part of the twentieth century, other laws began to be passed to protect the worker from injuries, such as safety laws and Workmen's Compensation Insurance. There was a tremendous development of the union movement, the effect of which was to raise the wages of the laborer commensurate with the increased living standards made possible by the improved technology.

Changes were taking place in Europe also. In some respects in the countries such as Germany there was in the late nineteenth and early twentieth centuries more paternalistic "social welfarism" than there was in the democratic countries—possibly to forestall further socialism. In the other countries these changes were to come, however, later—after 1930.

Education in the nineteenth century was primarily the history of the development of the national systems in all the various countries. The United States and Russia were to be the two countries which would make the greatest early progress. In the United States, the so-called "ladder" system was developed in which there was only one school system. The next rung of the educational ladder was to be made available when the previous rung had been completed. In the European countries, there developed a dual system of education, the one, an elementary school for the masses, the other, the secondary school for the upper classes. In the United States the public schools become universal, free, compulsory, and nonsectarian. Although there was compulsory education for a number of years in the European schools and soon there would be free education for the masses, it would be some time before there was to be widespread educational opportunities, even for those who could pay tuition, for European boys and girls of secondary school age.

The European schools have had a variety of methods of solving the problem of teaching religion, but in most cases it has been taught in the schools in cooperation with church authorities. France is an exception. The French national schools are completely secular. America is an example in which the schools are nonsectarian. The ideas of Pestalozzi, Froebel, and Herbart arrived on the American shores and Pestalozzianism was to influence elementary education in the normal schools and Herbart was to influence secondary education through the improved teaching methods.

American secondary education has gone through three phases of development. There was, first, the Latin grammar school which began to decline in the eighteenth century. Then the Academy, a privately operated secondary school, began to operate after the middle of the eighteenth century and became the predominant secondary school until around 1870. Last, the American high school started in 1821 and eventually became the predominant secondary school in America and almost universal after 1900. The American high school arose as an extension of the elementary school as a secondary school for the masses. However, its curriculum around 1900 had become largely college preparatory. Then forces began to operate which caused the curriculum to expand to meet the needs of a greatly increased number of boys and girls seeking admission. The enrollment of the secondary schools began to double each decade from 1890 (on through at least 1930) and larger and larger demands were made upon the high school to meet the increased number and the different kinds of students seeking to enroll in it.

In Europe during this time there were practically no changes in the elementary school. There were a few changes in secondary education toward the introduction of science and the establishment of the few academies and *Realschulen* with more practical, modern subjects. However, the opening up of secondary education for the masses on any practical basis was to be a phenomenon of the mid-twentieth century as far as Europe is concerned.

There were several educational leaders who played important roles in the United States during this period. Among these was Horace Mann with his influence on the development of the state school systems, particularly in Massachusetts, and in his influence toward nonsectarian education. Herbert Spencer, the British educator, in the latter part of this period stressed the practical knowledge of education and the preparation of pupils to be well adjusted individuals to the culture in which they would find themselves.

The outstanding figure as far as American education is concerned was that of John Dewey. John Dewey was a university professor of philosophy who became interested in education. He had studied Hegel's philosophy but broke with it and finally developed his own philosophy based upon an extension of Charles Peirce's philosophy, pragmatism. Dewey's point of view is currently called "Experimentalism." Dewey developed his philosophy out of a combination of the ideas arising out of democracy and the scientific method of solving the problems. Although Dewey was, to some extent, associated with the progressive education movement, he did not agree with the extreme elements of this movement and indicated this a number of times. Dewey's emphasis was on the development of an individual capable of reflective thinking, that is, of being able to solve the problems which he faces individually and in groups. There were some variations of Dewey's philosophy by his students and followers, such as Bode, Childs, and Kilpatrick.

There was also extensive development during the period of the nineteenth century of out-of-school informal educational opportunities. A great number of libraries and mechanics institutes were established. There was also the extension of mass circulation magazines and the mass-printing of cheap newspapers. There were also a great number of women's clubs and literary circles which were somewhat educational in nature.

The teaching profession as a whole was still at a fairly low level during this period. The systematic education of the teachers at a relatively high university level was not to begin until about 1910. Certification of teachers on a statewide basis was to be a development later in the period of the 1930's. The first education of teachers took place in the normal schools. These, in many cases, did not even require high school graduation. The emphasis was upon methods of teaching and upon the subject matter to be taught in the elementary schools rather than on a university-type education of the teacher. Some of the universities, however, did start to give work in pedagogy (or education) in the mid-nineteenth century, although this work was not highly regarded at this time. In the early twentieth century, there was a considerable rise in the standard of teacher education. The normal schools gradually became schools of collegiate grade; later, teachers colleges and universities. The minimum certification requirements of teachers was raised considerably until the degree requirement for both elementary and high-school teachers became fairly common.

The pay of teachers was still quite low compared with that of other learned professions, usually about that of the skilled craftsmen in each community—not the equal of other college-trained individuals based on equal length of training. There also was restriction of teachers' personal lives during this period. This personal restriction was much heavier upon teachers than upon other persons such as that upon the parents and other community leaders, for example. This was not to be changed until after World War II. Also, there were, during this period, wide-spread rules against women teaching after their marriage. This also has now been universally changed. Neither sex nor marital status is now a factor to be considered in filling teaching or administrative positions.

The complete freedom of the teacher and the complete autonomy of the teaching profession with respect to its own particular endeavors is still to be won. During the period up to 1930 freedom of teaching was a rather limited matter. In more recent years, freedom of teaching has been greatly extended but there are still restrictions in many communities.

SELECTED BIBLIOGRAPHY

Starred books most closely parallel the contents of this chapter.

General Books

Antieau, Chester J., and others, *Freedom from Federal Establishment*. Milwaukee, Bruce, 1964.

Bentwich, Joseph S., *Education in Israel*. Philadelphia, Jewish Publication Society of America, 1965.

*Boyd, William, *The History of Western Education*, 7th ed., revised and enlarged by Edmund J. King. New York, Barnes and Noble, 1965.

Brinton, Howard H., *Quaker Education in Theory and Practice*. Wallingford, Pennsylvania, Pendle Hill, 1949.

Brubacher, John Seiler and Rudy, Willis, *Higher Education in Transition: An American History: 1636–1956*. New York, Harper, 1958.

*Butts, R. Freeman, *A Cultural History of Western Education: Its Social and Intellectual Foundations*, 2d ed. New York, McGraw-Hill, 1955.

Carter, Harold J., ed., *Intellectual Foundations of American Education: Readings and Commentary*. New York, Pitman Publishing, 1965.

Cremin, Lawrence A., *The Transformation of the School: Progressivism in American Education, 1876–1957*. New York, Knopf, 1961.

*Cubberly, Ellwood P., *The History of Education*. New York, Houghton Mifflin, 1920.

Curti, Merle, *The Social Ideas of American Educators*. Chicago, Charles Scribners Sons, 1935.

Drake, William E., *The American School in Transition*. New York, Prentice-Hall, 1955.

Duggan, Stephen, *A Student's Textbook in the History of Education*. New York, Appleton-Century-Crofts, 1927.

*Eby, Frederick, *The Development of Modern Education*. New York, Prentice-Hall, 1952.

Education and Economics, Robert K. Hall, and J. A. Lauwerys, eds. The Year Book of Education, 1956. Yonkers-on-Hudson, New York, World Book Company, 1957.

French, William M., *America's Educational Tradition: An Interpretive History*. New York, Heath, 1964.

Frost, S. E., Jr., *Historical and Philosophical Foundations of Western Education*. Columbus, Ohio, Merrill, 1966.

Good, Harry G., *A History of American Education*, 2d ed. New York, Macmillan, 1962.

*Good, Harry G., *A History of Western Education*, 2d ed. New York, Macmillan, 1960.

Gross, Carl H. and Chandler, Charles C., *The History of American Education Through Readings*. Boston, Heath, 1964.

Gross, Richard E., ed., *Heritage of American Education*. Boston, Allyn and Bacon, 1962.

Hart, Joseph K., *Creative Moments in Education*. New York, Holt, Rinehart and Winston, 1931.

Hartford, Ellis Ford, *Education in These United States*. New York, Macmillan, 1964.

*Kirchner, Walter, *Western Civilization Since 1500*. New York, Barnes and Noble, 1958.

Knight, Edgar W., *Twenty Centuries of Education*. New York, Ginn, 1940.

Krug, Edward A., *Salient Dates in American Education, 1635–1964*. New York, Harper and Row, 1966.

————, *The Shaping of the American High School*. New York, Harper & Row, 1964.

Mayer, Frederick, *American Ideas and Education*. Columbus, Ohio, Merrill, 1964.

*Mayer, Frederick, *History of Educational Thought*, 2d ed. Columbus, Ohio, Merrill, 1966.

Meyer, Adolphe, *An Educational History of the Western World*. New York, McGraw-Hill, 1965.

*Mulhern, James, *A History of Education: A Social Interpretation*. New York, Ronald, 1959.

Muller, Herbert J., *Freedom in the Modern World*. New York, Harper & Row, 1966.

Power, Edward J., *Main Currents in the History of Education*. New York, McGraw-Hill, 1962.

Readings in Public Education in the United States, Ellwood P. Cubberley, ed. New York, Houghton Mifflin, 1934.

Readings in the History of Education, Ellwood P. Cubberley, ed. New York, Houghton Mifflin, 1920.

Rudy, Willis, *Schools in an Age of Mass Culture: An Exploration of Selected Themes in the History of Twentieth Century American Education*. Englewood Cliffs, New Jersey, Prentice-Hall, 1965.

Rusk, Robert R., *The Doctrines of the Great Educators.* New York, St. Martins', 1965.

Schaefer, Robert J., *William Heard Kilpatrick: An Appreciation. Teachers College Record,* Vol. 66. No. 4, 1965.

Sizer, Theodore R., *Secondary Schools at the Turn of the Century.* New Haven, Yale University Press, 1964.

Social History of American Education, Vol. I: Colonial Times to 1860, Vol. II: *1860 to the Present,* Rena L. Vassar, ed. Chicago, Rand McNally, 1965.

Thayer, V. T., *Formative Ideas in American Education: From the Colonial Period to the Present.* New York, Dodd Mead, 1965.

The Educated Man: Studies in the History of Educational Thought, Paul J. Nash, and others, eds. New York, Wiley, 1965.

The Secondary School Curriculum, George Z. F. Bereday and J. A. Lauwerys, eds. Year Book of Education: 1958. Yonkers-on-the-Hudson, World Book Company, 1958.

Wiggin, Gladys A., *Education and Nationalism: An Historic Interpretation of American Education.* New York, McGraw-Hill, 1962.

Paperbacks

Bailyn, Bernard, *Education in the Forming of American Society: Needs and Opportunities for Study.* New York, Vintage Books, 1960.

*Beck, Robert H., *A Social History of Education.* Englewood Cliffs, New Jersey, Prentice-Hall, 1965.

Boorstin, Daniel J., *The Americans: The Colonial Experience.* New York, Vintage, 1964.

Broudy, Harry S. and Palmer, John R., *Exemplars of the Teaching Method.* Chicago, Rand McNally, 1965.

*Cordasco, Francesco, *A Brief History of Education.* Paterson, New Jersey, Littlefield, Adams, 1963.

Essentials of History of Education, S. E. Frost. New York, Barron's, 1947.

Medawar, P. B., *The Future of Man.* New York, New American Library, 1959.

The New England Primer, Paul Leicester Ford, ed., Classics in Education No. 13. New York, Teachers College, Columbia University, 1962.

The Republic and the School, Lawrence A. Cremin, ed., No. 1, Classics in Education. New York, Teachers College, Columbia University, 1957.

The Rise of American Education. An Annotated Bibliography, Joe Park, ed. Chicago, Northwestern University Press, 1965.

SELECTED FILMS

Colonial Children   (11 min.)

Re-enactment, with authentic settings, costumes, and furnishings, of the home life and self-sufficiency of a family in a colonial New England during the late 17th century. Describes how colonial children received their education studying at home, and portrays the duties and chores of each member of the family. Reveals the spirit of helpfulness between families, and emphasizes the vital role of religion in the home.

Education in America: Twentieth Century Developments (Coronet)   (16 min.)

Education in America: The Nineteenth Century (Coronet)   (16 min.)

Education in America: The Seventeenth and Eighteenth Centuries
(Coronet)   (16 min.)

Germany: Feudal States to Unification (Coronet)   (13½ min.)
    Traces Prussia's growth in strength in the nineteenth century, shows how other German states were brought under its control and how, following Bismarck's policy of "blood and iron," she waged wars with Denmark, Austria, and France to establish a strong, unified German nation.

Horace Mann (Emerson)   (19 min.)
    Portrays important episodes in the life of Horace Mann, the "father of the common schools"; reviews his activities as teacher, lawyer, state senator, board of education member and college president; emphasizes his work in pointing up the need for well-built schools, good textbooks, democratic methods of learning, schools for teachers, and universal education in the United States.

Profile of Communism
    Part I. Reviews the history of communist ideology and practice from the nineteenth century until 1945.
    Part II. Communism in the Soviet Union in the post Stalin era. An examination of its effects on all aspects of Soviet life and institutions.

The American Education System   (29 min.)
    Teenagers from various countries discuss aims, standards, and other features of American high schools and colleges in comparison with schools of their countries.

The Red Myth (KQED, San Francisco)   (29 min. *each*)
    A series of thirteen documentary films dealing with the history of communism from Marx to Khrushchev and related information prepared by research in the Hoover Institute of War, Revolution, and Peace at Stanford University.

Revolts and Reforms in Europe (1815–1848) (Coronet)   (16 min.)
    This film presents an analysis of the struggle between the conservative landed nobility and the political and social reformers who agitated for more democratic forms of government. Focusing on France, the film also provides a view of the far-reaching consequences of similar movements in Germany, Russia, Austria, Italy, and Great Britain during this period.

Satellites, Schools, and Survival (NEA)   (28 min.)
    A pictorial history of education in the U.S. during the last half of the century. Points up the challenge of present problems. Shows close relationship of the American system of education to survival as free nation. Interviews supplemented by dramatized section on one school since 1900 and a present-day class at work.

School Days (University of Michigan)   (60 min.)
> Russian film on schools with English subtitles.

Section 16 (NEA)   (14 min.)
> Traces the history of public education in America from the Dame Schools of early New England through the colonial schools of Pennsylvania, the one-room schools of the Middle West, the mission schools of the Far West, the accomplishments of Horace Mann and other leaders in education, up to the public schools of today. Narrated by Raymond Massey.

Travel in America in the 1840's (Coronet)   (13½ min.)
> Through the colorful story of Matt, who travels from New York State to Illinois, students learn the significance of the changes in transportation that are beginning by the 1840's.

10

Contemporary
Comparative Educational Systems,
Twentieth Century: Germany,
France, and the United Kingdom

GENERAL PROBLEMS IN THE STUDY OF
COMPARATIVE EDUCATION

As noted in the earlier chapters, there tended to develop in the seventeenth, eighteenth, and nineteenth centuries, separate nation–states with very divergent cultural, political, historical, and social backgrounds. Each of these nations developed a tremendous pride in its own culture and its citizens developed a strong loyalty and patriotism. Each of these separate nations, out of its own background, attempted to find its own answers to the problems it faced. The field of education, like other areas, was approached differently by the different nations.

As the national systems of education began to develop in most of these countries in the nineteenth century, their features, as in other social institutions of these countries, were considerably limited and certainly in large part determined by the background factors in the particular and peculiar life of that nation. Although some educational reforms and practices moved from one country to another by a kind of cultural diffusion, in other cases, they were deliberately and consciously imported. At any rate, they tended to be modified to fit the local traditions or practices. If this did not happen, the innovation would tend to die out very quickly. In some cases the new developments arose in pockets and remained isolated, having only some residual effect on the rest of the country. This effect was greater when the organization of its school system was such that it could readily accept new practices from any source and adapt them to its use. Certainly this situation was more true of the American educational system during the nineteenth and early twentieth centuries than it was of any of the other systems discussed in these chapters.

Although it is true that the beliefs, prejudices, ideas, and habits of the peoples vary between countries, there are, of course, certain problems in regard to operating and establishing school systems which show a great deal of resemblance from country to country. Some of the organizational problems of school systems of all countries, for example, are: Who will control the schools? Who will pay for education? How will the control and financing be divided up among private and various governmental levels? The various countries of the world have solved these problems very differently, and these differences are found even when their political governments are somewhat similar. An example of this is the difference in control of the education by the Australian states and the American states. Even though in both cases there is a federal-type government, the state governments of Australia exercise much greater centralized control than do those of the American states.

One of the early problems to be solved (and this relates closely to the aims of education) is the relationship of the individual and his individual freedom to the units of government, to the religious institutions of the nation, and to the society as a whole. Depending largely on the history and general philosophy of the people, there are many differing answers given to the questions such as who will control and administer, and who will pay for education. The relationship between parents and children, between parents and the church, between families and local community, between political parties and the state, between local and central authorities, determine in large measure the final form of the organization or the national system of education that gradually develops. In the institutionalizing of education, regardless of the final form, the dominant social group attempts to shape the rising generation into a pattern which can be accepted as desirable by this particular group. The control of education depends upon the decision as to which group will participate in the control and how divisions of authority can be established. In the five nations to be discussed, varied answers to these questions are noted.

Education has become important in the life of every nation. It has been essential that some administrative machinery be devised to control and operate it so that, in some way or another, the "right" pupils will receive the "right" type of education from teachers who are deemed to be "right." [1] There are, however, different values in each country because,

---

[1] John F. Cramer, and George S. Brown, *Contemporary Education: A Comparative Study of National Systems*, 2d ed. (New York, Harcourt, Brace and World, 1965), pp. 4-22.

out of its own heritage, each country will determine what it considers to be the "right type" of education.

It is very difficult for one to argue from some objective point of view that there is a "best" educational system for *all* countries. It would seem that there might well be a "best" educational program that would fit a particular generation of a given country in order to develop the best interests of that country in light of its own particular type of governmental organization and its own set of values. This would not, however, mean that the program which is best for one particular country in light of its values would also be "best" for some other country in light of its values.

Numerous comparative studies have been made as to the cost of education and how this cost of education is related to the total income of the countries. There is probably no way in which a definitive study could indicate how much *should* be spent by a nation, i.e., what proportion of its income it can afford to spend on schools. It is probably true, however, that it can be demonstrated in terms of the later history of the country, that in its past, no country has ever spent all that it could on education, or all that it should in terms of its demonstrable needs, or in terms of how it could have improved itself for its own future. After an educational system has developed, there is usually a spurt in the development of that country. Furthermore, by the same token, many countries have declined where, possibly, they might not have if they had had sufficient foresight to have developed a better educational system.[2]

In modern times, the development of the concept of democracy as a way of life beyond that of being merely a political system, has had a strong influence on the educational philosophy and on the practices of education throughout the world. Both responsible governments and people in general are aware of the fact that in a nation where all citizens must take some measure of responsibility, they have to be educated for such intelligent citizenship. In many countries, this concept has been part of the force back of the development of a universal system of education cutting across class lines and economic status differences. This force has tended toward a breakdown of the special type of education existing largely for an intellectual elite. In certain places in the world in which universal systems of education have developed, as in countries with a totalitarian philosophy—with purposes quite different from those of a democratic state—there has been set up an educational organization which differed in structure and was organized for a number of different educational purposes.

Germany and France represent the more conservative and the least changed of the educational systems in the five nations to be discussed.

---

[2] Theodore Schulz, *The Economic Value of an Education* (New York, Columbia University Press, 1963).

The educational system of the United Kingdom represents that of a country which has made some change toward providing equal education for all through the secondary school age. The Soviet Union and the United States represent countries with school systems in which, at least theoretically, the same opportunity is available to all.

GERMANY (WEST GERMANY, FEDERAL REPUBLIC OF GERMANY)

The idea of a national school system controlled by state authorities originated in Germany. It is true that the Austro–Hungarian Empire did promulgate very early some laws designated to establish a national school system. However, these laws were not too successful. Signs of the idea of a national school system appeared as early as the sixteenth century in several of the German states when they began to establish state church-school systems. However, the country of Prussia (one of the most important Germanic countries) was the first modern state to inaugurate a truly national system without any direct church control.

Imperial Era (1870–1918). The German state was not amalgamated into a unified nation until after the Franco–Prussian War in 1871. Germany had suffered a terrible defeat under Napoleon in 1806 and the period from 1806 to 1871 was a period in which Germany attempted to reassert itself as the central power of Europe. Prussia, the strongest of the German states, eventually was able to obtain hegemony over the rest of the states and after the Franco–Prussian War with her victory over France, the twenty-five German states were brought together into an amalgamated German nation under the Hohenzollern dynasty. Bismarck, Prime Minister during much of this period, tried to get rid of the church influence. But in this he was unsuccessful and from then on he cooperated with the church officials but sought to oppress the socialists and any others who desired to bring about any kind of democratic tendencies. The spirit of the militaristic and nationalistic Prussia dominated the German Empire from 1871 to World War I.

The school system which had been developed in Germany was (as in most of the other European countries) definitely a "two-class" system. The objective of the Prussians, to become the model for the rest of the German school systems, was to produce on the one hand, a body of intelligent and highly trained experts, leaders, officers, and government officials to control the country and, on the other hand, a vast army of capable, obedient, and well-disciplined followers.

A few students were transferred to secondary schools from the elementary or special preparatory schools at age nine and there was practically no chance of admission after this time to the privileged system of secondary schools. In some few cases where students were permitted a late transfer from one type of school to another type, they were usually put back in their classes and therefore had difficulty catching up and meeting the requirements. The children of wealthier parents did not attend the regular elementary school, but attended a private preparatory school.

At the secondary level, Germany developed different types of schools, each quite distinctive in its curriculum and each playing its significant part. The first school developed for those persons not admitted to the privileged secondary system was the *Mittelschule*. This was a sort of a halfway house and gave some humanistic secondary education with one foreign language. It was a very popular school but did not include as many school years (to age 16 only) as the other secondary schools, led to no special privileges, nor did it permit the student to go to the university.

The *Gymnasium* was the secondary school of high prestige. Every boy and his parents aimed at entering him into a Gymnasium and everything was geared toward gaining entry for him at the age of nine. In the Gymnasium the curriculum was classical, with nine years of Latin, nine years of French and six years of Greek as the main subjects. There were other minor subjects. Every German scholar of note had been trained in a Gymnasium and there was a singular pursuit of knowledge and culture as the objective.

At the end of the work in the Gymnasium, at about age eighteen, the persons who successfully completed the course gained an *Abitur* or maturity certificate. This certificate opened up the prospect of an immediate middle-class civil service position. It also gave entrance to the University. The positions of higher civil service were restricted to persons who were graduated from the University.

Now as time went on there was pressure to add science and modern languages to the German curriculum. During this period it was impossible to break into the curriculum that had been established in the Gymnasium; therefore, the Germans established new secondary schools in order to comply with the pressures. (See Figure 10-1). The first one of these was the *Realgymnasium* which represented a trend in German education toward modern languages and science without the undue emphasis upon the classics. Rather than establishing this as an alternative within the Gymnasium, completely new schools were set up. The curriculum in these new schools dropped Greek, but still stressed Latin and the modern languages, and there were some science and mathematics given.

There was also the *Oberrealschule*. This school gave three to six years of Latin (and advanced classes on an optional basis) but its main subjects were the modern languages, sciences, and mathematics. All of

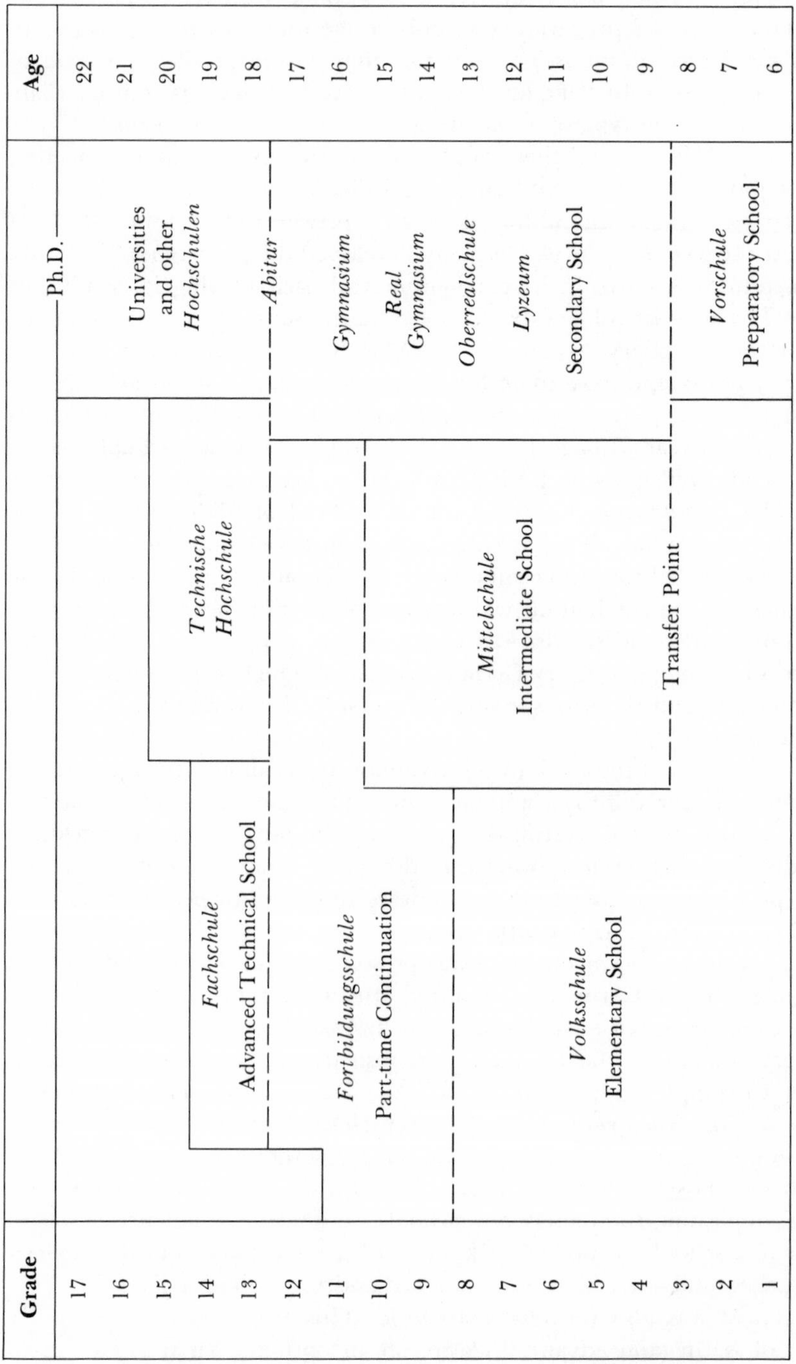
Age
22
21
20
19
18
17
16
15
14
13
12
11
10
9
8
7
6
Ph.D.
Universities and other *Hochschulen*
Abitur
Gymnasium
Real Gymnasium
Oberrealschule
Lyzeum
Secondary School
Vorschule
Preparatory School
Technische Hochschule
Mittelschule
Intermediate School
Transfer Point
Fachschule
Advanced Technical School
Fortbildungsschule
Part-time Continuation
Volksschule
Elementary School
Grade
17
16
15
14
13
12
11
10
9
8
7
6
5
4
3
2
1

FIG. 10.1 German schools under the empire, 1870–1918.

the schools did, of course, offer German literature, religion, history, music, and gymnastics. The students who went to the university came almost entirely from the Gymnasium, although a few of the students who graduated from the other secondary schools were able to pass the examination for admission.

Girls, in general, did not have as many educational opportunities in Germany as the boys. There were some good facilities for the girls and a few of the outstanding young women were able to secure admission to the university. Most of the Germans during this time held that the courses at the *Mittelschule* with emphasis on home economics and child development (as we would now call it) were sufficient for a girl. An institution was established called the *Lyzeum* which was the girls' secondary school corresponding to the Gymnasium. There was very little co-education in Germany, except in the small elementary schools in the country districts when there were not enough pupils to have separate boys and girls schools. In most classes even the teachers in a girls' school numbered more men than women.

On the other hand, the great masses of students in the pre-World War I Germany had their first full-time education in the *Volkschule,* the German general elementary school. After this, many of them would pass on to a part-time continuation of school called *Fortbildungschule*. It was felt that in this continuation school a liberal education should be gained in connection with the study of a vocation.

After being apprenticed in a recognized trade, the German student, usually male, attended the continuation school connected with their particular trade for three or four years, generally in the fourteen to eighteen year age bracket. He did this two half-days a week on his employer's time. The work included some study, now termed in the United States general education, German literature, history, music, and religion and, of course, the vocational trade itself. The vocational teachers in these schools were craftsmen out of the trades. These schools did have high educational standards. There were some continuation schools for girls in certain areas or occupations open to women, such as tailoring or lithography.

In addition to the part-time vocational schools, there were many full-time technical schools training students in more complicated professions such as agriculture, forestry, and some of the skilled trades or jobs in business and other important areas of the German economic life. These could be continued in an institution called the Technical High School (*Technische Hochschule*). These latter were of university rank and were similar to the Institutes of Technology, or even some engineering colleges in the United States even though they were named the German equivalent of the English "High School."

In the era from 1850 on to World War I, the German universities attracted students from all over the world because they offered very high

quality work in almost all of the scholarly fields. The fees were low even
for students from the outside. Unlike the English universities, there were
no residential colleges or dormitories and the students lived in private
homes. The only degree offered by these universities was the doctorate.
There were, however, numerous state examinations for licenses which
could be granted at certain stages to gain entrance to the professions.

The life in the *Gymnasium* for the secondary education student was
very stern and rigid, and the standards were rather high. But in the university, there were no additional requirements for admission (beyond the
Abitur), no required attendance in class, and the student usually lived a
very gay life. There was a great deal of drinking and duelling as a part of
university life. However, the examination at the end was very difficult
and exacting.

German universities were permeated with the nationalistic ideas
prevalent throughout the Germany of their times. There was a great deal
of discussion about Germany's importance in foreign affairs in line with
her past history. However, the pre-World War I German universities
stressed scientific research, and they had a very high level of scholarship.
The chief purpose of the German university was to train leaders and sub-
ordinates, immediately under the top leaders, for service to the state. At the
same time, the university attached great importance to learning for its
own sake and to the development of individual talents. The German
university of this period actually made great contributions to the whole
world culture. After World War I the breakdown in German education
at all levels, especially at the university level, left a large gap as far as the
world was concerned.

Weimar Republic (1918–1933).   Under the Weimar Republic, the Germans attempted to establish a democratic school system. The Weimar
Republic established after World War I was politically quite democratic
in form. The policy of this new German Republic was to establish a complete secular and universal school system in order to promote democratic
ideals and to provide for the development of democratic leadership.
There was much conflict, however, within the Weimar Republic from
the first between those persons who were interested in the old aristocratic
education along with the forces of the Junkers, or the military class, and
those who favored the development of truly democratic ideas and leadership. However, the Weimar Republic eventually fell because of economic
crises, one after the other, leading finally to a disastrous inflation. These
conditions in turn brought on the Nazis and the rule of Adolf Hitler.

At the time of the Weimar Republic there were twenty-six states,
each of which operated its own educational system. The central German
constitution under the Weimar Republic, and laws passed in accordance
with it, provided that there be at least eight years of elementary school

followed by training with a continuation school through the eighteenth year. In line with this, they abolished the old three-year preparatory school for the upper class, and the foundation school (now to be called *Grundschule*) was established consisting of four years of regular elementary school.

Each of the separate states was to work out the regulations for its schools. Most of the youngsters continued the second four years of their required education in the elementary schools rather than moving into other types of schools. Since the elementary schools had rather low prestige, the middle schools (*Mittelschule*) were again established to meet more practically the needs of many of the students. In 1925, Prussia established this six-year middle school based on a four-year foundation school which continued the students education to about age sixteen. There were still the old secondary schools (*Hohere Schulen*) which included the different forms of the *Gymnasien*, all of which lead primarily to competition for the examination and certificate called the *Abitur*.

The schools founded during the empire period were continued in the republic period, but two new types of secondary schools were added: The German secondary school (*Deutshe Oberschule*) and the *Aufbau* school. The latter enabled some children who had completed the seventh year of the elementary school to switch over and prepare for university admission by attending the *Aufbau* school for six years.

Those institutions established during the pre-World War I period, the six-year elementary school, and a six-year secondary school (based on a four-year elementary school) called the *Progymnasium*, the *Realgymnasium*, and other *Realschule*, were continued under the Republic. These also lead to a certificate of maturity but did not gain entrance to the university. They opened the way to certain lower administrative positions in civil service or business and they had a higher prestige value than the elementary school or the Mittelschule.

Under the Weimar Republic, the girls' education was reorganized somewhat upon the same basis as the boys' school with the name *Lyzeum* used in place of *Gymnasium*. There were also a few *Aufbau* schools for girls which lead to a maturity examination which would admit them to a university and to the higher levels of governmental service.[3]

The reason for the failure, or actually the lack of implementation, of many of the reforms (including education) of the Weimar Republic was the period of social unrest and economic difficulty. Due to the conditions imposed by the Versailles Peace Treaty after World War I, the German nation found itself in an impossible economic situation, the economic system broke down, then the government broke down, and the German Nazi

---

[3] *U.S. Department of Health, Education, and Welfare, Office of Education. Germany Revisited; Education and the Federal Republic* (Washington, Government Printing Office, 1957), pp. 18–24.

Party took over. After a period of time the schools were completely changed.

Nazi Education (1933–1944).   The objective of the Nazis was to achieve a totalitarian state. This would enable Germany to break out of its encirclement and get into a position of leadership in the world. Therefore, they wanted all the educational agencies to promulgate the Nazi doctrines. The liberal, democratic ideas of the Weimar period had to be checked and the people had to be lead into a new spirit of patriotism of Nazi variety.

The Nazi (National Socialist) Party was based on many socialistic principles but was nationalistic and authoritarian in the extreme. It was antidemocratic in all of its principles. At the top of the Party was the leader, *der Fuehrer.* The party developed the "Fuehrer principle" in which all persons were involved in a hierarchy of force, power, and leadership (a kind of modern feudalism). Basically, the Nazi movement was a movement of the middle class accompanied by suppression of the power of other groups. The upper militaristic class went along with it because of concessions made to their group. Meanwhile labor unions and other groups of the masses were suppressed ruthlessly, and all liberal ideas were crushed.

The general thesis of the period was that the welfare of the state came before that of the individual. Democracy was considered decadent and there was only one legal political party. No freedom of press or speech existed. Hitler wrote in his book, *Mein Kampf,* that he thought it to be nature's law that evolution produced stronger and stronger races. He argued that like attracts like, and that the weaker races would deteriorate and eventually disappear. Further, he declared that the strong must dominate the weak and that the mixing of races must be prevented otherwise all the development of the superior races out of an evolutionary background would be lost.

Students in schools were trained to be willing and uncritical servants of the state. All subjects taught were to incite necessary patriotism. Teachers had to be Nazi and, actually, they became officials in the Nazi government. They were required to teach as basic doctrines, racial purity and German superiority. Military force was exalted as was the belief that through military strength Germany might become great again. In reality, the change was more in the *spirit* than in the *structure* of education in the Nazi period.

There were, nevertheless, some changes in the administrative structure. A central national ministry took over the complete control of German education for the first time in its history. Out of the national Ministry of Education and Youth Welfare came all the instructions about courses, textbooks, and general procedures. A great deal of emphasis was placed upon physical training and other curricula elements deemed helpful in military situations. Any further increase in coeducation was discouraged. A very strong emphasis on discipline, including the use of corporal punishment with the student expected to take punishment without any sign of flinching was the order of the day.

Because Hitler overemphasized a racially pure and physically strong Germany, the intellectual aspects of the schools began to suffer considerably. Many of the outstanding teachers of the early period were Jews and not able to become Nazis. Twelve years of Nazi philosophy, from 1933 to 1945 produced a situation that made it very difficult for the German people to reorganize their educational system. After the Nazi military collapse in 1945, and with the occupation by the Allied forces, a new spirit made it possible for a different set of objectives to be set up for German education.

Post-World War II (West Germany) 1944. After a period of direct control separately by the Allied forces of France, The United States, England, and the Soviet Union in 1949, the new German Federal Republic in West Germany under the three Western Allies was set up, and under this republic education was again returned to state administration.

The portion of Germany ("East Germany") which was under the Soviet Union eventually organized into the German People's Democracy with a separate educational organization much similar to that in the Soviet Union. West Berlin, a part of Berlin islanded within East Germany, continued to be tied in with the West. East Berlin, a part of the former capital which had been under the Soviet jurisdiction became the capital of the East Germany section of Germany.

At the present time in Western Germany, the federal government plays no part in educational administration except to lay down certain general principles. In each of the *Länder* (*i.e.*, a German state), there has been enacted a basic education or school code. Since there are ten states in Western Germany plus West Berlin, each with their own educational system, there are eleven systems and a great deal of diversity. There are differences in curriculum, differences in textbooks, as well as in such policies as the handling of religious education.

It was soon found, even before the return to Germany's own government in 1949, that there ought to be some coordination among the states, and so there was established a Conference of Educational Ministers with a permanent secretariat located at Bonn. This conference still continues and through it the provision is made for reciprocity of examination certificates, and for the possible transfer of students from one system to another even before the examinations. The names of the schools in the post-war period (with the exception of those which have been reorganized recently under the *Einheitschule*) are very similar to those in the Weimar

Republic and in the empire days. The elementary school is the *Grundschule* taking pupils for either four or six years. In West Berlin, for example, it runs six years.

The instruction in a German elementary school is very thorough and a very high level of achievement is demanded. Heavy emphasis is placed upon learning to read well. However, there is instruction in other fields. For example, music is taught and there is a strong stress on physical education. Free expression in art is permitted and there is also an accent on dramatics. The necessity for hard work and discipline is still preached throughout the German schools much as it was in an earlier period of time. The schools still teach respect for God, the unity of mankind, and love for the Fatherland. There is a prominence given to these objectives in the primary and intermediate grades social-studies classes. International studies and cooperation with other people outside their own country are also stressed. Some of the newer ideas of teaching methods have gone into the new *Grundschule,* but very few changes have been made in the secondary school at this time, and practically none in the German university. There are some psychological services available in the schools since Germany has played an important historical role in the development of psychology. Education for the mentally handicapped and physically handicapped children, having been de-emphasized by the Nazi, is available again.

In three of the German states (or *Länder*), Bremen, Hamburg, and West Berlin, the *Einheitschule,* or comprehensive high school, in which all of the various secondary curricula can be taught in the same school, has been developed. In this plan, there are four years of *Grundschule* and the student then transfers to the secondary school level at about age ten. Previously he had stayed in the elementary school for another four or five years and then moved into the part-time continuation school when he went to work. Those who transfer to the secondary school at age ten are distributed to the *Mittelschule* and the *Höhere Schulen*. The *Höhere Schulen* will hold those youngsters for eight or nine years leading to preparation for matriculation examination. About twenty or twenty-five percent of those who start actually go on to the *Einheitschule* which provides for almost everyone in the same school.

There is no division in buildings or organization or types of secondary school. It is expected at age twelve, after two years in the lower division of the *Höhere Schule* that the secondary school pupils will transfer in one of three ways: (1) to the *Wissenschaftlicher Zweig* (or the general education branch) encompassing all of the schools leading to the Abitur or matriculation certificate; (2) to the *Technischer Oberschule,* or the secondary technical school in which the student will finish at about age fifteen after staying there for four years after a six-year preliminary instruction period; (3) to the *Praktische Oberschule,* similar to the modern

English school and the in-college preparatory branch of the American school. These students complete their work at age fifteen. It could be possible for some of them to transfer to the *Aufbau* form of the secondary school if they merited it. Parents could make a choice of the particular branch which they wanted their child to go into, but the elementary school authorities would have to ratify it. A transfer could be made after three months.

The different kinds of curricula all have similar type courses in the first year so that they could transfer readily. The authorities felt that more students would enter the practical school or the technical school but because of its high prestige value there is still a rush for the grammar school type. It is said that in recent years there has been some increase in the popularity of the practical branch. (See Figures 10-2 and 10-3 for examples of Hamburg and West Berlin.)

All of the German *Länder* still provide compulsory part-time vocational schools for those pupils between fifteen and eighteen who leave school and go to work. This is carried out in a continuation school and still permits the student to attend school to take both vocational and cultural work on an employer's time. There is full-time vocational training in the technical schools (*Fachschulen*). These generally admit students at the age of eighteen, who would therefore be on a par age-wise with university students.

FRANCE

French schools have developed out of the ideas found in French culture and, also, out of the political system which, since the time of the Louis', is based on centralization of authority within the national government. Even in passing through the period of the French Revolution and Napoleonic Era, and in all of the various changes back and forth from republics to monarchies, the centralized nature of the French government has maintained itself. Each new government, however much it might criticize the old, wished to retain the centralized power it took over in order to enforce whatever reforms it had proposed. Consequently, France resembles an authoritarian state in the extreme centralization of its controls. Their educational system is much more highly centralized than is that of Germany.

Because of the antagonism toward church authority (anticlericalism) arising out of the French Revolution and in the several French Republics which have followed, there has been a strong anticlerical movement.

Maturity Examination *Reifeprüfung*

Pupil's Age	Grade and Class	Classical Language Branch *Altsprachlicher Zweig*	Modern Language Branch *Neusprachlicher Zweig*	Mathematics Natural Science Branch *Mathematisch Naturwissen- schaftlicher Zweig*	General Education Secondary School Arts Branch *Wissen- schaftliche Oberschule Musicher Zweig*	General Education Secondary School *in Aufbauform Wissen- schaftliche Oberschule in Aufbauform*	Technical Secondary School *Technische Oberschule*	Practical Secondary School *Praktische Oberschule*
18	13							
17	12							
16	11							Practical Secondary School *Praktische Oberschule*
15	10							
14	9						Technical Secondary School *Technische Oberschule*	
13	8					Practical & Technical *Praktisch und Technisch*		
12	7							
11	6							
10	5							
9	4			Foundation School *Grundschule*				
8	3							
7	2							
6	1							

Fig. 10.2 Organization of education in West Berlin, around 1957.

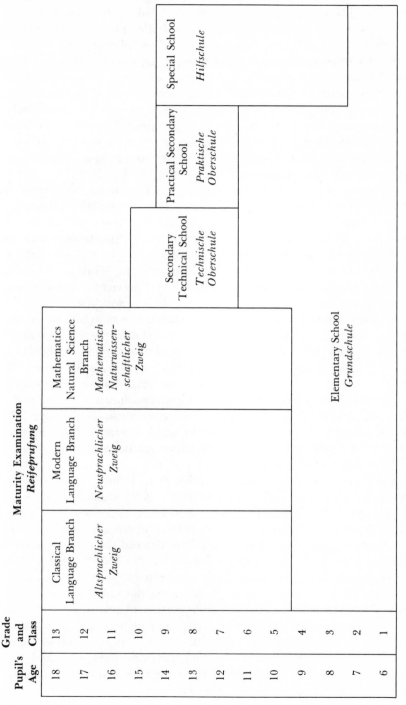

Fig. 10.3   Organization of education in Hamburg, around 1957.

The church has therefore played a much less important role in the development of French educational history than might be expected since France has been predominantly Roman Catholic. The system of education which France developed was thus a highly secular one. To this day, there is no religion taught in the French state schools. Thursday is a school holiday where parents who wish may send their youngsters to the churches in order to receive their religious education. There are, however, some private schools that youngsters may attend and receive religious instruction along with the rest of their courses. These may not have the standing of the state schools. Moreover, the graduates of these schools have to take the state examinations in order to establish any kind of credit or standing for their courses.

As in the other countries of Europe, the French system developed first as a dual school system with the elementary school, *L'Ecole Primaire,* for the lower classes and a system of secondary schools for the upper classes. As time went on with democratic reforms, proposals were made to establish a single unified school system termed *L'Ecole Unique.* Education in France is controlled from the top down by the Minister of Education together with an extensive staff of civil service employees and inspectors who see to it that the ministerial decrees are carried out.

In 1806 Napoleon brought all of secondary education under the one teaching body which he called the *Université de France.* This created a national monopoly over all the teaching of the secondary schools. It wasn't until thirty years later that there was any national concern with elementary education. It was then assigned to local communes, somewhat like the American counties. In 1845, elementary education was brought under the control of the Ministry of Education through the establishment of the academies in each of several regions of France. Later on as a part of the *L'Ecole Unique* movement, they were brought in more fully under the Ministry of Education.

For purposes of educational administration, France is now divided into nineteen regions called *Académies.* The regions are divided into the largest municipal or local government units of France, the departments. Each of the *Académies* has a university. The chief official of an académie is the rector who runs the university and is also the chief representative of the Ministry of Education in the region (or *Académie*). His appointment is made by the President of France upon nomination by the Minister of Education. He is appointed from among the university professors in that particular *Académie.* The major portion of this professor's time is given to the administration of secondary and higher education. These *Académies* have no autonomy. The rector merely acts as a representative of the Ministry of Education to carry out the educational edits as far as secondary education is concerned. The universities maintained in each *Académie* do have some autonomy, however.

The departments are political subdivisions but they are also given some educational responsibilities. These departments are actually governed by a prefect appointed by Paris as the representative of the Ministry of Education in order to carry out certain duties which relate to education. He has an educational council that has some advisory powers. The general departmental council may sometimes levy taxes for education. It is responsible for the upkeep of the buildings and administers the provisional board and room for the students who live in dormitories.

In France the local self-governments are the communes. These may be cities or there may be in part or all rural area and they have an elected council and an elected mayor. However, the mayors are responsible to the prefect of the department of the national government, so consequently do not have many discretionary powers whether in their political role or their educational role. There are local school boards that are appointed at the discretion of the president ex-officio who is also the mayor and they enforce the compulsory attendance law and perform a few other minor unimportant duties.

The French school system in the period prior to 1959, consisted first of a common primary school enrolling all youngsters from about age six to eleven. (See Figure 10–4.) At the age of eleven by means of a very severe examination system, the students were divided according to the schools in which they would be enrolled, with a larger number remaining on for the rest of their compulsory education period in the upper section of the primary school. The compulsory education age prior to 1959 was to age fourteen.

The secondary schools of France have traditionally consisted of two kinds; the Lycées and the Collège. The Lycées were the secondary schools of the highest prestige and had been established directly by the central Ministry of Education; the Collège was a secondary school of lesser grade established by the Department. Because of the higher prestige of the curriculum of the Lycées, the Collèges attempted to carry on the same curriculum so that the pupils could pass the same examinations. Thus, for all practical purposes, the schools became the same. However, the Lycée continued to attract the better students, had the better teachers, and enjoyed higher prestige, and perhaps maintained a higher standard of work.

As time went on, France accepted another kind of school somewhat analogous to the German *Mittelschule*. This was called the *"Cours Complémentaires."* These complementary classes were somewhat higher in standards of work than the upper levels of the primary school, but did not meet the standards of the Collèges or the Lycées. It was possible that persons could pass an examination after taking the complementary classes and enter the normal school (for elementary teachers) after the passing of the first baccalaureat examinations or to certain programs in the university after passing the second baccalaureat examination. At age fourteen

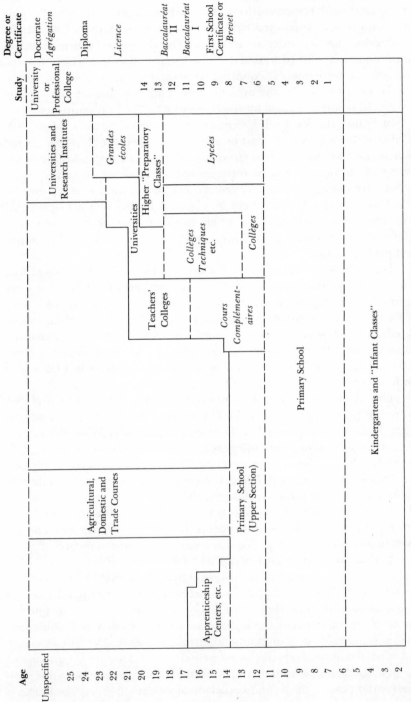

Fig. 10.4 Educational system in France—before implementation of 1959 reforms.

all students could take the first school certificate or the *brevet,* but in the Lycée this was of relatively little importance.

The first baccalauréat, as it was called before the 1959 reform, was taken at the end of the eleventh year of school, the sixth year in the *Lycée* or *Collège.* This examination eliminated a sizeable percentage of students of the secondary schools. The ones left would continue for another year and complete the second level of baccalaureat. Upon the completion of the second level of the baccalaureat, usually not achieved by more than sixty percent of the students left, they were then eligible for admission to some of the university classes. However, for many of the university programs, they needed to stay on in the higher preparatory classes for two years. These classes were available in connection with some of the *Lycées* or *Collèges.* The reasons for the necessity of some of these classes were that some of the engineering and technical schools required mathematics and other materials which were not sufficiently taught in the *Lycée* to get them ready for admission to the university.

In addition to the university there was also available, after finishing two years of preparatory classes, *Les Grandes Ecoles.* These were higher professional schools quite often operated by the civil service divisions of the ministries concerned. If persons were admitted to these schools they were actually on civil service and were paid while they were going to school. This was a very high level and high prestige type of course offering admission into many kinds of professions.

In the university after two or three years, a person could take an examination in order to receive a *Licence.* There were also other diplomas given from time to time indicating the completion of work such as in the *Grandes Ecoles.* These are not degrees in the American sense. A very high-level diploma, called the *agrégation,* was available after several years of highly concentrated study and a very high level of achievement.

This *agrégation* was sufficient to admit a teacher to high-level secondary teaching or to university teaching. Finally, at the top of the educational rung, was the doctorate.

There was also available in France for certain persons at about age thirteen, in the Collèges, the Lycées and, in some cases, the complementary classes, admission to the *Collège Technique.* This was a technical school which provided a higher level of secondary education leading to the engineering or scientific schools at the university level. Upon the completion of compulsory schooling at the age of fourteen, there were part-time courses, apprenticeships, and similar opportunities available for those people who were not going on to higher education.

Under the reform Langevin–Wallon plan, passed by the French Parliament in 1959, there were to be several changes in French education brought about gradually. (See Figure 10-5.) The changes affected only

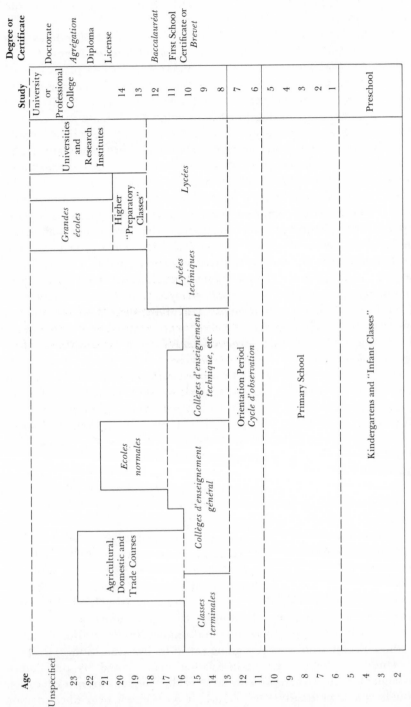

Fig. 10.5 Educational system in France—changes after 1959.

those pupils who entered school in 1959 and afterwards. This meant these forms would not affect the French schools very much until these pupils entered the secondary school five years later (in 1964). Although at age eleven, those still in school take an examination tentatively admitting them into one of several higher schools, the first two years of all these schools serve as an orientation period (*Cycle d'Observation*). During this period each of the schools was supposed to offer somewhat the same courses, making it possible to transfer students who have been incorrectly placed.

Basically, the *Collèges* of the higher secondary level were abolished and all the high-level secondary schools are now called *Lycées*. The old *Collège Technique* became the *Lycée Technique* and has high-level courses on the *Lycée* level. Another one of the schools abolished was the *Collège D'Enseignment Technique* and was similar to American technical institutes. Also gone is the *Collège D'Ensignment General* somewhat similar to the old complementary classes. Then there are the *Classes Terminales* or the old extended elementary school classes. All of the remaining schools are eventually to continue students until they are at least age sixteen. This will be the new school-leaving age, at which point all youngsters will take an examination for a school leaving certificate called *la brèvet*.

Prospective teachers who are now admitted to normal school without going through the *Lycée* must, as a part of the normal school course, complete the requirements for the baccalaureat before they can complete normal school. This raises the status of elementary teachers considerably but does not, as in parts of Germany, give them the university training which all the secondary teachers get. In France even the name applied to the teachers of secondary and elementary school is different. The one is *Le Professeur,* and the other *L'instituteur.*

Students are admitted to a university only after passing many difficult examinations. In addition, most of the universities, since World War II, have established a year called *L'Année Propadeutique* (Preparatory Year). At the end of this first year, there is another examination given to university students to determine whether or not they can continue at the university. This eliminates many persons whom the authorities think are not going to be successful in the examination to obtain the various university *licenses* and diplomas. It is very likely that the students who are successful in passing the second level baccalaureat represent the highest quality "secondary" education anywhere in the world. They have been successively winnowed out, the level required for passing being extremely high. However, the breadth of the courses that they have taken is quite narrow from the standpoint of American conceptions. They are largely the classical languages, French literature, mathematics, and the more "academic" of the sciences. There are practically no social studies or other subjects which would be considered in the United States to be "broadening."

The character of the French elementary schools is rooted in the nation's belief in the principle of "general culture." The French believe that the elementary school helps to preserve the national solidarity by giving all the children the common heritage of the French Nation, the use of the common language, and faith in the contribution of the cultural heritage of their country.

The enforcement of compulsory attendance laws in France is not very strict, particularly in some parts of the rural areas. Elementary schools are in session five days a week and the prescribed subjects are French, reading and writing, history and geography, arithmetic and the metric system, elementary science, moral and civic instruction, drawing, singing, and physical education.

In the French secondary education (the *Lycée*), the emphasis is to prepare the students for further study, and to give them the ability to acquire very highly specialized knowledge and vocational skills. Stress is placed on habits, logical and critical thinking, and speaking and writing well. The French educators show, by their actions at least, that they believe strongly in theories of mental discipline and automatic transfer of training which has been, at least in part, abandoned by other countries of the world.

There are very few electives in the French program, allowing for only minimal choice, aside from the required courses. In the older type of French secondary education, the choice lay between the classics curriculum, the modern letters curriculum, science, and the humanities. In the seventh year of the secondary school, since 1814, there has been prominence given to the study of philosophy not found in secondary schools in many other countries. The classes in the secondary school are numbered from the sixth (the lowest class) up to the first. The first is the sixth year of a seven-year course. In the final or terminal course in which philosophy is studied, mathematics and science are added above the first class in order to prepare for the second level of the baccalaureat. A baccalaureat certificate is actually university matriculation and is not to be confused with the bachelor's degree which is given in American and English universities after completion of a course of university studies.

One feature of French secondary schools, very different from the American high schools, is the number of subjects studied each year by French students. An American high-school student usually takes four or five subjects a year, usually five days a week for each. A French student, on the other hand, takes many more subjects throughout each year of the seven-year course, and most of these courses meet only two or three periods a week. It is not unusual for a student to be carrying twelve or more different subjects at one time in his secondary school course.

The atmosphere in the French secondary school is very stiff and formal with the teachers giving formal lectures and with the students taking notes much as in a formal university in England or the United States. The student keeps exercise books as an important part of the program. Very few textbooks or reference books are used or are available, and there are no school libraries. Primarily, the students copy the material dictated by the teacher rather than reading supplementary material. The examinations are of great importance in the student's educational career and the materials dictated must be the kind of work which is called for in examinations. Many of the students feel that they must memorize the subject matter even though perhaps this is not what the teachers of France wish them to do. Interestingly enough, in recent years (since 1956), the government has forbidden the requiring of homework in the elementary schools so all the work must be completed by the student before he leaves school. It is said that this is as yet not strictly enforced.[4]

The secondary school student in France spends more time in school than his American counterpart. The school year in France is only forty-two weeks and classes are in session six hours a day, five days a week. This is comparable, of course, to the usual thirty-nine or forty weeks in the city schools of America and the thirty-six weeks of many of the smalltown and rural schools.

THE UNITED KINGDOM: ENGLAND AND WALES

The United Kingdom of Great Britain and Northern Ireland consists of four parts; England, Wales, Scotland, and Northern Ireland. The customs and practices of the schools vary somewhat in each of these parts. Apart from minor organizational and cultural differences, the schools in Wales are operated very similarly to those in England.

The educational system of England is headed by the National Minister of Education with the National Government providing a considerable part of the financial support of all schools. The Local Educational Authorities (L.E.A.) handle the administrative details at the lower level. The British system of education can best be understood by realizing that it is based upon three important principles: (1) the retaining of as much authority as possible by the Local Educational Authorities, but with financial backing by the National Government; (2) the allocation of an

[4] U.S. Department of Health, Education and Welfare. *Education in France*, p. 70.

important part of educational activities to voluntary organizations, usually religious in nature but some merely private; (3) the very considerable freedom of the headmaster and the teachers in decisions on the details of class organization, curriculum, and teaching methods within their own school.

England had developed, largely through private and religious enterprise, a hodgepodge of schools without any attempt at bringing any order out of the system until about 1870. In the Education Act of 1870, it was made compulsory for primary schools to be established throughout the country. These were of the two types: (1) the council or provided school, established and supported in total by the local authorities; (2) the voluntary or nonprovided schools, most of which were operated by the religious groups. The Local Educational Authorities (L.E.A.) have paid the salaries of the teachers and the general cost of education, at least in part, over the years in the voluntary schools as well as in the provided schools. The difference between the two types was that the voluntary schools' sponsors had to raise the funds themselves necessary for the building of schools and their maintenance.

In the period just prior to World War II, the primary schools had, wherever possible, become more "child-centered," schools characterized by activity programs and special work in art and music, similar to trends which had taken place in elementary education in the United States. Very little change had taken place in British secondary education until the recent post World War II period; however, there are now most significant changes being made. Secondary education in England is no longer, as it was previously, the privilege of a very few persons; gradually it has been made available to nearly all, starting after 1944.

In the period prior to 1944, the date of the most important educational act in the educational history of England (to be discussed later), there had grown up in England over the years a patchwork of many kinds of secondary and post-primary schools. These schools, of course, had rendered a fine service to England in many ways, but it was felt when the Education Act of 1944 was passed that the system should be greatly simplified. This was done by providing basically three types of schools. This plan was later to be called the tri-partite system of education. The three types were: the secondary grammar schools, the secondary modern schools, and the secondary technical schools. It was expected in the planning stage that there would be four pupils in the secondary modern schools for every one in each of the other two types or, in other words, four out of six or two-thirds would be in the modern school. The L.E.A.'s were free to organize these schools in whatever way they wished. They could combine them into one general school, to be called the comprehensive school, or they might have separate schools located on the same single campus or be completely separated. Let us discuss each of these types in turn.

The Grammar School. The grammar-type of education had existed for many years in England and is famous throughout the world. In curriculum it corresponds most closely to the college preparatory courses in American high schools or to the special college-preparatory academies. After completing the primary education at age eleven or twelve, the grammar school pupils continue their schooling for six or seven (and sometimes eight) more years. They planned to either enter the university or take a relatively high position in banks or commercial establishments. The course of study in the grammar school consists of English language and literature, foreign language, science, mathematics, history, geography, and art and music—all studied over a period of years in a very formal academic manner. At the end of the first five years—at approximately age sixteen—the students would take an examination for the ordinary level "general certificate of education" (G.C.E.). The sixth form, for one to two years for the seventeen to nineteen year olds, caps the work of the school. This was usually a highly specialized course which gives the advanced pupils special training in a particular scholarly area plus special training for responsibility and initiative. At the end of this period, they would take the advanced level G.C.E. The grammar schools may be of three types: (1) the provided type, i.e., those set up and provided by the L.E.A.; (2) the voluntary type, i.e., operated by religious or other private groups; and (3) they may be the English Public Schools (really a private school of considerable prestige and with a long ancient history), to be discussed later.

The Technical Schools. The technical school is not entirely new; it developed from the so-called technical school which began to appear as a part of the "patchwork" in about 1905. These schools did some good work but they suffered from the disadvantage of being regarded by many persons as merely schools for artisans and domestic helpers. They admitted pupils at age thirteen after two years of post-primary education in the primary schools and were often housed in the senior technical school buildings with a tendency to be overshadowed by the senior schools. In some cases, the general education aspect of the work was subordinated to the trade training. In the new technical schools, the work was to be raised considerably in level so that it would be somewhat comparable with that of the grammar schools except with a different emphasis, and the general education aspect of the work would not be overlooked.

The English Modern School. This of course is still a controversial school in British education and there are many questions and problems with regard to it. Eventually all of the post-primary education had been planned to be organized on the basis of a secondary modern school (or as part of the comprehensive school as it becomes available) for those people who were not admitted to the grammar school or the technical schools. There are a few districts which have not as yet enrolled all of the post-primary persons in the secondary modern schools.

The modern school continues to be for students up to age fifteen. Later, perhaps, it is to be extended to age sixteen—when the compulsory education law has been extended to that age (1970?). It has been suggested that the vast number of persons entering this school will become workers in mills, factories, stores, plants, offices, transportation services, farms, personal services, and in the homes. Most of these schools are coeducational in nature. These schools also try to get the students interested in scholarly subjects, in books themselves, and worthwhile leisure activities. In recent years, the first two years of the secondary modern school have been made very similar to that of grammar schools, so there can still be some carry-over or transfer during this period where there have been mistakes in the "eleven-plus" examination used to determine whether pupils may enter the grammar-school section.

Subjects which are included in the English modern schools are many and vary from school to school, but they include English expression, social studies, health and physical education, games and sports, general science, general mathematics, arts and crafts, nature study, biology, history, geography, music, horticulture, literature, film appreciation, and a modern language which can be an elective.

In 1965 the Department of Education and Science issued a policy statement (known as 10/65) calling upon all Local Education Authorities to present plans to the Department showing how they would change the secondary schools under their direction to a system of comprehensive education, that is, of secondary schools enrolling all boys and girls in each area under one administration with neither selection nor segregated curricula. Under this provision, many local authorities have submitted plans, and have, upon approval, taken steps forward toward developing a complete system of comprehensive schools. There are many obstacles in the way such as opposition of the grammar school advocates, a lack of buildings adequate for comprehensive education and the lack of staff and finances for the increased numbers of persons under comprehensive education. Also, the entire movement became involved as a political issue.

In 1965, the Certificate of Secondary Education (C.S.E.) was set up to provide an examination for a school-leaving certificate for pupils who have been in the modern school (or comprehensive school) for five years.

The English "Public" School.   The "Public Schools" (really exclusive and endowed private schools) are, by far, the most distinctive feature of all British education. The development of these private schools, some of them founded hundreds of years ago, has been largely responsible for the

British tradition of education. They provide a high level of training in character building and the liberal studies, but this training has been available only to a few and somewhat exclusive group of pupils. According to some conceptions of general education, such training might be considered narrow.

The public school is defined as one which is represented on the Public School Governing Body Association or the Head Master's Conference. In general, in order for a school to qualify as a member in one of these two groups, it must be independent of any public grant or receive just a direct grant from the Ministry of Education. It must not get any money from an L.E.A. It must also supply evidence of the complete freedom of the school and of the head master.

One characteristic of most English Public Schools is the provision for boarding school education. Also, all of them have a prefect system whereby the older boys have a definite share in maintaining discipline and the general tone and mores of the school. Especially to be noted is the house system which attaches the boys to residence of one of the houses under a house master. Moreover, this has been imitated by many other grammar schools, both residential and day. In the public schools, there is a strong emphasis upon games, there is attention given to religion, and there is a great deal of importance attached by the boys to the corporate activities of the school.

Criticisms of these schools have been made regarding their exclusiveness, and their very conservative educational methods and ideas. The English people, in general, undoubtedly approve of these schools and the ideal of the "English gentlemen" which is upheld by these schools. Many persons felt, after World War II when the whole social climate of England was changing, that these schools would suffer a decline, particularly since the other schools were becoming better. However, the prestige and glamour of the "old school tie" is probably as high as it ever was. Many persons holding highest positions in government and business are from these schools, and those of most prestigious rank are, usually, from one of the older of these schools.

Critics maintain that the Public School system is wrong and that it has no place in democratic society. They argue that it maintains the lines of division between social classes because it is expensive and exclusive. There are, however, a few students who, on the basis of scholarships, have gained entrance to these schools. This is helping to break down class exclusiveness. Also, the fact that there have been students graduating from some of the other schools of equally good talent has helped modify the Public Schools' entrenched position.

The Independent Public Schools are then losing their monopoly of position in the civil service and at Oxford and Cambridge. Also, they are beginning to feel the financial strain of the additional expense of education without being able to raise their tuition. Some of them have applied for grants from the Ministry of Education and have become aided schools. In this case, they are no longer completely independent and have to open at least twenty-five percent of their available places to students nominated by the L.E.A. The larger ones, however, are completely independent and will probably continue to be so for some time. Whether or not in the far distant future, when the social changes taking place in England have continued still further, and the county secondary schools have become more efficient, the Public School will continue, is unknown.

There are very few schools in England which are coeducational. The Public School "tradition" was of course strongly against it and this has influenced other secondary education. English education goes back to the monastic traditions of past centuries and there was a relatively late educational emancipation of English girls and women. The girls' schools are mostly of recent origin and only after World War I were women even admitted to degrees at Oxford or Cambridge. In the reorganized system of secondary education, by and large, there have been separate schools for boys and girls; however, many of the modern schools and the new comprehensive schools are coeducational. Coeducation has been common in Scotland for some time and it will be interesting to see whether it makes any difference in the new system.

There have been in the past a great number of apparently unchanging features of British education. This had been so even with the reforms that have been made in the modern school, with the housing of modern schools with some of the grammar school persons in the same building (bi-lateral schools) and with the development of comprehensive schools.

One feature of the British school is the almost universal use of "streaming." "Streaming" is synonomous with "homogeneous" or "ability grouping" in the United States. After the students have been separated in terms of the kind of schools to which they will go, these groups are then divided further and put in separate classes (or streams) in terms of their abilities as measured by achievement, intelligence tests, or some other means. They continue for one year in this stream but, usually at the end of this year, there are readjustments of students into new streams. The study made by Pedley indicates that there are considerable changes in most schools at the end of each year in regard to the stream to which the student is placed as measured by his achievement.[5] Moreover, the author found in his 1967 visit to England, a movement in a few comprehensive schools to abolish streaming completely.

As was found in the American experience, ability grouping in practice has the difficulty of the school not being able to identify all the factors which allow for achievement, and particularly when there are factors which vary according to the subject being taught. In England, the adjustment of the individual student according to his ability in a partic-

[5] Robin Pedley. *The Comprehensive School*, p. 89.

ular subject is called "setting." This takes place mainly in mathematics, modern language, English, and science.

One of the big features of the secondary school, or of almost all schools in England for that matter, is the independence of the local headmaster. After the teachers have been employed, their salaries will be paid in an amount which has been set by the Minister of Education. The employing in the maintained schools has been done by the L.E.A. The secondary-school headmaster is perfectly free to operate the school as he and his faculty see fit. There is no required curriculum or required type of scheduling or anything; there is complete independence. The only course that is required in the provided secondary school is the common religious syllabus. While the schools are required to offer this, the students are not required to take it.[6] Of course, it should be noted since the student will eventually take a national examination for the ordinary level of the G.C.E. and, since the success of the student on this examination is widely considered to be an indication of the success of the school, this event constitutes in effect a kind of control.

Now, also there are Her Majesty's Inspectors from the Ministry of Education who do come around to the school. However, they consider themselves in the main there to help the teacher rather than to tell him precisely what to do. Because these inspectors are able individuals who have taught themselves and, because they travel from school to school getting new ideas, usually their ideas are rather well-accepted. They are not ignored nor are they considered to be in the position of issuing orders to the teachers or in prescribing the curriculum. In fact, in line with the tradition of independence of the school masters and school teachers in England, the teachers would probably not comply anyway.

In the private boarding schools of England the students have been organized in houses arranged by the dormitories in which they lived. These houses were concerned with student self-government including a system of prefects to take care of student discipline and other such matters. There was competition between the houses in sports and a great deal of school spirit centered around the houses. As England has changed from the exclusive private schools to the comprehensive schools for the masses many head masters have carried into the day schools the house concept. On entering the school at age eleven, or sometimes later, the students are assigned to one of several houses. The purpose to be served by these houses varies from school to school but usually competition in sports, some student self-government and guidance centers around the house system. It apparently serves a purpose in binding together youngsters from different walks of life and in the different curricula in the comprehensive schools.[7]

---

[6] Students actually are excused only by request of parent.
[7] Robin Pedley, *The Comprehensive School,* p. 128.

Further Education.   In England any education beyond the compulsory age is known as further education. So the sixth form of secondary schools, the advanced part-time continuation education, adult education, university education, and so on, are all considered to be further education. University education is highly specialized in curriculum and has been open in the past only to a very few. In the recent Robbins Report,[8] 1963, an effort is now being made to open up new university places to all those who desire to go and who can qualify by examination. This means almost doubling the number of places in the next ten years. New universities are to be added and some institutions are to be upgraded to university level. There is also to be an increase of education at the county level in the so-called county colleges. This was included in the Education Act of 1944 but has not yet been put into operation. This would allow for more advanced education in the various counties, such as vocational and other classes beyond the compulsory education age.

In England the training of prospective teachers (they are called the "intending teacher," as, in America, "teacher-in-training") is done in either of two ways. One is through university channels and the other is through "training colleges" which are similar to the American state colleges. In the university, upon completion of three-year degree, they can go one further year to the training school attached to it in order to take the courses in pedagogy, practice teaching, and so on, necessary to the teaching certificate. In the training colleges attached to the universities, the students pursue a three-year course in which they are prepared in their subject as well as in their education courses. These three years are in the process of being revised to four. The training colleges are to be called Colleges of Education with degrees to be awarded to the graduates by regional Institutes of Education.

There are other kinds of educational opportunities offered in England—special part-time adult courses may be offered by the L.E.A.'s as well as numerous classes offered by the Worker Educational Associations. There is British Broadcasting Company operated by the Department of Education; there are libraries, museums, and many other cultural groups. Education thus plays an important role in adult education as it does to the general populace.

See end of Chapter 11 for bibliographies and films for Chapters 10 and 11.

8 "The British Government Endorses the Robbins Report," *School and Society* (March 7, 1964), pp. 107–8.

11

Contemporary
Comparative Educational Systems,
Twentieth Century (continued):
The U.S.A. and the Soviet Union

This chapter presents the contrasting educational systems of the two most populous and advanced nations of the world. The United States of America and the Soviet Union, by historical accident, have been thrust into the forefront on the two sides of the East–West cold war, and, consequently, their educational systems have become of interest to each other and to other nations in the world.

THE UNITED STATES OF AMERICA

In Chapter 9, the story of how the American school system came to develop during the nineteenth century both in the elementary and secondary level was presented. By the beginning of the second decade of the twentieth century, there had developed in the United States to all intents and purposes, a complete "ladder" system of education from kindergarten in most areas, or at least from the first grade, through the university Ph.D. without any admission examinations or quota roadblocks and with, in many cases, little or no tuition, even at the university level (state universities).*

Education in the United States is very complex. The United States of America is a federal union of states and each of these has complete *legal* control of its own school system. In most of the states, control of education has been delegated by the state by law and through its consti-tution to local communities and there is a wide variety of different kinds of programs and procedures under which the schools are operated. Ac-cordingly it can be seen why it is inaccurate to speak of the "American school system." It should be noted also that, although legally the states are responsible for education that has been delegated to local com-munities, actually in the history of the United States, schools originated through the initiation of local communities with the states coming in at a much later date to exercise a minimum of control. How the school system developed is not that of the state first taking the initiative and then ask-ing the local communities to develop schools, but on the other hand, quite the reverse. The states were tardy in their interest and concern about schools.

Interestingly enough, the central government, although constitu-tionally prohibited from exercising any control of education, and since by the tenth amendment all powers not specifically given to Congress by the Constitution are reserved to the state and *education is not mentioned,* the federal government has, nevertheless, shown considerable interest in education over the years. Even before the formation of the federal United States of America, there was the land grant of one township in sixteen in the Northwest Territory, beyond the Appalachians and north of the Ohio River, for the benefit of schools. In 1860, there was the develop-ment of the land grant colleges in which each state was given a certain amount of land or an equivalent appropriation to establish a land grant college. In addition to operating schools in the various island territories not yet organized as states, the federal government also operates many schools for the training of its own personnel and for the military services. In recent years, the federal government has exercised an increasing con-trol over educational decisions by means of Supreme Court decisions in areas where fundamental constitutional questions of human rights were involved.

A look at the school systems, as found in states, reveals that there are certain features common to all the state systems. American education provides a universal program for all children beginning at age six and

* Many private institutions and some state schools require special examinations or have quota limits. In this case the student must attend another school open to him. Some state universities in the fifties and sixties have gradually raised their fees so that the costs have become more sizable. Community colleges are taking their place in the first two years of college with low tuition opportunities. The expense of living away from home is also a factor for many students.

continuing until age sixteen in most of the states and to eighteen in the remainder. In all of the states, this policy includes education for all. The percentage of the school population which remains in school for the entire twelve years has been constantly rising. Over ninety percent of the children between the age of five and seventeen are in school, a much higher percentage than that of any other country in the world. The percentage of Americans who continue on to college or to the university is also much higher than that of other parts of the world. As a matter of fact, this percentage of American boys and girls of college age who go on to college or to the university is higher than the percentage who go on to secondary schools in any country except, possibly, in the Soviet Union.

At the present time, the American elementary school is generally considered to include the first six or eight grades of the common school system, depending on the local organization plan. Increasingly, this is now becoming six grades. About half of the youngsters also live in school districts where they have the option of enrolling in kindergarten. In the United States, the elementary classes depend on the number in the age level within each part of the country. In the United States, over ninety-eight percent of children between the ages of six and thirteen are actually enrolled in school.

By and large, the principal aim of education in the elementary school is the education of the good citizen. The basic skills in the language arts, reading, writing, speaking, and listening are taught along with the mastery of arithmetic as being basic for all citizens. Courses in history, geography, science, health, and the arts and physical education are taught at appropriate times to most youngsters in American elementary schools. Most schools also teach many fundamental habits, ideals, and attitudes that every citizen needs. The basic purpose of the public schools then becomes one of integrating each individual into the life of the community and nation and of making him a self-controlled and self-directing citizen.

A hundred years ago, the elementary school was very traditional in terms of adhering largely to teaching the three "R's" out of a standardized text. It has now evolved to the much more complex and "progressive" school of today. In the United States educational control is based upon local autonomy (even though there is some state supervision); consequently, there is always a great deal of experimentation going on in all parts of the country with some communities trying out different types of organization and curriculum. In spite, however, of this local autonomy with no government agency to prescribe for the American school system—not even the states prescribing within a state—there are many more points of likenesses than of differences between any two American schools. A youngster moving across the United States is quite likely to find an elementary class waiting for him in which the instruction is very similar to that in the school he attended previously.

Because there are so many differences in the control of American secondary education in different parts of the country, it is even more difficult to show that any kind of a system of secondary education exists in the United States. The traditional four-year high school still enrolls about forty percent of the secondary-school pupils, the divided junior and senior high schools enrolls another slightly less than forty percent and most of the remainder are in the undivided junior–senior six-year schools. The administrative convenience or educational philosophy of the school boards of the local districts determines what kind of organization is selected. About eighty-two percent of all fourteen to seventeen year olds are enrolled in some type of secondary school.

In addition to the feature of the ladder type of education with no barriers, the other striking difference between American education and education abroad is the phenomenon of the locally elected board of education that legally owns and actually operates the school. This came about largely as an accident of history out of the New England town meeting. The educational precedents that were set in New England had a strong effect on what happened in other parts of the country (as illustrated in Chapter 9). In New England the town meeting—a "pure" democratic government, i.e., not using representations but all citizens—met, made the laws, and the executive decisions for the coming year. Among other things, the town meeting established schools. When the Massachusetts General Court (Legislature) decided the schools should become compulsory, they made the town meetings responsible. The town meeting would appoint selectmen to operate a school during the year while the town meeting was not in session. They also selected a group of persons called the school committee whose assignment was to operate a single school. Eventually then, these school committees provided the precedent for an elected board of education from each of the school districts to operate that particular school.

As the people in New England moved west, they took this idea of the school committee with them and as the new states were formed, school districts were formed in which the schools were established. When the principle of free education became established, the people then taxed themselves in order to pay the cost of their schools. The practice was developed and in operation long before the states themselves began to establish any kind of a supervision of education from the state level. However, during the twentieth century most of the states have established certain types of minimal standards for the schools within their borders. This started with an interest in the certification of teachers and led to the upgrading of the county schools, school bus transportation and, later on, in the improvement of teacher salaries through the giving of money to the school districts on some kind of an equalization basis. Only in the state of Delaware is the system partially *operated* from the state level.

The members of boards of education are not educators nor officials. They are ordinary citizens without any specific legal qualifications who have been elected by their fellow citizens to make the basic decisions in regard to schools. As a matter of fact, practically all the power is in their hands; however, they may delegate this power to the chief school officer, the school superintendent, who has been specifically trained and certified in order to operate the schools effectively and efficiently.

As has been indicated in Chapter 9, the early secondary schools of the United States prepared boys and, to a very small extent, girls for college. Girls were actually not admitted to the academy or to the Latin grammar schools until later in American history. The course of study was narrow and classical and offered no choice of subjects. Preparation for life was, of course, a by-product and bore no relationship to the subjects offered by the school. Less than ten percent of the fourteen to eighteen year old group was enrolled and this was a highly select minority. They were either extremely bright or the children of families on the higher economic levels. Chapter 9 told how the secondary school changed from the Latin grammar school to the academy and afterwards to the high school.

After the beginning of the twentieth century, the attitude toward secondary education began to change rapidly. Prior to that time even the high school was primarily a college-preparatory classical-type school. After this time, the public high schools were being established everywhere and no tuition was charged. Consequently, the children of all economic levels were now able to attend a free public high school, many of whom were not intellectually endowed, nor were they going on to college. In the year 1900, for example, about one-half million students attended the American secondary school which was about seven tenths percent of the total population of seventy-five million. In 1940 about six and one-half million students were enrolled, or five percent of the 130 million population. This meant that for each decade of the twentieth century through 1930, the high school was doubled, and between 1930 and 1940 it was again increased by fifty percent. It is estimated that in order to take care of this population the American people built on the average about three new high schools per day for five days a week during the school year with an average increase of about nine hundred new students per day. Today the high-school attendance in American communities is almost universal. In California, for example, it has been said that around ninety-three percent of eligible students are actually enrolled in high school.

The prevailing thinking in American education is that the "secondary school" is the name to be used for the formal secondary education institution for all adolescent youth. Secondary education begins with the onset of adolescence and continues to the post-adolescent period or an age range of about twelve to twenty years. Educationally, this would be from the seventh grade to the sophomore year in the university. The junior colleges and the first two years of the traditional four-year colleges are frequently discussed as essentially secondary in nature although they may cover the first two years of college or university work. This also can be correlated with the fact that when students finish the secondary school in Europe they are usually two years ahead in achievement over American students.

The average American high-school student takes only four or five subjects a year in addition to physical education or health. There are usually certain subjects that are required of all students and the rest are electives, "constants with the electives" curriculum. A list of the subjects actually required do vary somewhat from state to state and school to school, but usually includes at least three years of English and at least two years of social studies. Quite often a year of mathematics, a year of science, and, in some cases, two years of foreign languages may be added to the required list. This limiting of the number of subjects taken for a year is very different from many schools abroad where the youngsters take a good many more subjects which do not meet on quite as many days a week. This is particularly true of France, as discussed in Chapter 10.

The American secondary school has shown an enormous increase in the number of schools, and enrollments with an increase in the holding power (decrease in student attrition) during the high-school years. Also, there has been a striking increase in the number of courses that are offered as electives for students in the school. In some cases, some cities have developed specialized high schools, such as technical schools, commercial high schools, or home-economic high schools; however, the tendency in this country is toward establishing the comprehensive (or composite) high schools. Where previously there have been specialized high schools, the tendency has been recently to add the comprehensive programs to it. England is tending to develop the comprehensive high school, and this trend may be taken later in still other countries.

The American comprehensive high school includes in its offerings most of the various kinds of education offered in specialized schools, but brings them together in the same school. All the students in the comprehensive high school may take the same required courses, such as English, social studies, science, or mathematics. Then they may take whatever electives they need to meet their specialized vocational need or avocational interest. By and large, American opinion favors all secondary students attending the same kind of high school for democratic reasons. It is for this reason that there is not the difference of esteem between the various courses as there was in England where previously all students had to attend different schools in order to enroll in different courses according to whether they planned to go to the university or otherwise.

In the traditional high school, the subject matter was considerably compartmentalized. This is being modified in that the high schools have a tendency to offer social studies courses that would include history along with other social problems, and general mathematics courses combining various aspects of mathematics. Also, general science courses and surveys of physics- or biology-type courses have been experimented with in some schools.

Since the major purpose of the American high school has been that of preparing its students as citizens for democracy, most secondary schools have developed a wide variety of out-of-class activities in which opportunities are given to provide for leadership practice and development. Golf, cricket, rowing, and football have all been activities in the English public schools since the eighteenth century, and there was at least one student publication in Eton as early as 1786. By the nineteenth century student activities such as social clubs, history societies, political organizations, debating societies, began to appear in the secondary schools throughout the world with the possible exception of France.

The American high schools also showed early evidence of such extracurricular activities. The number and variety of these activities are much greater at present in the United States than anywhere else in the world. In addition to the athletic activities, there are musical, dramatic, debating and special interests clubs (such as science clubs, photography clubs), student publications, honor societies, service clubs, and homeroom organizations. Some of the schools have highly developed student governments and other student organizations which handle many of their own affairs.

The teachers quite frequently have assignments as faculty advisors to these student organizations and activities. Sometimes teachers are even hired because of their skills in conducting extracurricular activities. The student activities are usually financed through the membership fees paid to the over-all student organization, through club dues, or through paid admission to athletic contests, concerts, operettas, band concerts, and other money-raising activities. In some states, the board of education does provide part of the funds for athletic and other activities; in other states this is illegal. The amount of money handled in these student organizations is so great that many states have now provided for a regular audit of student funds, in some cases requiring it to be kept in a central treasury in the school's office.

The words, extra-curriculum and out-of-class activities, have been used so far in discussing these organizations. However, many authorities have felt that these are so much a part of the American secondary school curriculum, and so important in the education and development of the student, that they prefer to use a term such as "co-curricular" activities. There is no essential difference between the objectives of the program of faculty guidance in activities as compared to the regular classes. Only the content emphasis is different and there is more creativity and freedom of choice on the part of the student in the activity program.

The development of the American junior college or the community college is a phenomenon which is now considered. There is a question as to whether this should be counted as secondary or higher education. In some cases, it has been organized by the higher institutions in extension centers near the students' homes. In other cases, it has been organized by local or county boards of education as a continuation of grades eleven and twelve of the high school. Since it does require about the same courses of all students, it is justified to call it secondary education and it is more comparable within the last few years to the German gymnasium or the French Lycée or even the British "sixth form," than it is with the first years of a European university.

According to the United States Office of Education, there are over two thousand institutions of higher education in the United States. About one-third of these are actually publicly controlled, and the remainder are private or church-connected institutions. However, the publicly con- trolled institutions do enroll more than half of the students. In the year 1965–66 it was estimated that there were 5,570,000 persons enrolled in higher education in the United States. This was over twenty-five percent of the population of the college-age group. Around fifty percent of the age level actually continued, upon graduation from high school, into college, and around fifteen to twenty-five percent of the population age group were currently being graduated from college.[1]

There are a variety of higher educational institutions in the United States. In this respect the American colleges are something like the "hodge-podge" of secondary schools in England. The liberal arts college, the first to be established, is still flourishing. This college has no counter- part in Europe. Most of these are church connected or independent. Then there are independent universities that offer a wide variety of academic and professional work. The state universities have been growing in size and influence and offer many types of educational programs. The land-grant colleges or universities sometimes specialize in work in the technical fields of agriculture, engineering, home economics, and forestry, but they also may be a part of a larger university complex. In almost every state there have been institutions which started out as two-year normal schools and having grown into colleges of education, now exist as separate state colleges. These not only grant bachelor's degrees in the field of education, but offer some graduate work. There are some municipal colleges or universities with local financial control that offer

---

[1] Based on estimates of the National Education Association as reported in NEA Research Bulletin (May, 1966), p. 40.

both day and night courses in academic and professional fields. The locally controlled junior colleges have already been discussed.

In general, higher education in the United States is divided into two broad fields, the liberal arts and the professional. Each of these is further divided into undergraduate and graduate levels. The liberal arts program at the undergraduate level, whether or not found in separate institutions, is frequently divided into two levels: the first, two years and the second, two years. Quite often at the end of the first two years, an associate of arts or an associate of sciences degree may be earned and received. Some of the colleges divide their program into broad fields such as languages, literature, social sciences, sciences, mathematics, or fine arts. There are set requirements which specify that freshmen and sophomores take one or two full-year courses in each of three fields. Some courses, such as English or history are required of all with electives permitted in the other fields. This plan seeks to provide for the student's broad education before he specializes. In the European university, almost all the work is specialized. In the United States professional education is offered in a wide variety of fields and, in some cases, it may be pursued in separate institutions, or it may be attached to some university. Theology is found almost entirely in separate institutions. Quite often three or four years of liberal arts must be taken before admission to a professional school.

Graduate work requires completion of the bachelor's degree as a prerequisite for admission. A minimum of one year of graduate study with or without the submission of a written theses may lead to a master of arts degree. There are also master's degrees offered in the professional fields, such as master of education or master of engineering. The Ph.D. degree may be earned either in a liberal-arts discipline or in one of many professional fields. It is based on a minimum of two years of graduate study following attainment of a master's degree, including the preparation of a research project in the form of a doctorate dissertation. The American graduate schools are modeled very much on the German universities of the period of the 1880's. The American universities conceive of their functions as being instruction, research, and service. In the case of the state institutions, the responsibility for service is taken very seriously. Much of their work is providing surveys, research, and field service to various enterprises within their state.

The summer sessions, started largely as an extension activity, have now become a distinctive feature of higher education in the United States. Hundreds of thousands of students, young and old, go to the university and college summer sessions for periods of four to ten or eleven weeks during the summer vacation. A large number of these students are teachers working on advanced degrees or securing in-service training to keep them up to date in methods and content.

As lacking as the American schools still are in being able to meet the needs of everyone, and many persons of good potentiality are turned away largely for economic reasons, America's enrollment in schools at all levels is a much larger percentage of their population than that of any other country in the world. The percentage of our population which is educated as per any level above the elementary school is the highest of any country in the world.

THE SOVIET UNION AND ITS EDUCATIONAL SYSTEM

The Development of the Soviet Union (Russia). The country, popularly known as Russia, which has the largest political territory on earth under a common political authority is officially known as the Union of Soviet Socialist Republics; in short, the Soviet Union. The Soviet Union covers an area of nearly nine million square miles and in this territory there is almost every kind of climate, soil, and other geographic conditions imaginable. Much of the area is very thinly populated, particularly in central Asia and toward the north. In the mid-sixties it had a population of more than 225 million people living in an area about three times that of the United States. This country extends from the Baltic Sea in Europe to the Pacific Ocean in the east and from the Black Sea and the Gobi Desert in the south up to the Arctic Ocean. In this grand expanse it runs through hot deserts as well as fertile temperate areas and on into barren steppes. In the heavily populated regions around Moscow the winters are extremely severe making normal life very difficult during a large part of the winter season. The history of Russia as it has expanded from the area around Moscow and taking over this vast territory is quite similar to the western expansion of the United States with the frontier having also played an important part in Russian history.

There are perhaps over one hundred distinct nationalities in this large country. There are many languages and customs used in different localities. For example, the newspapers have to be published in about sixty-five different languages. There are five separate types of scripts used. Even in the fifteen major Union Republics, the major language is different in each of them. There are probably over 150 different languages spoken throughout the country but many of these are not even in written form. Looking at the population in another way, it ranges from very nonliterate type of people (such as the American Eskimos) in the far north to nomadic peoples in the south, and a wide range in religious differences, such as Lutherans, Roman Catholics, Orthodox Catholics, and Muslims.

Another factor must be taken into account in the total picture, however, about sixty-percent of the population are the Russians proper (the
Great Russians as they are called). It is the language of these people that
is the official language throughout the entire Soviet Union. Another
twenty percent are Ukranian Russians whose language is very similar to
that of the Great Russians. So this leaves only one-fifth to include all the
other nationalities.

Something of the history of Russia before Communism is of help in
understanding the country. Before 1905 the country was an absolute
monarchy. There was an hereditary Czar who possessed in his own person all absolute powers. In his operation of the country he was aided by
government officials who were appointed by him and were responsible
only to him, along with the Russian Orthodox Church itself, also under
his control. In this absolutistic regime there were a few persons of the
upper class who were well educated. There was some achievement in
scholarship and learning in the early Imperial Period. But the common
people, as a whole, were in a very state of ignorance and poverty.

There had been a revolution in 1905 and some limitations on the
powers of the Czar were imposed, but in reality not much had occurred.
During World War I a revolution occurred in several countries including
that of Russia. During this period of revolution single groups seized the
government in several countries and did away with all pretense of democratic forms. First, the Russian Imperial Government was overthrown in
February, 1917 by a group headed by Alexander Kerensky. But in Octo-
ber, 1917 the Bolsheviks ("majority"), a minority group lead by Lenin
and Trotsky, took control. This small group, in control of the country
ever since, regulates every single facet of government, culture, and propaganda.

Because it is such a diverse country, it has been organized as a federal
government. This consists of fifteen constituent republics that are called
the Union Republics and these correspond to the major nationality
groups. Within these fifteen Union Republics there are other small national groups which are organized into either "autonomous republics" of
which there are sixteen, or "autonomous regions" of which there are nine
and ten national areas. The "national areas" are something like the
American territories before they became self-governing. The Russian
Soviet Federated Socialist Republic, with its capitol at Moscow, also the
capital of the Union, is by far the largest of the republics and within its
boundaries there are about one-hundred nationalities and linguistic
groups.

The policy of the Czar was imperialistic and expansionist. The
Soviet Union has continued this policy. Territories have been added to
the Union which were never a part of Czarist Russia. The governmental
policy under the Czars was strongly nationalistic and a policy of

"Russification" was carried out. Although the Soviet Union did not attempt to ruthlessly bring about the Russification, there are many policies in force that indicate that the ultimate end of the government of the Soviet Union at present may also be Russification.

The study of the Russian language in every Republic is a compulsory subject at least by the third grade, even though in some of the republics they may teach in a native tongue in the elementary school. Even though local customs and languages are used, nationalism as such is discouraged or repressed except the nationalism of the total Russian Soviet Union. In many of the books that have been prepared for use in the schools, the greatness of the Russian people has been emphasized, and the importance stressed of the minority groups' opportunities to share in the glory of the great achievements of the Russian people. Proficiency in the Russian language enables a person to move up in the ladder of achievement. Most of the higher education is conducted in Russian. It is almost essential to be proficient in that language to hold down any important office in industry or government.

In light of what we know about education and schools reflecting the nature of a culture, it is not surprising that the main purpose of education in the Soviet Union is to promote and promulgate the Communist ideology. The thorough and intensive way in which this is done by controlling the particular version of Communist ideology that is given out at any time according to national policy is truly remarkable. In general, the relationship between the individual and the state in the Communist countries is very similar to that between the individual and the state in the fascistic-type countries. In the Communist countries the purpose of the schools is to become an instrument of indoctrination propaganda for the youngsters in school so that they will, in the process of being educated, become the prototype of the new Communist man. This propaganda education is carried on in every aspect of life—out of school as well as in school.

All the resources for communication as well as education are controlled by the relatively small elite of the Communist party. No dissident opinions are permitted to be expressed unless these opinions are better ways in which the Communist principles can be formed. There is some criticism permitted of officials but no criticism of the officially laid-down policy.

The Russian Communist party bases its ideas on the idea of a dictatorship of the proletariat, a laboring class. This concept envisages class warfare until the time when there is a one-class society—a government of workers. However, in the Soviet Union there has now arisen an elite of educated people and bureaucrats who are favored in many ways over the persons who work with their hands, laborers and farmers (peasants).

The Communist Party and the official policy of the Soviet Union (one and the same) have shown a number of changes as conditions have changed from the period of 1917 up to the present time. There have been some very important and unexpected shifts in the party line as situations arose requiring this. In some cases this meant that history had to be rewritten to be in accordance with the new line which the country and the party were pursuing.

Education In The Soviet Union. According to Cramer and Browne [2] the Soviets have analyzed education as being divided between *nurture* and *instruction*. *Nurture* is the process of bringing out the innate capacities of the individual. *Instruction* is giving him certain information and professional and technical training which he needs in the Communist society. The importance of heredity is not stressed nearly as much in the Communist world as it is outside. Until recently, the Lysenko theory of genetics rather than the customary Mendelian concept had been accepted. Since Khrushchev faded from power Lysenko has been de-emphasized, but there still has been no major change in the Soviet philosophy with respect to heredity.

According to the official Communist doctrine, heredity is not considered as important as it would be to those outside the Soviet Union. The Soviets believe the success of a person is based upon the success of the methods used with him. This places great responsibility on the teacher since they hold that all persons can learn, unless they have had some physical defect or brain damage. Lysenko's doctrine holds that children raised in a completely Communistic environment would be improved because of the characteristics which would be inherited through each generation. This, of course, has now been somewhat repudiated.

In recent years the Communists have had to add a third factor that can best be translated as *"self-training."* This places some of the deviations not on environment, nor on the inability to bring out the inate capacities, but upon the man himself as having certain weaknesses of character. A man may fail the State because of certain defects in his own self-training. So, the Communists are trying to control the environment and the structural process and, by stressing self-discipline, they hope to bring about the new Communist man which will be needed for the Communist world to come.

The power of the Communist Party and of the Soviet State is directed toward seeing to it that there is compliance on the part of the adults. However, the attitude toward children is not as harsh as it might appear from this. In the early period of the Communist State up to 1933, the teachers were considered leaders and directors of learning and not disciplinarians. After this period there was a return to a rather militarized

2 Cramer and Browne, *op. cit.*, p. 145.

system of discipline in the schools. However, there is no corporal punishment. The children are taught, of course, to consider Communism as the best of all possible systems and they are not permitted to have any contact with any divergent points of view. All the doctrines of Communism and the characteristics of the Communist Society are made as attractive as possible. The Communist Party, the persons in charge at least, believe that if an entirely new generation will grow up to know nothing else, they will believe in and support all the system's principles. They do use coercion on older people, but they feel that this would not be an appropriate way with young people to bring about the new Communist man.

The schools, at the present time in the Soviet Union, have at least two major purposes. The first one, and this is certainly all encompassing, is the agency of indoctrination for the basic ideas of Communism. Although Russian educators explain to visitors that the major aim of instruction is to understand the world and the cultural heritage of the present time, what is really meant is that the Marxist interpretation of these matters will be foremost. This differs widely from that which is taught by the "bourgeois" Western middle class. In order to become good Communists, people must learn how to read. Consequently, all people must become literate and publications are put out in great numbers so that persons can become indoctrinated through reading materials.

A second purpose of the Soviet system, and certainly this seems to have been quite successful, is to train the masses of people in the industrialization of the Soviet Union. Lenin had recognized this a long time ago—that in the modern world it is necessary to have the industrialized state—although the Russian state at that time was a long way from it. An industrialized Russian state would be necessary if it were to hold its own in a world which was hostile to Communism; therefore, the Russian people had to be educated to modern industrial procedures. The place of labor in society and the requirement of every individual to have some type of skill that will contribute to society, is an important stress in Soviet schools. Visitors in the Soviet Union are impressed how the energies of the nation are centered upon presenting education to its fullest efforts to obtain these two major purposes discussed here.

In the federal-type government of the Soviet Union there are two kinds of government departments. One is the all-union ministries. These ministries are comparable to those departments of the U.S. cabinet members whose authority extends across the entire nation. Second, are the Republic Ministries whose authority is confined to one Republic. As we see later, however, all fields of activity in the Soviet Union are supervised by a centralized national authority. The difference as can be seen lies only in whether or not authority is exercised through a ministry that is within each republic, or whether it is directly exercised on a national scale without going through a republic ministry. There is no all-union ministry of education in charge of elementary and secondary schools, though a few specialized secondary boarding schools are maintained by the all-union Ministry of Culture. In this respect on paper, Russia is similar to the United States in that the U.S. Office of Education has no direct charge of education.

In theory, each of the union republics has a large measure of autonomy as far as the machinery of administration of the elementary and most secondary education is concerned. In reality, however, an all-union ministry of higher education that is called the All-Union Ministry of Culture coordinates the work of the universities and specialized schools throughout the country. In recent years, they have established a Ministry of Higher Education in each of the fifteen republics, thus the All-Union Ministry of Higher Education operates through a Republic Ministry of Higher Education. A third all-union group, the Ministry of Labor Reserves, controls certain factors having vocational schools but does not contribute to their support. These are supported by money which is taken directly from the factories in which the schools are held.

The literature of education that is distributed by the Soviet indicates that there is decentralization of educational responsibility and control in order to permit each republic to work its own system of education adapted to national and other peculiarities. An observer, however, will notice that the curriculum and courses of study are very similar in all of the areas, regardless of the language or culture involved. Obviously, then, although responsibility is decentralized, authority is, in fact, highly centralized.

Periodically, conferences of the Republic Ministers of Education are held where uniform policies are agreed upon. These ministers, afterwards, carry them out in their own republics. All decisions in the republic are made in the Ministry of Education, no important decisions made at any lower level. This procedure results in a system of public schools, where its textbooks, and the courses of study are substantially the same throughout the entire Soviet Union. The amount of time to be spent on each part of the course of study, the dates of reviewing for examination are all determined by decrees issued by the ministries after they have agreed among themselves.

Perhaps of more importance than this aspect uniformity is by what means control is exercised in education as well as in other areas. Behind all government officials, looms the important policy decision-maker, the Communist Party. The Communist Party, itself, represents a small minority—probably not much more than five percent—and is controlled by a very small group at the top. Since almost all officials of the government are members of the Communist Party, policy making is controlled by the party rather than by the open free decisions of the ministry officials themselves.

Education in the Soviet Union is, of course, all public education. It is locally operated, although financed almost entirely from the Republic sources and is centrally controlled. No private schools of any type are tolerated. No religious education of any kind is permitted in the schools. The schools are completely secular. It might be considered that the teaching of Marxism is a kind of religion or doctrinal teaching. It is true, of course, that the Soviet constitution does guarantee freedom of religious worship, but religious teaching is discouraged even outside of the school. By and large the Soviet Union established co-education at a time when this was very rare in the rest of Europe. After 1943, in the larger cities, there was some separation of sexes.

In discussing the characteristics of the Soviet school we are discussing, basically, the school in the period after the Khrushchev reform. Khrushchev reforms are in the process, however, of being changed in some respect.

School is compulsory between the ages of seven and fifteen. Universally, in the Soviet Union, youngsters do not start to school before the age seven. Education before age seven is called "pre-school education" and for the most part there is a need for this. Even though the compulsory age for leaving school has been raised to fifteen this is not completely enforced as there are still youngsters, particularly in the rural areas, who do not attend up to age fifteen. Actually, there are not sufficient school buildings and teachers in order to enforce the law.

Soviet School Curriculum and the Examination System.   In the schools of the Soviet Union, as in many other European schools, there is no choice of subjects in the curriculum, except possibly the choice of a foreign language in the upper grades. This means that each pupil in the school follows exactly the same course. The curriculum in countries where Russian is not the native language differs somewhat from those schools where the native language is Russian. However, the schools throughout the area of the same language would be precisely the same. All the schools in the Soviet Union are comprehensive schools, and pupils are heterogeneous as to ability in both the elementary and the secondary school. A few persons with special talents may be separated out and sent to special boarding schools for this purpose in the top three years of the new eleven-year school.

There is first the elementary division that consists of four grades, then the middle school that now consists of the fifth through the eighth grade and, finally, what is sometimes called the senior stage, that of the upper three grades. The elementary school teacher is a general teacher for all grades except physical education. Emphasis during the first four grades is upon reading. Instructions concerning the teaching of reading say that the youngsters should learn not only to pronounce the word, but also the connection between things in the actual life about them. For this reason, then, the lessons are supplemented by demonstrations, field trips, and experiments. Many of the stories are dramatized in the early grades, and youngsters are taken to see plays performed by the various theatrical groups.

Moving into the social studies in the elementary grades, children learn about the geography, first, of their home district and then, in turn, of the region, of the republic and, finally, of the Union. They always study geography in connection with the economic implications involved and according to the Marxist interpretation of such things. In history, the child first learns about the nationality group to which he belongs. He soon branches out into the history of Russia, and then into that of the ancient and modern world. In the teaching of history, great care is taken to see to it that the historical events are interpreted from the Communist point of view. There are a great number of maps, charts, pictures, and films which are used in the classroom to illustrate the geographical and historical material. In addition, there are courses in arithmetic, art, music, and physical education. In the Soviet Union, the elementary school operates six days a week and there are twenty-four lessons in the week for the first and second graders, twenty-five for the third graders, and twenty-seven for the fourth graders. Each of these lessons lasts forty-five minutes with a ten minute break in between.

The basic textbooks used throughout the Soviet Union in both the elementary and secondary levels are the same although they are published in many languages and, of course, in five different scripts. Teachers are permitted to supplement the basic text with materials which they collect locally. The use of textbooks that are written in Russian and translated into native languages gives the idea that there is decentralization but this still means that there is uniformity in teaching throughout the Soviet Union.

Not all the stress in the schools is on the pure matter of study. There is a very careful organization of student self-government and other school organizations. There are science clubs, music clubs, dancing clubs. There are class committees. There is a school council to maintain order and discipline and many matters of that kind. Some of these matters are directed by the Young Communist group which is an organization of those carefully selected students who are trained to become Communist Party members. Apparently the educators in the Soviet Union believe that participation of the child in the operation of the school is a good way to achieve their educational aims.

The fifth grade, although a part of the eight year school is generally considered to be secondary education in the Soviet Union so there is a very intensive examination given at this time. At the end of the fourth, eighth, and eleventh years there are intensive examinations given. Interestingly enough, the questions for these examinations are issued publicly in the spring so that everyone knows what they are. These are very broad topics. There are cards which are made known to the students so they can prepare for them. On each card for the examination there are three general themes in a single school subject. For example, in geography the topics might deal with farming in the wheat area, with the canal system or with the problem of grazing lands. Each teacher works out a set of questions based on these topics. For his examination, the student draws a card and answers the questions thereon.

The examinations in the Soviet Union are oral with the exception of those in the Russian language and literature. There is an examining body made up of the school principal, the teacher of the class, two other teachers who are especially assigned, and a representative of the regional educational authority—possibly a school inspector. One child at a time is examined. A card is drawn out of the file for each of the subjects and each card contains three questions. He has to answer the question to the satisfaction of the committee and answer questions by the committee in regard to the answers given.[3] All marking in the Soviet Union on examinations or in class work itself is on the numerical scale with grades of five down to one, with five the highest. Very careful attention has been given by research groups in the Soviet Union with respect to the conducting of examinations including the establishing of rapport.

There is a great deal of material in the educational writings of the Soviet with respect to the problem of discipline and moral education. The Soviet leaders, at the present time, argue that the school children have not had sufficient experience and knowledge to make decisions for themselves and these decisions should be made by adults. They believe that if the community in which the children grow up—that is the school—is well ordered, they will soon begin to accept that pattern and will grow into the type of citizen who will accept the regulation of conduct by the state, including the conduct by the school itself. So a very great effort is made to have the youngsters eventually participate in the disciplining of those who fail to live up to the prescribed conduct of the school.

Soviet Secondary and Higher Education. The first half of secondary education is the last half of the eight-year school and quite often is combined with the elementary in a so-called incomplete school. In the complete school the second half of secondary education, three additional years making a total of eleven, are all combined in the same building which would be from the first grade through the eleventh grade.

Starting with the fifth grade, the teachers teach only the subject for which they are specialized. Teachers do not teach all day but teach as they are assigned, having certain free periods.

[3] See: Nellie Apanasewicz and Seymour M. Rosen. *Final Examinations in the Russian Ten-Year School.* (Bulletin OE-14126.) Washington, U.S. Department of Health, Education, and welfare, 1966.

In the period of the Khrushchev reform there was very heavy emphasis upon the place of labor in the development of nation in the Russian secondary school. A place was found in the curriculum for boys and girls to participate in some kind of vocational training. Furthermore, in order to stress the importance of labor, the youngsters who had gone out and worked in the labor batallion for two years after finishing the secondary school had a higher priority as far as being admitted to college. There is some evidence that there is a trend now to get away from this emphasis on active vocational skills on the part of all students.

The subjects in grades five, six, seven, and eight in the first half of the secondary school are mathematics (arithmetic, algebra, geometry and trigonometry), general science, history, geography, art or mechanical drawing, and the Constitution of the U.S.S.R. They, of course, still have the Russian language and, sometimes, their own native language. They take physics and chemistry in the sixth and seventh grades and physical education is taken by all. In social studies, the Soviet interpretation, of course, is still stressed.

In the second stage of the general education school which is grades nine, ten, and eleven, the youngsters who pass the examination to remain are those who are somewhat gifted. There is much more restriction with respect to the numbers attending the final three years of the secondary school than there is in the United States. However, very likely the number of students who do attend the secondary school in the Soviet Union after the compulsory attendance age is much higher than in most of the other European countries.

The examinations which are given at the end of the eighth and eleventh grades are very similar to the fourth grade examination. If a student fails an examination given at the end of the school year in June he can take another examination in August. If he fails a second time he must remain in the grade another year. There is also a possibility for double promotion or even being placed in a special school if he is very highly gifted. Of the youngsters who are permitted to take the tests, only a small number fail. The reason for this is that the teachers are held responsible for the failure of the child. Consequently, youngsters are usually not permitted to come for the examinations unless it is expected that they will be able to pass them. Since they already know what the general questions will be, and although they are very broad, it is easy to see why the teachers can select pretty well in advance those who are going to pass them.

The statistics on the actual numbers who go into the schools in the Soviet Union are difficult to obtain. It is thought by most observers that four out of ten of the students do continue into the senior part of the secondary school. There are no fees for education at any level from the beginning at age seven through to the University period. Furthermore, for able students at the University there is sometimes a subsistence or stipend paid to support the student while he is in school. Moving ahead on the enrollment of the secondary school, about one person out of ten enters into the technicums where he will be trained for some kind of vocational specialty. The people who are kept on the technicum have not been good enough to get in to the senior secondary school but they have done well enough to not be included in the labor reserves. The Soviet Union's higher institutions are actually for the training of specialties. They are not broad general trainings like the liberal arts colleges of America. At the top of the educational ladder is a group of people who are called a name which is difficult to translate into English. It could be called by the word "scientist" or "active scholars" or sometimes in English we translate this into "academician." Persons who have achieved this particular rank and position are of tremendous ability and their opinion is greatly sought. The ones who have reached this level are very secure and have a good salary.

Before a person enters the University in the Soviet Union he must choose what career or profession he wants to go into. And the University itself offers highly specialized training. Not only is it specialized in such areas as chemistry, but even more specialized within the area. It would not be chemistry but petroleum chemistry or a bio-chemistry. It would not be literature but classical literature or Russian literature, for example. Even in the medical school there is no such thing as a general doctor. Now the freedom of a choice for a student is to some extent restricted by the state planning in terms of availability of places. This means that only a certain number can be selected from those that choose a specialized area of study.

As has been said earlier, it is difficult to check the statistics in the Soviet Union and the statistics that we have are not always completely up to date. It may be that the current statistics are much better than we are indicating here.

Persons who have made a careful study of Soviet education feel that slightly less than half the age group was completing a secondary education program in the Soviet Union in the late 1950's as compared to about fifty-five percent in the United States. (Of course, figures for the U.S. are somewhat higher as Russia's may also be now!) Out of this group, it was thought, about one-third of the total age group had actually completed the regular secondary school. Of those who had completed the secondary school in the Soviet Union about one-fifth were admitted to higher education while almost fifty percent of the high-school graduates in the United States actually started work in a post-secondary school of some type.

About five percent of the college-age group in the Soviet Union completes university studies. More than fifteen percent of that age group in America actually complete the baccalaureate degree. Actually, no country of Europe approaches the quantity of record of either of these two countries at the secondary or college level. England, with its new approach toward the modern secondary school, is making a great effort to provide wide-spread educational opportunity to its youth of secondary school age. Up until recently less than ten percent of the age group in England and less than five percent in France actually took work in universities. However, a high percent of these do complete their work.

DEVELOPMENTS IN OTHER COUNTRIES

Although it is not possible in this short account to cover the tremendous diversity of systems existing throughout the world, there are a few countries that ought be mentioned because of certain features which are different than those which we have discussed.

Although education in England, Wales, Northern Ireland,[4] and Scotland are all under the British Parliament, there is a different tradition and a different system of schools in Scotland. The Department of Education and Science operates schools only in England and Wales and the Scottish Education Department is under the Secretary of State for Scotland. Further, separate laws have been needed in order to regulate the Scottish schools as compared to the British. In 1872, the Scottish Education Act transferred the administration of all schools from the Presbyterian Church to the State. The administration of the schools locally has paralleled in great measure that in England. In 1918 the administration was turned over to the county educational authorities as in England. All voluntary and denominational schools have been taken over by these educational authorities so that there is no dual system of education as still exists in England to this present day.

The traditions of the Scots are not that they are a very religious people but that they believe in religious freedom. Consequently, there is no such requirement in Scottish law as there is in England requiring that religious instruction be given in every school. Each of the local authorities can arrange for instruction if they wish. The Scottish schools have been more often co-educational than have their British counterparts. In many other respects the British education and the Scottish education have been quite similar, particularly in regard to the school-leaving age, and so on.

[4] Northern Ireland is a self-governing unit and has its own Ministry of Education.

The country of Australia is also interesting because its governmental form, a federal-type government, is somewhat similar to that of the United States. There may even be, in some respects, more decentralization as between the state and federal governments of Australia and Canada than there are in the United States. However, within each of the six Australian states there is complete centralization of education. Local authorities have very little to do with the operation of the schools. One of the reasons for this is that Australian states are still sparsely settled, since there are less than twenty million people in a country as large as the United States. Since most of these people live in the larger cities, it is difficult to maintain the schools in the small towns away from the cities.

Very little was done about this situation until, finally, the responsibility was turned over almost completely to the state authorities. Then new schools were formed and education advanced greatly. Consequently, we find very little sentiment for the decentralization of education in Australia as you would in England, for example. In many other respects Australia does follow the British system. With respect to the permitting of denominational schools and the teaching of religion in the schools they have very similar arrangements to that of the schools of England and Wales. The centralization of schools in Australia carries over to a very rigid inspectorial system of checking up on the teachers as well as the central administration of the schools otherwise.

In Canada, the schools developed much as in the United States with the local communities taking the initiative. When the Dominion of Canada was formed, only slowly did the school system become the responsibility of the Provinces of Canada. There is still much local control and operation just as there is in the American states. A unique situation, however, exists in Canada, particularly in the Province of Quebec, where there is the problem of language and the problem of differences in religion. Quebec is predominately French-speaking and Catholic. In order to provide education in this Province, it has been necessary that the schools be operated by the Church. Consequently, Quebec has two systems of education in every school district where there are the two languages and religion.

There is one Board of Education for the French speaking Protestants and other non-Catholics. The school districts, therefore, consist of those persons who choose their school systems. Persons who are neighbors may belong to different school systems and pay their taxes and are eligible to vote for board members of different school districts. This separation of the provinces into two systems goes up to the state authorities where at the national level the Council of Education consists of two parts—one for the French speaking Catholics and the other for the Protestants. The English "Protestant" group have had a tendency in recent years to enlarge their school system so as to provide for better services. However, the French speaking Catholic section tend to limit their system to the size of the parish which creates some difficulties in the terms of attempting to improve the quality of the school system. In the Province of Newfoundland, which has only recently been added to that of Canada, there is again the completely sectarian school system, although in this case there are seven different denominations which are involved in operating the only schools which are found in the entire province. Again, the districts correspond to the denominations but because of the segregation in terms of residency by religion it is found that there is not too much overlapping of the school district boundaries.

Numerous other examples could be given of ways in which, by historical accident or because of differing social conditions, various countries have organized to carry on their education in differing ways.

FREEDOM, EDUCATION, AND CULTURE IN THE CONTEMPORARY WORLD [5]

The extent of freedom in the major countries considered and the freedom of the teachers within those countries varies widely. In England, without question, the headmaster of the local schools has much greater freedom of operation than in any other country concerned. There is almost complete freedom of teaching in England, provided it is approved by the headmaster. The only restriction laid upon the headmaster of the secondary schools of England is the requirement to teach the agreed religious syllabus. The amount of freedom ranges all the way to much more detailed regulations governing the teaching in the United States, Germany, France, the Soviet Union, and in that order.

In the Soviet Union there is much more strict enforcement of the main ideas which the government plans to promulgate, namely that of Communism, than in any other countries. No possible deviation from the teaching of the approved point of view is tolerated in the Soviet Union as far as the teachers are concerned. In France and in Germany the teachers might be relatively free as far as their opinions are concerned but the curriculum is quite clearly and formally defined. In the United States there are about as many variations as there are school dis-

[5] The reader is invited to read in much more detail the book, Herbert J. Muller, *Freedom In The Modern World*, Chapters 5 through 6. These chapters do deal with the development of freedom in the twentieth century in most of the major countries of the world.

tricts with some school districts being quite restrictive as far as what teachers are permitted to teach and other districts being relatively free.

There has been, in the twentieth century in the United States, more or less restriction of the teachers from advocating or even teaching about the leftist points of view in economics and politics. The enforcement of this rule and the urgency of it has varied from time to time, depending on the situation. In the period of the Depression when the country was afraid that there might be a revolution, there was a possibility of great restriction in this area. Curiously enough, during World War II, there was not nearly as much restriction upon the ranks of the teachers as there had been during World War I and immediately following. The teacher who wished to advocate a pacifist or an anti-war point of view, however, was not tolerated. There were still some communities where fundamentalist religious ideas were predominant and evolution could not be taught, and there were certain other closed issues such as sex and economic problems.

When we come into the period of hysteria—the McCarthy era—there were serious restrictions upon the rights of the teachers. With the development of extreme Rightist groups in the United States in the late 50's there has been a serious restriction placed upon the teacher's right to choose textbooks and to teach certain matters in some communities. There have even been firings based upon the teacher's violation of certain canons laid down by the extreme group which has managed to capture a school board. There are some parts in the United States where the materials produced by the United Nations or UNESCO cannot be used in a school system. This is, certainly, restriction on the freedom of the teacher. By and large, though, the situation with respect to academic freedom and the personal life of the teacher is much better in the United States than it has been for a long time. In many cases it is fear plus the restricted mind of the teacher which provides the stronger ban (than do community pressures) on effective teaching of all points of view.

In the world in general, outside of the Communist countries and the dictatorships including that of Spain and Portugal, there has been more political freedom than possibly any time before the twentieth century. There has been a great extension of the right to vote, freedom of speech, and freedom of press has been pretty widely preserved. However, there are other aspects of the whole problem of freedom that need to be explored a little more fully. In a modern world where being well informed depends on the accessibility to information, it would seem at first as though this would be the freest of all possible worlds since we have a great deal of information being promulgated.

There are, however, certain limiting aspects. In the first place, much of the news tends to be sensational rather than a balanced reflection of what is happening. For example, there is emphasis on teen-age delinquency as opposed to teen-age achievements. This tends to give persons certain attitudes toward the teen-age problem which may not be based on a factual account. Secondly, the whole control of the news by relative large businesses which themselves reflect a business point of view tends to restrict the type of news and tends to place the opinion-making agencies in the hands of those people who have a particular point of view. This point of view quite frequently is not representative of the point of view of the people. A case in point was the almost unanimous opposition by the public press to the election of Franklin Roosevelt to each of his four terms when he proceeded to get a large majority.

This happens in many other areas as well. Some cynics think that the American people are pretty much controlled by the public-opinion media wherein the power structure determines the point of view they wish to expand. This is, probably, not true. Perhaps more serious is the inability of the typical citizen to weigh the evidence given him, to discount that which is very sensational, and to bring facts into balance. This has, of course, enormous implications for education.

There is also the tendency of the population toward the conformity of the larger group. This controversy rages back and forth, with arguments on both sides that are extremely difficult to reconcile. Culture has always had its conformist aspects. Certainly the people of the nonliterate times were conforming to their culture. Certainly the people of the mid-nineteenth century were conforming to the small local communities in which they are found. The difference in an interdependent, mobile population with mass communication facilities is that the area to which people conform now is geographically much larger. It is no longer restricted to the small community. There is, however, a question as to whether people are more conformist than they were. As a matter of fact, the affluent nature of our society permits people, if they wish, to be less conforming in their private lives than they have been in the past. Whether or not they choose to be nonconforming in intelligent ways is, of course, another question. But the potentialities and possibilities are there.

The whole movement toward the protection of minority rights and the civil rights movement in the United States, including that of the Negro vote, are examples of attempts to increase the freedom of persons who have been denied. Although the United States and other parts of the world have a long way to go to in setting up provisions whereby there are no restrictions placed upon a person because of his class status, national origin, color, or religious creed, certainly progress in the latter part of this century has been considerable.

In general, there are greater areas of freedom than ever before. There is the possibility that this freedom will further expand as certain laws which are now in the making in most countries are more carefully enforced and carried out. Certainly freedom is something which must be zealously guarded and perhaps fought for every decade. It is very easy for those in charge of the power structure to consider that they are so right that "error" must be put down at any cost. The only remedy for such an attitude lies, of course, in the conception that the other person must have the right to speak even though he is "wrong" because of the possibility that "he might be right." Even if he were not "right" he still should have the freedom to express himself as long as this does not jeopardize seriously the safety of the community in periods of crises.

SUMMARY

In Chapters 10 ond 11 the comparative approach has been used, involving primarily the five countries, Germany (Western), France, the United Kingdom, the Soviet Union, and the United States of America. Although there are some problems that are similar for each country, the solutions that the countries have chosen for their educational problems vary greatly with respect to the conditions and to the structure that has emerged in each of them. Each country has attempted to develop an educational system that is best for its values in terms of its structure.

In western Germany the traditions for the German educational system were laid down during the period of Imperial Germany, 1870 to 1918. Under the Weimar Republic some attempt was made to establish a more democratic school system. The Weimar Republic was doomed to failure because of economic reasons arising out of World War II and its school system also was unsuccessful. When Hitler established the Nazi Third Reich, he placed the school system under the central German government in a way which it had not been even in the days of the Empire. He attempted to use the school system as an instrument of the Nazi Party and of the German state. After World War II, in West Germany (later the German Federal Republic), an attempt was made under the three western Allies to set up a school system that would be adaptable to German conditions but still be democratic in its framework. Each of the states of Germany (or *Länder*) have been made responsible for its own school system. Germany has, until quite recently, tried to solve its problem of secondary schools by setting up parallel but separate schools for different purposes for each of the different types of students. There has been some recent attempt to establish an *Einheitschule* enrolling all students in the same institution, although still in separate programs.

Germany has always stressed part-time vocational education and its full-time vocational schools are of a quite high level.

France developed a highly centralized school system in order to teach French culture. A unified elementary school system, *L'Ecole Unique,* required all youngsters to attend the same elementary school. At about the age of ten or eleven, they were separated into those who went into the French *Lycèe* or *Collége* and those who continued in elementary school. Not until the reforms of 1959 was there any change in this division. Gradually France is changing over to a system whereby the boys and girls continue much longer in secondary schools but in different programs. Eventually, however, they will end up in a *Lycèe* for college preparatory purposes and in various kinds of Colléges. This return will be slowly placed into operation.

Discussion of British education was limited primarily to that in England and Wales. In the Education Act of 1870, primary schools were established, and made compulsory in each county. However, very little was done by the government to provide secondary education until after World War II. The Education Act of 1944 tried to establish three kinds of schools that would enroll among them all pupils—secondary grammar school, secondary modern school, and secondary technical school. However, the secondary grammar school still continued to be the school with the highest prestige. Consequently, there has now been a movement toward the development of the British comprehensive school that would enroll all youngsters in the same building, even though they would be taking any one of three programs—the tri-partite system in the comprehensive schools. Not all the systems have changed over to comprehensive. There is still considerable debate in England concerning its advisability. The English schools tend to classify all secondary students into ability groups known as "streams." By and large, in England, the schools are run by the Local Education Authorities with funds provided by the central Ministry of Educating. The headmasters in England have much more freedom with respect to their schools than do most other local schools throughout the world.

In the United States, the first completely ladder system of schools has been developed with no artificial restrictions placed from kindergarten through the university. Each of the various states of the United States has developed its own school system with some variations although there is a remarkable similarity among the various states. The United States developed a unique secondary school (the American High School), which, after 1870, practically replaced the previous types of secondary schools, the Latin grammar school and the Academy. The high school starting first as a noncollege preparatory became highly college preparatory and then gradually becomes more comprehensive in its scope beginning around the time of World War I. America educates a much higher percentage of its boys and girls at the secondary age level than any country in the world. Of the ones who graduate from high school, currently nearly half of them continue in some kind of post-high school institution.

The Soviet Union, an immense territory with many kinds of people and languages, has developed a remarkably unified culture under the control of the Russian Communist Party. The policy of Czar on Russification of the country has been continued by the Communists in the Soviet Union. Although the schools are ostensibly operated by the separate republics, but with a great deal of administrative detail left to local authorities, all higher policies, the curriculum, and so on, actually stem from central authority through the *de facto* control by the Communist Party of this and all activities (for that matter) in the country. Russia has made greater strides, perhaps, than any other European country toward educating a higher percentage of its pupils farther. This percentage would still be considerably less than that of the United States. Apparently, the standards of the Russian educational system are quite high.

Some attention has been given to education in Australia as an example of a country in which education is the responsibility of the state but still centrally controlled, to the problem of the bi-lingual situation in Quebec, Canada, and to the differences between Scottish and British education.

The modern period has been the period of a great deal of extension of freedom, but we have had the restriction of freedom during the Fascist period and in the Communist domination in the Soviet Union. There have also been situations in the free world where there has been restriction of open discussion with respect to controversial issues such as in the "McCarthy period" in America. The modern drive to protect minority rights, the freedom of the press, and the surge of other movements indicate that there is still much restraint of freedom in the world.

In the five major countries, the influence of certain trends or forces, also, can be discerned.

Nationalism. Nationalism has been a major force in the nineteenth century and this was continued to some extent in the twentieth. Most of the countries of the West extended and developed their school systems because they wanted to protect and develop their own national interests.

Ideology. The major force of the twentieth century was perhaps more ideological than it was social. France, England, and the United States were guided a great deal by the democratic ideas. There was a temporary interest of Fascism in Germany but with democracy now again playing an important part. In the Soviet Union, Marxist Communism dominates the ideology of that country and greatly affects the education.

Changing Purposes of Education. The new ideas that came about as a result of the development of democracy, the changing culture occurring in all of these countries, the industrialization with improved technology, automation, and changes in the philosophical approach to the nature of man and of values, and the new ideas which are arising out of research in psychology and the learning process—all of these caused a change in the purposes of education. There was much greater emphasis throughout the world on the education of the whole child and not just on intellect. People became concerned about the necessity for becoming interested in the individual differences among the children. There was more emphasis upon the meaning and the utility of subject matter rather than just memorization of the language in which the knowledge was written. These developments did not affect the countries the same, however, because of internal social conditions. The greatest amount of development of the trends took place in America and the least in Europe. Throughout all these countries, this was increasingly a period of rapid social change.

This change raises the question of the need for a different kind of education than that needed in a society that is static. In a static society, one can give the answers worked out in the past because they should continue to work equally well in the future. But in a changing society no one knows what the problems will be, let alone the answers. The school has had a difficult time maintaining itself in the uncertainties of this change. Further, the change raises questions about the nature of the schools at a time when the school had had great difficulties because of the rapidly expanding population and other forces which impinge upon it.

All countries of the world face the problem as to what kind of education is most desirable in a changing world; certainly none of them has reasons to be satisfied with the present conditions found in their schools.

SELECTED BIBLIOGRAPHY

Starred items represent books most helpful in relation to topics and countries in Chapters 10 and 11.

General Books and Periodicals

American Teaching About Russia, Cyril Edwin Black and John M. Thompson, eds. Bloomington, Indiana University Press, 1959.
Apanasewicz, Nellie, and Rosen, Seymour M., *Final Examinations in the Russian Ten-Year School* (Bulletin OE–14126). Washington, U.S. Department of Health, Education, and Welfare, 1966.

*Armytage, W. H. G., *Four Hundred Years of English Education*. Cambridge, England University Press, 1964.

Austin, A. G., *Australian Education, 1788–1900: Church, State, and Public Education in Colonial Australia*. Melbourne, Pitman, 1961.

Baron, George, *Society, Schools and Progress in England*. Oxford, Pergamon Press, Headington Hill Hall, 1965.

Bauer, Raymond A. and others, *How the Soviet System Works: Cultural, Psychological, and Social Themes*. Cambridge, Harvard University Press, 1956.

*Bayles, Ernest E. and Hood, Bruce L., *Growth of American Educational Thought and Practice*. New York, Harper and Row, 1966.

Beeby, Clarence Edward, *The Quality of Education in Developing Countries*. Cambridge, Harvard University Press, 1966.

Bentwich, Joseph S., *Education in Israel*. Philadelphia, Jewish Publication Society of America, 1965.

Bowen, James, *Soviet Education: Anton Makarenko and the Year of Experiment*. Madison, Wisconsin, University of Wisconsin Press, 1962.

Boyd, William, *The History of Western Education*, 7th ed., revised and enlarged by Edmund J. King. New York, Barnes and Noble, 1965.

Boyd, William, and Rawson, Wyatt, *The Story of the New Education*. London, Heinemann, 1965.

British Secondary Education: Overview and Appraisal, Richard E. Gross, ed. London, Oxford Press, 1965.

Comparative Education Review. (Official periodical of Comparative Education Society.)

Counts, George S., *The Challenge of Soviet Education*. New York, McGraw-Hill, 1957.

*Cramer, John F. and Browne, George Stephenson, *Contemporary Education: A Study of National Systems*, 2d ed. New York, Harcourt, Brace and World, 1965.

Crankshaw, Edward, *The New Cold War: Moscow v. Pekin*. Baltimore, Penguin Books, 1963.

*Cremin, Lawrence A., *The Transformation of the School*. New York, Knopf, 1961.

Daniels, Robert V., *The Nature of Communism*. New York, Random House, 1962.

Dent, H. C., *The Education Act, 1944: Provisions, Possibilities, and Some Problems*, 3d ed. London, University of London Press, 1947.

Drake, William E., *The American School in Transition*. New York, Prentice-Hall, 1955.

Ebenstein, William, *Today's Isms: Communism, Fascism, Capitalism, Socialism*, 2d ed. Englewood Cliffs, New Jersey, Prentice-Hall, 1958.

Education and the Development of Nations, John W. Hanson and Cole S. Brembeck, eds. New York, Holt, Rinehart, and Winston, 1966.

Fraser, W. R., *Education and Society in Modern France*. London, Routledge and Kegan Paul, 1963.

French, William M., *America's Educational Tradition: An Interpretive History*. New York, Heath, 1964.

Frost, S. E., Jr., *Historical and Philosophical Foundations of Western Education.* Columbus, Ohio, Merrill, 1966.

Gibson, A. Boyce, *Towards an Australian Philosophy of Education.* Sydney, New South Wales, Department of Education, 1962.

Good, Harry G., *A History of American Education,* 2d ed. Macmillan, 1962.

Halls, W. D., *Society, Schools and Progress in France.* Oxford, Pergamon Press, Headington Hill Hall, 1965.

Hans, Nicholas, *Comparative Education: A Study of Educational Factors and Traditions.* London, Routledge and Kegan Paul, 1951.

Harnwell, Gaylord P., *Russian Diary.* Philadelphia, University of Pennsylvania Press, 1960.

*Hartford, Ellis Ford, *Education in These United States.* New York, Macmillan, 1964.

Heath, Kathryn G., *Ministries of Education: Their Functions and Organization.* Washington, D.C., U.S. Department of Health, Education and Welfare, 1962.

Hook, Sidney, *World Communism: Key Documentary Material.* Princeton, Van Nostrand, 1962.

Huebner, Theodore, *The School of West Germany: A Study of German Elementary and Secondary Schools.* New York, New York University Press, 1962.

Humayun, Kabir, *Education in the New India.* New York, Harpers, 1957.

Hunnicutt, Clarence W., *America's Emerging Role in Overseas Education.* Syracuse, New York, Syracuse University School of Education, 1962.

Intellectual Foundations of American Education: Readings and Commentary, Harold J. Carter, ed. New York, Pitman Publishing, 1965.

Jackson, Brian, *Streaming: An Education System in Miniature.* London, Routledge and Kegan Paul, 1964.

Johnson, William H. E., *Russia's Educational Heritage.* Pittsburgh, Carnegie Press, 1950.

Kandel, I. L., *The New Era in Education: A Comparative Study.* New York, Houghton Mifflin, 1955.

*Katz, Joseph, ed. *Canadian Education Today: A Symposium.* Toronto, McGraw-Hill, 1956.

Kazamias, Andreas and Massalias, Bryon G., *Tradition and Change in Education: A Comparative Study.* Englewood Cliffs, New Jersey, Prentice-Hall, 1965. Pp. 182.

Kazamias, Andreas M., *Politics, Society and Secondary Education in England.* Philadelphia, University of Pennsylvania Press, 1966.

Kerr, Anthony, *Schools of Europe.* London, Bowes, 1960.

King, Edmund J., *Communist Education.* London, Cox and Wyman, Ltd., 1963.

———, *World Perspectives In Education.* London, Methuen, 1962. Pp. 380.

Krug, Edward A., *The Shaping of the American High School.* New York, Harper and Row, 1964.

Levin, Deaha, *Soviet Education Today,* rev. ed. New York, Holt, Rinehart and Winston, 1963.

London, Ivan D., "Improvement of Mathematics Teaching in Russian Schools." *School and Society,* Vol. 87 (June 20, 1959), 314–315.

Mackintosh, Mary, *Education in Scotland: Yesterday and Today*. Glasgow, Robert Gibson & Sons, 1962.

Mallinson, Vernon, *An Introduction to the Study of Comparative Education*. London, Heinemann, 1960.

Mayer, Frederick, *American Ideas and Education*. Columbus, Ohio, Merrill, 1964.

Medlin, William K. and others, *Soviet Education Programs. Foundations, Curriculum, Teacher Preparation*. Washington, D.C.. U.S. Government Printing Office, 1960.

Meyer, Adolphe E., *An Educational History of the Western World*. New York, McGraw-Hill, 1965.

Miller, T. W. G., *Values in the Comprehensive School: An Experimental Study*. Edinburgh, Oliver and Boyd, 1961.

Ministry of Education, *Schools in the U.S.A.: A Report*. Building Bulletin No. 18. London, Her Majesty's Stationery Office, 1961.
(May be secured from British Information Services, New York.)

Moehlman, Arthur Henry, and Roucek, Joseph, *Comparative Education*. New York, Dryden, 1952.

Moos, Elizabeth, *New Work-Study Program in Soviet Education*. New York, National Council of American-Soviet Friendship, 1965.

Muller, Herbert J., *Freedom in the Modern World*. New York, Harper & Row, 1966.

Nales, John N., *Schools of Democracy: An Englishman's Impressions of Secondary Education in the American Middle-west*. Lansing, Michigan, Michigan State University Press, 1962.

Ogilvie, Vivian, *The English Public School*. Macmillan, 1957.

Passow, A. Harry, *Secondary Education for All: The English Approach,* International Education Monographs, No. 3. Columbus, Ohio State University Press, 1961.

Phillips, Charles E., *The Development of Education in Canada*. Toronto, Gage, 1957.

Readings in Public Education in the United States, Ellwood P. Cubberley, ed. New York, Houghton Mifflin, 1934.

Redl, Helen B., *Soviet Educators on Soviet Education*. New York, The Free Press of Glencoe, 1964.

Research Section, Research Bureau, Ministry of Education, Government of Japan, *Education in Japan,* revised. Tokyo, Tokyo Kyoiku Kenkyuscho, 1956.

Richmond, W. Kenneth, *Education in the U.S.A.: A Comparative Study*. New York, Philosophical Library, 1956.

Rickover, H. G., *Swiss Schools and Ours: Why Theirs are Better*. Boston, Little, Brown, 1962.

Roberts, Henry L., *Russia and America: Dangers and Prospects*. New York, Harper, 1956.

Rosen, Seymour M., *Higher Education in the U.S.S.R.* Washington, U.S. Department of Health, Education and Welfare, 1963.

Rosen, Seymour M., *Part-time Education in the U.S.S.R.,* Office of Education, Bulletin 1965, No. 17. Washington, U.S. Department of Health, Education, and Welfare, 1965.

Rosen, Seymour M., *Significant Aspects of Soviet Education,* Office of Education, Bulletin 1965, No. 15. Washington, U.S. Department of Health, Education, and Welfare, 1965.

Rudman, Herbert C., *Structure and Decision-Making in Soviet Education*, Office of Education, Bulletin 1964, No. 2. Washington, U.S. Department of Health, Education, and Welfare, 1964.

*Rudy, Willis, *Schools in An Age of Mass Culture: An Exploration of Selected Themes in the History of Twentieth Century American Education.* Englewood Cliffs, New Jersey, Prentice-Hall, 1965.

Ruiz, Ramon Eduardo, *Mexico: The Challenge of Poverty and Illiteracy.* San Marino, California, The Huntington Library, 1963.

Secondary Education in Europe, James Greenleaf Umstattd, ed. Austin, Texas, The University of Texas Cooperative Society, 1956.

Soviet Education. (English Translation of the U.S.S.R. Monthly Journal, *Sovetskaya Pedagogiak,* Journal of the Russian Academy of Pedagogical Sciences.)

Soviet Education, George L. Kline, ed. New York, Columbia University Press, 1957.

Soviet Society: A Book of Readings, Alex Inkeles and Kent Geiger, eds. New York, Houghton Mifflin, 1961.

Thayer, V. T., *Formative Ideas in American Education: From the Colonial Period to the Present.* New York, Dodd, Mead, 1965.

The Changing Soviet School, George Z. F. Bereday, William W. Brickman and Gerald H. Read, eds. Boston, Houghton Mifflin, 1960.

The Educated Man: Studies in the History of Educational Thought, Paul J. Nash, and others, eds. New York, Wiley, 1965.

The History of American Education Through Readings, Carl H. Gross and Charles C. Chandler, eds. Boston, Heath, 1964.

The Politics of Soviet Education, George Z. F. Bereday and Joan Pennar, eds. New York, Praeger, 1960.

Thut, I. N., and Adams, Don R., *Educational Patterns in Contemporary Societies.* New York, McGraw-Hill, 1964.

Tucker, Robert C., *The Soviet Political Mind: Studies in Stalinism and post-Stalinism.* New York, Praeger Paperbacks, 1963.

Ulich, Robert, *The Education of Nations: A Comparison in Historical Perspective.* Cambridge, Harvard University Press, 1961.

UNESCO, World Survey of Education: Handbook of Educational Organization and Statistics, Part II, *Primary Education.* Paris, UNESCO, 1958.

UNESCO, *World Survey of Education: Handbook of Educational Organization and Statistics,* Part I. Paris, UNESCO, 1953.

Weinberg, Ian, *The English Public Schools.* New York, Atherton, 1966.

PAPERBACKS

A Firsthand Report on Soviet Schools, National Education Association, Division of Travel Service. Washington, D.C., 1960.

Baron, G., *Society, Schools and Progress in England.* New York, Pergamon Press, 1965.

*Communist Education, Edmund J. King, ed. Indianapolis, Bobbs-Merrill, 1963.

Crankshaw, Edward, The New Cold War, Moscow v. Pekin. Baltimore, Penguin Books, 1963.

Cros, Louis, The "Explosion" in the Schools. Paris, Sevpen (Oxford, Parker and Son), 1963.

Education in Britain. London, Her Majesty's Stationery Office, 1966.

Education in 1966: Being a report of the Department of Education and Science. London, Her Majesty's Stationery Office, 1967.

Elvin, H. L., Education and Contemporary Society. London, C. A. Watts, 1965.

*Grant, Nigel, Soviet Education. Baltimore, Penguin, 1964.

Harnwell, Baylord P., Russian Diary. Philadelphia, University of Pennsylvania Press, 1960.

The Incorporated Association of Assistant Masters, Teaching in Comprehensive Schools, A Second Report. Cambridge, University Press, 1967.

*King, Edmund J., Other Schools and Ours, rev. ed. New York, Holt, Rinehart and Winston, 1963.

*Lindegren, Alina M., Germany Revisited: Education in the Federal Republic, Bulletin 1957, No. 12, U.S. Department of Health, Education and Welfare. Washington, D.C., Government Printing Office, 1957.

*Medlen, William K. and others, Soviet Education Programs: Foundations, Curriculum, Teacher Preparation. Washington, D.C., U.S. Government Printing Office, 1960.

Moos, Elizabeth, Education in the Soviet Union. New York, National Council of American-Soviet Friendship, 1963.

*Pedley, Robin, The Comprehensive School, rev. ed. Baltimore, Penguin Books, 1966.

Rosen, Seymour M., Higher Education in the U.S.S.R. Washington, D.C., U.S. Department of Health, Education and Welfare, 1963.

Salisbury, Harrison E., A New Russia. New York, Harper and Row, 1962.

Salisbury, Harrison E., Russia. New York, New York Times Company, 1965.

Schwartz, Harry, China. New York, New York Times Company, 1965. Pp. 153.

Social History of American Education, Rena L. Vassar, ed., Vol. I, Colonial Times to 1860; Vol. II, 1860 to the Present. Chicago, Rand-McNally, 1965.

Solzhenitsyn, Alexander, One Day in the Life of Ivan Denisovich. New York, E. P. Dutton, 1963.

*Tyler, Ralph Winfred, Some Reflections on Soviet Education. Rochester, New York, Rochester Institute of Technology, 1962.

*U.S. Department of Health, Education and Welfare, Education in the U.S.S.R. Washington, Government Printing Office, 1957.

U.S. Department of Health, Education and Welfare, Japan: Three Epochs of Modern Education, Bulletin 1959, No. 11. Washington, D.C., U.S. Government Printing Office, 1959.

*U.S. Department of Health, Education and Welfare, Soviet Commitment to Education: Report of the First Official U.S. Education Mission to the U.S.S.R., Office of Education, Bulletin 1959, No. 16. Washington, D.C., U.S. Government Printing Office, 1959.

*U.S. Office of Education, *Education in France.* Washington, D.C., U.S. Government Printing Office, 1963.

*U.S. Office of Education, *Education in Scotland.* Washington, D.C., U.S. Government Printing Office, 1963.

Vigdorova, F., *Diary of a Russian School Teacher,* trans. from the Russian by R. Prokofieva. New York, Grove Press, 1960.

SELECTED FILMS

China Under Communism (Eastern Baptist College)   (22 min.)
    An uncensored, eye-witness report by an authorized U.S. Newsman permitted to travel in Red China.

Communism (Eastern Baptist College)   (32 min.)
    Film discusses the world-wide history and organization of the Communist Party; how its members operate in the United States to try to weaken and gain control of our political, social, and economic structure.

Communist Blueprint for Conquest (Eastern Baptist College)   (28 min.)
    Explains the methods and techniques used by the Communist to seize power in a country.

How Do American Schools Compare with Yours? (NET)   (29 min.)
    A forum with representatives comparing their schools with American. Includes Australia, Guatemala, Norway, and Turkey.

Passion for Life (Brandon)   (90 min.)
    A dramatic French film with English subtitles describing how a schoolmaster vitalized learning in a village. His activities are typical and represent a protest against the traditional French school. However, the film depicts some activities, such as the oral examination system, which are common in French schools.

Profile of Communism. Part I.
    Reviews the history of Communist ideology and practice from the nineteenth century until 1945.

Profile of Communism. Part II.
    Communism in the Soviet Union in the post-Stalin era. An examination of its effects on all aspects of Soviet life and institutions.

Public Schools of India (India)   (10 min.)

Red China (McGraw-Hill)   (54 min.)
    Fernand Gigon, from inside Communist China, examines the changes that have occurred under the Communist regime in the past few years; the relationship of Red China with the U.S., the Soviet Union, and other nations; Red China's growing strength and widening influence, and the threat it poses to world peace.

Russian Life Today Inside the Soviet Union (Bailey Films)   (21 min.)
    A revealing and objective study of the average Russian and his place in a communistic society.

School Days (University of Michigan)   (60 min.)
  Russian film on schools with English subtitles.

Schools of Mexico (Ind.)   (10 min.)
  Presents a comprehensive view of educational institutions, from the ultra-modern Ministry of Education in Mexico City to remote one-room adobe schools far in the interior. Includes normal schools, vocational and agricultural institutions and kindergartens.

Schools to the South   (15 min.)
  Efforts in various Latin American countries to improve their schools.

The American Education System.   (29 min.)
  Teenagers from various countries discuss aims, standards and other features of American high schools and colleges in comparison with schools of their countries.

The Challenge of Ideas.   (31 min.)
  An appraisal of the present contest between Western democracy and the Communist way of life. The threat to world peace by the aggressive nature of the Communist state is discussed.

The Difference Between Us. (NET Film Service)   (60 min.)
  A comparison of the secondary educational system in England and America.

The Soviet Challenge: The Industrial Revolution in Russia.   (20 min.)
(Encyclopaedia Britannica)
  This film was produced from several thousand feet of official Soviet motion pictures showing Russia's achievements and failures in their aim to become an industrial world power.

Village School (BIS)   (12 min.)
  This documentary illustrates the philosophy underlying the British system of education.

GENERAL BIBLIOGRAPHY

Historiography and Philosophy of History

For the interest of students who would like to delve more deeply into the problems of historical research and writing, the following is a list of significant books and articles.

A Study Guide for the "History of Education in the United States," *History of Education Journal,* Vol. X (Tenth Anniversary Issue, 1959), pp. 116–122.

An Anthropologist Looks At History, A. L. Kroeber, ed. Los Angeles, University of California Press, 1963.

An Introduction to the History of History, James Thompson Shotwell, ed. New York, Columbia University Press, 1922.

Anderson, Archibald W., "Is There A Functional Role for the History of Education?" *History of Education Journal,* Vol. I (Winter 1949), pp. 55–69.

Aron, Raymond, *Introduction to the Philosophy of History: An Essay on the Limits of Historical Objectivity.* Boston, Beacon, 1961. Pp. 351. (Paperbound)

Bailyn, Bernard, *Education in the Forming of American Society: Needs and Opportunities for Study.* Chapel Hill, North Carolina, University of North Carolina Press, 1960.

Barnes, Harvey E., *A History of Historical Writing,* 2d rev. ed. New York, Doerv, 1962. (Paperbound)

Barraclough, Geoffrey, *An Introduction to Contemporary History.* New York, Basic Books, 1964.

Barraclough, Geoffrey, *History in a Changing World.* Norman, University of Oklahoma Press, 1956.

Barzun, Jacques and Graff, Henry A., *The Modern Researcher.* New York, Harcourt, Brace and World, 1957.

Becker, Carl, *Every Man His Own Historian: Essays on History and Politics.* New York, Appleton-Century-Crofts, 1935.

Bellot, H. H., *American History and American Historians.* Norman, University of Oklahoma Press, 1952.

Benjamin, H. H., "An Approach to the Study of Causation in Educational History," *History of Education Journal,* Vol. VI (Fall 1954), pp. 137–152.

Benson, Lee, *Turner and Beard: American Historical Writing Reconsidered.* New York, Free Press, 1960.

Berdyaev, Nicolas, *The Beginning and the End.* New York, Harper & Row, 1952. (Harper Torchbooks, 1963.)

————, *The Meaning of History*. New York, Scribners, 1936.

Bereday, George Z. F., *Comparative Method in Education*. New York, Holt, Rinehart and Winston, 1964.

Berelson, Bernard, *The Social Studies and the Social Sciences*. New York, Harcourt, Brace and World, 1962.

Black, John Bennett, *The Art of History*. New York, Appleton-Century-Crofts, 1926.

Bond, Horace Mann, "The Role of the History of Education in Understanding the Struggle for Equalizing Educational Opportunity," *History of Education Journal,* Vol. I (Spring 1950), pp. 101–108.

Borning, Bernard C., *The Political and Social Thought of Charles A. Beard*. Seattle, University of Washington Press, 1962.

Brickman, William W., *Guide to Research in Educational History*. New York, New York University Bookstore, 1949.

Brickman, William W., "Revisionism and the Study of the History of Education," *History of Education Quarterly,* Vol. IV (December, 1964), pp. 209–224.

Burckhardt, Jacob, *Judgments of History and Historians*. Boston, Beacon, 1959.

Burke, Kenneth, *Attitudes Toward History,* Los Altos, California, Hermes Publicationa, 1959.

Bury, J. B., *A History of Freedom of Thought*. New York, Holt, Rinehart and Winston, 1913.

Butterfield, Herbert, *Man on His Past*. Cambridge, University Press, 1955.

Butts, R. F., and others, *The Rise of the History of Education in the Professional Preparation of Teachers*. Committee on Historical Foundations of the National Society of College Teachers of Education, 1957.

Carr, Edward H., *What is History?* New York, St. Martin's, 1961. (Also published by Knopf.)

Childe, V. Gordon, *History*. London, Cobbett Press, 1947.

————, *Man Makes Himself*. New York, New American Library, 1962.

Cochran, Thomas Childs, *The Social Sciences in Historical Study: A Report of the Committee*. Baltimore, Social Science Research, 1954.

Collingwood, R. G., *Essays in the Philosophy of History*. Austin, University of Texas Press, 1965.

Commager, Henry Steele, "Should Historians Write Contemporary History?" *Saturday Review* (February 12, 1966), pp. 18–20.

————, *The Nature and the Study of History*. Columbus, Nerrill, 1965.

Committee on Historical Foundations, "The Role of the History of Education in the Professional Preparation of Teachers," *History of Education Journal,* Vol. VII, Nos. 1, 2, 3.

Cremin, L. A., *The Wonderful World of Ellwood Patterson Cubberly: An Essay on the Historiography of American Education*. New York, Columbia University Teachers College, Bureau of Publications, no date.

Dawson, Christopher, *The Dynamics of World History*. New York, New American Library, 1956.

Dray, William H., *Philosophy of History*. Englewood Cliffs, New Jersey, Prentice-Hall, 1964.

Dutt, Rajani Palme, *Problems of Contemporary History*. New York, International Publishers, 1963.

Easton, Stewart, *A Survey of Ancient, Medieval, and Modern History.* New York, Barnes and Noble, 1963.

Fackenheim, Emil L., *Metaphysics and Historicity,* The Acquinas Lecture, 1961. Milwaukee, Marquette University, 1961.

Frost, S. E., Jr., *Historical and Philosophical Foundations of Western Education.* Columbus, Ohio: Merrill, 1966.

Gabriel, Ralph H., "Ideas In History," *History of Education Journal,* Vol. X (Tenth Anniversary Issue) 1959, 17–19.

Gallie, W. B., *Philosophy and the Historical Understanding.* New York, Schocken, 1964.

Generalization in the Writing of History: A Report of the Committee on Historical Analysis of the Social Science Research Council, Louis Gottschalk, and others, eds. Chicago, University of Chicago Press, 1963.

Gooch, G. P., *History and Historians in the Nineteenth Century.* New York, Longmans and Green, 1952.

Good, H. G., "Rise of the History of Education," *History of Educational Journal,* Vol. X (Tenth Anniversary Issue, 1959), pp. 7–16.

Gottschalk, Louis, *Understanding History: A Primer of Historical Method.* New York, Knopf, 1950.

Gray, Wood and others. *Historian's Handbook.* Boston, Houghton Mifflin, 1959.

Gustavson, Carl G., *A Preface to History.* New York, McGraw-Hill, 1955.

Handlin, Oscar and Burchard, John, *The Historians and the City.* Cambridge, Massachusetts: Cambridge University Press, 1963.

Hegel, Georg W. F., *The Philosophy of History.* New York, Colonial Press, 1899.

Hexter, J. H., *Reappraisals in History: New Views on History and Society in Early Modern Europe.* London, Longmans, 1961. (Also Harper's, 1963.)

Higham, John, and others, *History.* Englewood Cliffs, New Jersey, Prentice-Hall, 1965.

Hockett, Homer C., *The Critical Method in Historical Research and Writing.* New York, Macmillan, 1955.

Holmes, Brian, *Problems in Education: A Comparative Approach.* New York, Humanities Press, 1965.

Howe, George, and others, *Guide to Historic Literature.* New York, Macmillan, 1961.

International Congress of Historians of the United States and Mexico, *The New World Looks at its History.* Austin, University of Texas Press, 1963.

Kahler, Erich, *The Meaning of History.* New York, George Braziller, 1964.

Kazamias, Andreas M. and Massialas, Byron G., *Tradition and Change in Education: A Comparative Study.* Englewood Cliffs, New Jersey, Prentice-Hall, 1965.

Kent, Sherman, *Writing History.* New York, Appleton-Century-Crofts, 1941.

Kohn, Hans, *Reflections on Modern History.* Princeton, New Jersey, Van Nostrand, 1963.

Kraus, Michael, *The Writing of American History.* Norman, University of Oklahoma Press, 1953.

——, *The Nature of Culture.* Chicago, University of Chicago Press, 1952.

Lamprecht, Sterling, *Nature and History*. New York, Columbia University Press, 1950.

Mannheim, Karl and Stewart, W. A. C., *An Introduction to the Sociology of Education*. London, Routledge and Kegan Paul, 1962.

Maritain, Jacques, *On the Philosophy of History*. New York, Scribners, 1957.

Morrison, J. Cayce, "Public Education in the Phillipines—Footnote to the Future," *The Scientific Monthly*, Vol. 76 (April, 1953), pp. 197–202.

Neumann, Henry, "Should History of Education be Scrapped," *History of Education Journal*, Vol. I (Summer 1950), pp. 153–157.

Noble, David W., *Historians Against History: The Frontier Thesis and the National Covenant in American Historical Writing Since 1830*. Minneapolis, University of Minnesota Press, 1965.

Noble, Stuart G., "The Relevance of the History of Education to Current Problems," *History of Education Journal*, Vol. I (Winter 1949), pp. 78–80.

Peardon, Thomas Preston, *The Transition in English Historical Writing, 1760–1830*. New York, Columbia University Press, 1933.

Perkins, Dexter and Snell, J. L., *The Education of Historians in the United States*. New York, McGraw-Hill, 1962.

Philosophy and History: Essays Presented to Ernst Cassirer, Raymond Klibansky, and H. J. Paton, eds. New York, Harper & Row, 1963. (Harper Torchbooks)

Philosophy and History: A Symposium, Sidney Hook, ed. New York, New York University, 1963.

Powell, J. E., *The History of Herodotus*. Cambridge, University Press, 1939.

Power, Edward J., "Persistent Myths in the History of Education," *History of Education Quarterly*, Vol. II (September, 1962) pp. 140–151.

Renier, Gustaf J., *History: Its Purpose and Method*. London, Allen and Unwin, 1950.

Rickert, Heinrich, *Science and History: A Critique of Positive Epistemology*. Princeton, Van Nostrand, 1962.

Robinson, James Harvey, *The New History: Essays Illustrating the Modern Historical Outlook*. New York, Macmillan, 1931.

Rowse, Alfred L., *The Use of History*. London, Hodder and Stoughton, English Universities Press, 1946.

Russell, Donald W., "The Status of the History of Education in the Teacher Education Curriculum," *History of Education Journal*, Vol. I (Summer, 1950), pp. 144–147.

Sheehan, Donald and Strett, H. C., eds., *Essays in American Historiography: Papers Presented in Honor of Allen Nevins*. New York, Columbia University Press, 1960.

Smith, Page, *The Historian and History*. New York, Knopf, 1964.

Social Sciences Research Council, *The Social Sciences in Historical Study: A Report of the Committee on Historiography*. New York, Social Science Research Council, 1954.

Soderquist, Harold O., "Needed Research in the History of Education," *History of Education Journal*, Vol. I (Winter 1949), 80–83.

Some Twentieth Century Historians, Samuel W. Halperin, ed. Chicago, University of Chicago Press, 1961.

Stern, B. J., *Historical Sociology*. New York, Citadel Press, 1960.

Strout, Cushing, *The Pragmatic Revolt in American History*. New Haven, Yale University Press, 1958.

Teggart, Frederick J., *Theory and Processes of History*. Los Angeles, University of California Press, 1941. (Paperbound)

Thompson, James W., *A History of Historical Writing*. Vol. I. New York, Macmillan, 1942.

The Philosophy of History of Our Time, Hans Neyerhoff, ed. Garden City, New York, Doubleday, 1959.

Toynbee, Arnold J., *A Study of History,* Abridgement of Volumes I–VI. London, Oxford University Press, 1946. (Reprinted 1953.)

Toynbee, Arnold J., *Greek Historical Thought*. New York, E. P. Dutton, 1924.

Walsh, William Henry, *Philosophy of History: An Introduction*. New York, Harper & Row, 1960.

Williams, Lloyd P., "Educational History as a Humanistic Discipline," *History of Education Journal,* Vol. IV (Summer 1953), pp. 121–123.

Wish, Harvey, *The American Historian*. New York, Oxford University Press, 1960.

General Books

Anthropology and Education, Frederick G. Gruber. Philadelphia, University of Pennsylvania Press, 1961.

Atkinson, Carroll and Maleska, Eugene T., *The Story of Education*. Philadelphia, Chilton Books, 1962.

Audrey, Robert, *African Genesis: A Personal Investigation into the Animal Origins and Nature of Man*. New York, Atheneum, 1961.

Barclay, W., *Educational Ideals of the Ancient World*. London, Collins, 1959.

Boyd, William, *The History of Western Education,* 7th ed. New York, Barnes and Noble, 1965.

Brameld, Theodore, *Cultural Foundations of Education: In Interdisciplinary Exploration*. New York, Harper and Row, 1957.

Butts, R. Freeman, *A Cultural History of Western Education: Its Social and Intellectual Foundations,* 2nd ed. New York, McGraw-Hill, 1955.

Cubberley, Ellwood P., *The History of Education*. New York, Houghton-Mifflin, 1920.

Cubberley, Ellwood P., *Readings in the History of Education*. Cambridge, The Riverside Press, 1920.

Dodge, Bayard, *Moslem Education in Medieval Times*. Washington, Middle East Institute, 1962.

Durant, Will, *The Story of Civilization,* Nine Volumes. New York, Simon and Schuster, no date.

Education and the Development of Nations, John W. Hanson, and Cole S. Brembeck, eds. New York, Holt, Rinehart, and Winston, 1966.

Education in World Perspective, Emmet J. Hughes, ed. New York, Harper & Row, 1962.

Good, H. G., *A History of Western Education,* 2d ed. New York, Macmillan, 1962.

Gordon, Cyrus H., *The World of the Old Testament,* 2d ed. New York, Doubleday, 1958. Pp. 312.

Hart, Joseph K., *Creative Moments in Education.* New York, Holt, Rinehart, and Winston, 1931.

———, *A Social Interpretation of Education.* New York, Holt, Rinehart, and Winston, 1929.

Hawkes, Jacquetta and Wooley, Sir Leonard, *Prehistory and the Beginnings of Civilization. History of Mankind,* Vol. I. Sponsored by UNESCO. New York, Harper and Row, 1963.

Kerr, Anthony, *Schools of Europe.* London, Bowes and Bowes, 1960.

King, Edmund J., *World Perspectives in Education.* Indianapolis, Bobbs-Merrill, 1962. (Paperback)

Knowles, David, *Saints and Scholars: Twenty-five Medieval Portraits.* New York, Cambridge University Press, 1962.

Kropotkin, P., *Mutual Aid: A Factor of Evolution.* New York, Knopf, 1916.

Meyer, Adolphe E., *An Educational History of the Western World.* New York, McGraw-Hill, 1965.

Muller, Herbert J., *Freedom in the Ancient World.* New York, Harper & Row, 1961.

———, *Freedom in the Modern World.* New York, Harper and Row, 1966.

———, *Freedom in the Western World: From the Dark Ages to the Rise of Democracy.* New York, Harper and Row, 1963.

Myers, Edward D., *Education in the Perspective of History.* New York, Harper and Row, 1960.

Peterson, A. D. C., *A Hundred Years of Education.* London, Gerald Duckworth, Ltd., 1952.

Power, Edward J., *Main Currents in the History of Education.* New York, McGraw-Hill, 1962.

Smith, William A., *Ancient Education.* New York, Philosophical Library, 1955.

Thut, I. N., *The Story of Education. Philosophical and Historical Foundations.* New York, McGraw-Hill, 1957.

Weimer, Hermann, *Concise History of Education.* New York, Philosophical Library, 1962.

Wilds, Elmer H. and Lottich, Kenneth V., *The Foundations of Modern Education,* 3d ed. New York, Holt, Rinehart, and Winston, 1961.

Pertinent Paperbound Books

Acton, Lord John, *Essays on Freedom and Power.* New York, Meridien, 1955.

Albright, W. F., *From the Stone Age to Christianity,* 2d ed. Baltimore, Johns Hopkins Press, 1940.

Asimov, Isaac, *The Well Springs of Life.* New York, New American Library of World Literature, 1962.

Beck, Robert Holmes, *A Social History of Education.* Englewood Cliffs, New Jersey, Prentice-Hall, 1965.

Blake, Raymond Jack, *A History of Education Through Time Lines.* Palo Alto, California, The National Press, 1962.

Bobbs-Merrill Reprint Series in the Social Sciences.
  (Examples pertinent to the history of education):
  Barnett, H. G., "Invention and Cultural Change"
  Herskovits, Melvill J., "The Processes of Cultural Change."
  Holmberg, Allen R., "Adventures in Cultural Change"
  Megger, Betty J., "Environmental Limitation on the Development of Culture"
  Sahlins, Marshall D., "The Origin of Society"
    Reprint: The Scientific American
    September, 1960
  Steward, Julian H., "The Economic and Social Basis of Primitive Bands"
  White, Leslie, "The Symbol: The Origin and Basis of Human Behavior"

Bowra, Cecil Maurice, *The Great Experience*. New York, New American Library, 1958.

Broudy, Harry S. and Palmer, John R., *Exemplars of Teaching Method*. Chicago, Rand McNally, 1965.

Burrell, Sidney, *Elements of Western Civilization,* Vols. I and II. San Francisco, Chandler, 1959.

Butterfield, Herbert, *The Origins of Modern Science, 1300–1800,* rev. ed. New York, Collier Books, 1962.

Castle, E. B., *Ancient Education and Today*. Baltimore, Penguin Books, 1961.

Cheney, L. J., *A History of the Western World: From the Stone Age to the Twentieth Century*. New York, The New American Library, 1959.

Childe, V. Gordon, *Man Makes Himself*. New York, New American Library (Mentor Book), 1951.

———, *The Prehistory of Europe Society*. Baltimore, Penguin Books, 1958.

———, *What Happened in History*. Baltimore, Penguin Books, 1961.

Cordasco, Francesco, *A Brief History of Education*. Paterson, New Jersey, Littlefield, Adams, 1963.

Cramer, John F. and Browne, George S., *Contemporary Education: A Study of National Systems,* 2d ed. New York, Harcourt, Brace and World, 1965.

Culture and the Evolution of Man, Ashley Montagu, ed. New York, Oxford University Press, 1962.

Dobzhansky, Theodosius, *The Biological Basis of Human Freedom*. New York, Columbia University Press, 1960.

———, *Evolution, Genetics, and Man*. New York, Wiley, 1955.

Downs, Robert B., *Books that Changed the World*. New York, Mentor, 1956.

Dudley, Donald R., *The Civilization of Rome*. New York, New American Library, 1962.

Frost, S. E., Jr., *History of Education*. New York, Barron's, 1947.

Golding, William, *Lord of the Flies*. New York, Capricorn, 1955.

Great Teachers, Houston Peterson, ed. New York, Random House, 1946.

Hatch, Edwin, *The Influence of Greek Ideas and Usages Upon the Christian Church*. London, Williams and Norgale, 1904.

Hitti, Philip K., *Islam and the West: A Historical Cultural Survey*. Princeton, New Jersey, Van Nostrand, 1962.

Hunnicutt, Clarence W., *America's Emerging Role in Overseas Education*. Syracuse, New York, Syracuse University Press, 1962.

International Education: A Documentary History, David G. Scanlon, ed. New York, Columbia University Press, 1960.

Kirchner, Walther, *Western Civilization to 1500*. New York, Barnes and Noble, 1960.

———, *Western Civilization since 1500*. New York, Barnes and Noble, 1958.

Kristeller, Paul Oscar, *Renaissance Thought: The Classic, Scholastic, and Humanistic Strains*. New York, Harper and Row, 1961.

Low, D. M., *Gibbon's The Decline and Fall of The Roman Empire*, One Volume Abridgement. New York, Holt, Rinehart, and Winston, 1960.

Man, Culture, and Society, Harry L. Shapiro, ed. New York, Oxford University Press, 1960

Marrou, H. I., *A History of Education in Antiquity*. New York, New American Library, 1956.

McNeill, William, *History Handbook of Western Civilization*. Chicago, University of Chicago Press, 1953.

Montagu, Ashley, *Man: His First Million Years*. New York, New American Library, 1959.

Montagu, Ashley, *Man in Process*. New York, American Library, 1961.

Power, Eileen, *Medieval People*. Garden City, New York, Doubleday, 1924.

Ralph, P. L., *The Story of Our Civilization*. New York, Dutton, 1959.

Sedillot, Rene, *History of the World in 240 Pages*. New York, New American Library, 1951.

Slater, Robert Lawson, *Can Christians Learn From Other Religions?* New York, Seabury Press, 1963.

Smith, Preserved, *The Age of the Reformation*. New York, Holt, Rinehart, and Winston, 1920.

———, *The Enlightenment: 1687–1776*. New York, Collier Books, 1962.

———, *Origins of Modern Culture: 1543–1687*, Vol. I. New York, Collier Books, 1962.

Social History of American Education, Rena L. Vassar, ed., Vol. I, *Colonial Times to 1860;* Vol. II, *1860 to the Present*. Chicago, Rand McNally, 1965.

Sources of Western Civilization, Daniel McGarry, and Clarence L. Hohl, Jr., eds., Two Vols. Boston, Houghton Mifflin, 1962.

The Renaissance Philosophy of Man, Ernst Cassirer, Paul Kristeller, and John Randall, Jr., eds. Chicago, University of Chicago, 1948.

Thompson, Merritt M., *The History of Education*, College Outline Series. New York, Barnes and Noble, 1958.

Ulich, Robert, *Education in Western Culture*. New York, Harcourt, Brace and World, 1965.

Wallbank, Thomas Walter and others, *Civilization: Past and Present*. Chicago, Scott, Foresman, 1962.

West, Charles C., *Communism and the Theologians: Study of an Encounter*. New York, Macmillan, 1958.

INDEX